The Art of Human-Computer Interface Design

The Art of Human-Computer Interface Design

Edited by
Brenda Laurel

S. Joy Mountford,
Manager of the Human Interface Group,
Apple Computer, Inc., conceived of
and technically supported the development of
this book

ADDISON–WESLEY

Boston • San Francisco • New York • Toronto • Montreal
London • Munich • Paris • Madrid
Capetown • Sydney • Tokyo • Singapore • Mexico City

Library of Congress Cataloging-in-Publication Data
The Art of human-computer interface design / Brenda Laurel, editor.
    p.   cm.
   "S. Joy Mountford, Manager of the Human Interface Group, Apple Computer Inc., conceived of and technically supported the development of this book."
   Includes bibliographical references.
   ISBN 0-201-51797-3
   1. Human-computer interaction.   2. User interfaces (Computer systems)   I. Laurel, Brenda.   II. Mountford, S. Joy.
QA76.9.H85A78   1990   90-34470
005.1—dc20   CIP

Cover concept: Gitta Salomon
Cover photograph by Lynette Molnar
Cover design by Copenhaver Cumpston
Text design by Mike Fender
Set in 10-point Sabon by DEKR

Text printed on recycled and acid-free paper.

ISBN 0201517973

14 1516171819 CRS 04 03 02 01

14th Printing   November 2001

Focal Point is a trademark of Activision, Inc.
IBM 3270/PC and IBM PC are trademarks of IBM
IMAX and OMNIMAX are trademarks of IMAX Systems Corporation
MacDraw and MacPaint are registered trademarks and MacWrite is a trademark of Claris Corporation
MacRecorder is a trademark of Farallon Computing, Inc.
MCI Mail is a trademark of MCI Communication Corporation
MicroPhone II is a trademark of Software Ventures Corporation
Microsoft Excel, Microsoft Windows, Microsoft Word, and Power Point are all registered trademarks of Microsoft Corporation
NeWS is a trademark of Sun Microsystems, Inc.
Nintendo is a registered trademark of Nintendo
Officetalk is a trademark of Officetalk, Inc.
PDP-12 and VAX are trademarks of Digital Equipment Corporation
Pepto-Bismol is a registered trademark of Morton-Norwich
Phone Slave is a registered trademark of Active Voice, Inc.
Pillsbury Doughboy is a trademark of Pillsbury
Pole Position and Pong are trademarks of Atari
Post-it is a registered trademark of 3M
PostScript is a registered trademark of Adobe Systems, Inc.
Prototyper is a trademark of Smethers Barnes
Rocky's Boots is a trademark of The Learning Company
Showscan is a trademark of Showscan Film Corporation
Sideband is a trademark of Nexus
Space Invaders is a trademark of Taito America
Star is a registered trademark of Xerox Corporation
Trust and Betrayal is a trademark of Mindscape
UNIX is a registered trademark of AT&T
VisiCalc is a trademark of Lotus Development Corporation
Volkswagen is a registered trademark of Volkswagenwerk Aktiengesellschaft

Warranty Information

All implied warranties on this manual, including implied warranties of merchantability and fitness for a particular purpose, are limited in duration to ninety (90) days from the date of the original retail purchase of this product.

Even though Apple has reviewed this manual, Apple makes no warranty or representation, either express or implied, with respect to this manual, its quality, accuracy, merchantability, or fitness for a particular purpose. As a result, this manual is sold "as is," and you, the purchaser, are assuming the entire risk as to its quality and accuracy.

In no event will Apple be liable for direct, indirect, special, incidental, or consequential damages resulting from any defect or inaccuracy in this manual, even if advised of the possibility of such damages.

The warranty and remedies set forth above are exclusive and in lieu of all others, oral or written, express or implied. No Apple dealer, agent, or employee is authorized to make any modification, extension, or addition to this warranty.

No licenses, express or implied, are granted by reason of this book describing certain processes and techniques that may be the intellectual property of the author or others.

Some states do not allow the exclusive or limitation of implied warranties or liability or exclusion may not apply to you. This warranty gives you specific legal rights, and you may also have other rights which may vary from state to state.

CONTENTS

Introduction

What's an Interface?

WHAT DO INTERFACE DESIGNERS DO? Where in the process of product development do they do their work? What parts of a product concern them? Upon what principles and intuitions do they base design decisions?

We must begin, predictably, by defining what we mean by the human-computer interface. When the concept of the interface first began to emerge, it was commonly understood as the hardware and software through which a human and a computer could communicate. As it has evolved, the concept has come to include the cognitive and emotional aspects of the user's experience as well.

Although the "old-timers" in the industry (people over thirty) remember teletypes, many people today equate the interface with the screen. The noun, *interface,* is taken to be a discrete and tangible thing that we can map, draw, design, implement, and attach to an existing bundle of functionality. One of the goals of this book is to explode that notion and replace it with one that can guide our work in the right direction.

That direction, the goal of all our efforts, is to empower the user. But empowerment itself is a notion that must be unpacked. A new version of my favorite word processor offers me twice as many options as its predecessor. Theoretically, I can now customize my environment and achieve more complex and sophisticated goals. But the plethora of options—and the interface conventions that I must learn in order to deploy them—leaves me bewildered and tired. Psychologists call this an increased cognitive load. I call it trouble. True, the new, improved product offers me more power over my final product and my working environment. It offers me more degrees of freedom. But all is lost when the cost to me is too great. I retreat from the "improvements" and limp along, employing the tiny domain of functionality that I already know how to use. For empowerment to occur, more powerful functionality must go hand in hand with greater ease of use.

What is a human-computer interface? How can we think about it so that the interfaces we design will empower users?

The primitive notion of the interface as a screen or membrane holds important seeds of truth. Forgetting for a moment the enhancements we have made to the definition in recent years, let's begin with that notion. We naturally visualize an interface as the *place* where contact between two entities occurs. The less alike those two entities are, the more obvious the need for a well-designed interface becomes.

An interface is the contact surface of a thing. The world is full of them. A doorknob is the interface between a person and a door. The steering wheel, accelerator, clutch, and other dashboard instruments are the interface between a driver and a car. A space suit is the interface between an astronaut and the void. What gives these interfaces their shape?

The shape of the interface reflects the physical qualities of the parties to the interaction (the interactors, if you will). A doorknob is hard and firmly mounted because of the weight and hardness of the door; it is round or handle-shaped because of the nature of the hand that will use it. The doorknob's physical qualities also reflect the physical aspects of its function. It is designed to be turned so that the latch is released and so that it is easier for the user to pull the door open.

A point that's often missed is that the shape of the interface also reflects who is doing what to whom. The doorknob extends toward the user and its qualities are biased toward the hand. The door will be opened; a human will open it—the human is the agent and the door is the patient of the action. In a high-security government office I visited the other day, there was no doorknob at all. I was screened by a hidden camera and the door opened for me when I passed muster. My sense of who was in control of the interaction was quite different from the way I feel when I enter a room in my house. In the office, the door—representing the institution to which it was a portal—was in control.

An interface is a contact surface. It reflects the physical properties of the interactors, the functions to be performed, and the balance of power and control. This notion of human-computer interfaces is a place to begin; when you have finished reading the book, you hopefully will have formulated a better definition.

Human-computer interface design is an ad hoc discipline. It arose to solve a problem. As computer technology has become available to more and more people in a greater variety of devices and contexts, the need for accessibility, ease of use, and user engagement has grown more and more pronounced. As the nature of the problem has been explored and articulated in greater detail, people with a greater variety of skills and points of view have become involved.

At first, the goal of interface studies appeared to be consciousness-raising—teaching engineers how to be sensitive to users' needs and to design products to meet them more effectively. In the eighties, the discipline of human-computer interface design has separated progressively from the domain of software and hardware engineering. What will the field of interface design become in the future?

An interesting possibility is that the discipline of human-computer interface design will disappear. We continue to demonstrate to ourselves—through both our successes and our failures—that the first and most important question to ask is, *what does the user want to do?* The process of interface design, as explained by Don Norman and others in this book, returns again and again to this fundamental question. Perhaps in the future we will finally give up the illusion of applications engineering and interface design as being two separate things. The designer of interactive systems will be a superdesigner with the skills of an engineer, an artist, and a psychologist. More likely, the designer will be a team of individuals who, like the playwright, director, actors, technicians, and scenery, light, and costume designers in the theatre, will contribute different skills toward the realization of a common vision.

Building that common vision is what this book is about.

Brenda Laurel

About the Book

This book was originally proposed by Joy Mountford as part of an interface training course sponsored by the Human Interface Group at Apple Computer. The initial idea was to collect some of the distributed expertise and wisdom about interfaces inside Apple into a book that could be used to train current and future Apple employees. Brenda Laurel was hired to serve as editor. The project quickly began to grow into an idea for a trade book that would give Apple authors a chance to publish some of their work on interface design. When we became serious about creating a book on human-computer interfaces for both educational and professional markets, we realized that we needed to include non-Apple perspectives as well in order to provide a well-rounded and thought-provoking treatment of the topic. We put out a call for abstracts to Apple people and a wide variety of non-Apple interface workers and thinkers. We selected a group of abstracts that

Joy Mountford

we felt provided good coverage of the domain, ending up with about a 50-50 mix of Apple and non-Apple authors.

When first drafts were completed, they were distributed among the entire community of authors for peer review. In December of 1988, we all met at Asilomar for an intensive three-day conference, during which a group session was held on each chapter. We also discussed the book's broad

Brenda Laurel

themes and built in cross-references that would establish connections among ideas. At the end of the conference, the group reorganized the book's structure. Each author went away with a hefty list of recommended changes and new ideas to consider. Second and third drafts were produced and edited throughout the spring and summer of 1989.

From the beginning, we have tried to encourage our authors to reach for the "big ideas" in interface design. Looking at the existing books on the topic, we felt that there was a need for a book that surveyed the enormous diversity of philosophies, design methods, and technological approaches that have evolved over the last few years. As interface designers ourselves, we have been struck by the ever-widening circle of domains and approaches that are coming into view as important contributors to the art of making computers easy to use.

To that end, the book contains work from people in fields that are not yet widely associated with interface design, including drama and narrative, industrial design, animation, and cognitive and interpersonal psychology. We have also surveyed new modalities and media that will be incorporated into the interfaces of the future, from speech and gesture to video and television.

You will also notice that the articles in the book are of varied types, including research papers, case studies, surveys and tutorials, theoretical discussions, opinion pieces and sermons, interviews, first-person observations by working designers, and even some humor. Each section of the book contains chapters of several types. The variety of chapter styles reflects a variety of approaches, each of which can contribute useful ideas. You will also notice that the authors disagree in many areas. Good arguments—

supported by logic, evidence, and passion—bring the key issues into high relief. We have included conflicting views in order to stimulate thinking and to motivate research.

Acknowledgments

We wish to thank all of our authors for their diligent and enthusiastic contributions and their patience with the process. Within Apple, many people have championed the book along the way. We especially want to thank Dave Nagel, Harvey Lehtman, Gene Pope, Martha Steffen, and the senior staff at Apple, including Jean-Louis Gassée and Larry Tesler, for all their efforts. Roy Pea of the Institute for Research on Learning, Don Norman of the University of California at San Diego, and Larry Tesler of Apple's Advanced Technology Group contributed valuable editorial insights. Howard Rheingold lent us his superb interviewing and writing skills. Kevin Broun of the Apple Library gave us invaluable help with our references. Sara Mead, Lori Weiss, Pat Ricci, and Jo Ann Vander Vennet solved both strategic and tactical problems. We are extremely grateful to Steve Stansel and Linda O'Brien of Addison-Wesley for their unflagging support. Finally, we thank Apple Computer for funding development and production, including our conference at Asilomar, and for having the vision to sponsor a work that contains a wide variety of points of view.

Brenda Laurel
S. Joy Mountford

Creativity and Design
Introduction

WHY DID THEY DESIGN IT LIKE *THAT*?

Voiced in tones of baffled disbelief, this is a question that many computer users have asked. After all, there are so many bad interfaces around, with such obvious problems. Even the Macintosh—that paragon of good interface design—even the Macintosh has its warts! The infamous Font/DA Mover. The bewildering Installer Utility. Or everybody's favorite wart: ejecting a diskette by dragging its icon to the trash can. What were they thinking of when they did *that*?

Because the chapters in this section deal with how to solve interface design problems, it's important to begin with an understanding of why such obvious problems may be so difficult. Thus, I'm going to tell you how the Macintosh trash icon came to be used as a disk ejection mechanism. It's a good illustration of the difficulties involved in designing an interface for even a simple task.

The Truth about the Trash

The use of the trash can to eject a disk was present from the very beginning of the Macintosh interface. As is usually the case in interface design, it's important to understand the situation. The original Mac had no hard disk; only a single diskette drive. When a diskette was in the machine, a diskette icon would be displayed and a list of its files would appear in a window. Because most users typically would switch back and forth between several

Thomas D. Erickson

Advanced Technology Group
Apple Computer, Inc.

diskettes during a session, it was deemed appropriate for the Mac to keep a memory image of the lists of files on the various disks, regardless of whether the diskette was actually inserted in the drive. Diskettes that the Mac "knew about," but that weren't actually in the drive, were represented by grayed-out diskette and file icons. Thus, a user could select a grayed-out file icon and open it, and the Mac would eject the current diskette and prompt the user to insert the proper diskette. This was all well and good, and made life easier for the user.

There was one drawback. Often, during the course of a session, the user would finish using a particular diskette. The actual diskette could be ejected, but the grayed-out diskette and file icons would remain, taking up both limited screen space and memory. To reclaim valuable space, the now-unwanted list of files represented by the grayed-out icon could be thrown away by dragging it to the trash. Thus, when users decided they were really finished with a diskette, they had to do two things: use the eject command to get rid of the physical disk, and throw away the memory image of the disk by dragging it to the trash.

This annoyed one of the programmers. Why should users have to do two things to accomplish one, frequently desired, action? Clearly, if users are going to discard the image of the diskette that's in memory, they're not interested in keeping the physical diskette in the Mac's drive. Thus, the now-infamous shortcut: dragging the icon of the currently inserted diskette to the trash can would both eject the physical desk and delete the memory image. From the programmer's viewpoint, it was a logical extension of existing functionality. And convenient. After all, wasn't making things easier for the user what the Mac was all about?

The programmer's decision caused a dispute within the design team. In particular, objections were heard from the member of the team, a non-programmer, who was responsible for testing the interface and taking the user's point of view. It was agreed that the tester try it out until the next release. After a week of using it, she couldn't give it up. The rest is history.

I like this story because it is a good example, in miniature, of the realities under which the design process must operate. Not the design process as it ought to be, perhaps, but the design process as it really is. The problem was relatively simple: give users a simple way of ejecting a disk and freeing up memory. But there was no simple, obvious solution. The possible solutions—do nothing, eject via the trash icon, or create a new command or icon for ejection—each had its own trade-offs. Doing nothing retained simplicity and ease of learning at the expense of ease of use. Ejection via the trash icon provided the desired functionality without adding a new interface element, but it compromised the consistency of the trash can's behavior. Creating a new interface object increased ease of use and maintained behavioral consistency at the expense of increasing the number of interface objects. Finally, arriving at a solution involved the interaction—requiring communication and agreement about methods of evaluation and criteria for success—of two people with very different backgrounds.

The point here is not whether the solution was a good one. Rather, the point is to highlight the multiple difficulties of interface design.

Why Interface Design Is Hard

Interface problems are often obvious. Solutions are less obvious. It may be difficult to find a solution that solves a particular problem without creating new problems. Even then, a separate solution for every problem would result in an interface of such complexity that it would be unusable. What is really needed is a solution that elegantly solves a range of problems. Such solutions are exceptionally difficult to find.

The difficulty of interface design is compounded by the fact that virtually all solutions are compromises. Solutions are shaped by a multitude of problems that are invisible to those outside of the design process. A wonderfully intuitive solution doesn't matter if the system architecture doesn't support it, or if the resulting code takes up too much memory or runs too slowly. Other problems stem from the basic capabilities of humans, and the requirements of the tasks users wish to do. It doesn't matter if the interface responds instantly, if the user can't use it. Solutions to an interface problem involve compromise. But how do designers determine what an acceptable compromise is? How do designers figure out acceptable trade-offs between speed and intuitiveness and other seemingly contradictory values and requirements?

Not only does the sheer number of requirements increase the difficulty of interface design, but the variety of sources from which the requirements come requires that successful interface design be a multidisciplinary process. The multidisciplinary nature of interface design introduces problems that are political in nature. Psychologists, graphic designers, writers, industrial designers, and programmers all have essential contributions to make to the design of an interface. Yet each discipline has its own priorities and perspectives, its own methods, its own criteria for success. Often these are in conflict with one another. Whose priorities are most important? Whose perspectives are most valuable? Whose criteria for success should be met? Figuring out how to resolve conflicts between differing approaches is not easy.

There are three sorts of reasons why interface design is difficult. First, quite simply, it's hard to come up with good solutions. Second, there are so many competing desiderata involved in interface problems that any solution is bound to be a compromise. The problem here is one of evaluation: how do designers figure out which compromises will fly, and which are to be avoided? The third reason for the difficulty of interface design is that it's interdisciplinary and highly political.

Making Interface Design Less Difficult

The chapters in this section provide a look at the methods of some of the most skilled and experienced interface designers in the business. The interface designers contributing to this section come from a variety of backgrounds: industrial design, programming, writing, psychology, and graphic design. Most contributors have experience in two or more of these fields. Most contributors have also had the experience of working on interdisciplinary teams. As a result, the chapters in this section contain a broad array of ideas, methods, perspectives, and approaches. Whether you are a designer who wants to broaden your repertoire of methods, or simply a user who wants a better understanding of the design process, this section has a lot to offer.

Here's a sampling of questions addressed by the chapters in this section: What does the evolution of language suggest about ways in which the Macintosh interface might evolve? What can interface designers learn from fields like animation, theater, and architecture? Why do designers from different disciplines have such trouble communicating, and what can be done about it? What happens when you give a programmer and a graphic designer the same interface problem and let them duke it out? Why is cardboard an important interface design tool? People talk about *interface metaphors*, but what exactly are they and how do you design a metaphor? Everyone agrees that consistency is a Good Thing, but how can consistency be conserved when each release adds new features? How on earth can designers do all the testing and tweaking they advocate, when the program isn't working until the week before it ships? Everyone agrees that it's essential to involve users in the design process, but how do you do that?

If you're intrigued, read on. The chapters that follow address these questions and many others.

An Interview with
Don Norman

Prologue

*"WHAT DO YOU THINK is most important about the interface?" I asked
Don Norman.*

*"What do I think is most important about the interface?" he parried, with
a puckish grin on his face, "nothing—everything."*

*I was supposed to interview Norman for this book, but it turned into a
lengthy discussion, lecture, polemic. The interview went on for a long
time, but Norman told me to throw away most of it.*

*"Skip the off-the-top-of-the-head conversation," he said. "I just want the
important points and philosophy to come across. A writer is a designer,
but of text, not of things. So think of the end users, the readers: What
do they need to get out of this? How should we interact with them? My
bet is that the typical reader is in a rush, or bored, or impatient: So get
their attention, and keep it short. Give the critical points and stop.*

*"But speaking of 'off-the-top-of-the-head' things, one problem with design
is that it tends to be done by people who have off-the-top-of-their-heads
ideas and beliefs about imaginary beasts they call 'the users.'*

*"An amazing world. All these people who study what is needed, and all
these people who actually build the stuff—two different communities.
They don't understand one another, and certainly don't talk to one
another.*

"With some notable exceptions, of course.

Howard Rheingold

Donald A. Norman

5

"What's wrong with interfaces? The question, for one. The interface is the wrong place to begin. It implies you already have done all the rest and now you want to patch it up to make it pretty for the user. That attitude is what is wrong with the interface. Actually, that attitude is what is wrong with design—all design, whether of homes, offices, showers, auto dashboards, television sets. And of course, the worst offenders of all, computers.

"The only good thing I can think of about computer interface designs is that the Museum of Modern Art doesn't yet give prizes for them or exhibit elegant examples. Like they do for watches and toasters and fountain pens. Once they start to do that, that is the end of functionality."

Cultivate Sensitivity to Design

I wrote *The Psychology of Everyday Things* because I wanted to show that design is a pervasive influence on daily life. Everything we use is designed by somebody. Any person who wants to design for others must develop a high degree of sensitivity to the nuances of good and bad design—from shoelaces that are so long you trip over them to pens that don't leak in your pocket. Take out a pen and look closely at it; right now, I can see at least nine different design features on the pen in my hand, from the ridge along one side that helps me grasp it to the little hole at the top that equalizes atmospheric pressure so the pen won't leak in an airplane.

Noticing and analyzing the design features of the everyday environment is a way of developing sensitivity to the designed world in which we live and work. When you start to design a computer system, your habitual use of this exercise will have sensitized you to many issues. Empathy can be cultivated by performing countless thought experiments, observations, hands-on experiments. Think of the frustrations you encounter and tuck them into your memory so that you will be sensitive to analogous frustrations on the part of computer users.

Remember that every interface designer is a system designer. Nothing can be designed in isolation. Look at home audio systems or television systems. Each component might have been designed perfectly in isolation, but when you try to connect your VCR and television and stereo, it's a holy mess. With a computer, you buy your computer and keyboard display and printer and disk drives and network connections and telephone modems and game controllers and pointing devices, and try to hook them up. It's a bigger mess. What is all this crap about simple, "intuitive" systems? A designer with some degree of sensitivity will understand that the cables are often the first part of the design that the user encounters, and this encounter sets the tone for the initial stages of the interaction. A negative tone. And the problem here seems to be that each thing is designed in isolation, without sufficient thought to the total picture, the total system the users will see.

One heuristic in developing this kind of sensitivity is to look at the whole task—not just the thing you've been asked to design, but the whole task your potential user wants to accomplish. This means that members of the team must encourage themselves and one another to ask questions. There is no such thing as a stupid question.

Yes, designers have to concern themselves with other problems: materials, time pressures, technology, and economics are real constraints. Saving money by doing something one way rather than implementing a design that might be better from the user's perspective is legitimate only if it is a deliberate, intelligent design decision. It shouldn't be done out of ignorance of the best way to do a chosen task.

Interact with the Task, Not with the Computer

The computer industry focuses an enormous amount of energy on the human-computer interaction. That's a lot better than no concern at all, but I think it's the wrong focus. *We ought to be asking what tasks people need to accomplish, what tools are most appropriate for those tasks.* We need to ask those questions with the entire working environment in mind, with an eye toward the effects our tools will have on that environment. Real tasks are not done solely by individuals but by groups of people, usually within organizations. The task completion takes place in a certain space, with certain people, over a certain period of time. Useful tools will have to support this kind of cooperative and interactive work.

It's also important to remember that in real organizations, cooperative work is not always so cooperative. This person is trying to get promoted, that person is competing with a peer, this one wants to gain recognition for his division, another wants to prove that her hypothesis is better than another. All sorts of tensions exist within organizations, and the people who design tools to be used in those environments must be sensitive to the task in its largest systemic sense.

The effects of a tool upon a task are often overlooked in the design process. When you introduce a new tool or a radically improved tool into an organization, you will change the way people do the task for which you designed the tool. Introducing computer systems has implications throughout the rest of the organization; it might even cause the whole system to fail. I have seen very good systems fail because their designers didn't take into account the social interactions and the way the tool changed life for the users.

People and Tasks Come First; Interfaces Come Second

The usual concerns of interface designers—creating more legible type, designing better scroll bars, integrating color and sound and voice—are all important considerations. But they are secondary. Improving the way people can use computers to think and communicate, observe and decide, calculate and simulate, debate and design—these are primary.

Human interface design is an exciting challenge precisely because the goal is to change the world by improving the way real people accomplish their tasks in classrooms, offices, factories, homes. New ideas, new technologies, new cultures, new jobs, new industries, new world views will be the eventual results of well-designed computer interfaces. Finding ways to help people cooperate with one another is the designer's highest challenge. User interfaces and computer technology and all the tools we use to think with are part of an evolutionary process. Designs that work change the way we think, and that enables us to design more effective systems.

The first principle of human interface design, whether for a doorknob or a computer, is to keep in mind the human being who wants to use it. The technology is subservient to that goal. This is more than a heuristic; think of it as a world view. The mental skill of putting yourself into a person's position in a specified environment and trying to model the way a tool is used from the potential user's point of view is a very general skill. You can practice it when bathing, when opening your mail, when dialing the telephone.

How To Go About Design

Cultivate sensitivity to design. Yeah, I already said that. But I want to emphasize the point again: it's that important.

And get a design team that includes cognitive scientists (or at least a psychologist or anthropologist) and programmers and industrial designers. People who have some exposure to all of these fields and are sensitive to the separate viewpoint. And start the human-centered part of the design first—before the technological stuff.

Test the ideas with users at all stages in the design process, from conception to end product. Which means you need rapid prototyping tools. The Lisa was done this way, and many of the proper lessons spilled over into the Macintosh.

And don't think you can get away with designing something and then, when it is done, turning it over to the psychologists for approval. Barf. The problem with turning nearly finished products over to someone to review them is that then those reviewers are outsiders. Their comments will be viewed with suspicion. All that effort you put into the design, and these ill-informed, fuzzy folks do nothing but criticize. Clearly they are incompetent. And even if the designers agree with some of the critiques, it is too late. By this time, the design is more or less frozen.

The best way is to integrate all the necessary knowledge and experience in the same team. Better yet, the same person. If you can get it in each individual, then you win. I think this means we need a profession of interface design, in which each member is trained in design, cognitive science, and programming. These design teams will have a richer common language—they'll be able to communicate better and make better decisions on crucial human interface issues.

Task Analysis: Do User Testing First

Task analysis is the formal name for the methodology of studying what users need to do and the ways in which they do their tasks. An excellent way to begin learning about the methodology and process of task analysis is to read *The Human Factor* [Rubenstein and Hersh, 1984]. The authors work for DEC, so they understand the computer side of the problem. Their textbook case of successful human interface design illustrates how the critical skill in task analysis is understanding what the user is trying to accomplish.

John Gould et al. of the IBM Research Labs wrote an excellent paper about the use of task analysis in designing a new kind of communication system [Gould et al., 1985]. Their objective was to design a voice message system for the Olympic participants in Los Angeles in 1984. The participants would be able to receive messages from family, friends, coaches, and fans all over the world. One constraint was that the potential users were not highly technologically literate. And obviously the users spoke many different languages. Moreover, they would undoubtedly be in a hurry when they used the system. So the designers designed mock-ups, which they put in the halls of their IBM research facilities. They brought people in to try using the different versions, and they discovered a great deal just by paying attention to the way people used the cardboard mock-ups. Then they went out to some track meets and installed prototypes. And then they interacted with the Olympics people, talked to them about how they might use such a system.

The point is that these designers didn't just think about what was needed; they acquainted themselves with the needs of athletes and the kinds of messages that their colleagues and families sent to them. They went through many redesigns using this process, and the final result was a successful message system that conveyed tens of thousands of messages. Computer interface designers could do worse than imitating the procedures described in this article.

Most people seem to think that user testing is what you do after you've solved the major problems and you want to see how well your design works, so you can tweak it in various ways in response to feedback from users. No: that is too late. Good task analysis means continual user testing, starting as soon as the work begins. Key elements of the design should emerge from the task analysis, rather than being shaped to fit the results of the user testing.

The Designer Is Not a Typical User

Designers may think of themselves as typical users, and maybe they were before they started, but after they have thought about the task for as long as you need to for proper design, they are no longer typical, they can no longer understand the average user: *they know too much.*

Designers are confident. Users, however, are often fearful. Fear is an important element in every novice computer user's first attempts to use a new machine or new software: fear of destroying data, fear of hurting the machine, fear of seeming stupid in comparison to other users, or even to the machine itself.

Another aspect of task analysis involves developing a sensitivity to the environment in which computer systems will be used. Computers are used in environments that are unlike anything you've dreamed of in your laboratory or production facility.

And no single individual (or even a team) can be like all the potential users. It is not a designer's fault that he or she is twenty years old with perfect vision, but it is a good reason for that designer to include in the task analysis us old folks who wear bifocals. I have to tilt my head way up in the air in order to read all that lovely small type on the screen through the bottom lenses of my glasses. You can't appreciate the problems of an older person, or people in a loud, badly lit office or a cramped space where people are in danger of tripping over cables, until you spend some time watching people do their jobs in real offices, classrooms, factories.

The best kind of task analysis is in the field. You have to learn how to watch people. It can help to bring in a trained observer—an anthropologist or psychologist or sociologist who knows about the people who are under study can make videotapes of typical interactions and show you how computers are used in the environment for which your design is destined.

The Future

In the future, I want less emphasis on "interfaces" and more on appropriate tools for the task. More on user-centered design. Less emphasis on technology; more on people, and groups, and social interactions. And tasks.

No matter which way the scientific fashions may change in the future, the skill of systematically studying the way people do things is sure to remain central to the interface design mission. It's more than a skill. It's a way of looking at the world.

Interface and the Evolution of Pidgins:

Creative Design for the Analytically Inclined

Thomas D. Erickson

Advanced Technology Group
Apple Computer, Inc.

THERE ARE MANY METHODS of pursuing design. The question of how to get new ideas, or how to approach an idea from a different direction, is one that designers must answer repeatedly. There are dozens of books on visual thinking, drawing, lateral thinking, creative blockbusting, and other ways of better using your neglected right hemisphere. There are even books on how to whack and kick yourself into that crazy, flexible, and fun creative mode. They're all carefully crafted to coax you away from your comfortable, cautious, rational approach to problem-solving.

But what if you don't want to go?

What if you're unrepentantly analytic? What if your idea of having a good time is to read the dictionary, looking for words you don't know? What if your verbal and math test scores are off the scale, but your attempts at realistic drawings resemble those of two-year-olds? What if your right hemisphere was irredeemably damaged in a tragic childhood accident? What if you're inhibited, inflexible, and don't want to look silly? What if you've just got a bad attitude?

Is there no hope?

There *is* hope. This chapter describes a method of pursuing creative design that is pleasing to the analytically inclined. To the best of my knowledge, it has no widely known name, because no best-selling books have been written about it. However, for the purposes of this paper, I will call it design by symmetry.

This chapter plays two roles: it illustrates the conceptual approach of design by symmetry; and, in the process, it tosses out some ideas about how the Macintosh interface might evolve.

Design by Symmetry

Most approaches to creativity in design advocate throwing out rules and juxtaposing concepts that are essentially different in the hope that a new point of view, or a new concept, will serendipitously emerge (see the next chapter, "Tools and Techniques for Creative Design," for examples). In contrast, this chapter describes the technique of applying extended, precise analogies to design problems. Because the term *analogy* can be used to refer to anything from the vaguest likeness to a mathematically precise relationship [see Polya, 1957], and because the extended and rigorous nature of the analogies pursued are central to this technique, I shall use the word *symmetry* to designate an extended, highly precise analogy.

Design by symmetry works by juxtaposing concepts that are similar at a very deep level—the concepts are symmetric in terms of some deep structure or underlying process. Once the underlying symmetry is established, the designer attempts to extend the symmetry farther, using what is known about one domain to suggest new ideas about the other. Where traditional approaches to creative design require playfulness and produce new ideas via inspiration, design by symmetry requires analysis and produces new ideas by extrapolation.

This is all rather abstract. Let's look at an example of how design by symmetry works on a real problem. The problem is one that, as you may imagine, many people have been worrying about: how should the Macintosh interface evolve so as to accommodate the increasing demands being made of it?

Symmetry: The Macintosh Interface as a Language

In the late 1700s, explorers, traders in sandalwood, and immigrants began to make contact with the members of the oceanic culture of the South Pacific islands. Sometimes the contacts were fleeting, as in the case of explorers, and sometimes they were more permanent, as with immigrants and traders. These contacts are of interest because they required the members of two radically different cultures to communicate, even though there was no common language. A language had to be invented. Such languages are variously known as *trade languages, contact vernaculars,* or *pidgins.*

Pidgins—which have developed in many times and places throughout the world—share a number of characteristics. First and foremost, pidgins are easy to learn. Ease of learning is the *raison d'etre* of a pidgin; its users are typically those who lack the time or inclination to learn a language— they simply want to get on with business. The other characteristics shared by pidgins are clearly related to their ease of learning. Pidgins employ only simple sentences, with very regular, if awkward, syntax. For example, a plural of a word might be formed by repeating it. Pidgins have no tenses— all statements are present tense. Pidgins have a very limited vocabulary, which may be buttressed by the use of pointing and other gestures. Finally, pidgins typically allow their speakers to deal with a very narrow segment of the culture. Though you can't discuss philosophy, make puns, or express the subtleties of the extant culture using a pidgin, you can bargain for food, trade for goods, or make travel arrangements.

What does this have to do with the Macintosh? The Macintosh interface is much like a pidgin. First and foremost, the Macintosh interface is easy to learn. Ease of learning was the driving force behind the development of the Macintosh interface; it was targeted at users who lacked the time or inclination to learn about a computer—they simply wanted to get on with business. Like a pidgin, the Macintosh interface has a simple, noun-verb syntax: first you select the object, then you specify the action to be carried out. The Macintosh interface has almost no tense—most of its commands take effect here and now. A user cannot issue a command and specify that it will take place at some point in the future, with the exception of being able to tie a few actions to the next start-up via the "Set Startup" command and settings in "Chooser." The Macintosh interface also has the limited vocabulary characteristic of pidgins, and is extended by using simple pointing and dragging gestures. Finally, like a pidgin, the Macintosh interface has distinct limitations in its communicative power—you can get your basic tasks done, but that's about it.

I have made the case for the existence of an underlying symmetry between the Macintosh interface and a class of simple languages called pidgins. The next step is to examine other characteristics of pidgins and see what sort of insights they can provide about the Macintosh interface and the various ways in which it might develop.

Extending the Symmetry

Pidgins have another characteristic: under proper circumstances, pidgins spontaneously evolve into a more complex type of language called a *creole*. This is particularly interesting *vis à vis* the Macintosh interface, because the characteristic ways that pidgins evolve into creoles may tell us what properties a linguistic system—or an interface—must have for it to become a powerful communicative device while remaining relatively simple and easy to learn. First we'll look at when and how pidgins evolve into creoles, and then, extending the symmetry, we'll examine some ways in which the Macintosh interface might evolve.

The evolution of pidgins into creoles is relatively rare. It thus behooves us to look at the conditions under which such evolution does occur. Creoles develop in two types of situations: pidgin speakers may be deprived of the opportunity to use their mother tongue, or pidgin becomes so widely used in the community that it becomes natural to use it in the home. The first situation often occurred as a result of the slave trade in the Caribbean, when slaves from the same areas were deliberately separated to reduce the possibility of an uprising. In more recent times, rapid modernization, such as in New Guinea, has resulted in the intermingling of such a large number of linguistically distinct groups that no single one emerges as dominant, and a pidgin becomes an important, and high status, community language. These and other observations suggest that the prerequisites for the evolution of a pidgin into a creole are: 1) lack of a fully-developed common language; 2) lack of a dominant, "full-featured" language that could become a common language; and 3) cultural pressures for a more complex communicative system. It is worth noting that parallels to these pressures exist in the computer world. There is clearly no interface *lingua franca*, nor even a clear candidate for one. Yet there certainly do seem to be pressures for more power in human-computer communication.

Now let's look at how a pidgin evolves into a creole. One of the most fascinating aspects of the change from pidgin to creole is that—regardless of the sophistication of the adults—the transformation from pidgin to creole occurs only in the speech of pidgin-speaking children. Adults who are pidgin speakers remain pidgin speakers for life, even in the presence of children who have become creole speakers. This spontaneous emergence of a more complex language, from the mouths of babes, as it were, suggests that the features of creoles are fundamental to a powerful, yet simple, communicative system. The following features spontaneously emerge as part of the pidgin-to-creole evolution: complex syntax—for example, devices for marking relative clauses; past and future tenses; and a much larger vocabulary.

The next step is to consider how these characteristics of creoles map onto the Macintosh interface. Clearly the Macintosh interface has a very simple syntax, essentially noun-verb. The appearance of more complex syntax in pidgin-to-creole evolution suggests that a more complex syntax is not necessarily an evil. For example, one element of syntax that emerges during the evolution of a creole is a relative clauses mechanism. Although this could be interpreted in several ways, one possibility is that because relative clauses allow speakers to embed comments in a sentence, a general means of annotating objects would be a useful way of extending the power of the interface without overburdening the user.

The appearance of tense in creoles is easy to extend into the Macintosh interface. Time should become an integral part of the interface. For example, it should be possible to tie a command to any possible future event, not just start-up, or to tie it to an actual time, as in: "Call up the Applelink electronic mail system and download my mail at 3 a.m. every morning."

Although the development of complexity, richness, and range in creoles is predictable, the particulars of such developments are not. The expanded size of a creole's vocabulary results from a number of different mechanisms. One way creoles expand is that new words are coined. Obviously, new words mean new actions and new objects in the Macintosh interface. It also suggests that a useful addition to the interface would be a way of dynamically creating new vocabulary; that is, an integrated macro capacity. Such a capacity ought to provide for the creation of both objects and actions, and ought to allow them to be used just as existing objects and actions are used. Another way a creole's vocabulary expands is that the meanings of existing words become more general—they are used in a wider variety of situations and for a wider variety of purposes. This suggests that a natural way of extending the interface is to transpose familiar interface objects to new contexts, where they may play similar roles.

This symmetry could be extended much further. Our treatment of the roles of syntax, tense, and vocabulary expansion in the Macintosh interface has been cursory. More is known about pidgin-creole evolution [for example, see Holm, 1988] that could be extended into the Macintosh domain. However, for the purposes of illustrating design by symmetry, our example is sufficient.

Note that many of the specific features suggested by this symmetry are already appearing in the Macintosh interface; for example, the "Set Start-up" command corresponds to an instance of allowing tense in the interface. But it is only one instance of tense; many more can be imagined. The real value of the design by symmetry method in this case is that it provides a framework for the evolution of the interface.

Properties of Symmetries

Three characteristics distinguish design by symmetry from most other methods of fostering creativity in design. First, as noted above, design by symmetry tends to produce a conceptual framework, as well as new ideas and expressions. Because one of the banes of interface design is creeping featurism—the proliferation of individually desirable, but collectively unmanageable features—a method that encourages a coherent approach to adding features is surely of great value.

Second, design by symmetry is ideally suited for cross-disciplinary work. The Macintosh-interface-as-language symmetry draws upon work in linguistics and anthropology for its substance. Other symmetries may draw on other disciplines. For example, Susan Brennan in her chapter examines the implications of a symmetry based on research in psycholinguistics: interface-is-conversation. She explores how what we understand of human-human conversational interaction may be extended to human-computer interaction.

Third, once a symmetry has been discovered, it has the potential of being extended in many directions. For example, the Macintosh-interface-as-language symmetry could also be extended in a different direction. It would be interesting to study the cultural conditions that promote the evolution of creoles; this might shed light on conditions that would foster the evolution of computer interfaces. Lest the notion of cultural effects on interface evolution seem entirely academic, note that one reason for the continued consistency of the Macintosh interface across products from thousands of developers is that the Macintosh "community"—end users, developers, reviewers—has bought into the ideas of ease of use and consistency. It is likely that sociologists and anthropologists could discover quite a bit about what sort of things might promote the health of the "Macintosh culture," and thus the health of the interface.

Creativity in Design

Design by symmetry is just one method of fostering creativity in design. In spite of my tongue-in-cheek opening comments, I think that all methods—be they left-brained, right-brained, or harebrained—can be of immense value to the designer. New ideas and new perspectives are always in demand.

Tools and Techniques for Creative Design

"A WEEKDAY EDITION OF *THE NEW YORK TIMES* contains more information than the average person was likely to come across in a lifetime in seventeenth century England" [Wurman, 1989]. The world is rich with data, rapidly becoming more varied in media type—sounds, photos, FAX, computer-generated images, telephony, as well as text flood our lives. The challenge is how to best present and represent such data within the interface, to transform it into useful information.

For computer users, much so-called information is virtually inaccessible, not only because there is so much of it, but also because the many types of information formats and delivery systems are not integrated at the interface. Electronic mail, for instance, comes in a bewildering assortment of flavors: screen text, voice, or paper print-out; usenet, MCI, or interoffice e-mail; personal messages, electronic conferences, or bulletin boards. Telecommunications, service industries, entertainment companies, and educational institutions will use tomorrow's personal information environments to store and present enormous worlds of data. Several business areas do not yet provide extensive computer access to their workers; for example, theatrical production, fast-food chains, creative art and design companies, travel-related industries, bookings, and merchandise ordering in retail sales. Future interfaces need to incorporate new information types and to accommodate new types of users with additional customized real-world interface metaphors that make information easy to find and use.

S. Joy Mountford

Human Interface Group
Apple Computer, Inc.

With the onslaught of more varied information and application types, there is a great need for guidance in generating more creative, usable interface designs. We need techniques to help us do a better job of visualizing the look and feel of potential interfaces. Such interface prototyping tools as HyperCard have been a great step forward in enabling graphic designers to demonstrate their ideas, but we need even more powerful tools with which to emulate the "feel" of the interface in the hands of new users with new uses. A limited number of computer tools are available to assist in the design process (see the chapter by Wagner in this volume), but even fewer exist to help us decide which ideas are worthwhile.

The science and art of computer interface design is a relatively young discipline within a world of more mature design traditions. There are few success stories for interface designers to learn from, compared with traditional disciplines such as mathematics and biology. There are even fewer principles that can help us predict the behavior of our clients, the users. We have much to learn about interpersonal communication, group behavior, aesthetics, showmanship, and users' adaptability to change. Some of our new interface ideas will come from people who study thought, language, entertainment, and communication, as well as from people who study hardware, algorithms, data structures. We need to find better mechanisms for facilitating collaboration among designers from both artistic and scientific points of view, as articulated in "The Role of the Artist in the Laboratory" [Buxton, 1988].

This paper examines the emerging discipline of interface design in terms of established disciplines, the present state of the art, and techniques for generating new ideas. Looking to the past, we can identify mature design disciplines in other fields that can inform our own. The first section of this paper examines the areas of "traditional" animation, theater, architecture, industrial design, and information display for techniques and approaches that can be of use to human-computer interface designers. The second section looks at the more contemporary tools of metaphor and user observation. The final section of the paper surveys some techniques for designing the interfaces of the future through brainstorming and the creative juxtaposition of ideas.

New Wine from Old Vats

FILM

Table 1 shows an insightful historical timeline indicating some of the changes that have occurred to various communication crafts as they moved from being inventions to being art forms (this table is taken from *The Elements of Friendly Software Design* [Heckel, 1984]). Heckel views "software as a newcomer to communication crafts." It is interesting to note that one of the most recent "arts" to change its form is filmmaking, which

Writing	Painting	Film	Drama	Photography	Architecture	Music	Computers
3300 BC Egyptian hieroglyphics	**20000 BC** Cave Paintings of Lascaux, France	**1884** Thomas Edison demonstrates kinetoscope	**600 BC** First Greek amphitheatre built for festival of Dionysos	**1839** Daguerre announces his photographic method	**2700 BC** Pyramids at Sakkara and Gizeh	**2000 BC** Invention of the Egyptian harp	**450 BC** First abacus
2300 BC Maxims of Ptohhotep	**3000 BC** Egyptian tomb paintings	**1903** Edwin Porter's *The Great Train Robbery*	**550 BC** Introduction of the chorus in Greek plays	**1861** Mathew Brady's civil war photographs	**400 BC** Parthenon Athens	**1306 AD** First pedal organ	**1864** Charles Babbage's analytic engine
1500 BC Development of phonetic alphabet	**1100 AD** Invention of oil paints	**1915** D.W. Griffith's *Birth of a Nation*	**442 BC** Sophocles' *Antigone*	**1882** Eastman develops Kodak camera	**1100 AD** Development of flying buttress	**1404** First clavichord	**1955** First commercial mainframe computer
800 BC Library of Assyria founded	**1497** Da Vinci's *Last Supper*	**1927** First Sound Movie: *The Jazz Singer*	**1580 AD** Establishment of the first repertory companies	**1902** Stieglitz's "Spring Showers"	**1400** Completion of Chartres Cathedral	**1520** First violin	**1958** Fortran: First high level language
1440 AD Gutenberg's invention of moveable type	**1654** Rembrandt's *Portrait of Jan Six*	**1941** Orson Welles' *Citizen Kane*	**1603** Shakespeare's *Hamlet*	**1947** Ansel Adams' Yosemite photographs	**1920** Invention of pre-stressed concrete	**1602** Monteverdi's first opera, *Orfeo*	**1975** First Personal Computer
1605 Cervantes' *Don Quixote*	**1937** Picasso's *Guernica*				**1936** Frank Lloyd Wright's "Falling Water"	**1720** J.S. Bach: *Well-Tempered Clavier*	**1978** VisiCalc
1719 First Modern Novel: Defoe's *Robinson Crusoe*						**1824** Beethoven's Ninth (Choral) Symphony	**1979** WordStar

Table 1: Most communications crafts started as inventions and evolved slowly in the direction of an art form. Software is a newcomer to the world of communications crafts. Reprinted by permission of Warner Books, Inc., from Elements of Friendly Software Design, *copyright © 1984 by Paul Heckel.*

likewise had its roots as an engineering discipline. Originally movies were viewed as having a fixed window within which some action occurred; they were often nothing more than continous slideshows of information. The roots of filmmaking changed with the production of *Birth of a Nation* by D. W. Griffith in 1914. Engineers who had controlled films actually lost out to those who saw the artistic possibilities for film. Griffith's success began the relatively recent tradition of films as an art form, communicating directly to an audience.

The next "new" communications medium is likely to be that of software design. Like film, software was originally dominated by those who knew how to program, but this has now expanded to include a much larger audience. The first most widely used successful piece of software was VisiCalc™, which was considered "friendly" and usable by a wide audience who had hitherto found financial packages rather cumbersome. Tools such as HyperCard™ have made the price of entry into so-called "programming," or rather scripting, much more accessible to a range of new, more artistic, skill sets. It would serve interface designers well to learn from the lessons of filmmaking, to facilitate the best growth directions for interface design. Our new interfaces will serve as future vehicles of communication to a large audience, the world's users.

ANIMATION

Walt Disney Studios produced their most famous animation classics long before computer animation existed. Disney's goal was to create an animated form of communication that was as new in the 1920s as computers were in the 1960s. Both are powerful communicative forms that rely heavily on the use of graphics. We employ limited animation in the Macintosh interface today—the zooming effect for opening and closing of files, for instance. New uses for animation in human-computer interfaces are explored in the chapter by Baecker and Small in this volume. Tomorrow's personal computers have the potential to create animations rich enough to allow users to actually interact with dramatic dynamic events. The principles developed by the Disney animators, who worked without automated assistants, are likely to prove quite useful in interface design.

A set of twelve principles of animation is detailed in *Disney Animation: The Illusion of Life*, by Thomas and Johnston [1984]. Anticipation, for example, is a motion characteristic that can both provide information and produce powerful dramatic effects. Disney's animated characters exaggerate the way bodies prepare to move forward by pulling backwards slightly beforehand. Anticipation "telegraphs" the character's intent, adding visual continuity and a sense of realism that carries the audience forward with the character. Disney also used sound quite effectively to represent such aspects of events as position, direction, and speed of motion. Sound can be similarly applied to interface events to establish continuity and provide information for the user (see the chapter by Mountford and Gaver in this volume). Each of Disney's principles of animation contains valuable insights and techniques for interface designers.

THEATER

The dramatic arts are full of promising ideas for interface design. Contemporary discussions of software agents with humanlike qualities brings one to consider exactly what makes characters effective and believable (see the chapter by Laurel in this volume). A recent research project at Apple called Guides demonstrated a way of searching a database with the help of different personal viewpoints. These personal guides gave users their individual viewpoints of a encyclopedic slice of Grolier's American history. Initial studies indicated that users found the guides engaging and informative (see the chapter by Oren et al. in this volume). Dramatic stories and characters are familiar and effective mechanisms for structuring thought and behavior. We have barely begun to scratch the surface in applying this body of knowledge to computer interface design.

Drama has the power to *engage* audience members both emotionally and cognitively. Interactive plays and novels are beginning to be studied to see what facets make them more or less effective with readers and viewers. By isolating the key factors contributing to audience involvement and participation, we can discover techniques for enhancing direct engagement through human-computer interfaces [Laurel, 1986].

ARCHITECTURE

Architecture and interface design have an important goal in common: to create livable, workable, attractive environments. The principle of "form follows function" maintains that the form of objects should follow their functional requirements. The architectural movement towards functionalism was initially contested in Victorian England, as the industrial age was trying to hide the impact of industrialization on people's everyday lives. Le Corbusier was initially viewed with skepticism when he proposed that a house was a *machine for living*, as opposed to the traditional idea that a house was a shelter. He likened a house to a ship or bridge in its function. Likewise, we are only just beginning to conceive of computers as extensions of our functional everyday lives.

The listing of all the requirements to be met on an architect's design project have become known as *programming*. The more precise these definitions can be made on a project, the less likely it is that variations will occur among the different contributors to any design project. In architecture, these requirements are often referred to as *constraints*, just as they are known to interface designers. In order to make the process of designing within constraints as systematic as possible for architects, Alexander [1964] devised a set of steps for listing all functional requirements for a given architectural design problem. As an example, he specifies 21 requirements for designing a tea kettle. He then studies the interactions between the requirements and groups them into related clusters that form a hierarchical order of relationships that will govern the final design.

Managing trade-offs becomes rather difficult when the architect cannot control all of the variables. For example, requirements for plenty of natural light and interior quiet may be in conflict. If the windows must face a noisy street for the best light, then a trade-off decision must be made. Such trade-off decisions can be made in isolation by even an inexperienced designer, but experienced designers can often generate better alternatives because they have a better feel for the relative importance of the various requirements. Experience can lead to more graceful solutions. As Pile observes:

Satisfactory performance is invariably a matter of meeting a number of requirements—a vast number in the case of complex designs. The various requirements may be in conflict so that different satisfactory solutions can result from differing emphases on differing requirements. One most satisfactory solution only can emerge in the limited context of one particular evaluation of the relative importance of various desiderata. [Pile, 1979]

Alexander captures some of the wisdom of an experienced designer in his formal methodology. It can improve the performance of the inexperienced, and can help even an experienced designer make a more systematic analysis of the consequences of alternative solutions. This approach is controversial because it says little about beauty, harmony, or pleasure. Even so, it can be a spur to creativity in the fields of both architecture and interface designs.

INDUSTRIAL DESIGN

The experience of designing real-world objects for everyday use has a lot to teach us about how to design usable interfaces for software. Those designs which endure the test of time are mostly those that are reliable, offering straightforward ease of use and pleasurable user experiences. The chapter by Vertelney and Booker in this volume suggests principles and techniques of industrial design that can guide our interface work.

INFORMATION DISPLAY

In applications ranging from statistical graphics to scientific visualization, computers are used increasingly as tools for creating graphical displays of information. Often, however, the designers of such displays fail to take advantage of the techniques developed in "traditional" information display disciplines. The graphical prowess of today's computers has encouraged the production of a plethora of unreadable graphics, characterized by Tufte as "chartjunk" [see Verity, 1985]. Tufte goes on to observe that "people who don't see particularly well are designing interfaces to graphics machines. People have been doing books for 500 years and much wisdom has come from all that activity" [Tufte, 1983]. Not just interface designers, but American culture as a whole, seems to undervalue the established disciplines in this area—in Japan, for instance, there is an Annual Statistics Day contest and celebration! Experts in traditional fields like statistics and cartography can provide wisdom and techniques to the designer of graphical information displays (see figure 1).

The domain of classical mathematics employs a linear language of symbolic expression that is poorly suited to the representation of parallel events and processes, yet this is often the first "language" adopted by interface designers—the software for creating 3-D graphics on a leading graphics workstation, for instance, requires the user to define figures and specify

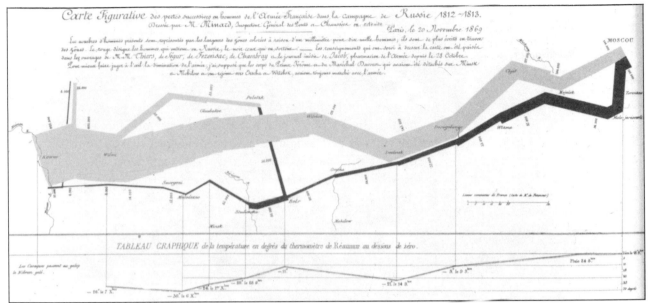

their movements mathematically at the interface. A conversational metaphor provides a good alternative to the formal language of mathematics. Smalltalk, for example, exemplifies an object-oriented approach where "objects" are given "messages" specifying their desired behavior, placing the emphasis on "communication" among the elements of the program.

Within statistics, Deken [1985] takes the conversational motif a step further by proposing three types of agents to assist users in the analysis and evaluation of data. *Data-item agents* could capture data and verify its "fit" by applying expertise in handling approximations and noticing relationships among data. This data-item agent could likewise communicate with an *organizer agent* that could create an organizational structure for the data. A *reporter agent* could take care of providing a variety of useful representations of the data to the user, even to the point of suggesting relevant questions. Deken's model illustrates a dynamic and conversational approach to data transactions, borrowing from the dramatic arts in its use of the behavioral associations among actors/agents.

Most people have experienced the situation in which a good diagram can explain more than the prose one would use to describe it. Why and how a good diagram works, however, is poorly understood. A picture is not always worth a thousand words, and even great scientists could benefit from the support of artists in visually representing their work (see figure 2).

A general observation is that perceptual codes in diagrams convey less information than symbolic ones. Symbolic representations elicit conscious cognitive processing, whereas analogic, pictorial ones are perceived more

Figure 1: A map of the progress of Napoleon's invasion of Russia. Expert cartographers and statisticians can create graphical displays that are packed with accessible information. "Napoleon's March to Moscow: The War of 1812." Edward R. Tufte, The Visual Display of Quantitative Information. Cheshire, CT: Graphics Press, 1983.

Figure 2: A sketch from Galileo's analysis of the strength of a beam. The sketch obscures its information content with a welter of irrelevant detail. Obtained from the Ann Ronan Picture Library, Somerset, England.

automatically. A map, for example, provides specific locational information using grid coordinates, which for some people is more useful than analogic spatial arrangement. Examples of frequently used perceptual codes are contour mapping, color coding of electrical systems, and auditory tone distinctions used in telephone systems. Venn diagrams are used to represent inclusion—a notion that is difficult to communicate through natural language, especially when more than two sets are involved. Flowcharts provide visual representations of connectedness and sequence. In musical notation, symbolic codes (the forms of notes themselves) give specific information about pitch (through the position of a note on the staff) and duration, and the perceptual effect of "blackness" on the staff provides general information about the speed of the music.

Such principles of information display as the effective use of perceptual and symbolic codes can be applied to a variety of problems in interface design. Successful graphic and layout techniques can even make computer programs easier to visualize. For example, Fitter and Green [1979] have found that understanding is enhanced when different programs are represented in ways that are as perceptually distinct as possible. Baecker and Marcus [1989] similarly have applied knowledge about information display to the task of visualizing programs written in C.

Contemporary Interface Design Tools: Metaphor and User Observation

In addition to the wealth of wisdom to be gained from the study of design in other traditional domains, the discipline of interface design has developed some methodologies of its own that are worth reviewing. Related to the notion of borrowing techniques from other domains is the idea of creating interface metaphors that can anchor users' understanding of the computer to something with which they are already familiar. Conversely, studying people as they perform familiar, well-understood tasks can provide valuable insights about possible ways to represent tasks on the computer.

INTERFACE METAPHORS

Interface design is a relatively new human endeavor and has benefitted much from the application of metaphor in helping interface designers who understand it mainly by virtue of being human:

> The metaphor is perhaps one of man's most fruitful potentialities. Its efficacy verges on magic, and it seems a tool for creation which God forgot inside one of His creatures when He made him. [y Gasset, 1925]

Metaphors are powerful verbal and semantic tools for conveying both superficial and deep similarities between familiar and novel situations. We are generally unaware of the extent to which metaphor is embedded in our thought and language (see Erickson's chapter on metaphor in this volume). As MacCormac describes them, "Metaphors not only communicate suggestive and expressive meanings but they also become iconic objects through their fusion of sense with sound" [MacCormac, 1985].

The Macintosh computer interface is a well-known example of the successful use of various metaphors to facilitate new users' understanding of the computer and its functions. During the development of the Lisa interface, Apple designers found that the "desktop metaphor" was preferred by users to a form-fill-in dialog box. Much of the ease of use of the Macintosh interface is attributable to the correspondence between the appearance, uses, and behaviors of such interface objects as documents and folders and their real-world counterparts; conversely, user difficulties are often attributable to differences between them.

Although some find the use of interface metaphors to be too constraining (see Nelson's chapter in this volume), designers can optimize the cognitive value of metaphors and minimize difficulties through careful selection and implementation. As Lakoff and Johnson [1980] observe, metaphors do not imply a complete mapping of every concrete detail of one object or situation onto another; rather they emphasize certain features and suppress others. Thorough examination of a candidate metaphor helps designers to discover its inherent selectivity and use it to their advantage.

OBSERVING REAL-WORLD TASKS AND ENVIRONMENTS

Development of some worthy "new" ideas for introduction into the electronic world can come from careful examination of the "traditional" ways of performing tasks. As Don Norman exhorts elsewhere in this volume, designers must sit down in offices, factories, and schools and watch the problems people encounter and the tools they use to solve them in their everyday work and education.

Observation of a person at a traditional physical desk reveals typical and extended ways of working that are not supported by a computer system. For example, the person may start writing a small Post-it™ note to carry with them, then on another plain piece of paper draw a map sketch, and on another plain piece of paper paint in different colors. Today, trying to do the same thing using a computer is immensely more complicated. Typically, different applications have to be launched separately depending on the kinds of data to be created; writing, drawing, and painting are all separate applications and different data types. Individual elements must be pasted together, sometimes requiring that they be transformed into new data types, in order to create a finished document.

The observations above have led to the further refinement of a set of interface ideas often referred to as the *plain-paper metaphor*, likening the screen to a blank sheet of paper. Currently, users must break their work up into separate tasks and perform each within its associated environment—taking the tasks to the tools. The plain-paper metaphor would reverse this process by bringing the tools to the task. "Virtual" tools could be designed to correspond to "real-world" uses.

Metaphors have two distinct but related uses in interface design: as cognitive aids to users, and as aids to creativity for designers. Metaphors can help designers to use their own, often unconscious expectations to create new information links and mental structures. The creative use of metaphor and other techniques for formally facilitating creativity are reviewed in the next section.

Techniques for Generating New Ideas

No one really knows where good ideas come from or what actually makes them "good". Novelty is desirable, and so is a close fit between the idea and some real-world problem. Leverage and generality are also important. So where do these novel, useful, high-leverage, general ideas come from? What follows are some suggestions on how to stimulate thought by looking at the world in unusual and nontraditional ways.

Some people believe that new ideas are almost always the result of collisions—juxtaposition or recombinations of ideas [Koestler, 1964]. Consciously creating juxtapositions of normally unassociated referents may suggest new, previously unsuspected hypotheses about how to approach or solve a problem. Adams [1986] provides a series of brainstorming steps that can help designers expand existing metaphorical elements and generate new ideas. Designers can be encouraged more formally to think more broadly and openly about their interface designs by engaging in lateral thinking exercises. What follows is a series of interface design exercises based on Adams' axioms, many of which illustrate ideas that have been considered in the design of past interactive systems.

New Uses for the Object   Consider the "desktop" interface. What else could a desktop be used for? People often use a real desk as a space for communication—laying out papers and showing intermediate stages of their work, marking them up together, putting them in a different order. The "desktop" could be used similarly as a space for shared work and as a communications area.

Adapt the Object To Be Like Something Else   What if we adapt our "desktop" to be more like a kitchen? In kitchens, we find lots of basic and specialized tools that are used to create a myriad of different items (food). The same ingredient creates different foods when different tools are applied to it. For example, grating a carrot can produce fine-grained garnishes, but placing it in a blender produces juice. If we could identify or create some similar basic ingredients to serve as building blocks, they could serve as models for building better general-purpose tools. How would these ideas change the "contents" and organizational structure of an interface?

Modify the Object for a New Purpose   What happens if we add the desire of providing information about the larger environment to our "desktop"? We might employ environmental sound, as in a real office, to provide information about adjacent activities. We might treat windows as periscopes or portholes through which we can observe or even travel to other parts of the environment (rather like Smalltalk project Views/Rooms from Xerox PARC).

Magnify—Add to the Object   We could add various features to the "desktop" that are already present in a real desk; for example, a drawer with scissors, glue, tape, and other tools (PARC Cypress, 1977, and Apple II

Jane, 1983, are examples). We could add features like phones, calendars, diaries, FAX, newspaper service, or shopping lists. These items would enhance and extend its functionality.

Minimize—Subtract from the Object We might pare away the desk until all that is left is the "desktop" and a drawer with blank sheets of paper and a pencil in it. What could be accomplished with only these items? (This is usually described as the "plain paper metaphor," an idea that may actually predate the notion of separate applications.) This helps prevent the mind-set of always adding more and more isolated pieces of technology.

Substitute Something Similar A "desktop" may not be a useful metaphor for every user in every task domain. What about a delivery service? Instead of things like files and folders, the interface could be organized in terms of trucks, routes, and ordering systems. The trash can could become a dumpster. Another interesting metaphor is the idea of an interface with peel-off transparent layers.

Rearrange the Data What if we reorganized the basic layout of the "desktop" so that the scroll bars were at the top (as in Smalltalk) and the menu bar was at the bottom? Among other things, we may discover such biases as a layout for right-handed people. We might also use the same technique to generate ideas for designing an alternative interface for left-handed users.

Reverse or Transpose the Information Turning the metaphor inside out creates some interesting ideas. What would happen if windows were views from files to the desktop rather than the other way around? What if everything were circular rather than rectangular in form? What if we were to view the desktop from below rather than above? What if we saw it from very *far* above—what else would come into view? Ideas of different visual lenses come to mind; for example, fisheyes and magnifiers.

Combine the Data into an Ensemble What larger metaphor might the "desktop" be a part of? Beyond its area is perhaps a virtual office, a whole building-full of data-rooms, cities, or worlds of information. How might this larger metaphor be represented? How would the desktop fit into it?

Role Playing

In addition to Adams' exercises, thought provocation through role playing [von Oech, 1986] might help designers to create, evaluate, and develop ideas by assuming different points of view. Often it seems that the only point of view we have time for is the defense of our own existing positions, roles, and ideas. It is too easy to get blinded by our own myopic view.

Deliberately assuming different roles can be both creative and liberating. Von Oech describes four characters that are active in all of us to varying degrees and, depending on our job descriptions, that are allowed in different proportions to work on a problem:

The Explorer: This character gathers information on an issue, researching the problem before the solution set exists. Activities include reading, asking others about their views, and deciding which issues need additional work or definition.

The Artist: This character generates new ideas in the problem-solving phase. This phase is the most energetic and active. New problem definitions, potential solutions, and alternative next paths for action are produced.

The Judge: This character evaluates and filters the ideas that have been generated. At this stage some ideas must be discarded—a task that is less appealing to creative folks. New ideas won't emerge if the Judge is in charge at the beginning of the brainstorming process.

The Warrior: This character champions a particular idea and sets the course for the next round of problem-solving. This includes planning how the idea will be tested, evaluated, and developed.

Creative problem-solving can be enhanced by exercising mental agility— the ability to move easily between different roles. No one of these four types of characters can make an idea succeed without the other characters' participation. Knowing how and when to change character roles is crucial. A useful exercise is to take 30 minutes to brainstorm and to plan out a solution to any particular problem, alternating roles between the four described characters every 7 minutes. This approach can demonstrate how each of the different roles contributes to the overall decision. We have tried such exercises at Apple and have found that the transcripts of such role-playing sessions offer much food for thought even later.

ENHANCING CREATIVITY

Is creativity a talent, accessible only to a gifted few, or is it a skill that can be learned? This question has been debated and researched from a surprising variety of angles, from discussions by theorists such as Koestler [1964] and Harman and Rheingold [1984] to practical brainstorming and unblocking guidebooks from applied imagineers such as von Oech [1986], Adams [1986], and McKim [1972]. Current research into the cognitive underpinnings of human learning is making important contributions to the study of creativity. Books and exercises for enhancing creativity are worthwhile for interface designers, especially those connected with visual thinking [Hanks and Belliston, 1980] and right brain exercises [Edwards, 1986]. They all serve as platforms for individual and group exercises that can help us better understand our users' needs and propose some usable and creative solutions to their problems.

As software becomes a more powerful and pervasive tool for communicating and learning, the need will increase to find new ways to look at interfaces and their designs. Interface designers can learn from the past successes and failures of other design/communication disciplines. The idea of *visual thinking* as promoted by Arnheim [1969], McKim [1972], and others emphasizes the success designers can achieve by educating themselves in new perspectives. The development of new prototyping tools and hardware platforms with greater capabilities, as well as techniques for using traditional design knowledge with new creative methods and fresh perspectives, will facilitate the design of exciting new interfaces.

Interface designers must live in both the present and the future. While we are working on our present interface problems, we should be thinking about how to create tools to better build on our knowledge and make it reusable and available to others. The best contribution that we can make to the understanding of the communication interface is to create and build tools to be better able to do our own jobs. Right now we are just beginning to discover what these tools should be, creating specifications for their design, and experimenting with new methodologies. In the future, we will be challenged to make the most of this power to pass on our understanding both to other designers and to new users in the form of new, more powerful, more easily learnable, and more engaging ways to use computers.

Interdisciplinary Cooperation

#$(*&% @ to You, Too!

IN THE EARLY DAYS, computers and software were designed by engineers for engineers. Nowadays they are designed by teams that include psychologists, artists, and writers, as well as engineers and programmers. Because many of these alliances are new, misunderstandings naturally arise. Here is a typical exchange between a graphic designer and a programmer.

Scott Kim

Look Twice, Inc.

Designer: I'm interested in computers. Can you help?

Programmer: Gladly! What would you like to know?

Designer: What can I do with this computer?

Programmer: Anything you want.

Designer: Marvelous! Show me a page of text.

Programmer: Okay.

Designer: But that looks ugly.

Programmer: That's the font that's built into the machine.

Designer: I guess that's the way computers look.

Programmer: No, you could change the font, too.

Designer: Okay, let's redesign it.

Programmer: But it would take a lot of work. And besides, I don't see anything wrong with this one.

Designer: *Can't you see what's in front of you?*

Programmer: *Can't you tell me the rules?*

Both people walk away frustrated. The programmer feels annoyed that the artist doesn't appreciate the work involved; the designer feels outraged that the programmer cannot see the obvious. Yet both people started with good intentions. What is going on? How can such situations be improved?

This article is about interdisciplinary cooperation and how to make it work better. The ideas are based on my recent studies at Stanford University as an interdisciplinary graduate student in computers and graphic design. I conclude that disciplines are like cultures: for disciplines to work well together they must learn to appreciate one another's language, traditions, and values. I raise these issues here because human-computer interface design is a particularly interdisciplinary field. For interface design to thrive, many disciplines must cooperate.

Different Disciplines Have Different Priorities

Different disciplines have different priorities, different thinking styles, different values. When people from different disciplines get together, their values collide. What one person finds valuable others do not even notice. And they do not notice that they do not notice.

I first understood this effect some years ago when I started as a graduate student at Stanford. Computer science professor Donald Knuth had just developed a programming language for typeface design called Metafont. I liked Metafont's mix of artistic and technical considerations.

Metafont allows a designer to design a typeface by writing a program, rather than by drawing shapes on paper. Programming a typeface allows a designer to make systematic variations—like changing the thickness of all strokes—without having to redraw each letter individually. Knuth's dream was to enable designers to express the structural ideas of their typefaces in a precise notation akin to music notation.

As the resident programmer/artist I had the pleasure of demonstrating Metafont to many outstanding typeface designers. Over and over I heard the same demand: make it more visual. Designers said they would prefer to work directly with images on the screen, rather than type programs to produce images.

The obvious solution was a more graphic version of Metafont, similar to computer-aided design or painting programs that are common today. But I felt there was a deeper issue. I decided to keep probing.

The key question seemed to be "What is the difference between the thinking styles of a computer scientist and a graphic designer?" (Here I am lumping the concerns of typeface designers with the concerns of visual communicators in general.) The computer science department proved a hostile environment for thinking about this question. The art department was no better. Each found the other way of thinking incomprehensible.

The explanation was simple: computer scientists and graphic designers have different priorities. Computer scientists value the program and how it works; graphic designers value the picture and how it looks. This difference is the primary source of misunderstanding between computer scientists and graphic designers.

In computer science, the life or death struggle is getting the program to run. The entire programming environment supports this single task. Other things matter also—a computer will not run without electricity—but those jobs can be delegated. Until the program works, a programmer feels obsessed. It is hard for a programmer to say "Oh, my program crashed, no problem. I'll just go home and come back tomorrow." If you want to talk to a programmer, it is important to know that you will not be trusted unless you have written a program. The program can be simple; all that matters is that you have experienced the basic drama of programming.

In graphic design, the life or death struggle is getting the picture to look right. The entire studio environment supports this single task. Other things matter also—a painting will not survive without proper paint chemistry— but those jobs can be delegated. Until the picture works, an artist feels obsessed. It is hard for an artist to say "Oh, my composition doesn't balance, no problem. I'll just go home and come back tomorrow." If you want to talk to an artist, it is important to know that you have not gotten down to the real business until you start looking at pictures. It does not matter what you say; the proof is in the portfolio.

Programs and pictures—each of these priorities is so obvious to someone within the discipline that it goes without saying, but so foreign to someone outside the discipline that it is almost unthinkable. As a result, outsiders not already attuned to the priorities of a discipline have difficulty breaking in.

Any self-respecting programmer will probably be outraged that I have reduced programming to mere coding. Isn't solving the user's problem the true priority of programming? Likewise, designers will be outraged that I have reduced design to mere production. Isn't clear communication the true priority of design? In both cases I emphasize the bottom-line survival priorities of a field rather than the conceptual goal-oriented priorities, because it is the survival priorities of a field that shape its culture.

Once I had isolated the issue of priorities, I was free to wonder what would happen if priorities were rearranged. Metafont is a computer scientist's approach to a graphic design task. The reverse of computer-aided design is design-aided computation. What would be a graphic designer's approach to a computer science task? This led me to my dissertation, which asks how computers might be different if they were designed for use by visual artists.

Flexible Humans and Rigid Disciplines

Here is a theory of disciplines that explains why miscommunication between disciplines occurs.

DISCIPLINES DEVELOP WHEN FLEXIBLE HUMANS MEET RECURRING SITUATIONS

When a human encounters a new situation, the human must invent a new response. If the situation occurs repeatedly, the human may find it more economical to develop a single habitual response than to invent a new response each time.

If the repeated situation affects many people, society may find it worthwhile to teach the habit as a practice. If the practice is worth improving, society may find it worthwhile to create a field of study around the practice. The field of study is a discipline.

Disciplines, like all human tools, are by nature rigid. A hammer must be hard, or it does not work. A theory must be precise, or it cannot be tested. A discipline must have traditions, or it cannot be passed on. Rigid tools give humans leverage.

Every Discipline Has a Hierarchy of Priorities Derived from the Survival Needs of the Original Situation

The same holds for habits or practices. In life itself, priorities include eating, sleeping, and breathing. In driving, priorities include staying on the road, having enough gas, and not colliding with other cars. In computer science, priorities include getting programs to run, not losing data, and keeping programs maintainable. In graphic design, priorities include anticipating the appearance of a printed piece before it is printed, communicating instructions accurately to printers, and visual consistency.

Priorities pervade every aspect of a discipline, including social organization, physical artifacts, training procedures, and specialized language. Priorities are not necessarily easy to meet; but because they are a matter of survival, enormous effort goes into their maintenance.

Everyone must eat, so society is organized to deliver food. Cars need roads, so an enormous network of roads webs the nation. Programs must be maintainable, so programmers organize programs according to conventions of structured programming. Colors must be printed accurately, so printers use special language for naming colors.

When a Discipline Becomes a Way of Life, Priorities Become Invisible

The nature of habit is to be unconscious. If you had to think about every footstep, walking would be mentally exhausting.

When you are surrounded by people who share the same habit, the habit becomes accepted as part of the natural order of things. It is hard to hear your own speech as having an accent, unless you have learned more than one way of speaking. Likewise, it is hard for programmers to remember that not everyone thinks in sequential logical terms, and for graphic designers to remember that not everyone looks for visual patterns.

Current society links personal identity to job category. You are not a person who drives buses; you are a bus driver. You are not a person interested in philosophy; you are a philosopher. Because jobs are linked to physical survival in the form of money, disciplinary priorities become personal priorities.

The invisibility of disciplinary priorities is both good and bad. On the one hand, they allow people within the same discipline to communicate more efficiently. On the other hand, they prevent people from noticing that their responses may no longer be appropriate.

When Priorities Are Threatened, Survival Feels Threatened

When people from different disciplines get together, their priorities are bound to misalign. The mismatches lead to the upsetting feeling that what one person considers important is being ignored by the other person.

This would not be a problem except for two points: because people identify with their disciplines, the insult is taken personally, and because priorities are invisible, the matter is not available for discussion. Each person feels personally attacked, and cannot figure out why.

I want to emphasize that interdisciplinary miscommunication is a direct result of the rigid nature of disciplines. It is not anybody's fault. It is not to be taken personally. And it is not insurmountable.

Why You Should Stick Your Nose into Other People's Business

Interdisciplinary cooperation sounds good in principle. In practice, there are many doubts.

IT'S NOT MY JOB

Certainly your first responsibility in a work situation is your job. But part of your job is to know what is not your job. Unless you understand where your job ends and someone else's begins, you will try to do work that is beyond your ability. And you will miss opportunities for creative synergy.

For instance, programmers who do not understand the contribution of artists to visual interface design often try to design screen layouts themselves and resist suggestions for improvement. Graphic designers who do not understand the capabilities of computers often design for the screen as if it were paper and miss the visual continuity problems of a dynamic medium. Together, a programmer and a graphic designer can create something much stronger than what either could create alone.

YES, BUT IT REALLY IS SOMEONE ELSE'S JOB

You may be right. But sometimes circumstances force us to do jobs outside our area of expertise, especially in small companies or innovative projects.

YES, BUT MY JOB REALLY IS SELF-CONTAINED

It is true that some jobs require less cooperation than others. If you are working by yourself on a job with tightly defined goals, you may have little need to talk with others. Talking with others can still help by giving you new ways of thinking about your discipline.

I ALREADY KNOW WHAT I NEED TO KNOW

No job in the computer industry stays the same for long. Job definitions keep changing as computers themselves change. For instance, technical writers need to keep learning more about graphic design as publishing software unifies text and illustration.

I Can't Afford the Time

Of course you cannot spend all your time learning about other disciplines. Decide for yourself how much time you can afford, then think about how to use it efficiently. If you never take time to explore, you will never find out what you are missing.

I Can't Go Back and Get Another Degree

Social pressures make it seem like you have to study for years before you are qualified to ask questions. The truth is that beginners often ask the most profound questions. And you do not have to be an expert to make good use of expert advice. You need to learn only as much as you find useful. No matter where you are, you can always make the best use of what you know.

I Tried, But I Couldn't Make Sense of the Jargon

People within a discipline often have trouble communicating what they know to outsiders. This is frustrating to everyone. Your best guide is probably someone from your own discipline who has already learned the new jargon.

I'm Scared of Looking Stupid

To take the pressure off yourself, imagine you are a reporter assigned to do a story on this other discipline. Ask intelligent questions readers might be interested in. Insist the answers be in terms that you, as a representative of your readers, can understand. If that is still too scary, take along a bodyguard. Treat your subject as you would like to be treated if the roles were reversed. If someone came to you and cheerfully mentioned that they would love to learn about a subject you know well, how would you respond?

I Can't Think That Way

You may feel like you cannot think about some other discipline, but such feelings are probably due to early discouragements ("math isn't lady-like," "art is for sissies"). Given enough support, there is no reason you cannot learn anything you want. Imagine you are an actor playing the role of an expert in another discipline. Rise to the occasion despite feelings of insecurity.

When I Need to Know, I'll Hire a Specialist

That is fine, as long as you know enough about the specialty to bring the specialist in early enough. A good solution is to talk to the specialist at the very beginning of a project, to figure out when the expertise will be most helpful. The specialist must also know about your area; otherwise, communication will be difficult.

How Do I Know It Will Be Relevant?

You don't. It is a risk. But not risking can be risky too. So you might as well give it a try. No one can judge relevance but you. And you cannot make judgments until you have collected all the facts impartially. Collect now, judge later.

This Is How We've Always Done It

Consider changing. Human-computer interface design is certainly improving, but without better interdisciplinary cooperation the field will continue to suffer large holes. For instance, most psychologists studying computers assume text dialog or window/menu interfaces. But these are only two possible interface styles among thousands. Unless psychologists talk to designers who are free to imagine alternate interface styles, their studies have no basis for drawing general conclusions.

It's Too Hard

It was once. But it does not have to be. That is what this paper is about.

How To Be an Interdisciplinary Ambassador

Disciplines are like cultures. For disciplines to work well together they must transcend national boundaries and learn to appreciate one anothers' cultures. Here are six steps you can take to improve interdisciplinary understanding.

1. **Patriot.** Start by being proud of your own discipline. If your discipline is systematically undervalued, you may find this exercise difficult. But before you can appreciate others you must be able to appreciate yourself.

   Think of a patriot. Appreciate the struggles and triumphs of your people. Recall what first interested you about your discipline. List persuasive reasons why your discipline has tremendous value. Value your discipline without devaluing other disciplines.

2. **Tour guide.** The first step towards interdisciplinary understanding is to welcome visitors from other disciplines, just because they are who they are, whether or not you understand anything about their culture. Interdisciplinary communication can happen only where there is unconditional respect.

   Think of a tour guide. Your job is to make your guests feel comfortable, learn a bit about them, and share aspects of your land they will find interesting. Your job is not to criticize your visitors for being from the wrong place, to convince them that your way is right, or to protect your secrets.

3. **Traveler.** The next step is to learn about other disciplines. Interdisciplinary understanding can happen only when both disciplines have experienced the other's culture.

Think of a world traveler. Make plans to visit another discipline. Read about the discipline's history, learn a bit of the language, talk to travelers who have been there before. Live as a native. Be open to new experiences. Do not only eat hamburgers. Replace fear of the unknown with curiosity and a spirit of adventure. Once you start traveling, you will find yourself in the company of other travelers.

4. **Pen pal.** Interdisciplinary relationships are based on personal relationships. Start building your worldwide community one person at a time.

"I'm interested in hearing about what you do, and telling you about what I do. I realize we come from different backgrounds, but there's no reason we can't be friends. Your way of thinking is just as valid as my way, I can learn to appreciate its value, and it will be valuable for me to understand it. Ask me anything you want to know about my discipline and I will do my best to answer."

5. **Ambassador.** The next step is to establish diplomatic relations between pairs of disciplines.

Think of an ambassador. Learn to speak both languages. Learn to live in both cultures. Work with people in both disciplines toward common goals. Be committed to overcoming inevitable disagreements. Diplomacy is a slow process of building trust. Building trust requires active testing of faith. Do not accept simple answers. Question everything and do what it takes to find out the truth.

Diplomatic relations are difficult if the two disciplines are fighting over the same turf, so do not wait until a crisis before you step in. To maintain neutrality, an ambassador should not be in a power relationship with either discipline.

When explaining one discipline to people in another discipline, your first responsibility is to explain persuasively why they need to know about this other discipline, not to turn them into instant experts. Start from where they are. Use examples they care about. Show the effects of the other discipline on their discipline. Demonstrate the bad consequences of ignoring this other discipline. Outline the general principles of the other discipline; avoid details. Standard introductory courses probably will not work, because they are often addressed to people who are already in the same frame of mind as the discipline.

6. **World citizen.** Think of the world as your home. Take pleasure in the diversity of cultures. Borrow freely from all disciplines. Get help when

you need it. Where one discipline is weak, look for another that is strong. See to it that all disciplines benefit. Assemble interdisciplinary teams that work together as equals from the beginning. Agree on goals early.

When disciplines merge, the results can be outstanding. The painting program MacPaint, which gave thousands of people their first positive experience of computers and of art, came from a tight collaboration between software artist Bill Atkinson and visual artist Susan Kare.

Yes, this is an ambitious charter. My purpose here is to give you all the options. You do not have to do it all. Any piece is fine. And you do not have to do it alone. We are all in this together.

How to See the Nose on Your Face

As you reach out to other disciplines, it is important to keep noticing the assumptions in your own discipline that might limit your view of the world. Seeing your own assumptions is like seeing your own nose. It is such a constant part of your visual field that you have to do something special to become aware of it, like close one eye, cross your eyes, or focus unusually closely. Here are games to bring your assumptions into focus.

BE PLAYFUL

Nothing locks in assumptions like seriousness. Put aside practicality for a moment and take an irreverent attitude toward your discipline. Tell someone about your discipline as if it were astonishing news: "You'd never believe it!" Describe everyday practices as if they were strange alien rituals. Chuckle at the little absurdities of your discipline. Spout technical jargon. Apply the full weight of your discipline to a simple everyday activity, making it hopelessly complex.

TELL THE STORY OF YOUR LIFE

How did you get to be where you are now? Telling the story of your life helps remind you (and others) of the choices you made along the way to your current occupation, and of your identity as a human being apart from your work. Recall early delights that got you interested in your current field. Take turns with other people telling life stories and listening. You will be fascinated by the curious similarities and differences.

TELL THE STORY OF YOUR DISCIPLINE

Disciplines spend so much time defending their boundaries that we forget that the boundaries are arbitrary and can be changed. Research the history of your discipline. How did it start? What was the original question? Whose big idea was it anyway? How have its boundaries changed over time? Why did it evolve the way it did? Imagine how it could have evolved differently had circumstances been different. Imagine how it might change. When historians five hundred years from now look back at our times, how might they tell the story of your discipline?

Draw a Map

The quickest way to sound like an expert in a field is to know how it is organized. Draw a map showing your discipline and how it is divided into different factions. Draw neighboring disciplines. Label mountains, rivers, cities, and wilderness.

Write a Tour Guide

Pretend your discipline is a foreign country. Write a tour guide for visitors. Design a poster that will attract interest. Rave about scenic wonders. Draw a state flag. Include a short dictionary of useful phrases. Give tips on local customs. Offer package tours. Make up tacky souvenirs.

Write an Emergency Guide

It takes years of training to become a doctor, but everyone needs to know first aid. Write a one-page guide to your discipline in the style of the first aid guides that appear at the beginning of some phone books. It does not have to be serious. Give short, clear instructions on what to do in crisis situations. Include diagrams.

Argue Persuasively That Another Discipline Is Far More Important Than Yours

In this book you will find arguments for the importance of many different approaches to user interface design, including industrial design, writing, computer games, sound, gesture, psychology, drama, help systems, and education. Choose an approach that you find boring. Enthusiastically list reasons why that approach is the most interesting and important of all, while the approach of your discipline hardly matters. Enjoy demolishing any pompous self-importance your field may have developed.

Imagine How People in Other Disciplines Would Solve a Problem in Your Discipline

Changing your point of view is a basic technique of generating new ideas. Use the friction between different disciplines to spark new ideas. By systematically trying out other points of view, you can overcome limitations in your own point of view. For further ideas on creative brainstorming, see Mountford's and Erickson's chapters in this volume.

Interdisciplinary People . . .

. . . carry messages between castles.

. . . fall in the cracks.

. . . build bridges so others may cross.

LIST ALL THE ROLES YOU PLAY THROUGHOUT THE DAY

You are already interdisciplinary, by virtue of the many roles you play through the day: friend, spouse, parent, child, driver, pedestrian, student, teacher. Even the simplest job usually requires several distinct skills. How do you juggle all these roles? What do you do when they overlap? What are the priorities in each situation? Interview yourself as if you were the world's leading expert on juggling roles.

LIST THE PRIORITIES OF YOUR DISCIPLINE

What are the most important priorities to teach beginners in your field? Order priorities by importance. For each priority, recall a story that explains its importance. Compare how the same priorities look to beginners and experts.

REMARKS

The assumptions of different disciplines are usually compared only in jokes about different people's stereotypical responses to the same situation ("A doctor, a lawyer, and a politician were walking down the street . . ."). Such jokes perpetuate the belief that people cannot change. The purpose of these exercises is to replace stale cynicism with fresh imagination.

The Center for Explanation and Other Fantasies

Here are some other interesting opportunities I see for future interdisciplinary work.

PROVIDING INSPIRING EXAMPLES

Traditional schools and businesses discourage interaction between disciplines. To raise our hopes of what is possible, we need inspiring examples of good interdisciplinary work. Search out and document existing interdisciplinary work. Compare how people in different disciplines approach the

. . . sit on the fence.   *. . . wear many hats.*   *. . . see more than one point of view.*

same problem, as Arent, Vertelney, and Lieberman do in their chapter in this volume. Set uncompromisingly pure goals, even if the scope of the project has to be narrow. Teams work best if they are small, allow everyone to participate equally from the beginning, and can agree early on common goals.

Raising the Lowest Common Denominator

Interdisciplinary work often flounders for lack of adequate tools. For instance, a graphic designer cannot participate in graphic user interface design without adequate graphic prototyping tools. To raise our expectations of what is practical, we need better everyday standards. Research the minimal requirements of each discipline. Build the minimum requirements into everyday tools and procedures. Set standards that are universally accepted, even if the details have to be compromised. Standards work best if they are expressed precisely, presented in language that users understand, and adapt well to particular cases.

Changing Organizational Priorities

Large-scale change requires clear commitment from those in charge. An organization's structure must reflect its priorities or it will not be effective. When Alan Kay set up the group that created Smalltalk and the much of desktop metaphor at the Xerox Palo Alto Research Center in the early 70s, he built the importance of the user interface into every aspect of the group. The group opened the door to a constant stream of young users, hired people with backgrounds in music and philosophy, designed a dedicated personal computer with a large bitmapped screen, and pioneered a simpler type of software environment. In contrast, most computer research centers are closed to outside users, hire only engineers, use existing machines, and build on layers of complex software designed for sophisticated programmers. In such an environment it is hard for user interface design to be a priority.

INTERDISCIPLINARY DISCIPLINES

Several existing disciplines study relations between different social groups. Anthropologists and sociologists document cultural behavior. Organizational development people assemble teams in business. Educators and psychologists analyze different thinking styles. Journalists and writers present specialized topics to general audiences. All of these fields can contribute to better interdisciplinary cooperation.

THE CENTER FOR EXPLANATION

I see a new profession emerging: interdisciplinary connectors who are skilled at explaining any discipline to any another. Such connectors would help members of an interdisciplinary team communicate with each other.

This brings me to the Center for Explanation. Writers, illustrators, and filmmakers all learn to tailor explanations of ideas to particular audiences. Usually the explanations follow rigid explanatory conventions. For instance, popular science is usually presented in a slightly detached authoritative voice that says "isn't science wonderful," whereas academic science is usually presented in a dry formal voice that says "I'm so objective." Only parodists break the conventions.

Nowhere is there a place to explore explanatory styles themselves freely. Occasionally a new explanatory style will sweep a field, as happened with graphical techniques and statistics. But these are isolated instances. The Center for Explanation would systematically explore all possible ways of explaining an idea, both after the fact for a general audience, and during the process for a specialized audience.

RETHINKING *INTERDISCIPLINARY*

I have always been proud to be interdisciplinary. But the word makes me feel scattered. To find out why, I listed all meanings of *interdisciplinary*. They are cartooned on the previous pages.

I concluded that the word is backwards. *Interdisciplinary* means you cut up the world into disciplines, then try to glue it back together. The word maintains a fragmented view of the world, even though it advocates unity. The opposite approach might be to call an interdisciplinary field a *generality*, and to characterize anyone who specializes in only one aspect of a generality as being *subgeneral*.

There is only one world. Disciplines are ways for people to subdivide the world. If you treat disciplines as primary divisions you can build bridges between particular disciplines. But if the disciplines move, the bridges no longer connect anything. It is better in the long run to let disciplines play a secondary role, and to build bridges between people on the basis of mutual understanding and respect.

Two Disciplines in Search of an Interface

Reflections on a Design Problem

COMPUTER PROGRAMMERS AND GRAPHIC DESIGNERS appear to operate in distinctively different worlds. Yet as computer systems become more graphic and communications media more interactive, experts in the two disciplines find themselves increasingly called upon to deal with the same subject: the design of interactive graphical software. Can this shotgun marriage be made to work?

The literature provides little documentation of the actual analysis and decision-making processes used by programmers and graphic designers in the development of interactive applications. Each profession has a stereotypical view of the other: graphic designers are "beautifiers" who make things look pretty after they are made to work; programmers are "feature-freaks" who could care less how a thing looks as long as the code is elegant. Such stereotypes don't arise from thin air, but we felt ourselves to be exceptions to them—new members of the rare species of eclectic interface designers. Nevertheless, we wondered if the thinking styles lampooned by the stereotypes might lurk beneath the surface of our brave new ethos. We resolved to find out.

Arent is an experienced graphic designer in the Human Interface Group at Apple Computer, where his primary role is to improve visual communication in interfaces. Lieberman is an experienced artificial intelligence researcher (and programmer) who is currently working in the area of interactive tools for graphic design. I (Vertelney) posed Arent and Lieber-

Laurie Vertelney
Michael Arent
Advanced Technology Group
Apple Computer, Inc.

Henry Lieberman
Visible Language Workshop,
Media Laboratory
Massachusetts Institute of Technology

Figure 1: The original Map interface.

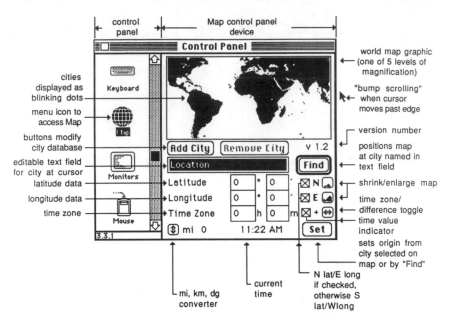

man a user interface problem—the redesign of the interface of an existing Macintosh control panel module called Map—and recorded their thought processes as they worked on it. I limited the two sides to exactly four hours to perform the design task in hopes of forcing the key issues to the fore.

When I got together with the two sides to compare notes after the design task was accomplished, I discovered both common ground and radical differences in their approaches. This experience, I think, can function as a parable for others, and it suggests that an actual comparative study of the design process, under controlled conditions accompanied by user testing, might provide extremely useful insights for both the software and interface design communities.

The Map Problem: A Benchmark for User Interface Design

The design example, Map, is an interactive interface to a database of cities represented by visual points on a world map. In this program, the user may view latitude, longitude, and time zone information for any location selected on the map. Once a location is established, the user can view time and distance difference information between it and another location. We started with an implementation that was originally designed by a programmer without feedback from graphic designers, then considered how it might be redesigned (see figure 1).

I chose Map because it is representative of the typical problems interface designers encounter on a daily basis. The original programmers labored under the constraints of a Macintosh control panel module[1]. This meant it

---

[1] A control panel module is a component of the Macintosh Control Panel, that portion of

had to fit in a small fixed rectangle of screen space, and such interface luxuries as pull-down menus were prohibited. These constraints, together with the Macintosh interface guidelines, forced compromises that may have adversely affected the quality of the interface. Nevertheless, these are the kinds of trade-offs that interface designers face constantly. There are always *some* resource constraints, be they of limited development time, screen space, memory, processor speed, or just the complexity of the interface itself. As Chris Crawford argues eloquently (see Crawford's chapter in this volume), the process of grappling with constraints often can lead to design creativity. As you will see, each interface designer approached the constraints from a different perspective.

A Comparison of Design Approaches

What were the areas of the interface analyzed by the two interface designers, what were the perceived problems, and what paths did they follow in terms of resolving those problems?

The problems and their solutions can be mapped onto three primary criteria in software interface design:

- **Usability:** Can users easily learn and efficiently interact with Map to get to the desired information?
- **Functionality:** What functions and controls are available to allow optimal use of the Map database?
- **Visual communication and aesthetics:** How do the visual appearance and spatial location of the elements of Map optimize functionality?

As you will see in the following text and visual examples, the graphic designer and the programmer approached the Map redesign problem by concentrating in different proportions on each of the criteria.

USABILITY

In a typical "we need it yesterday" design situation, Arent, the graphic designer, started the redesign process by assuming the given functionality and application type of Map. He also assumed the constraints of the Macintosh interface; that is, he followed the guidelines for consistent "look and feel" with the rest of the Macintosh interface. He looked at how the existing interface could be improved. Arent began to critique the interface by imagining scenarios of different users interacting with Map for the first time and immediately discovered some usability questions: "What do the

the Macintosh interface which allows users to observe and change system-wide parameters, such as the speed of mouse-tracking and the volume of speakers. Setting the time on the system clock is a function of the Control Panel, which led to the inclusion of the Map program with its database of time zones. The Macintosh interface guidelines constrain a control panel module to be entirely self-contained inside a pane of the Control Panel's window.

Figure 2: Arent's critique of the existing Map interface.

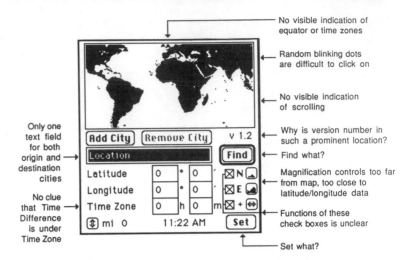

No visible indication of equator or time zones

Random blinking dots are difficult to click on

No visible indication of scrolling

Why is version number in such a prominent location?

Find what?

Magnification controls too far from map, too close to latitude/longitude data

Functions of these check boxes is unclear

Set what?

Only one text field for both origin and destination cities

No clue that Time Difference is under Time Zone

random blinking dots on the map (cities in the database) indicate—can I easily interact with them?"; "How can I get other views of the map, such as a magnified view or a view of the parts of the default map that are not visible?"; "What does the Set button set?"; "Once location and time information are determined for one city, how can I compare it with information from another city?" (see figure 2).

Arent: I tried out the original Map program against a series of "what if" user scenarios to highlight problems with the design. I found that the functionality was adequate for the most part but usability was hampered by poor visibility, spatial arrangement, and representation of the controls and indicators.

In contrast, Lieberman initially performed none of the steps Arent performed. He did not make an element-by-element critique of the original interface, nor did he analyze it for consistency with the interface guidelines. *He simply threw it out.*

What irked Lieberman was that he thought the original interface *did not satisfy a user's needs*, rather than that it contained troublesome elements or violated interface guidelines. This was especially bothersome to him because he saw himself as the kind of user such an application would be intended for. He reconceptualized the problem in terms of his own needs, and proposed an alternative design.

Lieberman: As a frequent traveler who must sometimes work on the road, I could sympathize with a potential user who uses Map during travel. The most serious conceptual deficiency I found was the underlying assumption that there would be a single destination city. Rather than set the origin each time I change location, I would rather program an entire multiple-destination itinerary in advance, including my estimated

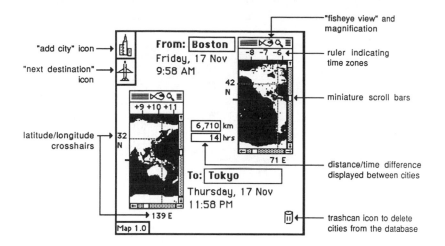

"add city" icon →

"next destination" → icon

latitude/longitude crosshairs

"fisheye view" and magnification

ruler indicating time zones

miniature scroll bars

distance/time difference displayed between cities

trashcan icon to delete cities from the database

Figure 3: Lieberman's redesign of the Map interface.

departure times. The system should automatically change the origin city as I travel from place to place, by reading the system clock.

Although the multiple destination idea seemed to offer a genuine breakthrough in the usability of the program, Lieberman did not develop it further due to the time constraints (a situation often faced in the "real" design process). Instead, he chose a compromise solution to usability problems: he replaced the single map and city display with two independently scrollable maps and displays (see figure 3).

The "design by critique" strategy employed by Arent is a good way to approach a redesign problem hampered by time constraints. Assuming the integrity of the underlying functionality, "design by critique" allows the interface designer to concentrate on usability and consistency issues. The disadvantage of "design by critique" is that it becomes difficult to correct major functionality problems. Lieberman chose to challenge the underlying specifications in his approach, but as you will see, he maintained most of the functionality of the original Map program while developing a conceptually new "look and feel."

FUNCTIONALITY

Arent began using the controls to see if he could understand the functionality of Map. Some controls were invisible, some were hidden, some had nonstandard representations, and others were unclearly labeled. To evaluate the various functions, he laid out all the functional components of the Map interface in a schematic diagram. As a result of the schematic, he decided not to add to the functionality but rather to eliminate a couple of components that he felt were of low priority, such as the time-zone indicator and mile/km/degree converter, in order to make better use of the constrained screen space allotted to Map (see figure 4).

Figure 4: Arent's redesign of the Map interface.

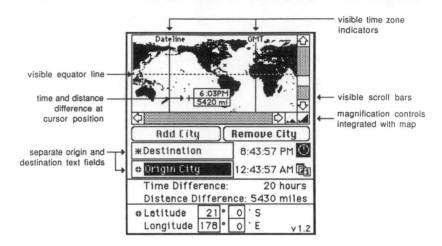

visible time zone indicators

visible equator line

time and distance difference at cursor position

visible scroll bars

magnification controls integrated with map

separate origin and destination text fields

Arent: I mapped out both the visible and hidden components' parts in a schematic diagram. I then began questioning their functionality as well as their spatial arrangement and representation. I discovered that Map was much more powerful and complicated than I had anticipated. There was plenty of opportunity to simplify it both functionally and visually.

Lieberman, meanwhile, decided not only to improve the usability through a radically different conceptual layout of the functionality but also to add to the functionality. He decided to add controls in the form of icons to add destination cities easily as well as to switch to the next origin/destination city combination in the case of multiple destinations. He also added a trash can icon as a means of deleting unwanted cities in the database. Finally, he embellished the two map displays with a ruler-like indicator displaying time zone information.

Lieberman: I felt strongly that both the origin and the destination information should be visible at once, rather than having to toggle between them. Having just one map always hides the information about the other city and confuses the user about whether he or she is in "origin mode" or "destination mode." Having two maps makes the relationship between the cities more visually apparent.

Given the time and space constraints, the real functionality issue for both the graphic designer and the programmer was *trade-offs*. In order to overcome space constraints and make Map a more powerful tool, Lieberman implemented what Arent termed "Macintosh slang." For example, Lieberman miniaturized the scroll bars (at the cost of making them smaller targets for mouse clicks) to enable two map views to fit into his new conceptual layout. He also used icons in the title bar of each map and stole the trash can icon from the Desktop (see figure 3). Such decisions are heretical to the Macintosh Interface Guidelines, but Lieberman felt they were justified.

To maintain the traditional "look and feel" of the Macintosh interface, Arent adhered to the standard Macintosh conventions. His efforts to improve the interface were concentrated primarily on simplifying functionality; that is, establishing two text fields for simultaneously displaying the names of the destination and origin cities as well as developing a clearer spatial arrangement of the visual elements (see figure 4).

VISUAL COMMUNICATION AND AESTHETICS

How did the graphic designer repair the visual communication and aesthetic problems he found with Map? Arent's redesign proceeded in two stages. In the first stage, he used the schematic layout of all the visual components and concentrated on the *communication* aspects of the interface.

Arent: What is each interface element trying to communicate to the user? Are users likely to have the same interpretation of each element as the designer intended? Are elements that are trying to communicate related concepts in close spatial proximity to one another? How do all the visual elements work together in the context of the total layout of the interface?

The elements that didn't pass the test were replaced, wherever possible, with those drawn from the standard Macintosh user interface conventions. A second design stage was necessary for spatially organizing all the elements and arranging them to fit in the size-constrained screen space. Figure 5 shows four successive views of the final interface layout with "backtracking" occurring between the third and fourth views to make room for necessary interface elements that didn't fit.

On many occasions, information could be displayed either iconically or as text, at the discretion of the designer. Surprisingly, the programmer's design made more extensive use of pictorial information in some ways than that produced by the graphic designer.

Lieberman: I resolved to show as much information visually on the map as possible, rather than off in separate text boxes. To indicate latitude and longitude, I put crosshairs on the map, labeled with the numerical values. I felt there should be some graphic indication of time zones, so I used a "ruler" similar to those found in drawing programs. Greenwich and the Date Line would be indicated on the ruler. More accurate would be to draw the time zone boundaries directly on the map.

The graphic designer indicated that he did not feel compelled to use graphics in every possible situation. Sometimes the functionality of a button labeled with text is more immediately understandable by the user than an icon whose meaning is subject to interpretation and learning. But this argument depends on the recognizability of the icon and whether the software is distributed across national or cultural boundaries.

Even when the respective designers were trying to accomplish the same

Figure 5: Progression for Arent's redesign. Note backtracking between the third and fourth stages

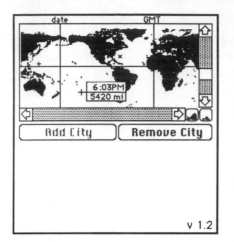

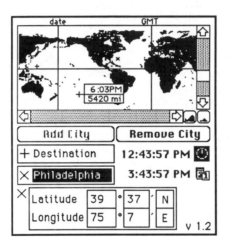

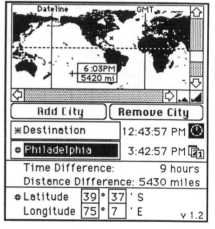

goal, the designs differed—and each designer could offer a plausible justification for his choices. For example, Lieberman decided to reverse the colors of land and water on the map.

Lieberman: *I drew the maps with oceans represented as black and land as white. I wanted the most important semantic relationship, namely cities on land, to be rendered as black on a white background, as is most Macintosh graphics and text.*

But Arent took a graphic designer's perspective and chose to focus on the visual effect of the color choices.

Arent: *Black was used for land masses as a means to emphasize the city dots; that is, white dots appear larger and more prominent on a black background than black dots of the same size do on a white background.*

How does one decide which of these seemingly equally justified but conflicting choices is correct? This dispute cannot be resolved *a priori*, so the experimental approach of user testing is called for. See the article by Gomoll in this book for a detailed discussion of user testing and its effect upon design decisions.

Issues and Lessons

WHERE DOES THE "USER'S VIEWPOINT" COME FROM?

Both designers tried to be sensitive to what they thought was "the user's viewpoint," but just how did they decide what an eventual user might think? An interface designer might look to three possible routes to the user.

First, interface designers can consider *themselves* as potential users. This is what Lieberman did. How well this works depends upon how closely the interface designer's experience and interests match those of a majority of "real" users—that is, potential buyers of the product. When there is a good match, the close coupling of designer and user viewpoints can result in an excellent design. Lieberman's travel and interface design experience worked fairly well in this case, but this approach is fraught with danger. The problem is that programmers are usually *too* expert, and can easily fail to empathize with the needs of beginning or occasional users.

Second, interface designers can *simulate* potential users. Designers can go through the exercise of pretending to be a user and step through what they perceive to be typical user scenarios. This can reveal problems and opportunities that would otherwise be ignored. That is how Arent approached the problem. His relative lack of programming expertise was in fact an advantage during this process, as it more closely approximated the computer skills of typical users.

But neither of these alternatives is as reliable as actually *asking real users!* Significantly, it occurred to neither of the design teams to query real users about any of the issues they were considering. Again, it's somewhat unfair to expect them to, because the exercise was not set up to accommodate user testing. But again, there's perhaps a lesson in that, because user testing needs to be planned into the design process from the start. The role of well-planned and well-executed user testing throughout the design process cannot be overemphasized.

This point was driven home to us when we later posed the same design problem to another programmer, an experienced developer of commercial Macintosh software. Almost at the start of his design process, he made provision for something that, we were embarrassed to admit, was not only absent in the original but was totally ignored in all of our redesigns—Help. Despite the fact that we all share a belief in the need for good documentation, we had all failed to consider what would happen if the user didn't know what to do next. Certainly, user testing would have uncovered this problem at the first sign of confusion.

WHEN IS IT RIGHT TO CHANGE THE RULES?

After seeing Lieberman's design, Arent complained that Lieberman wasn't playing by the (unspoken) rules. His design departed so much from the original that the graphic designer felt almost tricked. He felt that had he been explicitly given the option of a total redesign, he too would have come up with something radically different. He did not see it as his task in this exercise, nor are interface designers routinely given that option in practice.

But that's just it! If an interface is not meeting the user's needs, it doesn't matter how well-designed, aesthetic, or consistent it is—it's just wrong and needs to be redesigned. Lieberman's challenge to the problem drew praise from Don Norman as "standing up for the user" (see Norman's chapter in this volume). The lesson is that interface designers should always consider it their job first and foremost to meet the user's needs, rather than simply to implement a certain set of features or a certain interface style.

There's another lesson here as well. Arent was also justified in claiming that graphic designers are often put in a difficult position. In many organizations, graphic designers are often treated as "firefighters"—called upon in an emergency to repair disasters not of their own making, under severe time constraints. This situation precludes the kind of comprehensive redesign that Lieberman attempted.

Programmers and managers have a tendency to feel that the role of the graphic designer is to provide cosmetic improvement; that is, to "pretty it up after the programming is done." Graphic designers see their role in broader terms—the design of visual forms to facilitate communication. This broader role encompasses the behavior of an interface as well as the way in which its appearance affects communication. Graphic designers can and should be involved in conceptual-level interface design decisions.

As a result, was Lieberman's redesigned interface better than that produced by Arent? Not necessarily. The graphic designer's training and expertise in visual communication made some aspects of his interface decidedly superior. Some users we consulted informally showed a strong preference for Arent's version. Lieberman eventually ran afoul of both some accepted visual design practices and the Macintosh user guidelines. Other differences reflected fundamental trade-offs that depend upon priorities and tastes.

Related to the issue of challenging the specifications is that of adherence to a set of standard conventions for interaction. The success of the Macintosh is due in no small part to the consistency of its user interface (see Tognazzini's chapter in this volume), which makes learning and using of the computer much easier. But slavish adherence to a set of rigid conventions can also be a damper to realizing optimal functionality and effective visual representation.

Interface guidelines, such as those formulated for the Macintosh, may constrain the exercise of creativity, but they can also be of great value to the designer. They both express and help to set user expectations through consistency, allowing the designer more reliably to predict user behavior. They also remove at least some of the burden of making trade-off decisions from the individual designer's shoulders. Even when a designer decides to "break the rules," it is worthwhile to analyze the rule being broken to discover its original purpose and to predict the effects of violating it.

Collaborative Design: Breaking Down the Stereotypes

Our results were less dramatic than they might have been in that both the graphic designer and the computer scientist produced designs that failed to elicit any really serious negative criticism from the other camp. They also failed to exhibit strong biases commonly held to be stereotypical of people of their professions.

One might have expected a hard-core programmer to propose a command-line interface devoid of visual interaction. This might indeed have happened had we chosen programmers whose experience was primarily with mainframes. One might have expected the graphic designer to spend all his effort on appearance and display some naïveté about the functionality of interaction. This might indeed have happened had we chosen a graphic designer whose experience was limited to print media.

That each designer did show some sensitivity to concerns usually thought of as the other's domain we attribute to the fact that a new discipline of interface design is emerging where the need for both perspectives is acknowledged. The chapter by Scott Kim in this volume is a manifesto for this kind of interdisciplinary collaboration. The best work in interfaces will come from those who bring the best of both graphic design and computer science approaches to interactive graphical software.

Acknowledgments

Lieberman's research was supported by a grant from Hewlett-Packard. The Visible Language Workshop is supported by grants and equipment from HP, Apple, DARPA, IBM, NYNEX, and Xerox.

We would like to thank Joy Mountford for initiating the collaboration among us, and Brenda Laurel, Chris Crawford, Don Norman, Scott Kim, Christopher Fry, and Muriel Cooper for helpful feedback.

Designing the Whole-Product User Interface

USER INTERFACE IS MORE THAN SOFTWARE—it includes every interaction that a user has with a product. Industrial design, traditionally concerned with product packaging, can play a valuable role in user-interface design by extending the user interface to the physical product and beyond. This chapter discusses the concept of the whole-product user interface. Traditional industrial design techniques are examined in light of their applicability to the design of user interfaces. Illustrations are used to guide you through the design process.

Laurie Vertelney

Advanced Technology Group
Apple Computer, Inc.

Sue Booker

Special Projects, Apple Products
Apple Computer, Inc.

User Interface + Industrial Design = Whole-Product User Interface

Until recently, industrial designers designed the product packaging of computers, and user-interface designers focused primarily on software design. But as technology continues to evolve, this distinction will blur. The Lisa and Macintosh computers were among the first to use software commands to replace mechanical switches. Examples of this include: turning the computer on and off, ejecting disks, and dimming the screen. Computers are becoming smaller, more affordable, and more personal. We now find them embedded in familar products like coffee machines and wrist watches, and soon they will become a pervasive feature of the environment (see Negroponte's sermon). As a natural consequence of these trends, industrial designers are becoming more involved in user-interface design. In the future,

ID is the design of the product packaging (left).

UI is the design of the interaction that the user has with the product (center).

ID+UI = whole-product user interface (right).

we will think of the user interface as the entire experience that a user has with a product—including the software, product packaging, marketing, training materials, and support.

A Little History

Before the industrial revolution, craftsmen both designed and built products. This enabled them to focus on the requirements of the individual user who purchased their services. But the industrial revolution spelled the demise of the craftsman, who could not match the speed and repetitive accuracy of the machine. The activities of designing and building could no longer be the responsibility of a single person. Products were no longer designed for a single client, but rather for the masses. The conception of form and the act of making the form became clearly separate activities, thus requiring the skills of many specialists to carry out an envisioned product.

How could the relationship between the craftsman and end user be maintained as more and more people became involved in the design process? A discipline emerged to assume the role of designing products that could be used by the masses and produced by industrial manufacturing processes: industrial design. The industrial designer acted as a liaison between the potential users and the manufacturer of a product. The industrial designer concentrated most specifically on the physical housing of a product, but was also frequently involved in how the user interacted with it through advertising, merchandising, production, and distribution.

What Is Industrial Design?

Industrial design, sometimes referred to as *product design*, is the design of things that people use. Industrial designers concern themselves with several aspects of a product's design: its form, function, and user interface.

Consider the telephone. The *form* of the telephone determines the way that it looks and feels—its weight, the choice of materials, and other physical considerations. This is what most people associate with industrial design. The *function* is what the product is supposed to do. Telephones are supposed to transfer speech over distance. In order to ensure that the telephone functions properly, the designer must be concerned with how the user interacts with it. This might include the rationale behind the placement of the keypad, the location of the handset, the sounds users hear when placing a call, and other interaction considerations. Because industrial design involves designing both for form and function, user interface is a natural extension of the industrial designer's domain.

Here are some examples of industrial design:

Before: There was one designer working for one user.

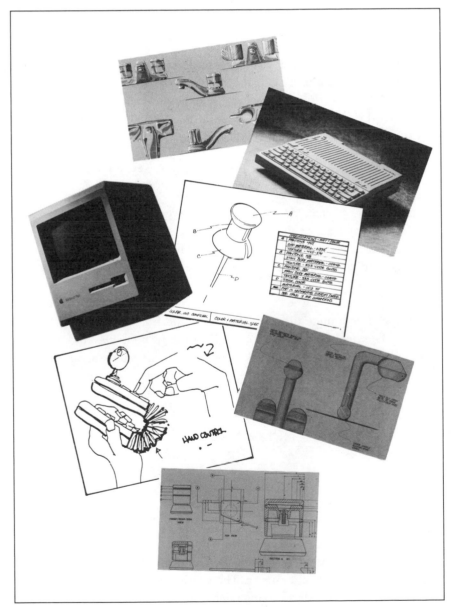

After: There are now many designers working for many users.

The industrial designer is a liaison between manufacturing and the masses

Why "Good" Industrial Design Is Important

You may have noticed that certain models of telephones seem to work better than others. It's not usually because one brand actually *functions* differently from another—more often, it's because one is easier to use or feels better than another. For example, some poorly designed telephones have incorporated the hang-up switch in the handset. Users often find themselves accidentally hanging up in the middle of a conversation because they hit the switch with their hand or their chin. What about those stylish little novelties that look like a shoe or a boat but that force users to talk into a spiked heel or tail rudder? These telephones still function as telephones—Willie can still talk to Aunt Reba in Arkansas—but the form sometimes gets in the way of the function.

Good industrial design is transparent. Users should be able to utilize a product without fumbling with the form for the sake of trendy styles or features. Although it's "transparent," good industrial design often stands out in a world where poor design abounds (see Norman's sermon elsewhere in this volume).

What Does This Have to Do with User Interface Design?

Surely there are scenarios similar to the above telephone examples in the computer user-interface domain. Have you ever noticed a user struggling with a user interface while attempting to get a task done? Combine a horrible user interface with terrible industrial design—have you ever used a VCR?—and you'll find that it's impossible to get the product to function at all.

A collaboration between the industrial designer and the user interface designer will help unite the form, function, and user-interface aspects of a product. The industrial designer, versed in the technologies and materials of the physical product, can make good design decisions about how the product should be packaged. The user-interface designer can devise interaction techniques that are transparent and that enable users to access the functionality of the product without tripping over the interface. Together, these skills can create a well-designed experience for users. Let's look at an example of how an industrial designer might contribute to a user-interface design project.

A Design Scenario

Product Definition

The client is a reputable banking firm. In the initial design stage, the client presents a description of the product—an automatic bank-teller machine (ATM)—to an industrial designer. The specification is probably a written manuscript. The bank has a fair understanding of what the ATM should

The client consults a designer with a design problem.

do, how much it should cost, and so forth, but does not have a clear notion of how the ATM should look or behave. The industrial designer can help clarify design objectives even at this early stage of the product's conception by sketching as the client describes the desired product. Visual facilitation can be useful, especially if there is a large group of people involved in the specification process.

RESEARCH

Once the team envisions the ATM from a common perspective, it is much easier to begin research. Having a shared representation of the product can clarify misconceptions that otherwise might have led the group down divergent research paths. Designers can even facilitate the design process by visualizing planning schedules and resources for the team.

The designer figures out what is needed to solve the problem.

BRAINSTORM

During the brainstorming process, many loose, uncommitted ideas are generated. The main purpose of brainstorming is to generate as many ideas as possible, in the hope that one will lead to a satisfactory solution. The industrial designer can quickly sketch or build rough mock-ups of what the ATM might look like, often generating dozens of designs over the course of a day. The more ideas that are communicated early in the design process, the more likely it is that one will evolve into a satisfying solution.

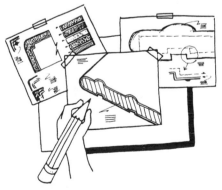

The designer generates many solutions to the problem.

GENERATE DESIGN SOLUTIONS

The favored ideas from the brainstorming stage are refined in this stage. Designs are thought out more thoroughly and made into drawings and sketch models. The purpose of this phase is to examine promising ideas more closely by testing whether they are feasible.

During this stage, the industrial designer will have generated several cardboard mock-ups of the ATM, perhaps trying out a variety of screen or keypad positions, money-handling devices, and even flipbooks of potential screen interactions.

ANALYZE

Once several mock-ups of the ATM have been generated, it is possible to begin evaluating and comparing them against the initial design constraints. Sometimes even these rough sketches or mock-ups provide enough information through visual representation for decisions to be made about the proposed designs. The bank can be brought in for a midpoint review to determine which ideas should be further refined, ensuring that the client and designer are seeing eye to eye.

Brainstorm sketches or thumbnails are refined to work out the details.

The solutions are measured against the design constraints.

Designers use many techniques to make the model look and behave as if it were real.

Watching users fumble with tasks can help designers eliminate flaws.

PROTOTYPE

Prototypes or models of the preferred designs are then generated. They attempt to approximate the finished product in as realistic a way as possible, without actually implementing the product. In this phase, the industrial designer builds a believable model of the physical housing of the product, including buttons, knobs, or other physical devices. He might also create screen designs, animations, or interactive demonstrations of how the product should respond to the user. Sometimes these models look so real that they fool even the client.

TEST

Once the ATM has been prototyped, it is often possible, and always desirable, to test the design for design flaws (see Gomoll's chapter). There are several advantages to testing a prototype. Because the industrial design and user-interface design have been integrated into the prototype, it is possible to test how well they work together; that is, do users move smoothly between software interactions and mechanical interactions such as those required to deposit money into a savings account? It might also be possible to test how the environment affects the design by moving the prototype into a bank and checking for glare, wear, aesthetic integrity, and user acceptance.

REDESIGN

If the prototype is tested and found to be unsatisfactory in some way, it is redesigned. If time and budget permit, the redesigns are tested again. Allocating plenty of time to product testing and redesign helps ensure a well-designed product. Those designs that pass user testing are then evaluated by the client. The client's preferred design solution goes on to the next stage.

IMPLEMENT

The final design must be converted into a form that can be manufactured. The industrial designer has produced drawings, renderings, models, and draftings that describe the form of the ATM, as well as computer animations, screen dumps, or storyboards that demonstrate the user-interface specifications. These are passed on to an individual or group who will see the product through the development process. All of these visual specifications can save time and money during the implementation process.

Interdisciplinary Design Teams

Having integrated the industrial designer into the user-interface design process, one can imagine the following scenario:

An interdisciplinary team has assembled a prototype of a design for the ATM. The industrial designer has constructed a cardboard mock-up of the ATM, complete with buttons and deposit and withdrawal slots. He, or possibly another user-interface designer, has generated screen designs of all of the possible display interactions for a predetermined user task, such as withdrawing $20.00. A simple paper flipbook might be used to illustrate the software user interface. A more powerful example might be a computer animation that is projected onto the display of the ATM.

Typical users are then brought in to act out the task, using the prototype as if it were the real ATM product. The industrial designer and the user-interface designer play the part of the computer, flipping between screens, pushing and pulling money in and out of deposit and withdrawal slots, and so forth.

A psychologist is responsible for constructing the test and observing the users' interaction with the machine. A video recording of the dramatic simulation can provide additional valuable feedback. The team can use this information to see how the entire user interface functions as a whole.

The bugs are ironed out in the re-design phase.

In a Nutshell

- The industrial revolution gave rise to the discipline of industrial design. Computers have given rise to the discipline of user-interface design. Because computers incorporate industrial design features, a new discipline has emerged that is the combination of these two.

- A well-defined process is used to solve traditional industrial design problems. This process, as well as the unique design skills of the industrial designer, can be of great value when designing a user interface.

- Simulation and user testing of both the industrial design and user-interface design aspects of a product can be done simultaneously to create an integrated product.

The design is passed on to others who will actually build and market the product.

Working with Interface Metaphors

Thomas D. Erickson

Advanced Technology Group
Apple Computer, Inc.

"METAPHOR," someone recently said to me, "seems to be the holy grail at Apple." It's true. Just about everyone at Apple knows the phrase "desktop metaphor" and fervently believes that a good metaphor is essential to an easy-to-use human interface. But just as the grail proved to be elusive, so is the knowledge of how metaphor really works.

The goal of this chapter is to provide designers with a deeper understanding of what metaphor is, and how to use it when designing an interface. First, we look at some of the characteristics of metaphor in language. These characteristics provide insights on how metaphor works in an interface. Next we look at an example of a poorly chosen interface metaphor and how it decreases the usability of the system. Finally, a design example is used to illustrate a method for coming up with interface metaphors and to present some rules of thumb for evaluating their value.

The Ubiquity and Invisibility of Metaphor

Many people think of metaphor as a flowery sort of language found chiefly in poetry and bad novels. This is not correct. Metaphor is an integral part of our language and thought. It appears not only in poetry and novels, but in our everyday speech about common matters. Mostly we don't notice; metaphor is such a constant part of our speech and thought that it is invisible.

The ubiquity of metaphor in language is convincingly demonstrated in the delightful book, *Metaphors We Live By* [Lakoff and Johnson, 1980]. The authors show that many of our basic concepts are based on metaphors. For example, without any intention of being poetic or fanciful, we speak of argument as though it is war. Arguments have *sides* that can be *defended* and *attacked*. Facts can be *marshaled* to support one's *position; strategies* can be employed. If a position is *indefensible*, one can *retreat* from it. Arguments can have *weak points*—they can even be *destroyed*; arguments can be *right on target*; arguments can be *shot down*. There is a whole web of concrete military language that we use to describe the rather abstract process of having an argument. It's also important to note that we don't just <u>talk</u> about argument as though it were war: being in an argument <u>feels</u> like a conflict; when we *lose* an argument, we <u>feel</u> bad.

The metaphorical way in which we talk and think about argument is the rule, not the exception. For example, the goal of this chapter is to provide a *deeper* understanding of metaphor. (Rather than just providing a *surface* treatment or *getting our feet wet*, I'd really like to *get into* the topic. Yet metaphor contains unexpected *depths*. Although we must avoid *getting in over our heads*; still, it would be nice to *plunge in* and *get to the bottom* of things.) In the next sentence, I say that we're going to *look at* metaphor as it's used in language. You *see*, we often speak of understanding an idea as seeing an object. Thus we may want to take a *closer look* at something, *shed some more light* on it, or *approach it from a different direction* so as to get a new *perspective* on it.

A word that is used in a metaphorical way is usually just the tip of the iceberg. A metaphor is an invisible web of terms and associations that underlies the way we speak and think about a concept. It is this extended structure that makes metaphor such a powerful and essential part of our thinking. Metaphors function as natural models, allowing us to take our knowledge of familiar, concrete objects and experiences and use it to give structure to more abstract concepts.

Metaphor in the Interface

The characteristics of metaphor in our language are the same ones that govern how metaphor works in an interface. Just as metaphors invisibly permeate our everyday speech, so do they occur throughout the interfaces we use and design. Just as we use military terms to make the rather abstract process of arguing more tangible, so we use object and container terms to make the Macintosh file system more concrete. And just as we experience arguments as real conflicts, most Macintosh users believe that when they move a document icon from one folder to another, they are really moving the document itself (what is "really" happening is that a pointer to the file is being moved—of course, *pointer* is a metaphor too . . .).

Because we use metaphors as models, an interface metaphor that suggests an incorrect model can cause difficulties for users. Consider the following scenario:

A visitor arrives. As previously agreed, she phones from the lobby to tell me she has arrived. However, I've stepped away from my desk for a moment, so the voice mail system answers:

"I'm not here now. But if you'll leave a message after the beep, I'll get right back to you."

She does so, and is quite properly annoyed when I show up in the lobby half an hour later and ask what kept her.

What neither of us knew was that there was a half hour delay between when she left the message in my mailbox and when it became available to me. Why the delay? The voice mail system resides on a machine in another building and, under conditions of heavy use, it can take as much as half an hour to notify me of a message.

It's easy to blame the system, but the real problem is that the system's metaphor has failed. The instruction manual and the on-line recordings inform users that they have *mailboxes* in which *messages* may be *left*. When the caller reaches the system, she hears a message in the callee's voice, saying "I'm not *here* now," followed by a beep—just as with an answering machine. A very clear model is presented: the caller has reached the callee's desk; the callee is not there; but the caller may leave a message in a *mailbox* that seems to act just like a conventional answering machine. Unfortunately, the model is incorrect. It provides no way for the users to understand that there might be a time lag between when a message is left in a mailbox and when the mailbox's owner can open it and find the message.

A more accurate metaphor would be an answering service metaphor. Messages would be left with an answering service, which would then forward the message to the appropriate person. Though this might not lead the user to expect a delay, it does provide grounds for appropriate suspicions when it becomes clear that something is wrong. The system need not even be redesigned for this metaphor to be used. Individual users could invoke the answering service metaphor just by having someone else record a message for them: "Tom's not at his desk. If you leave a message after the beep, I'll forward it to him." This is a small change, but it gives the user a different, more accurate model. No longer does the voice and language suggest that the message has reached its destination; instead, it's clear that an intermediary has the message and that it still must be forwarded.

The example of voice mail is a good one for several reasons. First, it clearly illustrates how an interface metaphor can provide the user with a model of the system, and how differences between the user's model and the real thing can cause problems. Second, it illustrates that a metaphor can make a difference even when there are no graphics or text associated with the interface. Too many people think that interface metaphors exist, or are important, only when icons and graphics are used. Finally, the example is good because it's so universal. Nearly everyone who uses this voice mail system has a message that presents the wrong model.

Why don't people use the more accurate metaphor? There are several possibilities. Many users don't understand how voice mail really works— they believe that the system's metaphor is real, that messages are really left in the boxy phones sitting on their desks. When incomprehensible delays occur, well, that's just the way high-tech stuff is sometimes. But that's not the full story, because even those who understand how the system really works continue to present the wrong model. Some of these users may not understand the purpose of an interface metaphor. They blame the hardware, and it doesn't occur to them that something as nebulous as a metaphor could in any way compensate for something as real as slow hardware. Finally, even users who understand that an interface metaphor should provide the user with a good model of the system may not know how to go about finding better metaphors.

Coming Up with Interface Metaphors

How do you come up with appropriate metaphors? This section describes the process of generating interface metaphors and applies it to a simple design problem. Although the design example is both hypothetical and oversimplified, it illustrates a useful approach to designing with metaphor.

Here's a brief overview of the process. Because the purpose of an interface metaphor is to provide users with a useful model of the system, the first step is to understand how the system really works. Second, because no metaphor can model all aspects of a system's functionality, the designer must identify what parts of it are most likely to give users difficulty. Finally, once the designer has identified the sort of model required, metaphors that support that model must be generated.

FUNCTIONAL DEFINITION

To create a model of something, obviously you have to understand how the thing itself works. This includes not only what the system can do but when that functionality is available to the user and how quickly the system can perform various functions. Some of this information may not be available in the system specification; nevertheless, it is essential, and the interface designer must either experiment with the system or probe the appropriate technical people to obtain it.

Now let's take a look at our example. Because we're using a fictitious, over-simplified example, the functional definition process is easy: we just make up the specifications. To make the example somewhat more realistic, rather than starting from scratch, we will assume that we are going to add new functionality to the Macintosh.

In the Macintosh, data is shared between applications by copying and pasting. However, this can be cumbersome if the data in the source document is continually changing: every time it changes, you have to recopy it and then repaste it. Let's assume that our task is to automate this process. Users will be allowed to define links between parts of different documents, so that when a change is made to data in the source document, the change is copied automatically, sent over the link, and then pasted automatically into the receiving document. For the purposes of this example, we'll impose three constraints. First, links have directionality—that is, data can go only one way along a link: from source to recipient, or from beginning to end. Second, links can be one to many: one piece of data may be at the source end of many links, so that a change to it is sent to many different documents. Third, we'll assume that we can't guarantee that a change in data at the source end of a link can be transmitted instantly to the destination end of the link—there may be a time lag.

IDENTIFY USERS' PROBLEMS

The second step is to figure out what users have problems with. What aspects of the functionality are new to them? What may look familiar, but will really be different? The best way to do this is to observe users (see Gomoll's chapter in this volume). Watch them using similar functionality and see what problems they have. Describe what you're doing and see if they understand. Show them prototypes of your system and watch them try to use it (see Wagner's chapter in this volume for a description of prototyping). Each of these methods has its drawbacks, but any is better than just guessing.

What do users understand and not understand about the functionality of links? For the purposes of this example, we'll just guess. Users may not understand that links have directionality—that data can flow one way along a link, but not the other. Or, users may not understand that links are one-to-many: data at the source end of a link may show up in many different documents. There are other likely problems that would most appropriately be identified by working with users, but these two will serve our purposes.

METAPHOR GENERATION

The first step in generating metaphors is to note what metaphors are already implicit in the problem description. Because we use metaphors to talk about abstract concepts, it's almost certain that metaphors are lurking about in the description of the functionality. However, because the functionality is usually defined by technical people who aren't representative of end users, the metaphors are often inappropriate. Nevertheless, it is important to identify these metaphors if only because unrecognized metaphors, may limit the variety of metaphors you generate.

In the description of our example, we are using a metaphor. We speak of the functionality in terms of *links between* documents. We say that links have *sources* and *destinations* and that data is *sent along* the links. It is important to recognize that there are other possible metaphors. Perhaps data could be conceived of as flowing through pipes. Or one could imagine electronic connections—a link could be created by wiring it up. Or a link could be thought of as a path, and special porters could carry data along it. But note that these metaphors—"pipes," "wires," and "paths"—are all special cases of the "links" metaphor. Each is a special type of *connection* metaphor. It may be useful to look for metaphors that focus not on connections, but on the properties of the data at either end of the link.

Mountford's chapter in this volume describes various techniques that can be used to generate new metaphors. However, one particularly useful approach is to focus on the user problems you've identified and look for real-world events, objects, or institutions that embody some of the characteristics that users find difficult to understand. These make good candidates for new interface metaphors.

For example, what are some real-world things that exhibit directionality? Rivers flow in one direction; TV images are transmitted from a broadcaster to a receiver; newspapers are mailed from a publisher to subscribers; forces like gravity and magnetism have direction. Similarly, TV broadcasts and newspaper editions also originate from one point and end up in many places at once; rivers generally do the opposite; and gravity and magnetism don't work at all.

It should be possible to generate dozens of potentially useful metaphors. For the purpose of keeping this example brief, we'll look at only three: links (because with the advent of commercial hypertext this is an increasingly popular metaphor), TV broadcasting, and newspaper publishing.

Evaluating Interface Metaphors

Once several metaphors have been generated, it's time to evaluate and choose one through which to express the new functionality. For our purposes, we'll take our original metaphor—links—and the TV broadcasting and newspaper publishing metaphors described above. Here are five questions for evaluating the usefulness of an interface metaphor.

AMOUNT OF STRUCTURE

How much structure does the metaphor provide? A metaphor without much structure may not be very useful.

One problem with the links metaphor is that it doesn't have much structure. If you ask users what a "link" is, you'll get a lot of different answers—users don't have a clear notion of what a link is. Links can be one-way or two-way. Links may imply data flow, or they may just be physical connections. When users think of links, they may even think of chains, sausages, or golf. There's nothing in the links metaphor that suggests the directionality or one-to-manyness of the flow of data that the users need help in understanding.

In contrast, users know a lot about TV broadcasting and newspaper publishing. For example, newspapers have editions, subscribers, editors, delivery people, and delivery routes; they may be found at newsstands; and so on. TV broadcasting has networks, stations, channels, *TV Guide*, TV receivers, reruns, serials, shows, VCRs, and so on.

APPLICABILITY OF STRUCTURE

How much of the metaphor is actually relevant to the problem? What is particularly important here is not what is irrelevant, but things that might lead the user in the wrong direction or raise false expectations.

For example, in comparing TV broadcasting and newspaper publishing, note that the broadcasting metaphor may lead the user astray because broadcasting implies instantaneous transmission of the data; in contrast, everyone knows that newspapers take a while to get delivered.

REPRESENTABILITY

Is the interface metaphor easy to represent? Ideal interface metaphors have distinctive visual and auditory representations, as well as specific words associated with them.

This is another area where the link metaphor is weak. Even assuming that users understand that "link" means a "connection over which data can flow," what does a link look or sound like? In contrast, the broadcasting metaphor has many possibilities for representation; for example, a TV set for a receiver, a broadcasting tower for a transmitter, sounds for indicating transmission. The newspaper metaphor also has possibilities—one could imagine sounds and images of a printing press for the source end of the link and a newspaper as the receiving end. There are also rich vocabularies specifically associated with broadcasting (transmitting, receiving, tuning, reception range) and newspapers (publishing, issues, editions, circulation, delivery).

SUITABILITY TO AUDIENCE

Will your audience understand the metaphor? A metaphor may satisfy all the other criteria, but if your users don't grasp the metaphor, it's useless.

Suitability would, for example, probably rule out the use of pointers (in the computer science sense) as a metaphor for links, even though they do indicate directionality. In evaluating suitability, it is once again important for the designer to involve the user in the design process. It is exceedingly easy to become convinced of the suitability of a metaphor that, when tested on users, turns out to evoke completely inappropriate associations.

EXTENSIBILITY

What else do the proposed metaphors buy you? A metaphor may have additional bits of structure that may be useful later on.

For example, it would be nice if links worked across networks. Because both broadcasting and newspaper publishing work across large distances, it's likely that they have structures that can provide a degree of support for data sharing across machines. For example, one might imagine each server on a network having a *newsstand*, which would be the recipient of *publications* from other machines.

It's also important to notice ways in which the metaphor may extend itself. For example, the broadcasting metaphor might encourage a use of the link functionality in a way that is very different from the data sharing that it was originally envisioned as supporting. It's easy to imagine users deciding to use the link functionality presented via the broadcasting metaphor to browse among the different *channels* available, just as they would switch from one TV channel to another. This sort of behavior seems much less likely to occur with the newspaper publishing metaphor.

What's Next?

Which metaphor should we choose for our example? It's not clear. To enable us to really address the question, the problem definition needs to be more detailed, more metaphors need to be generated and evaluated, and end users need to be consulted and observed throughout the design process.

Once a metaphor is settled on, it must be integrated into the interface. Although a discussion of this is beyond the scope of this chapter, one point should be made. Using the above criteria to select a good metaphor will be of little use unless the metaphor is used to its full extent. That is, having chosen a metaphor with a lot of structure, use as much of the structure as possible in the interface. Similarly, having chosen a representable metaphor, be sure to make full use of those representations.

Although the injunction to use and represent a metaphor fully may seem obvious, it's astonishingly easy to find examples where it has been ignored. For example, many HyperCard stacks start out using a book metaphor, usually by presenting a book-like background, but then fail to include such basic elements of books as page numbers, tables of contents, and indexes. Similarly, actions such as going to the next page are often represented by dissolving from one page to the next, rather than by using a visual effect to indicate that the page is being turned. These are all small details, but, as we saw in the voice mail interface, small details can make big differences.

Summary

Although metaphors are everywhere, they are often difficult to notice. They are present whenever we speak or think about abstract concepts. Metaphors serve as natural models; they allow us to take our knowledge of familiar objects and events and use it to give structure to abstract, less well understood concepts.

Metaphors exhibit these same properties in interfaces. To the extent that an interface metaphor provides users with realistic expectations about what will happen, it enhances the utility of the system. To the extent it leads users astray, or simply leads them nowhere, it fails.

Designers need to do several things when working with metaphor. They need to notice what metaphors are already present in the system. They must understand the system's functionality. And, most important, they need to know which aspects of the functionality users may not understand. Armed with this knowledge, the designer can search for metaphors that best support the areas in that the user's understanding is the weakest.

Consistency

ACHIEVING CONSISTENCY IN A STABLE SYSTEM is a difficult enough task. Trying to do so in the rapidly evolving world of computers can be positively Herculean.

An important aspect of consistency was defined by Smith et al. [1983] in this way: "Consistency asserts that mechanisms should be used in the same way wherever they occur." I would add, by inference, "and *when*ever they occur": first release or fifth release.

Well, that makes it all rather simple, doesn't it? Just don't change anything, and you will be able to maintain perfect consistency! Unfortunately, the computer industry is still in its infancy. Before we can polish and fine-tune the current generation of a given system or application, we are often driven by market pressure to release the next generation, with new metaphors, objects, and behaviors. With so much movement, how can we hope to maintain complete consistency?

We can't. Instead, we must pick and choose which aspects of consistency are most important to maintain. Many principles can help guide those choices. Some are obvious; for instance:

- Follow published guidelines whenever possible.
- Don't change something unless it really needs changing.
- Add new skills to the user's skill set rather than expecting the user to modify existing skills.

Bruce Tognazzini
Product Engineering
Apple Computer, Inc.

A few principles appear to be less obvious. It is these I have chosen to highlight.

Two Principles for Change

The following two principles, taken together, offer the designer tremendous latitude in the evolution of a product without seriously disrupting those areas of consistency most important to the user:

1. Consistent interpretation of user behavior by the system is more important than consistent system objects or behaviors.

The computer system sends information to the user via text, graphics, sound, etc. The user sends information to the computer via the keyboard, mouse, etc. In both cases, the *receiver* of the information applies specific interpretations to the sender's message: "He pressed the second key on the third rank of the keyboard. I'll place an 'A' character in the text buffer and on the display. . . ."

In the real world, the *content* of the communication between a given sender and receiver changes often. The *sender's method of transmission* will also change, but seldom. The *receiver's interpretations* will rarely, if ever, change: the receiver will not unilaterally decide to interpret time as "time stated minus one-half hour," then yell at his or her spouse for arriving half an hour late.

If the system as sender acts in some new way, people may at first be startled, but they will soon learn how to interpret that new behavior. If a system object has changed appearance, people do not go into a blind panic—they learn the meaning of the new appearance. But if the system suddenly interprets the user's pressing Command-R, which used to mean "readjust the margin," to mean "remove everything from my hard disk," the user is going to be more than a little upset.

2. If you must make a change, make it a large and obvious one.

Designers often fear making changes that are highly visible. Yet these are just the sort of changes that cause no confusion: Faced with an entirely new appearance for a program, people will just sigh and begin learning what's new. But inject the word "not" into the question, "Do you want to save this document before closing?" and it could take the user several lost documents and a few trips to the dealer to trace down the real culprit: the designer.

What starts out as a conscious skill quickly becomes automatic. Questions such as, "Do you want to save . . . ?" are soon no longer read. The "OK" button is clicked or Return key pressed with no conscious thought. Even after the user realizes that the computer has presented a subtly new question, the task of adapting to the change has only begun. Now he or she must somehow block the automatic response long enough to unlearn the old habit and acquire the new.

A Combination of Ingredients

Taken together, these two principles offer the designer a great deal of freedom: **You can change the entire look and feel of an application as long as you honor the user's previously learned interpretations and subconscious behaviors.**

Put in oval windows. Change from a dialog box offering a list of specifications to a directly manipulable object. Go from 2D to 3D. Just don't make the left-arrow key make the pointer go to the right. Don't shuffle all the tools around in a palette so that the user depending on spatial memory keeps selecting the wrong one.

Consider your car. Let's say you got it back after its 30,000 mile service and found they had added anti-lock brakes and hidden, retractable wings, all for under $100. You would probably be quite happy. But now let's say that they switched your gas and brake pedals and *didn't charge you anything at all!* Think you'd be thrilled? And yet, it is so easy for designers to change the "pedals" around on the keyboard that it's done all the time.

Consistency also derives from what users *expect* to happen as a result of their actions. Coined by W.A.S. Buxton, the term *consistency with expectations* implies a principle for those occasions when consistency seems inconsistent, or vice versa. Before any product ships, take time to do user testing with the target population. Find out what users expect, what would stimulate them to change their expectations, and what would make such a change worth the trouble.

Prototyping:
A Day in the Life of an Interface Designer

AS ONE OF THE FIRST icon and window graphics designers for graphical interfaces, I have used some pretty archaic computer tools over the years. Even today, I still use paper and pen for design in addition to my computer tools. I am not a programmer, though I do extensive prototyping. Given that, how would life change if I had the "perfect" prototyping tools just for me? Well, look over my shoulder for a moment and I will show you my "perfect world."

Annette Wagner
Product Engineering
Apple Computer, Inc.

I am a Macintosh interface designer in a meeting with a project team working out the interface for a drawing application. The team includes a product manager, software engineers, and writers. As the meeting progresses, the team is working on the interface for an alignment dialog that interactively shows how objects will align on the screen. Everyone gets into the discussion, waving hands, drawing on the shared electronic whiteboard, and describing behaviors and layout verbally.

My electronic drawing pad is in front of me, and I can rapidly sketch the ideas from the meeting on the pad with a stylus. One part of the shared whiteboard mirrors what I draw on my pad, so that the team can see what I have so far. The pad has a complete palette of tools, including customized palettes of interface elements that can be drawn on the pad to create windows and menus. I can use the faint grid to line things up to, or I can

79

draw where I will on the page. There are as many pages as I might need to draw on; a click on the page corner flips through the pad to a new page or back to a previous page.

When the meeting is over, I return to my office, download the drawings I have made in the meeting, and fire up my prototyping environment. Objects from the drawings can be selected and grouped together. Squares can be replaced with windows. Icons can be added to demonstrate a particular idea. A "zoom close" animation can be scripted in. Groups can be linked together in a sequence, can share common information, and can be activated through scripts. Within minutes, the drawings from my meeting have been turned into a *visualization*.

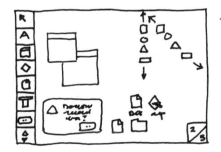

A visualization *is a minimalistic prototype useful for demonstrating and capturing ideas. Visualizations provide a mechanism for allowing team members to see a literal representation of what they have been talking about. Initial interface ideas don't need to be detailed; a simple reiteration of ideas in a format that people can see is best. Think of the visualization as a "for example" generator. Many times, seeing an idea that has had only verbal description can enable people to make a better design decision. Visualizations can also be shown to real users to get feedback. Even if the user cannot interact with the visualization, the concept can be demonstrated.*

An important benefit is the speed at which new team members can be integrated as a result of the history portrayed by the visualizations.

Visualizations require very quick turn-around to be useful. They are linear, with little branching, no interactivity, and little scripting or programming. It's as if you took that napkin you drew on at lunch and turned it into a very simple animation or simulation. The idea is to capture the idea and put it in a format in which it can be examined, and to iterate those steps as many times as possible.

A month of feverish work has gone by. I have been providing visualizations at every meeting. As the project has evolved, the wealth of visualizations has replaced the written specifications of the human interface. And, because of the variety of ideas produced, the interface is further along than we had expected and more fun!

Now we're up against our first deadline; the product review is next week. We need to demonstrate the various interface proposals to management. Back in my prototyping environment, I load up several visualizations and look them over in a reduced "show page" format. I drag pieces of visualizations around on my storyboard to sequence elements and lay out branching. As I put together different elements in this storyboard fashion, I swap in interface graphics from my library and add scripts to make an *interactive prototype.*

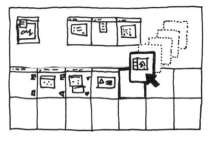

The interactive prototype allows team members and users to "try out" the interface and get their hands dirty. The intention is to provide a one-way path that demonstrates how a chunk of an interface is going to work. For example, the prototype might show a ruler dialog in which most of the dialog works but which is not yet an entire application interface. With an interactive prototype the team can start to "feel" how an interface is going to behave.

This level of prototype is fairly hard-wired because turn-around time is still critical. Interactive prototypes have minimal branching and scripting to make the interface seem fairly realistic. There is a library of reusable basic "interface behavior" scripts and interface graphics that can be added as necessary.

Prototypes should be easily distributed. Each interactive prototype should end with a "comments window" in which the user can enter feedback on the prototype. The easier it is to gather comments, the more you will get. The more comments you get, the more data you have. This provides a way to test out theories and possible implementations before too much time is invested in a particular idea.

The interactive prototypes are done. Before the review, the team hands out a written specification and a set of interactive prototypes that parallel and demonstrate the specification.

Finally, the review is here. With the shared whiteboard, everyone at the review can easily see the interactive prototypes on the room's large wall screen. The pad can be handed to people for them to try out the prototype, or they can try it out on one of the screens embedded in the table. It is easy to get straight to the heart of the concerns, as everyone has a clear concept of what the team is attempting to do. With easy access to the history of visualizations and the interactive prototypes, controversial areas are resolved more quickly and to everyone's satisfaction.

Once the review is past, it is time for the team to iterate the design and begin to focus on the final interface. Soon the team has narrowed down the interface designs to one proposal that encompasses the necessary functionality, appears to work smoothly, and is understandable. Or is it? It's time to do user testing.

In conjunction with another member of the project team, I take one of the interactive prototypes and start linking chunks of prototypes together into a *user testing prototype*. When I'm done, I end up with two user testing prototypes. Next I link in more complex programming modules that give the prototype enough "real" functionality to complete a task. Finally I link in the testing modules to collect data.

User-testing prototypes *are the most complex prototypes to create, as they require a fairly complete interface implementation and should be somewhat robust. Sequences that can be sketchy in the interactive prototypes should be complete in the user testing prototypes. For example, if the user is expected to swap disks to complete a task, then the functionality for ejecting and requesting disks should be part of the prototype. For some user tests, facilities for collecting different kinds data may be needed. Read the chapter by Kate Gomoll for more on user testing. The main emphasis with this kind of prototype is to build something with which the user can complete a typical task.*

This implies an ability to take the interactive prototype and extend it with programming modules to complete the functionality. This includes code to fake behaviors such as disk insertion and ejection, status messages, error alerts, dragging, resizing, scrolling, and even a desktop.

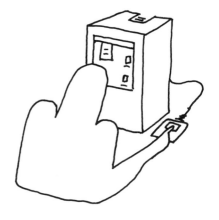

User testing is complete and the results have been evaluated. All the hard work of prototyping has paid off. User testing presented us with some surprises, and with a few iterations, the improvements to the interface will be complete. Now I can devote my time to "filling out" the interface with error messages, final interface artwork, and the other implementation details that round out an interface. And someday, the product will ship.

Now that you've had a chance to see what my perfect tools might be like, you might wonder how I prototype today.

Keep in mind as I describe my current tools that I am not a programmer. Tools like MacApp™ and Prototyper™ are beyond my limited programming ability. If I did have a programming background, MacApp would be an excellent object-oriented environment to work in, as it provides routines for standard menus, windows, and so on, and some facility for creating new elements. Prototyper, though not object-oriented, is useful for designing standard Macintosh interfaces, but it has no facilities for designing new interface elements.

Today I use a variety of tools to produce prototypes. I make drawings and quick visualizations with felt tip pens and pads of marker paper. There is no computer interface yet to compare to this method for capturing ideas in meetings. But once the drawings are on the paper I cannot go back and move the shapes around, reuse portions, or add scripts.

The level of integration that allows for easy, fast iteration of ideas doesn't exist with today's tools, even though iteration is critical to good interface design. I can capture ideas only as fast as I draw, and if I am the only one who brings a drawing pad, then I am the only one drawing. Shared whiteboards where everyone can contribute would help, but the closest thing to a commonly available shared whiteboard is a electronic whiteboard that makes copies. And the copies are static.

Visualizations need to get into the computer to be useful. I can use a scanner to scan in drawings and visualizations, but most times it is easier to recreate the drawings in a paint application than to turn scanned images into clean art, especially if I am working in a well-defined interface like the Macintosh. I keep a large selection of ready-to-use interface elements in my computer scrapbook, everything from title bars to trash can icons. Recreating visualizations on the computer slows down the process of prototyping, leaving less time for thinking of new ideas.

For interactive prototyping, I currently use HyperCard. I can set up a template stack that imitates the Macintosh desktop, complete with a menu bar, gray desktop pattern, and icons. However, HyperCard is not the easiest tool to use to produce prototypes of the Macintosh interface. There are no standard methods for producing menus, icons, windows, or basic behaviors. One can script elements together, but too often extensive knowledge of programming is needed to make certain behaviors work correctly.

HyperCard stacks are easily distributed, and adding in a "comments" card is a simple task. It is possible to show a user a stack or to produce a prototype stack that someone else can walk through with minimal help. But to do substantive user testing, I cannot produce a robust enough HyperCard prototype without extensive scripting and external code. There are no testing modules one can roll in or easy ways to collect data. When I reach the stage of user testing today, I must enlist an experienced programmer to write code to collect data and add minimal functionality.

The skill set of an interface designer can encompass programming, graphic design, industrial design, experimental psychology, cognitive psychology, and so on. If we are to support this range of skills, tools must have several entry points. That way, I can use a drawing pad and you can write scripts. And, regardless of what tool I use, I will still be able to produce a prototype.

Some Techniques for Observing Users*

THE WORD IS OUT: Users should be involved in interface design. But how many people practice what they preach? Until I started observing users, I didn't know the excitement, the value, and the ease of involving users in design. Each time I set up an observation, I find myself discovering something new about the way people think and work. I've become such an advocate that I try to observe users at every stage of the design process: brainstorming, prototyping, building, and evaluating.

When our group at Apple began to design an interface for on-line help, we decided to involve users in the project right away, before we had a prototype. To find out what kind of help users really need, we watched and listened to people using Macintosh applications. We noticed that people ask several distinct types of questions when they need help. These question categories gave us an idea for a menu scheme and provided the structure for our help interface.

Since that initial brainstorming session, we've been asking users to try out each of our design iterations. And we've learned a great deal. We've seen users interacting in ways we couldn't predict ourselves; we've found out what works and what doesn't; and we've saved ourselves a lot of time. By observing users early and often, we've been able to catch problems in

Kathleen Gomoll
Advanced Technology Group
Apple Computer, Inc.

Kathleen Gomoll
Advanced Technology Group
Apple Computer, Inc.

---

* Note: Significant portions of this chapter were published by Apple Computer as a Developer's Technical Note.

the prototype stage, rather than waiting until just before the product ships. (For more information about the On-line Help project, see the chapter by Abi Sellen and Anne Nicol.)

This chapter is an outline of the steps I typically go through when conducting a simple user observation. This isn't the only way to observe users; in fact, it's one of the least scientific ways. But if you try this technique, you'll get lots of useful data for designing and revising your interface.

Ten Steps for Observing Users

The following instructions guide you through a simple user observation. This observation is not an experiment, so you won't get statistical results. You will, however, see where people have difficulty using your product, and you'll be able to use that information to improve it.

You may want to ask pairs of people to work together on your tasks. You'll find that people working in pairs usually talk more than people working alone, and they also tend to discuss features of the product and explain things to each other.

These instructions are organized in steps. Under most of the steps, you will find some explanatory text and a bulleted list. The bulleted list contains sample statements that you can read to the user. (Feel free to modify the statements to suit your product and the situation.)

1. SET UP THE OBSERVATION

Write the tasks. To prepare for a user observation, you'll want to design some tasks for a user to work through with your product. These tasks should be real tasks that you expect most users will do when they use your product. Design tasks that focus on the part of the product you're studying. For example, if you want to know whether your menus are useful, you could design a task that requires the user to access the menus frequently. After you determine which tasks to use, write them out as short, simple instructions.

Recruit the users. When you look for users, try to find people who have the same experience level as the typical user for your product. Be careful not to recruit people who are familiar with your product or your opinions about the product.

Set up a realistic situation. An ideal setting for user observation is a quiet, enclosed room with a desk. Create an environment that is natural but free from interruption by getting users away from phone calls and other distractions. Although you can observe users quite effectively without using any special recording equipment, you might want to use a tape recorder or video recorder to record the session.

2. DESCRIBE THE PURPOSE OF THE OBSERVATION (IN GENERAL TERMS).

Set the users at ease by stressing that you're involving them in your design process. Emphasize that you're testing the product, not the users. For example, you could say:

- You're helping me by trying out this product in its early stages.
- I'm testing the product; I'm not testing you.
- I'm looking for places where the product may be difficult to use.
- If you have trouble with some of the tasks, it's the product's fault, not yours. Don't feel bad; that's exactly what I'm looking for.
- If I can locate the trouble spots, then I can go back and improve the product.

3. TELL THE USER THAT IT'S OK TO QUIT AT ANY TIME.

Make sure you inform users that they can quit at any time if they find themselves becoming uncomfortable. This is not only an ethical observation technique, it's standard professional practice. Users shouldn't feel as if they're locked into completing tasks. Say something like this:

- Remember, this is totally voluntary. Although I don't know of any reason for this to happen, if you become uncomfortable or find this objectionable in any way, feel free to quit at any time.

4. TALK ABOUT AND DEMONSTRATE THE EQUIPMENT IN THE ROOM.

Explain the purpose of each piece of equipment and how it will be used in the observation. (Hardware, software, video camera, microphones, etc.) If you're using a computer, determine the user's previous experience with keyboards, computers, this computer, similar software, etc. Demonstrate the use of any equipment that users will need in order to complete the tasks.

5. EXPLAIN HOW TO "THINK ALOUD."

Ask users to think aloud during the observation, saying what comes to mind as they work. By listening to users think and plan, you'll be able to examine their expectations for your product, as well as their intentions and their problem-solving strategies. You'll find that listening to users as they work provides you with an enormous amount of useful information that you can get in no other way.

Unfortunately, most people feel awkward or self-conscious about thinking aloud. Explain why you want them to think aloud, and demonstrate how to do it. For example, you could say:

- I have found that I get a great deal of information from these informal observations if I ask people to think aloud as they work through the exercises.
- It may be a bit awkward at first, but it's really very easy once you get used to it.
- All you have to do is speak your thoughts as you work.
- If you forget to think aloud, I'll remind you to keep talking.
- Would you like me to demonstrate?

6. EXPLAIN THAT YOU WILL NOT PROVIDE HELP.

It is important that you allow users to work with your product without interference or extra help. This is the best way to see how people really interact with the product. For example, if you see a user begin to have difficulty and you immediately provide an answer, you will lose the most valuable information you can gain from user observation—where users have trouble, and how they figure out what to do.

Of course, there may be situations in which you will have to step in and provide assistance, but you should decide what those situations will be before you begin observing. For example, you may decide that you will allow someone to flounder for at least three minutes before you provide assistance. Or you may decide that there is a distinct set of problems for which you will provide help.

As a rule of thumb, try not to give your users any more information than the true users of your product will have. Here are some things you can say to the participant:

- As you're working through the exercises, I won't be able to provide help or answer questions. This is because I want to create the most realistic situation possible.

- Even though I won't be able to answer most of your questions, please ask them anyway. I'll note your questions and answer them later.

- When you've finished all the exercises, I'll answer any questions you still have.

7. DESCRIBE THE TASKS AND INTRODUCE THE PRODUCT.

- Explain what the participant should do first, second, third. . . .
- Give the participant written instructions for the tasks.
- Describe the general function of the product.
- **Important:** If you need to demonstrate your product before the user observation begins, be sure you don't demonstrate something you're trying to evaluate. (For example, if you want to know whether users can figure out how to use certain tools, don't show them how to use those tools before the observation.)

8. ASK IF THERE ARE ANY QUESTIONS BEFORE YOU START; THEN BEGIN THE OBSERVATION.

9. CONCLUDE THE OBSERVATION.

When the observation is over:

- Explain what you were trying to find out during the observation.
- Answer any remaining questions the participant may have.
- Discuss any interesting behaviors you would like the participant to explain.

- Ask the users about their overall impressions, as well as any details they would like to discuss.

10. USE THE RESULTS.

As you observe, you will see users doing things you never expected them to do. When you see users having difficulty, your first instinct may be to blame the difficulties on the user's inexperience or lack of intelligence. But the purpose of observing users is to see what parts of your product might be difficult or ineffective. Therefore, if you see a participant having difficulty or making mistakes, you should take note and attribute the difficulties to faulty design, *not* to the participant.

It's a good idea to keep a record of what you found out during the observation. That way, you'll have documentation to support your design decisions, you'll be able to see trends in users' behavior, and you'll be able to tell others how real users helped you to design your product. After you've examined the results and summarized the important findings, fix the problems you've found and have users try it out again. By involving users more than once, you'll see how your changes affect their performance.

Users and Contexts
Introduction

MY FATHER WAS A CITY PLANNER. When I was a kid, I was fascinated by one particular photograph on his office wall. It was a view of the state capitol in which the foreground was occupied by a roughly constructed outhouse, complete with the traditional half-moon cut-out icon. One day I asked him about it, and he explained that the outhouse had been constructed by the Appalachian occupants of a downtown housing project. When these folks moved into the then-new apartment building, the first thing they did was to remove the indoor plumbing, which was of no apparent use to them, and sell it. They used part of their earnings to construct the familiar outhouse facility and called the rest profit.

This story demonstrates a particular kind of intersection: the encounter of a distinct population (in this case, rural poor Appalachians who had migrated to the city) with an environment that was not specifically designed for them (the "generic" housing project). What happened with the outhouse illustrates a typical result of such encounters: that which is unfamiliar, even though it may be potentially empowering, is rejected, and other materials are transformed into familiar objects that meet the same needs.

People transform their interfaces. Interfaces also transform their users. Studying the ways that distinct user populations think about and interact with interface environments can reveal these dynamics in dramatic ways.

Brenda Laurel

91

Who Uses Computers for What?

If the young discipline of interface design can be said to have traditions, one of them is the limited number of perspectives from which we normally frame interface design problems. At the micro-level, we look at individual users in user-testing situations, deriving "anecdotal" information from individuals and "scientific" information by applying statistical tools to groups of individual results. At the macro-level, we think about task domains—either tasks in the real world that we hope to facilitate or tasks that are unique to the computer.

A perspective that is often neglected (because it is hard to see) is the middle ground where task and tool domains—that is, contexts—and distinct user populations intersect. For instance, how are tools that are not specifically tailored to the needs of fiction writers (for example, word processors and outlining programs) actually used by them? What can be discovered by observing how educators design programs to enhance the learning process for kids, and how can we employ those observations to make other types of programs easier to learn and use? What sorts of tools, facilities, or formats might be of global value or appeal? The goal of this section is to illustrate how these perspectives can inform the design process.

The following chapters detail the experiences of a variety of users and designers whose perspectives generally are not well understood by interface designers, including children, teachers, computer game designers and players, fiction writers, gorillas, and professionals in the architecture-engineering-construction industry. Contexts include computer-based entertainment, learning, research, and hypermedia. Relatively new interface domains, including user programming and computer-supported collaborative work (CSCW) are also explored. The section can be viewed as a sampler of middle-ground perspectives. It includes individual and group users, technical and artistic applications, work and play, males and females, children and adults, and humans and animals.

You should also note some of the users and contexts that we have *not* included:

- Users of distinct hardware/OS platforms other than Macintosh (MS-DOS, workstations such as Sun and NeXT, etc.)

- Specialized business contexts and users (except as CSCW)

- Vertical professional and scientific contexts and users

- Artists other than writers (for example, graphic artists, animators, musicians, multimedia artists, and video artists)

- Special needs populations (for example, differently abled people and seniors)

- Distinct cultural and social groups (as distinguished by geography, life-style, history, politics, and other cultural dimensions)
- Custom systems for public access, such as arcades, amusement parks, and hands-on installations in museums

Which features of an interface are most valued by users with distinct characteristics and specialized tasks? Which features give them the most difficulty? Where is more flexibility required? Where is there *too much* freedom—and what kinds of user constraints might actually enhance creativity and productivity? Studying the kinds of users and contexts that are treated in this section, as well as those listed above, can provide surprising and illuminating answers.

Where group, task, or paradigm identification is strong, *local ways of doing things* evolve (comparable to the notion of "pidgins" as developed in Tom Erickson's creativity chapter). Interface metaphors will tend to be drawn from—or evolve toward—the task domain or user context (see Mountford's creativity chapter). The chapters in this section demonstrate the art of observing, analyzing, and making use of such "local cultures."

Sometimes the same interfaces work for everybody and sometimes they don't. Where is a "generic" interface best, and where is a "varietal" interface required? By studying a variety of users and contexts, we should be able to devise a methodology for systematically answering this question.

The chapters in this section could be characterized as *interface anthropology*. Observations from one user/context intersection (for example, kids using learning-oriented software) can inform the design of interfaces for other populations and tasks. Like cultural anthropologists, we will often find native "informants" to be indispensable in guiding our explorations. When we have amassed enough experience with diverse users and contexts, we can begin to learn when and how to extrapolate. Most important, we can learn to broaden our focus to include not only the well-explored sites, but also the vibrant new villages of activity within the larger cultures of computing.

Koko's Mac II:
A Preliminary Report

Project Koko

APPLE COMPUTER'S VIVARIUM PROGRAM has been working with the Gorilla Foundation to provide a gorilla named Koko with a voice. Apple has designed and built a special Mac II enclosure and written software which will allow Koko to activate a voice by touching icons on the screen. With this tool, the Gorilla Foundation can modify the information presented to Koko, and collect and analyze Koko's use of the system to gain further insights into language acquisition by higher-order primates.

Mike Clark
Tom Ferrara
Dave Jones
Ann Marion
Kim Rose
Larry Yaeger
Vivarium Program
Apple Computer, Inc.

Koko, the Gorilla Foundation, and the Desire for a Voice

Since she was one year old in 1972, Koko has been learning a version of American Sign Language (Ameslan), and now has a vocabulary of over 600 words. The Gorilla Foundation was formed to continue this training and the related research, and Project Koko is now the longest uninterrupted study of ape language abilities ever undertaken [see Patterson, 1987]. The research findings of the Foundation offer strong support for the notion that, when immersed in an environment rich in interactions with speaking humans, not only can gorillas comprehend and react to spoken English, but they can also invent new gestures, translate from English to Ameslan, and converse at a high level of abstraction. The dedication of researchers Dr. Francine (Penny) Patterson and Dr. Ron Cohn is no less impressive— since lowland gorillas have a life span of more than fifty years, the re-

*Photo courtesy of the Gorilla
Foundation/Ronald Cohn.*

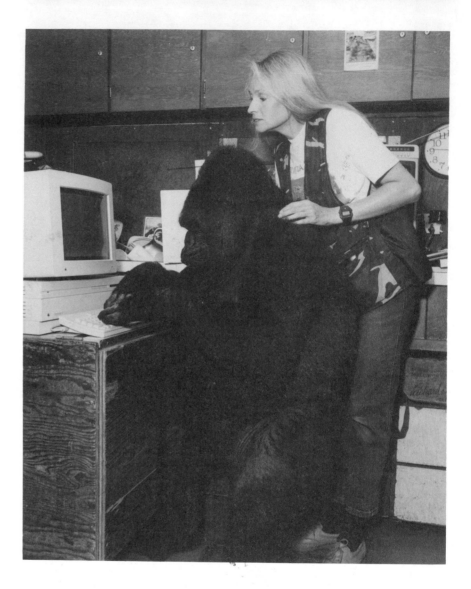

searchers have basically committed the rest of their lives to studying Koko
and a male gorilla, Michael.

At one time, when Project Koko was still on the Stanford campus, Koko
had access to a voice synthesis unit which she used to enhance her communication skills. However, when the Foundation moved to Woodside
Koko lost access to this device. The loss was traumatizing—when Koko
was asked what she wanted for her birthday, she signed, *Voice*! The researchers were also disappointed to lose this basic tool and have been
seeking a way to reinstate this capability.

With the system we've designed, Koko's researchers from the Gorilla
Foundation can display icons for Koko to select, manipulate the icons

available to her, and record both her and the researchers' use of their systems. This last function will give the Gorilla Foundation its first computer tool to completely record and analyze Koko's communications. Dr. Patterson (Executive Director of the Gorilla Foundation) serves on Vivarium's Advisory Board, and will provide regular feedback on Koko's use of the system. Dr. Patterson believes that by enabling Koko to use spoken language, new ground can be broken in interspecies communication.

Koko's Macintosh

Koko uses a standard Mac II enclosed in a special gorilla-proof housing. The enclosure is constructed of 1/2″ polycarbonate and will be bolted to the floor of Koko's trailer. Access to the computer is provided through a special touch screen designed to withstand the 2,000 pounds of force an excited gorilla can potentially generate. The computer has two video cards and is shared by Koko and the researcher.

What We Hope to Learn

Alan Kay notes that, "Since we're doing a project simulating animals, we should have at least one animal on our advisory board!" We further expect to gain some insights into what kind of iconic representation scheme will allow Koko to do sophisticated retrievals. Will she be able to use the interface we've designed to navigate successfully? Are there any ways in which we can extrapolate from the results of this experiment to make systems more accessible to novice *human* users?

A continuing exposure to Koko's use of language can provide insight into the nature of her cognition and brain function; we expect this to continue to be of interest and value, especially since we provide the Foundation with copies of some of the date/time-stamped files of her speech and the researchers' notes. The nature of the world model that Koko has built in her brain/mind is very much of interest; presumably, use of language requires some internal world model. Larry Yaeger, Principle Engineer of the Vivarium Program, has embarked on a project to build simulated critters that build and use internal models of the world. Larry is basing his work on neurophysiological data and neural network models, but we believe that phenomenological input regarding this issue from natural sources (such as Koko) will be of great value.

What We Have Already Learned

In the process of developing the tools, Vivarium engineers Mike Clark (Systems and Electronics), Tom Ferrara (Mechanical), and Larry Yaeger (Software) have had a number of challenging experiences. Above all, the personal experience of participating in this research—meeting Koko and communicating with her—has been truly awesome.

Systems and Electronics

Mike Clark has spearheaded system design since the project's inception. The Gorilla Foundation had an existing proposal to develop a large keyboard for Koko, but during initial discussions Mike Clark determined that everything that the Gorilla Foundation wanted to do (and more) could be done with a Mac II, a large touch screen, and a HyperCard-style button interface. At the first meeting Mike demonstrated a HyperCard stack that spoke all of the words from the book *Koko's Kitten* [Patterson, 1985], spoken by his niece and digitized by his son.

Mechanical Engineering

The most important consideration in all of the mechanical design aspects was for the safety of the gorilla. A typical gorilla response to anger or excitement is to run full speed and backhand the object of the anger. For Koko, this means a 260-pound animal running at about 20 miles per hour, swinging her arm with a force comparable to a 10-pound shotput traveling at 100 miles per hour. Accordingly, Tom Ferrara faced a significant design challenge in developing the workstation—a Mac II computer, a 19″ Sony monitor, and a touch screen—into a package that could withstand these extreme forces. Failure of the physical system could only be tolerated if it did not endanger Koko in any way.

The most difficult design consideration was the part of the system with which the gorilla actually comes in contact: the touch screen. Most touch screens are thin, to minimize the visual parallax between the image on the screen and the point of contact. But we needed a thick piece of glass to withstand Koko's potential force. Mike spent over a month talking to the Gorilla Foundation and the Los Angeles Zoo to determine the right combination of materials. A standard MicroTouch capacitive screen optically bonded to a one-inch thick piece of tempered glass was finally selected. It is interesting that the parallax through a one-inch piece of tempered glass is not as bad as one might predict when operating the system from the floor. Behind the touch screen is mounted a standard 19″ Sony Trinitron from SuperMac Technology.

Design of the computer's enclosure proved almost as challenging. We needed an enclosure that would withstand Koko's excitement and absorb the shock of any blows she might deliver. After debating and testing a number of designs, Tom finally built the enclosure of an inner framework made from 1″ × 2″ solid 6064-T6 aluminum, covered by a 3/8″ polycarbonate sheet. The Monitor is mounted on a sliding assembly that is dampened with gas struts with 3″ of travel. This provides shock absorption in the event that Koko should throw her weight into the screen area. The final unit as delivered is 28 5/8″ tall × 21 1/4″ wide × 39 1/4″ long. Passive ventilation is provided by slots which are designed to channel any foreign materials (bananas, feces, etc.) away from the CPU. Koko has a standard Mac II CPU consisting of 5 megabytes of memory, a 40-megabyte hard disk, and a SuperMac Spectrum/8-color card, connected through the floor of Koko's trailer to the researcher's monitor and keyboard.

In the process of designing the physical system, Tom Ferrara had to concern himself with both durability and ergonomics. He felt that the project helped him to gain a better understanding of human-computer interfaces, especially in terms of accommodating users who may not have the physical ability to use a keyboard or manipulate a mouse, but who can point.

Software User Interface

Using SuperCard, Mike Clark developed three applications specifically to familiarize Koko with the touch screen interface. The first is four digitized animal pictures that make the animal's sound when touched. The second shows a picture for each letter of the alphabet (developed by the Gorilla Foundation) and speaks the name of the picture when it is pressed. The final application is called KokoPaint. It is a simplified color painting program which allows Koko to select from a few colors and finger paint with them.

Linguistic Research

The primary application specified by Gorilla Foundation staff is a research tool. This computer tool replaces and replicates handwritten notation methodologies familiar to Penny and Ron, and represents the first computer software tailored to their specifications. As such, it offers exciting unforeseen potentials as well as new questions for the researchers. The Vivarium staff is eager to evolve the tools as the Gorilla Foundation evolves in their own thinking. This is only the beginning.

Larry Yeager experimented with HyperCard and SuperCard, but he ultimately opted to write a custom Mac application for Koko entitled "Lingo." The interface presented to Koko is simple, consisting primarily of uniformly shaped, regularly spaced buttons—rectangular regions on her touch-screen display—that, when pressed, cause the playback of a sampled-sound resource corresponding to the selected button. Each button corresponds to a single word and may display text, a full-color picture, or both. Sampled sound was selected over phonemic speech generation early on, primarily for the improved clarity of speech. This rapidly led to a discussion of who would serve best as Koko's voice, and we decided to find a way to let her make the selection herself. The voices of four human females were recorded with MacRecorder and later played for Koko, who ultimately selected one of them as her own.

Anticipating a maximum vocabulary of between 500 and 2000 words (Koko's common-use signs and the total number of uniquely identifiable signs she has evidenced, respectively), specific, strategically placed buttons on the screen were set aside to perform a forward- or backward-paging function, hopefully allowing Koko to flip between screens of words. Additionally, at the request of the Gorilla Foundation, a sentence button was incorporated that accumulates the individual words as they are pressed and when pressed itself produces a sentence consisting of these words played rapidly in sequence.

The interface just described is presented to Koko on a "Subject screen" which she uses to make her word selections. A separate "Researcher screen" displays Koko's word selections and permits the recording of contextual notes by observers. The Researcher screen is a standard Apple RGB monitor fed by a cable out of the bottom of Koko's workstation. The keyboard cable also extends out the bottom, and the keyboard, mouse, and second monitor form a second workstation for the researcher.

Through various menu options, the Researcher can employ a number of tools for laying out and manipulating the Subject screen and for saving and restoring these layouts in a convenient fashion. Several characteristics of the interface could not be predetermined—for instance, most useful button size, optimal number of buttons per screen, the relative usefulness of text versus images for the buttons, the desirability of playing a sound immediately upon each button's press versus delaying until the sentence button is pressed, and so on. The solution was to make such features easily modifiable through menu selections and simple dialogs from the Researcher screen. Tools for editing the words, sounds, and images associated with the various buttons are provided directly within Lingo to help the researchers design and experiment with the Subject screen layout. Alternate layout configurations may be saved and opened in the usual Macintosh manner through the File menu.

The system displays the subject's and researcher's entries and voicing of Koko's selections and records them in a pair of archival data files—the Subject Archive file and the Researcher Archive file—for subsequent linguistic and behavioral analyses. Every utterance (button press) made by Koko is separately date/time-stamped; the researcher's notes are date/time-stamped and archived once per line. The configuration of the Subject screen along with any changes made to it is also archived in simple TEXT files which may be examined in any word processor. Fresh transcript files are automatically opened and closed every time Lingo is launched.

What Has the Gorilla Foundation Learned?

At the time of this writing, Koko has not yet used her complete workstation; Ron and Penny are hard at work gathering all the images and sounds for the new workstation software, and the final screen layout is being designed. Koko has only used the stand-alone Mac II for voice selection. Even with only two brief sessions totaling less than one hour with the Macintosh, however, significant results have already been achieved. Through the voice-selection exercises, Koko was able to solve a complex conceptual problem presented to her in spoken English by a computer, without prior training or the aid of visual markers of any kind. The accomplishment of this task illustrates that a gorilla has cognitive capacities for:

1. Comprehension of spoken language: Koko responded to the recorded statements and grasped the task requirements.
2. Self-concept: Koko employed the sign "myself" to refer to one of the voices when it spoke both the query and concept sentences.
3. Auditory discrimination of human voices: Koko responded differently to the four voices.

Next phases of the computer-language project will allow Koko to use the voice she has selected to create her own spoken statements [for further reading, see Patterson and Cohn, 1989].

What Does the Gorilla Foundation Hope to Learn?

The first research project is to develop a user interface that will allow Koko to navigate between screens. The entire vocabulary of over 600 words cannot effectively be displayed for Koko on her screen all at the same time. We must therefore design a way to represent to Koko where she is in relation to the other things available to her and how to get to them. In addition, we need to provide Koko with a way to indicate thought completion. After the user interface issues have been resolved, then the main research task of communications research can begin.

Once Penny and Ron saw Koko's Macintosh, they began to see possibilities for using it that extend beyond those originally imagined. They began thinking about the possibility of empowering Koko to control her environment. Could our engineers make it possible for the Mac to control the lighting in Koko's room so that Koko could control lighting herself? Could she learn how to operate the interface they designed? Could Koko control her curtains, raising and lowering them at will? Currently she orders around researchers to do these tasks for her—would she perform them herself if she could?

In Conclusion

Designing Koko's workstation and software has already led to some insights regarding user interface issues in hardware and software design. And the manner in which Koko now interacts with her Macintosh, its rather special workstation, and its software will undoubtedly yield even greater insights into these issues.

The exciting implications of applications designed to empower Koko directly is surely what stirs our imaginations. But this will not be accomplished overnight. To empower any individual through the computer medium requires much thought and exploration. The road to empowerment is a long one, full of slow, personal realizations and learning—on the part of both users and designers. The Vivarium Program is involved in long-term collaboration with end-users of special needs, our primary association being with an elementary school. Our experience shows that it takes three years to familiarize new computer users with this novel medium and to involve them in the process of redefining it. The way one does one's work changes as the computer is used, and such changes in working style cannot be made to happen quickly. The Koko project has required several years of conversations and prototypes involving the Gorilla Foundation researchers to design and develop the system. Now that they have a system, the process will not end; as soon as the system is in use, the researchers will undoubtedly begin to see ways to transform and customize it. We hope that these new tools will illuminate whole unforeseen areas of research on gorilla intelligence and culture. We hope that once the goals of the researchers have been met, we can see how to include Koko herself in the evolution of these computer tools and interfaces.

Perhaps the most enlightening aspect of this work will be the greater understanding we obtain of the nature of intelligence through this ongoing study of language and its use. Through such studies of alternate cognitive systems we should be able to develop a better understanding of human cognition and communication. Perhaps we may then apply this understanding to the development of functional artificial intelligence, or, at the very least, come to know ourselves better. And if we are able to see the human species as part of a continuum, rather than uniquely set apart, perhaps we will become more aware of our place in the world's ecosystem—and the need to act accordingly.

Lessons from Computer Game Design

Rationale

THE STUDENT OF USER INTERFACE DESIGN who sets aside old prejudices can learn a great deal from computer games. After all, games operate in a more demanding user-interface universe than other applications. The user of a word processor evaluates the quality of its interface not in absolute terms but in terms relative to the alternatives. If the user interface allows the user to perform the job more easily than, say, pencil and paper would, then it's good enough. The user of a word processor has no choice but to get the job done and is interested in finding an easier way to do it.

The user of a game feels no compulsion to play the game. If the game's interface is clumsy or confusing, the player simply abandons it. Thus, a game's user interface must pass not a relative test but an absolute test, and a harsh one it is. The user interface must be not merely functional, nor even just easy to use—it must also be fun!

This point is borne out by historical experience. Computer games have always been at the forefront of the user interface revolution. Although it is true that many user interface innovations first appeared in academic and research environments, the first commercialization of many innovations appeared in games. Scrolling windows, joysticks, trackballs, point-and-click interfaces, double-clicking, click-and-drag—various representations of these ideas appeared in games such as *Eastern Front (1941), Pinball Construction Set,* and *Rocky's Boots* long before the Macintosh interface was introduced.

Chris Crawford
Computer Game Designer

Some General Lessons from Game Design

I will begin with some elementary lessons that applications developers and interface designers can learn from game designers.

MOVE AWAY FROM THE KEYBOARD

The first lesson is to move away from the keyboard as the primary input device. Games have long relied on the joystick as their sole input device. The discipline imposed by this primitive device has forced game designers to hone their interface design skills; thus, when the mouse arrived, game designers were quick to master its possibilities. Many games on the Macintosh can be played with no keyboard at all.

Obviously, there are many applications (word processing providing the best example) in which the keyboard must be given primacy. Many serious applications rely heavily on the manipulation of text, and the keyboard is usually superior to the mouse for such applications. Yet, even in word processors, the keyboard can be given too much emphasis. Compare the interface designs of the word-processing software products with which you are familiar. Some place almost exclusive emphasis on the keyboard, via keystroke commands and embedded control codes. Others accomplish many of the same tasks, such as centering a line of text, without undue emphasis on the keyboard (through ortho-Mac-ish direct manipulation operations), and their user interfaces are accordingly cleaner.

PLACE GREATER RELIANCE ON GRAPHICS AND SOUND

Concepts are often better represented through sounds and images than through words. Games have always relied heavily on graphics and sound because game designers know them to be more directly communicative than unadorned text. Some designers think that graphics and sound are of primarily cosmetic value. This misapprehension is understandable, given the gratuitous nature of graphics in many games. The simple truth is that a graphic is often able to express a concept *directly* where text talks about it indirectly. This indirection of text robs it of expressive clarity. The power of graphics is expressed in the old English teacher's dictum: "Don't talk about it, **show** it!"

EMPHASIZE INTENSITY OF INTERACTION

A third lesson from computer games emphasizes the speed and intensity of the interaction between the user and the computer. Game designers have learned that they cannot leave the user in the lurch waiting while the computer goes off to process something. A good program establishes an "interaction circuit" through which user and computer arc in apparently continuous communication. Although it is entirely fair for the user to freeze the circuit in order to pause and think, the computer deserves no similar luxury. The user needs fast response from the computer because a delay of even a second is often enough to break the user's concentration and disturb the continuity of the game. This lesson is easily misunderstood by those who miss its fundamental asymmetry. The goal here is not to have the user frantically processing words or crunching numbers in the adrenalin-charged style of Space Invaders™. Rather, the ideal is to have the computer moving at a speed that doesn't inhibit the user.

The Central Problem: Increasing Complexity

It seems to me that the central user interface problem of the personal computer industry is, how can we design interfaces to enable the user to control the more complex tasks that will be made possible by the more powerful hardware of the future?

VOCABULARY EXPANSION

A loose linguistic model can help us understand the problem. The user "talks" to the computer, telling it what to do, usually in a custom language designed for the application. The ease of learning this language is identical to the ease of learning the application. But as the feature set expands, the vocabulary of the language must expand with it. After all, it does the user no good that the program can "tri-axially fromangulate" his spreadsheet data if the command "tri-axially fromangulate" is not a part of the user interface. How then can we expand the vocabulary of the user interface?

CLASSIC SOLUTION #1: COMMAND LINE INTERFACES

The archaic solution is a command-line interface, such as is found in CP/M and MS-DOS. This user interface is quite easy to program, but it is now widely recognized as inadequate. The problem is that the user has no way of knowing the vocabulary and syntax of the language used in the command-line interface, and so must guess, often with disastrous results. A variety of crutches (for example, reference cards, on-line help systems, and shells) have been developed to ameliorate the situation, but they are palliatives. As the vocabulary expands with the feature set, the user must spend more time searching through the reference card or on-line help documents to find the desired command. The command-line interface works well in a tight environment populated by a small number of heavily used commands. In such an environment, the user will memorize the command vocabulary and syntax and will have no problems with the interface. Such tight environments are of historical interest only; our problem concerns environments that are entirely the opposite of these.

CLASSIC SOLUTION #2: MENUS

The second classic solution uses menus to explicitly declare the options available to the user. In effect, the on-line help system becomes the user interface. The user sees options and makes a choice. This solves the worst problem of the command-line interface. But the classic menu structure has its own problems. First is the matter of screen space. If each option were presented with a full explanation of its import, the screen would fill with just a few options. The alternative, to present terse contractions of the options, robs the menu of its major advantage of being self-explanatory.

The second and third problems with menus are related: how does one present a large vocabulary through menus? One approach is to have long menus, and this gets us into the second problem. Once a menu gets longer than, say, ten items, it grows cumbersome. The user must scan through each item on the list, and the list is so long that the scanning becomes tedious. Moreover, in any given situation, many of the items that we might place on the menu are not of interest to the user at that time, so the user must waste time reading and rejecting irrelevant options.

The alternative is to nest the menus, allowing each menu item to bring up a new menu. This ensures that the user will see short menus populated with pertinent items. But it creates its own problem: menu navigation. The user can easily take a wrong turn in traversing the menu tree and become lost. Providing "quick escape" options that return the user to the base level helps somewhat, but does not entirely solve the problem.

THE MACINTOSH INTERFACE: A FINELY BALANCED SET OF COMPROMISES

The standard Macintosh interface uses a variety of techniques to minimize the problems listed above. It relies heavily on a nested menu system, but the main menu is spread sideways so that it doesn't dominate the screen. The secondary menus are instantly available and pop in and out to conserve screen space. There is also a provision for tertiary menus. However, the size of the menus does enforce terseness in naming menu items, to their detriment. More complex menu options will raise a dialog box that allows a diversity of options, subsets of which can be mutually exclusive or nonexclusive as needed.

Although the basic Macintosh interface design is flexible and extensible, it has at heart a two-word sentence structure. That is, it works best when the user selects something in the window by clicking on it and then selects a verb from the menu to act on the selected object. The system begins to gum up when more complex expressions are demanded of it. This is most obvious when we note the evolution of dialog boxes in Macintosh applications. Some have become large enough to fill the entire screen. Even worse, we are now beginning to see nested dialog boxes.

THERE'S A PATTERN HERE

In examining these three interfaces, we see a clear pattern: each one is targeted for a certain range of hardware power and vocabulary size. The command-line interface works well with small machines and, say, a dozen commands. The menu interface requires a little more hardware and can comfortably handle a few dozen commands. The Macintosh interface demands much more hardware and can push the vocabulary size up to, say, a hundred commands. With extensions, the Macintosh interface could well handle more, but it is straining even now.

This pattern suggests a way to characterize the nature of the problem we face. Our task is to design new interface structures that will allow larger vocabularies; we concede that they will consume more hardware resource in the process.

Another Set of Compromises

I offer another set of compromises that extends the range of our working vocabulary. My concept is not quite original, having been anticipated by earlier work. It is instead a different twist on other ideas.

The first notion I use is an explicitly linguistic approach. The user is going to talk to the computer, so he might as well use a sentence. People know what a sentence is; they are comfortable with the concept. So in this interface they will talk to the computer by building sentences.

Sentences are composed of words; the user will select words from menus. The problem to avoid here is the profusion of lengthy or nested menus. My solution—and this is the heart of the interface design—is to provide an intelligently chosen set of options. If we imagine the vocabulary of the interface to reside in an internal dictionary, we will not have the user flip through the virtual pages of the dictionary searching for the correct word. Instead, we will have the software do most of that job for the user. The software will examine each word in the dictionary, evaluating its applicability to the situation at hand. If the word makes sense in the context, it will be presented as an option.

A word that is presented as an option will go into a window or pane that holds the entire set of contextually acceptable words. The user will simply click on the desired word. The chosen word will then be attached to the sentence that the user is building. This is the second important feature of the design—showing the user the sentence in construction. This solves, in a very intuitive fashion, the problem of menu navigation that deeply nested menus encounter.

Only three special buttons are needed to complete the interface. The first is a backspace button that cancels the last selected word. The second is a cancel button that cancels the entire sentence. The last is an execute button that activates the command if it is complete.

A WORKING EXAMPLE: *TRUST & BETRAYAL*

The user interface described here has been implemented in my game *Trust & Betrayal*. The interface used in the game has a few twists not described earlier, foremost of which is the use of icons in place of words. I would advise against the use of such icons for general-purpose work, but it does have one advantage. A regular English word carries a great deal of undesirable connotation with it, connotation that might interfere with the narrow use of the word in a computer program. An icon is more clearly defined and controlled by the designer.

The other twist in *Trust & Betrayal* is the use of spatial sentence structures to assist in the player's understanding of the syntax of the language. The icons in the sentences are organized in structures that suggest the relationship between the elements of the sentence. There is no reason why such a system could not be used with normal words; the designer could simply use common sentence-diagramming structures.

The following screen shots show a short sentence being constructed in *Trust & Betrayal*. The available words are presented in the left pane; the sentence being built appears in the upper right pane. For purposes of clarity, the other portions of the screen display have been removed. In the first screen shot, the user, represented by the horned creature in the upper right

Figure 1

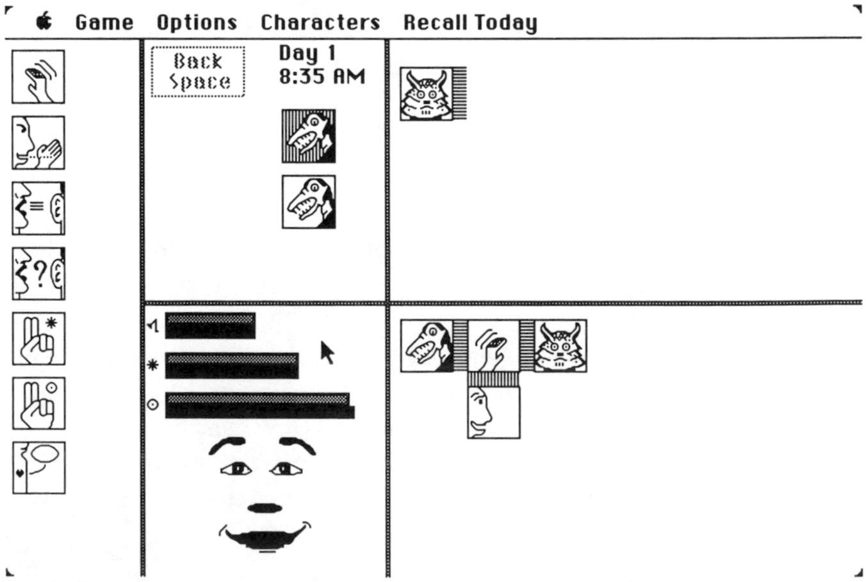

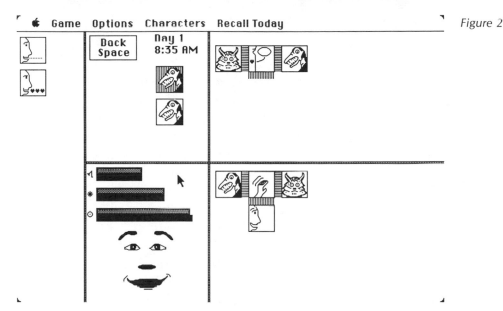

Figure 2

pane, is considering a verb (see figure 1). Note that the subject of the sentence has been filled in automatically for the user.

The user elects to express a feeling to the other character. When this verb is selected, the object of the verb (the other character) is filled in automatically. After all, the other character is the only person in the room; to whom else would the user speak? The user now must choose the feeling to express. There are only two choices: to make small talk, or to flatter the other character (see figure 2). The user clicks on "flatter."

The sentence is now complete. It says "Vetvel flatters Skordokott," as shown in figure 3.

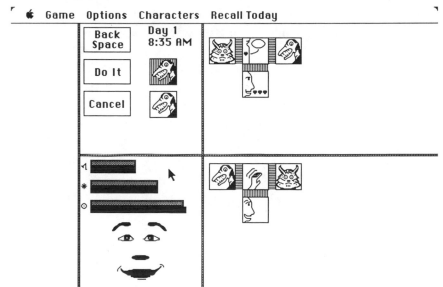

Figure 3

STRENGTHS OF THE INTERFACE

This language-oriented interface enjoys as its primary benefit a much larger vocabulary than can be supported by current interfaces. My experience shows that it can handle an 80-word vocabulary with ease, and my hunch is that it could handle up to 512 words before breaking down.

It handles this larger vocabulary while greatly reducing (not eliminating) some of the problems that cripple other interfaces. For example, menus in this design are really lists of contextually acceptable words. Such menus tend to be short, because contextual considerations will eliminate most of the vocabulary. Although the design relies on nesting of menus, the nesting doesn't confuse the user because the direct representation of the sentence under construction clearly shows the user's situation.

Especially gratifying is the automatic elimination of user errors. This design makes it impossible for the user to say something nonsensical. There will never be an alert box telling the user "You haven't specified what to find," or something similar. It simply can't happen. The user can still say wrong things, but not nonsensical things.

Finally, the design does not consume excessive amounts of screen space. The basic system can be executed in less than 30K pixels, about one-sixth of a standard Macintosh screen.

WEAKNESSES OF THE INTERFACE

The weak link in this interface design is the contextual rejection of words in the dictionary. This can fail in several ways. Some situations might have little context associated with them, in which case most of the dictionary would be available; this would swamp the user. Moreover, the design would have to use a scroll bar or other window-searching technique to allow for those cases in which the number of words available exceeds the capacity of the window.

The real killer is the software that searches the dictionary. It must scan the entire dictionary and apply the contextual considerations. This is itself a complex task. Many of the design considerations traditionally made explicit in the user interface would be implicit in the search routine. Worse, the routine must execute very quickly, perhaps in half a second. After all, the user cannot be asked to wait longer than that after choosing a word. This problem imposes the upper limit on the size of the vocabulary. Until we have faster processors, the dictionary-searching routine would run too slowly to allow a large vocabulary.

A Final Note

Computer games, we must admit, can be silly, stupid, childish, and wasteful of time. But the harsh competitive environment in which game designers operate has nourished the development of sound concepts of user interface design. The serious student of interface design could spend a profitable afternoon playing games—for evaluative purposes, of course.

Interfaces for Learning:
What Do Good Teachers Know That We Don't?

Anne Nicol
Human Interface Group
Apple Computer, Inc.

AMY IS USING LOGO for the first time. She can look up at the board in the front of the lab where her teacher has written a list of "commands" that she can use. She types FORWARD 20. The "turtle" moves vertically on the screen a short distance, leaving a visible trail. Amy then types RIGHT 20 and the turtle rotates slightly to the right. "Huh? I told him to go right! But he just stayed in the same place. What's the matter with this turtle?!"

Across town, Sonny is using a science program on the Macintosh to learn about electricity. By "dragging" the mouse from a battery to a bulb and back again, he can set up a circuit. If he does it right the bulb lights up. He watched Carlo do it and now it's his turn. He carefully draws the line from the battery to the bulb and draws another line back to the battery. Nothing happens. He "erases" the whole thing and starts over. This time it works and the bulb lights up. He tries it again, but it fails. This seems to get him into a somewhat haphazard mode of trying things at random, with some successes, but no discernible pattern.

For years, I've been watching children using computers to learn a whole range of subjects and ideas—from programming to history to creative writing. Children work miracles with the machines and overcome all kinds of obstacles that would stymie their parents and teachers. But what interests me are the places where they stumble or get off-track. I learn from the mistakes children make and the misconceptions they develop as they use

113

computers. And what I learn often has relevance for adults as well as for children, for experts as well as novices.

My observations have led me to believe that "interfaces for learning" have special design requirements above and beyond the considerations we make in building good electronic tools for professionals and casual users. When the user is naive with respect to underlying concepts (not just the use of the program), the interface needs to reflect teaching principles and models that might be unnecessary in programs geared towards more knowledgeable users. A good example may be found in user observations made during the development of the Grolier/Americana browser (see the chapter by Oren et al. in this volume). In this design, users are led by "guides" (characters representative of the early 1800s) through series of related articles about American history. But it seems that the ability to appreciate the connections among the articles depends on prior knowledge of the period. In fact, one of the questions users asked frequently was, "Why did the guide bring me to this article?"

Although educators and child development experts have had increasingly important roles in building educational software, their influence on interface design, particularly in tool environments, is less apparent. Word processors, science simulations, database browsers, and programming environments are examples of tools. As computers are integrated into the classroom, I suspect that tool software will be used more frequently and in many more parts of the curriculum.

There is a tendency to assume that all we need to do is provide a good tool and the child's natural curiosity and motivation will take over. Users are left on their own; they are expected to "discover" concepts and principles by exploring the environment. But, as Jerome Bruner—a careful student of discovery learning—says, "Discovery favors the well-prepared mind" [Bruner, 1962]. In years of watching and supervising other teachers, and in my own teaching experience, I have observed that children are most likely to make their own fruitful discoveries when they work in contexts that have been carefully constructed by teachers and other experts to facilitate discovery, and when there are models available to help show the way.

In designing interfaces for learning, we need to take into consideration the same principles that good teachers use when they prepare a child for new discoveries. In this chapter, I will be looking at four ways in which interfaces can be designed to support learners:

- By giving cues and overviews that serve as advance organizers for learners new to the territory—**unfamiliar territory**

- By careful modeling and facilitation of the problem-solving process—**modeling process**

- By using movement and animation accurately to represent **changes in state**
- By using interaction in ways that capitalize on the user's intelligence—**interfaces as coaches**

For illustration, I will refer to several existing software packages: Discovery Lab, LOGO, Bank Street Writer, and HyperCard.[1]

Discovery Lab represents a large and varied class of educational software designed to let learners simulate the scientific process. As a tool, it lets the user design and conduct experiments within certain constraints. Whereas the other software packages that I am using as illustrations are primarily tools, Discovery Lab includes specific scientific content as well as tool-like functionality. Bank Street Writer is a word processor developed at Bank Street College of Education and designed especially with children in mind. LOGO, a computer programming language sometimes called "baby LISP," was also designed for children. Of the four selections, HyperCard is the one system not designed originally for children. HyperCard is already being used extensively for educational development, however, and represents a new class of tool—a hypermedia construction set, according to its creator, Bill Atkinson.

Unfamiliar Territory

The interface is a means by which computers and users communicate. Notice in our everyday communication that when the purpose is to accomplish a task, we are perfectly capable of interacting in an abbreviated style, filling in the gaps, making up for syntactic and semantic shortcuts—as long as we are talking about something we know well. Listen, for example, to the kitchen conversations of short-order cooks or to the cryptic dialog over the taxi driver's radio. But if we are in unfamiliar territory and do not already have a model for the domain, we need better and more complete communication in order to carry out the task. We need to be given some structure ahead of time to help us understand. Educational researchers call this type of preparation "advance organizers."

MAPS AND TUTORIALS AS ADVANCE ORGANIZERS

One way to elaborate the communication about the application domain is to give more information about the context. Maps and tutorials can be designed to let users know how the territory is laid out and what kinds of

---

[1] *Discovery Lab* is published by Minnesota Educational Computing Corporation, St. Paul, Minnesota 55112. The version of *LOGO* referred to in this chapter was published by Logo Computer Systems, Inc. and Apple Computer, Inc. *Bank Street Writer* is published by Broderbund Software, Inc., San Rafael, California. *HyperCard* is published by Apple Computer, Inc., Cupertino, California 95014.

Figure 1: Menu titles for HyperCard.

File   Edit   Go   Tools   Objects

actions are possible, but they have limitations, too. It is hard to make a useful map of an application that is essentially a tool environment, although this is certainly an area in which expert teachers could help interface designers.[2]

Tutorials have the disadvantage of not being context-specific: they can't provide the help when and where you need it. Observing adults who were new to HyperCard and to hypertext in general showed us that even the most carefully illustrated and demonstrated concepts seemed too abstract to the uninitiated. Learners wanted (and needed) to *do* while they were being tutored; and concepts had to be simplified to the point of distortion in order to be presented at once in a single overview.

MENUS AS ADVANCE ORGANIZERS

New users of an application often skip the manual, tutorials, and other aids and browse through the menus to get an overview of the program's functionality. But menus are not often designed to provide conceptual structure for someone who doesn't already know the domain. Our research at Apple reveals that even experts can have trouble understanding the logic behind menu groupings: they don't know why certain functions are in a given menu and they can't remember what items are in what menu.

More carefully designed menus could help novices organize their understanding of the program and its domain. Ideally, the learner could begin to build a useful mental model on the basis of the menu organization and content alone. In HyperCard, the content of some of the menus is confusing for a person just learning to be an author, but the menu titles provide cues about the domain (see figure 1).

There are the standard File and Edit menus, followed by HyperCard's distinct Go, Tools, and Objects menus, which communicate three basic and perhaps new notions for users of HyperCard: (1) you will be moving around in HyperCard, (2) you can build things yourself, and (3) there are special things—buttons, backgrounds, etc. (novel concepts for many users)—that need their own menus. A third-grade user of HyperCard suggested, "There ought to be 'Create a Sound' . . . you could put 'New Sound' in the Objects menu" [Nicol, 1989]. This comment tells us something about the way the

---

[2] *Educational Technology*'s special issue on Hypermedia (November, 1988) includes compelling examples of the influence teachers can and should have in designing interfaces to hypermedia databases.

child understands the authoring elements in HyperCard; it may even suggest the usefulness of the menu in organizing those elements for him.

Process Models

A child using tool software like LOGO, Bank Street Writer, Discovery Lab, or HyperCard is engaged in problem solving. What are the prerequisite problem-solving skills that an expert might bring to the situation? And how might the interface support the non-expert or learner? To illustrate design principles, I am going to use Discovery Lab, an application in which the problems to be solved and the processes to get there are more constrained, because its purpose is explicitly to support the novice scientist.

First, problem solvers need to formulate an appropriate definition or representation of the problem [Hawkins, 1986]. In Discovery Lab, the "problem" is to describe a set of organisms by their reaction to the independent variables—light, temperature, moisture, food and sound. That is, the user must design an experiment. Figures 2–4 show the sequence of screens the student uses to set up conditions for the experiment. As decisions are made by the user, the graphics reflect the choices. Thus, the program leads the learner to an appropriate representation.

Even having defined a problem, learners sometimes have trouble knowing what to do first, how to sequence, and how much time to spend on different parts of the problem (in short, planning). The Discovery Lab interface addresses these problem-solving skills by (1) limiting the options at the start and (2) ordering at least some of the steps for the user.

Finally, the Discovery Lab experimenter is required to report findings and evaluate results. Evaluation of the solution is a final and essential step in successful problem solving, and needs to be supported by learning software.

In sum, learners need cues about how to define and represent problems, how to start, how much effort to put on different parts of the task, and how to evaluate their work. In less-structured situations, such as word processors and programming environments, what are some ways to provide such cues or models of process? It turns out that modes have potential here. Bank Street Writer, LOGO, and HyperCard all use modes that may be able to help learners make critical distinctions in representing their problems.

In LOGO's turtle graphics, for example, a typical problem is to write a procedure that will draw a figure on the screen. In understanding the problem, the learner must distinguish between the procedure itself and its result upon executions (see figures 5 and 6).

Editing is always a mode in LOGO, but the user may enter the mode explicitly by using the command "EDIT" or more subtly and temporarily by typing "TO ____," which signals the beginning of a procedure definition.

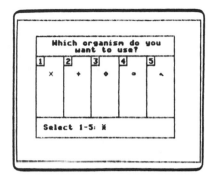

Figure 2: Decision 1—Choose subject organism(s). Source: Discovery Lab, Minnesota Educational Computing Consortium, 1984 ©.

Figure 3: Decision 2—Choose variables. Source: Discovery Lab, Minnesota Educational Computing Consortium, 1984 ©.

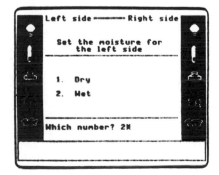

Figure 4: Decision 3—Choose conditions. Source: Discovery Lab, Minnesota Educational Computing Consortium, 1984 ©.

Figure 5: The LOGO procedure to draw a square.

```
TO SQUARE
REPEAT 4 [FORWARD 40 RIGHT 90]
END
```

Figure 6: The graphic produced as the procedure "SQUARE" is executed.

My conclusion, after watching new learners struggle with the distinction between defining and running a procedure, was that shifting modes was useful in structuring the problem. But, at least for new users, entry into and exit from a mode should be very explicit.[3]

Early versions of Bank Street Writer had two major modes: writing and everything else. In writing mode, the screen was essentially a blank space; the user could type and delete characters and move about using the arrow keys. The Escape key changed modes and brought up the menu that provided both editing and file and disk management functions (see figure 7). In this mode, the user could only activate commands from the menus; no text could be entered into the document, but blocks of text could be moved, deleted, and so forth.

To a skilled writer who uses less modal word processors, the modes seem cumbersome. But from a teacher's point of view, I can argue that as my young students learn to write, I want them to focus separately on two parts of the process—getting words out to express their ideas and *then* evaluating, organizing, and editing what they have written.[4] The modes support this approach to learning how to write.

It turns out that there were two reasons for the modes in Bank Street Writer: one was pedagogical, as I have suggested here, and the other was the memory limitations of the computer. As the program was revised for more powerful computers, the modes became less distinct. These changes were the subject of much debate among the educators and designers

Figure 7: Menu titles for the Bank Street Writer.

```
File   Edit   Spell   Options   Disk   Quit
```

---

[3] These observations were conducted at Yale University in 1984 and are reported in two unpublished papers, "LogoBugs: Things That Confuse Young Children" and "Watching Children Learning Logo." Later, I made modifications in the LOGO interface to test my hypotheses. This work was reported at the Western Educational Computing Conference, Los Angeles, 1986: "Exploring the match between LOGO symbolics and children's mental representations."

[4] It can be argued that the inability to edit can distract from the task of "getting words out," too. The role of other variables, such as the task orientation and the sophistication and experience of the user, could be identified through user observation.

involved[5] and, although there is a growing body of research on the use of word processors in learning to write, I am not familiar with any studies that directly address modes in relationship to the writing process.

Gavriel Salomon carries the discussion of tools serving as process models one step further when he describes what he calls "artificial intelligence in reverse" [Salomon, 1988]. The hypothesis is that "human thinking can come to simulate computer 'intelligence.'" Under certain conditions, which Salomon describes and justifies, the operations of a computer tool presumably can be internalized by the learner. To test this theory, Salomon conducted experiments in which students used a computer tool called the *Reading Aid* while reading computer-displayed texts. The role of the *Reading Aid* was to suggest reading strategies and provide "explicit metacognitive guidance" during the process of reading. Children who used the tools not only engaged in more "metacognitive" behavior (devoted more time to reading, reported they were more "mindful" of the reading task, and gave better ideas on how to help a nonreading friend), but they also scored higher on tests of reading comprehension. Further analyses related the improved scores directly to the display of metacognitive skills. Salomon refers to the "intellectual partnership" between the learner and the tools, saying that the latter can become "relatively novel cognitive tools."

Changes in State

In LOGO, when a child types "Right 360" she has every reason to expect the turtle to turn a complete circle to the right.[6] But the command is executed so quickly that the motion cannot be perceived. Even for less than full rotations, the actual movement of the turtle is imperceptible. More expert LOGO programmers probably appreciate the speed, but for the learner the correspondence between the written command and the execution of that command by the turtle needs to be obvious.

The general principle is not that interfaces for learning should be slower, but that movement and animation should be faithfully employed to support the learner's understanding of critical concepts. In building educational Stackware in HyperCard, for example, the interface designer could make good use of HyperCard's visual effects[7] to help the user understand how the information (not necessarily the stack) is organized.

Children love to use the visual effects in building their own stacks. I

---

[5] Smith, Franklin E. 1989. Personal communication.

[6] Actually, *very* new users expect the "LEFT" and "RIGHT" commands to behave similarly to "FORWARD" and "BACK," as shown by Amy's confusion in the example at the beginning of the chapter.

[7] HyperCard visual effects are animations that appear as the user moves from one card to the next. Examples are wipes to left or right, iris open or close, "barn doors," etc. Visual effects are initiated by scripts and can be made to occur at different speeds.

watched one boy spend nearly ten minutes editing the visual effects for one card. By using a series of effects, one after the other, he was able to create the impression of an explosion. But do new authors recognize the value of the visual effects in helping users understand movement through the information? Nothing in the HyperCard interface itself encourages an author to use visual effects meaningfully.

Another place where special attention needs to be paid to the interface is when movement and animation are used in simulations. At the beginning of this chapter, I recounted my observation of Sonny's experience with software simulating the wiring of batteries and electric lightbulbs.[8] Although the software included some technically snazzy ways of manipulating the variables, the animation on the screen didn't help the user learn from his mistakes. Sonny's problem was that the wires were not always connected correctly to the positive and negative nodes of the battery. But Sonny wasn't getting any visual cues to help him see what was wrong. True, we might have the same problem in the real world, but can't we expect educational computer simulations to be *more* useful than actual trial and error?

Movement and animation are often gratuitous enhancements of the interface at this stage of the technology. We need to develop our understanding of how we perceive motion, what meanings we attribute to it, and how animation can have a more integral role in achieving interface goals (see the chapter by Baecker and Small in this volume). As this understanding grows, we should be able to incorporate animations into the interface that are instructive as well as enticing.

Interfaces as Coaches

Many interfaces have more signs of intelligence than we tend to realize. They possess a store of wisdom about the domain that they share with the user in the form of defaults. For example, to set the parameters for printing in Bank Street Writer, the user answers a series of questions, one by one.

As a learning tool, this interface may be superior to a form like the MacWrite print dialogs because it calls the user's attention systematically to each consideration that must be made in producing a finished document. At the same time, it supplies a set of defaults that serve as models or standards for the beginning writer.

The potential for more dynamic ways of tutoring learners is enormous, even in some of the simplest existing systems. Good teachers use students' mistakes as teachable moments. On the computer, mistakes can set the stage for learning by trial and error. And alerts and error messages become

---

[8] This observation was made while children were using an experimental piece of software that had not yet been formally released. The software has since been modified in response to classroom observations.

an opportunity for providing highly contextual support for learning processes. But most error messages are written with little attempt to explain why the error occurred and give little constructive advice on how to avoid the error in the future (see the chapter by Sellen and Nicol in this volume). I would like to see an experiment comparing two versions of the same program. One group of subjects would use the version with the original error messages (typically written by the programmer), and another group would use a version in which messages for the same errors had been written by a teacher experienced in the content domain of the program. I suspect that there would be significant differences between groups, especially if subjects were new to the domain.

The tone of the interface with regard to users making errors and fixing them is important too. Learners need to be encouraged to take risks. In LOGO's turtle graphics, the most common error message is "I DON'T KNOW HOW TO ___," signifying that what the user has typed has not yet been defined as a primitive or a procedure. True, this message is not self-explanatory to new users, but children learn what it means pretty quickly. The point is that the turtle seems to take a little of the blame, and the overall metaphor (that the user is teaching the turtle/computer how to do things) puts the user in a powerful role.

To be able truly to coach or tutor a novice, the system needs more intelligence than we see in current applications. A discussion of intelligent tutoring systems and the design of user interfaces for those systems is beyond the scope of this chapter.[9] But it *is* relevant to my thesis that the research scientists and programmers who are involved in building intelligent tutoring systems all seem to acquire a new respect for teachers. In the process of trying to build systems that have (1) subject matter expertise, (2) an understanding of individual differences and abilities in learners, (3) awareness of principles of teaching and learning, and (4) the talent to put all this together at the right time and the right place, they are realizing that there are indeed many things that good teachers know that we don't.

Lessons

There are several places to go for the lessons that will lead to better design of learning tools. Of course one can turn directly to the children and let them experiment with new interfaces. They are, after all, the users; and it is critical that the software be both accessible and engaging. As an advocate of early and continual user involvement in design, I certainly see the need for getting feedback from the children. But who should interpret children's

---

[9] For overviews of the issues and current state of the art, see *Artificial Intelligence and Tutoring Systems*, by Etienne Wenger [1987] and *Artificial Intelligence and Education, volume 1*, edited by Robert Lawler and Masoud Yazdani [1987].

responses and interactions with the computer? Developers can look to teachers and psychologists for assistance. These are the experts who can evaluate the child's response in the context of the goals and objectives of the curriculum.

But long before there is something to take to the children, designers could begin in the classroom by watching good teachers teach. Look for the ways they set up the environment and prepare their students for new concepts. Watch how they coach and guide students; observe the models they put forth for inquiry.

In designing new tools for learning, we need to be familiar with more than just the content of the application. We must also learn to appreciate the ways in which learners construct new concepts so that we can design interfaces that at least support and perhaps even enhance those learning processes.

Lessons Learned From Kids:

One Developer's Point of View

THE FIELD OF CHILD DEVELOPMENT is not a new one. Scores of articles and books document how children develop both intellectually and physically. Researchers watch children playing and learning and then develop theories to explain their observations. Until very recently these theories of child behavior and development were built on observations of children who did not have access to electronic interactive learning environments.

We know very little about how young children use electronic interactive devices or whether having access to these devices provides them with new opportunities for thinking and learning. We do not know enough about what kinds of interfaces work well for children and how or if their preferences differ from adults. Clearly, more research is required in these areas. What we find out may cause us to change our current theories of intellectual development. Children themselves won't change, but their actions and how we interpret them may.

For a number of years I have created electronic interactive learning environments and products for children. Observing how children respond to technology-driven environments and products has been a critical phase in my design development process. I have not fashioned any formal theories, but in creating products that children can enjoy and use I have learned a few lessons about how people, particularly children, respond to and use technology. Here are some of the lessons.

Joyce Hakansson
President, Joyce Hakansson Associates

> **LESSON:** Kids love the challenge and excitement of games. When a game is appealing and provides steadily increasing levels of difficulty, a child's interest lasts for a long time.

Chris Crawford has covered the topic of games in another section of this book, so I will limit my comments to one aspect of games—the role that scores and achievement levels play in a child's enjoyment of an activity. While watching children play computer games, we found that kids under the age of six ignore scores entirely. They concentrate on the game and are pleased when they can make something happen on the screen. Then, quite suddenly, sometime around their sixth birthday, a change takes place. Not only does the child keep close track of points, but if the game doesn't keep score, he or she often will make up a scoring system. Kids really want to be able to measure themselves and want to be able to compare themselves with others. Teachers have told me that in the classroom when a program does not have a score or provide levels of achievement (for example, Ace, Master of the Universe, Rank Beginner), their students will invent levels. "I got to the third clue," ". . . the second problem," or ". . . the red door" is heard as kids leave the computer laboratory.

> **LESSON:** In the early days people thought that the technology was too complicated and inappropriate for young children. It turns out that what was inappropriate and daunting to kids was simply the amount of text on the screen.

Colorful graphics, sound, speech, animation—all of these are excellent ways to communicate ideas and information, and all are possible on computers. All of these are also attractive to and appropriate for children. Screens filled with printed words can provide information and ideas, but not in a way that is generally appropriate for kids. Screen after screen filled with text makes *me* tired—imagine how it affects a five- or six-year-old. In the early days of personal computing, all we had were screens filled with words, and they created impossible barriers for the children who were beginning and early readers. When we finally created programs that replaced the text screens with activities that were graphic and approachable, we found that children, even very young children, could use the technology.

LOGO's turtle graphics and screen paint programs were among the first activities to demonstrate how well young children responded to the computer. Today we see children as young as two using a mouse to move a cursor around the screen, using pull-down menus to open a program and drawing with the tools in a paint program. Do they understand it all? No, not any more than they understand everything about a book. But they know how to open a program and get back to it just as they know how to open a book to get to the pictures. Sometimes they open the book upside-down or backwards. Sometimes they get lost in the computer program, but they are learning from both experiences and should not be denied either one.

> **LESSON:** Computers can provide kids with unique opportunities for cooperative activities.

Research studies have shown that in classrooms where students use computers there is more social communication and cooperative problem solving than in other classrooms [Office of Technology Assessment, 1988]. This is exactly the opposite of the effect predicted by early opponents of technology, who warned of classrooms filled with isolated students staring blankly at video screens.

Maybe kids work together because the computer is new, and when they focus on it they shed their shyness and forget the old rules that inhibit collaboration. Maybe it happens because of the simple fact that there are usually too few computers in the class, and the scarce resources have to be shared [Office of Technology Assessment, 1988]. For whatever reason, we should recognize an opportunity and encourage it by designing collaboration into programs. Some new systems—networks, for example—will offer interesting opportunities. A group writing project could be carried out where everyone has access to outlines and manuscripts, and each student chooses to add to the text or edit what has been written. A word processor could have an interface that encourages this kind of collaboration. I can imagine young authors deciding whether they want to write with a "group font" or have their own personal fonts.

Many activities could be used to foster cooperation and collaboration, including simple games, simulations, and projects such as the writing one described above. The computer environment has already demonstrated its ability to get kids talking together, and we can now provide them with opportunities to work and play together as well.

> **LESSON:** Girls are as capable as boys at understanding and using computers. Boys, more often than girls, become focused on their computers.

Computer games are created for young boys. Ask the marketing department of any computer software company if you have any doubts. Better yet, look at the games. If there is a real difference in the fantasies of boys and girls, most computer games, with their action and destruction, are planned for the boys [Malone, 1980].

I have found that there is little difference in the way young boys and girls respond to computers. Some kids like computers more than others, but in the primary grades gender does not seem to be the deciding issue. By the time children have reached junior high school there is a real difference in the number of boys and girls participating in computer classes and other computer-related activities. Somewhere between the third and tenth grades girls learn or decide that computers are not for them. Gender as a factor in computing is apparent in later years as well—many more men than women are graduating with advanced degrees in computer science [Markoff, 1989].

Many of the reasons for the apparent gender bias in computing have to do with our culture. Women are not encouraged to learn about machines, and computers are machines. Being analytical, mathematically proficient, and having the ability to use logical thinking skills are not the traditional traits we associate with desirable women, but we do assume that one needs these traits to use a computer successfully for something more than data entry. As long as girls in their teens aspire to be accepted and desirable, and as long as their role models are the ones presented in TV situation comedies, the situation will not change.

Most adult women can't use computers, and many actually feel frightened by them. Mothers can't help their daughters. The girls need role models—women teachers who are computer enthusiasts, for instance. Girls need to understand the opportunities that technology offers, and they need to be ambitious enough to want to take advantage of these opportunities. This is a job for guidance and career counselors, parents, and classroom teachers alike.

The notion that computers are for boys is reinforced all the time. Sarah, a nine-year-old girl, complained when she saw a newspaper article about a popular computer game machine, headlined, "Every Boy Wants One." She wanted one, too. The fact is, however, that of the more than 15 million game players sold, most of them were sold to boys, and most of the programs are designed for, and sold to, boys. Because of their more extensive experience with computer games, boys have learned and are more comfortable with traditional computer interfaces. What is daunting to a girl, or to any novice user, has been overcome by boys in pursuit of computer game experiences that are geared to traditionally male themes of conflict, competition, and sports. To interest girls in computer games, developers need to broaden the variety of themes and activities and to create interfaces that are easier to learn and use [Cignarella, 1989].

It would seem that the differences we observe between boys and girls are the result of the content and marketing of computer games and cultural stereotypes that discourage computing for girls, rather than any intrinsic factors. These problems are self-perpetuating; to solve them, new models must be created.

> **LESSON:** Kids can use a variety of input devices, if the choice of device and its design are well-tailored to the activity, the context, and the way kids learn.

My observations of children have demonstrated that they can use a variety of input devices, including keyboards, joysticks, touch screens, digitizing tablets, speech, and mice. Children are not always secure enough with words to use a standard keyboard comfortably. It is difficult to think of a word, dissect it into its parts (letters), and then reconstruct it on a keyboard, letter by letter. It is much easier to use point and select inputs, in part because they allow the child to select from existing choices, rather than requiring that the child create an answer.

In 1979, I was hired by Children's Television Workshop, the creators of *Sesame Street*, to design and create, in ten months or less, a computer gallery at Sesame Place. Sesame Place is a play park for children aged 3 to 13 and their families. The idea of creating an electronic play center using computers was unique and challenging; there were no models for it.

I hired a small staff and we worked hard to construct a facility that opened on time and is still being used today, nine years later. Many of our design decisions had to do with how to structure the computer hardware and software to make it attractive and easy to use. Fifty-six micro-computers in housings specially designed to be safe and durable filled the space.

We designed our own keyboards. Kids are not typists, and the computer's keyboard said "serious, work-related, adult." Food and drinks could be brought into the computer gallery. A sticky drink spilled on a keyboard would kill it. We used a flat and washable keyboard with colorful graphic overlays. Originally, we wanted the special overlays on each keyboard to match the program running on the computer, but we found it too expensive.

We were, however, able to make one special overlay for a program called "Dial a Muppet" (originally created by Christopher Cerf). We put a picture of a big telephone with four large keys on the keyboard. On each key there was a picture of a Muppet character. When the child played the game, a digitized "operator's" voice said, "Press a Muppet key." When a child made a choice the operator said, "Wait one moment." Then the same Muppet character's picture was drawn on the screen and a digitized Muppet voice spoke one of the phrases stored in memory. It was a popular activity for all ages; the youngest visitor could use the program without adult help. Even computerphobic adults could use the programs without fear of making a mistake and looking foolish.

We made one standard design for the keyboards. The keys were large and well spaced to make them easy targets for little fingers. We arranged the keys on the overlay alphabetically, reasoning that young children would have less trouble finding letters if they were in alphabetical order. It made great sense to us as adults, but it didn't work that way for children. We thought that the alphabetical keyboard would work even better than a QWERTY keyboard because we assumed that a child would know, for example, to look near the middle of the keyboard to find the letter *n*. In fact, we discovered that, no matter what letter they were looking for, most children started every search with the letter *a* and then moved letter by letter through the alphabet. It was only the exceptional child that took advantage of the organization of the letters on the keyboard to shorten their search time.

Keyboards are not necessary to use a computer. Having designed interactive products for a variety of situations, including classrooms, amusement parks, personal computer systems, and hand-held interactive toys, I have observed children using a wide variety of input devices. Obviously, the place and the purpose should dictate the type and design of devices used. Of the currently available devices, the mouse and point-and-choose inputs work best for a wide range of situations. Even very young children can use the mouse. If the program is aimed at young children, objects on the screen should be large and distinct enough to be easy targets.

Most video-game machines and some computer activities use joysticks. Joysticks work better for kids than keyboards, but they still present problems. Kids have a tendency to twist and change the position of a hand-held joystick, particularly when they get involved or excited by an on-screen activity. When that happens, pushing up on a joystick may suddenly move the cursor on the screen to the left or right, not up as anticipated. Young kids, as well as nervous adults, become frustrated when they can't figure out what is wrong. They have difficulty correcting the problem, even when it has been pointed out to them. Because of these drawbacks, the mouse is often preferable to the joystick.

> **LESSON:** Children will develop a new literacy as a result of interacting with media-rich environments.

We have already seen how responsive kids are to video games; they are much better at them than adults. Kids respond to all of the information presented; graphics, sounds, and movements. They quickly develop "video literacy."

Since 1982, I have worked on the design and production of dozens of software products for children, two years old through adults. The products have been computer activities, interactive videos, and hand-held electronic toys. I have found that the best products have been developed by a production group including an artist, a writer, a musician, a content specialist (a geographer if the subject of the program is geography), and a programmer.

If interesting and engaging interactive environments are to be developed, the production elements must be of the highest quality. High quality in this case does not mean the most expensive technology, but people who are excellent at their ability to communicate and integrate their skills. In order to produce a product that attracts and appeals to the target population, a product's visual images, sound, and content all must blend together to provide users with the sensory information they need to interpret and respond to the program. We are developing information environments. Text is used when necessary to convey information, but it is only one of many ways in which to communicate with children.

> **LESSON:** Kids are able to think in novel and unsuspected ways, but they need tools to facilitate and support them.

Kids respond well to situations that allow them to function in ways that are natural to them. They listen and talk before they read and write. Even very young children are fascinated by and are able to talk on the telephone. When the technology is perfected, kids will have no trouble with voice-activated and voice-recognition systems.

Children surprise us constantly. Back in the early '60s, every kindergarten teacher in the country started the year teaching the alphabet, safe in the knowledge that only a few of the entering students would be able to recognize and recite the letters all the way from a to z. There were those who thought that the reason young children did not know the letters of the alphabet was that they were not able to learn them until they were five, or maybe even seven. The imaginative and effective use of a relatively new technology—television—led to *Sesame Street*. A few years later, a new generation of kindergarteners entered school knowing the alphabet and numerals well enough to force a nationwide change in the kindergarten curriculum.

We now have available a much more powerful technology that can include and extend television. We should not underestimate the potential it has for expanding a child's capability to learn and understand all kinds of information. As new and more powerful interactive systems are created, designing interfaces that will work for children will be a challenging and exciting job. We almost certainly will have to reexamine our existing models of child development, reevaluate school curricula, and be prepared to be surprised at what children can do.

How I Learned to Stop Worrying and Love HyperCard

A First-Person Account of a Paradigm Shift

USER CONTROL. Consistency. Modelessness. Forgiveness. Feedback.

It seemed hopeless. How would I ever adapt? Everyone was raving about HyperCard. And I hated it! After working as the writing manager for a year and a half on *The Human Interface Guidelines: The Apple Desktop Interface*, I knew what a good interface was. And HyperCard didn't have it.

I couldn't believe the buttons! When you clicked on them, nothing happened! No highlight, no cursor change, nothing. Not only that, but you only clicked on an icon *once*. Not twice, but once! I was highly skilled in the art of double-clicking. It drove me nuts either to end up somewhere that I wasn't trying to get to or to be wasting all that good double-clicked energy. Talk about energy crises.

Then there were the scroll bars. There weren't any. And the resizable windows. You couldn't. But worse than that was the auto-save. Who said the user was in control? We did. And before HyperCard, we were right. But now, HyperCard was in control. It saves your work whether you want it to or not. Make a backup before you begin, or else!

Even more disastrous was the "Delete Card" menu item. Not only was there no verification prompt, you could not undo a deleted card. Once it was gone, it was gone!

Talk about modelessness. Take the script editor. As modal as they get.

Jason Gervich
*Software Publications
Apple Computer, Inc.*

This baby's so modal that you have to use the keyboard equivalents just to cut and paste.

Yes, it seemed that Armageddon was here. The mouse had roared. One cutesy little graphics program written by a guy in a basement[1] had toppled the interface we knew and loved. How did it happen?

Why did we work so hard to come up with an interface that was supposed to be consistent among all applications? Why did we practically threaten developers with exile in MS-DOS-land if they didn't follow our interface religiously? Why was Sculley letting Atkinson single-handedly destroy all our hard-earned success in evangelizing the interface? Was HyperCard an IBM conspiracy? My paranoia seemed to know no limits. These were tough questions and I had to get the answers.

I read and reread the *Guidelines* to see if there was some way to interpret them to allow for such bastardization of the canon. There wasn't. No consolation there.

What puzzled me even more was how self-respecting Apple employees who should know better could go around singing the praises of this heresy. They professed to adhere to Apple Values, yet they were out there committing treason.

I was still no closer to an answer. Then it hit me. An absolutely brilliant strategy was revealed to me as I stared at the Home card with its cute little buttons and nonexistent scroll bar. IGNORE IT and it will GO AWAY. I did. It didn't.

I buried my head in the sand of my next projects, writing programming overviews for the Macintosh and IIGS. The purpose of these books was to explain and encourage the adoption of the Apple Desktop Interface as well as to provide developers with a technical overview as to how to go about writing the code. Upon the completion of these projects, I was given the *HyperCard Script Language Guide* as one of my new assignments. My head-in-the-sand strategy was suddenly rendered inoperative. I had to confront the beast head on.

Being a hands-on kind of guy, I prepared myself to start learning HyperCard and HyperTalk. At first I was just a browser, using HyperCard for my ToDo list and calendar. I still hated the buttons that didn't highlight when I selected them, and I usually double-clicked them out of habit, occasionally finding myself in some unknown quadrant of hyperspace. Greatly intimidated by the auto-save and the non-reversible Delete menu item, I was a very conservative hyperspace navigator. When I expressed some of my hyperfears to the writer of the *Script Language Guide*, he

---

[1] Ed. Note: Bill Atkinson, the guy in question, was also instrumental in designing the very interface that the author is attached to. As Larry Tesler puts it, "When them that made the rules break the rules, people get upset."

suggested that I modify the buttons and the Delete menu item to make them function the way I wanted them to. Needless to say, I jumped at the chance to right the wrongs that had been inflicted upon me and (as I imagined) countless thousands of other HyperCard users.

Being thus liberated (a little knowledge being a truly dangerous thing), I went crazy checking the "Auto Hilight" option on every button that I could get my mouse on. I became a button crusader. I absolutely loved that black veil of darkness that would enshroud each button when I (single-) clicked on it. But now it was time to get serious. I was initiated into the mysteries of "DoMenu" and was shown how to write a script that brought up a "Delete this Card?" dialog box. After testing the script, I immediately pasted it into my home stack and heaved a great sigh of relief. Not only had I been able to rectify one of the worst sins of HyperCard, I had customized my environment and taken a giant step forward for Hyperkind. The user was in control again! I didn't realize it yet, but now I was hooked.

Bolstered my previous conquests, I continued my assault on the HyperCard interface. I had always wanted to be able to print a range of cards starting with the present card, but nooooooo. HyperCard forced me to print either one card manually or the entire stack. But I wanted to print only the next two or three weeks of my calendar, not the entire year. So . . . .

I began to write a script that would let me print a specified number of cards starting with the current card. After about a week, I had completed the script. It even told the user how many pages it was printing and when the task was completed. I showed my printing utility to the head of the department; she liked it so much that she had it incorporated into our department's HyperCard phone book stack. I began to dream of other utilities that I could create, perhaps I could even . . . .

My mouse had roared—I had learned to stop worrying and love HyperCard.

Note: The fact that I was ultimately seduced by the empowerment that HyperCard can bring to a user should not be construed as endorsement or approval of what I see as the deficiencies of the HyperCard interface. Rather, this chapter's focus is on the paradigm shift that took place when I attempted to make the transition between a known, familiar interface to one with significant variations and anomalies.

A Writer's Desktop

THE MACINTOSH WAS BORN OF METAPHOR: the screen was no longer flat vertical phosphor; it became a desktop. Here my files hide in folders. I have access to tools: a file clerk (Disktop, Find File), a calculator, a phone book. Some of these used to reside under the Apple menu and now live inside HyperCard.

The transition from old technology to new is eased by metaphor, which is, in the modern critic I. A. Richards' words, a "borrowing between and intercourse of thoughts" [Preminger, 1974]. A metaphor is made up of two parts, tenor and vehicle, which together sometimes state in an illogical and bizarre fashion that one thing is really something else (his fingers are sausages, but never the other way around). The soul of a Macintosh, the "purport and general drift of thought regarding the subject of the metaphor" is the tenor, "that which serves to carry or embody the tenor as the analogy brought to the subject." Mac's desktop and file folders and trash can make up the vehicle. Even my word processing software breaks my text into pages that do not really exist until I print.

Over time, tenor and vehicle lose sight of one another: the metaphor becomes real. Eventually the Mac desktop is all the desktop there is. I think it's worth pausing to ponder the origins of metaphors, because they hide beneath the surface of all our language.

For example, from time to time I take note of various tools sitting on top of my desk as I contemplate the difficult and tortuous course of a story.

Rob Swigart

Novelist and Software Designer

135

Charles Dickens at his desk. Note the familiar objects, including the trash can! From a pen and ink sketch by W. Steinhaus.

My desktop, the real desktop, not the metaphorical Macintosh, offers a distraction. It occurs to me, looking at pads of yellow paper, the can full of pens, the wooden container for paper clips, the Post-it™ pad and the clear plastic box full of rubber bands I seldom use, that many writers are superstitious about their desktops. A meticulous straightening of pencils, for example, or a shuffling of paper, is a ritualistic action to stave off the terror of the void. The void, of course, is blank paper, or the blank screen and the insistently flashing cursor (or, in some other circles, the Cursing Flasher).

I imagine Charles Dickens seated before a surface of leather and inlaid woods, inkpot at the ready, quills sharpened and lined up. No metaphors for him. (Of course, under all this real stuff hides yet another layer of metaphor—for instance, paper is "really" papyrus, a plant, and ink is "really" an encaustic painting, which involves the fixing of colored beeswax with heat . . . but that's another story.) All real stuff there: to one side is his stack of finished manuscript, the pages neatly aligned, corners straight, the ink dry in steady lines of cursive, waiting for the appearance of a messenger boy to carry them to the printer, where the cursive will be given, through the medium of a typesetter, the regularity of type. This month's installment is nearly ready for the magazine, but now a difficult passage confronts him, from *Our Mutual Friend,* perhaps. Heaps of dust, the drowned body in the river, the identity of a character. He pauses, mumbling.

The paper is blank. He chews on the end of the quill, spits out a few fragments of feather.

He, too, may have paused to stare at these ritual artifacts and perhaps reflect on how their use affected the way he created his stories. So many pages to a chapter for this month's installment—so many words to a page at so many pence a word to keep the story going.

Contrary to current mythology, writing is not an entirely "organic" process. The product is shaped by its tools in ways unconscious and unsuspected. The movement of the hand manipulating the quill pen, the play of muscle and tendon as the mind directs words to flow from the tip, the pauses to dip for more ink, all impact the outcome. How long is a chapter? The answer may lie in how fast the writer can move his pen across the page in legible sentences as much as in the demands for completeness of a scene or the rigors of character development. After all, the monthly installment is due. He can write fast, scratching away at the paper, but not that fast. Eventually he must stop, because his time is up or his hand is too cramped to move any more. So, that's a chapter.

The relatively slow movement of the hand (compared, for example, to the speed at which one can type) leaves mental time for longer, more intricately constructed and elaborately rhetorical sentences than are encouraged by a faster medium. Homeric similes were Homeric and long and elaborate because they aided memory in an age when writing did not exist at all, and everything had to be memorized and recited. For Homer, a long simile took up easily memorable space in the narration and often became a story in itself, a hunting scene or a battle. With text the simile grew shorter.

So this morning I looked at my desktop. I had come to a crossroads in the novel. The screen was blank (not behind where I was in the story, but ahead of that place, or, more accurately, to the right and below that flashing cursor). I tried the usual formulae: I stretched. I looked out the window. I turned on my radio scanner and listened to police broadcasts. I took off one shoe and scratched the bottom of my foot.

I rearranged my desktop. Because I now work with a Mac II, that meant moving a few icons on the screen, choosing different shades for scroll bars and menu items. Then I thought maybe I could try a different pattern for the desktop itself, a picture perhaps, or a nice fractal pattern. Time passes quickly when I have this kind of fun.

This is the confession, of course: I am a techno-junkie. If I were Dickens, and someone announced a fantastic new quill pen made from dodo feathers, I would be the first to dip one in my inkpot (the ink probably composed of some new longer-lasting and quicker-drying formula of yak blood and silkworm hairs).

I began to consider these new tools I use, and how they affect the way I write. For example, my handwriting is atrocious; it takes me forever to scratch out a word; my hand cramps up, and when I'm done, I can't read what I've written. Furthermore, handwriting doesn't look like real writing, because real writing is published. The letters are neat.

When I wrote with a typewriter, my work was immediately in print: Typing is instant publication. So I wrote my first novel in the days of the typewriter. Granted it was, by then, an electric typewriter. The keys fell easily to the touch. The fingers danced. But I had worked for years with (Gods!) a manual typewriter. When I worked as a newspaper reporter, the ancient upright Smith-Corona filled the newsroom with clacking. I thought of Clark Gable in "Teacher's Pet" rattling away at a furious pace with his reporter's two-finger hunt and peck. But my book was electric. (Now the newsrooms are so quiet!)

I had a formula: for the soundest ecological reasons—to save trees and eschew waste—I typed single-spaced, with miniscule margins. I calculated between six and seven hundred words to a page. One page would made a chapter, a quick narrative stab. The medium determined my form. One hundred of those pages made a book (60,000 to 70,000 words). All I had to do, then, was write three of those pages a day, and in a little over a month I had the first draft of a novel. "Please," my editor said some years later, "don't send me anything single-spaced. My eyes can't read that well any more."

But by then I was using a computer. A different medium, and a different shape to the chapter. The computer didn't care if I double-spaced or not. It had different constraints. My chapters now were twelve kilobytes long, because that was the longest file I could have on disk with my Apple II and Easywriter 1.0. I felt it was inelegant to break chapters into two or more files. Not to mention the hassle of making changes.

So I would write a chapter on the computer and print it out (back to wasting paper, but I wasn't doing the typing any more!) The next day I would go over the paper version of the chapter, making editing changes with a red pencil, and I would then enter these changes into the computer. This ramped me up to plunge into the next chapter. It was an effective system, despite the weirdness of looking at a forty-column screen in all upper-case letters, with capitals displayed in inverse video. There was something satisfying about writing on the computer. It seemed to allow text to go through a phase-shift. I began to imagine that typewritten text was somehow solid, almost like granite—difficult to change, intractable. Once typed, a book had to be retyped; in effect recreated. The personal computer changed that. Words and phrases, sentences and paragraphs flowed; they found their own level. In other words, they became liquid—more energetic and easier somehow to shape. Editing became a continuous, fluid process, not a cut and paste labor. The screen is impermanent, organic, transient. Its content is electron and phosphor dot, painted in quantum events, constantly refreshed. This is why using the computer is so refreshing.

Paper is solid, hard, irreducible. Once applied to that surface through printing, text is frozen, but until that time it is dynamic and alive on screen. Printing performs what physicists call a phase-shift on text, from liquid to solid. This means of course that spoken text is the gas-phase, the expansive, evanescent, transient form. In other words, speech is, quite literally, hot air!

What has happened, as Paul Saffo has pointed out in his column in *Personal Computing*, is that paper itself has become interface instead of storage. It is meant to be viewed and discarded, not filed [Saffo, 1987 and 1988]. It may be losing its solidity, becoming the equivalent of some kind of superconducting medium, an uncontainable textual plasma.

Suddenly, though, it seems that the computer metaphor is beginning to catch up with itself. The metaphor is becoming a medium: text, graphics, color, sound, even animation begin to shape the information. I can easily add graphics to a text, and if I want to present my creation through the screen (which seems to lie somewhere on the desktop), why, then I can give my audience a multimedia interactive experience. A little bit like movies? Oh, no. Not another metaphor! Don't tell me the screen has become a, uh, a screen? Dickens certainly would never have suggested his audience come into his office at Gad's Hill to look at his desktop.

But now it is true. Information is shaped by this new medium. The way we perceive it is changing. We can have video bits (what I call *drits* for dramatic units, as I call short screens of narrative *nits*, for narrative units) mixed with our own sense of direction through a forest of brief narrative, pictures, demonstrations, voices telling us things. The novel will unravel into something rich and strange indeed, something beyond the novel—the new medium of the computer itself: a hypertext environment that allows not only text, but deconstructed, nonlinear, multimedia interactive narrative, to evolve, to offer up to the reader (now no longer a reader, but a user, an audience of one who participates in the presentation and perhaps even the course of the narrative) narrative in text *nits*, graphics, animation, sound and music, a sense of personal involvement in the rhythm and flow of narrative, a choice in the order and intensity of the story. This is a medium that I have explored for some years and that continues to fascinate me. If the paper page has become interface, then the screen has in an odd way also become paper, a mass storage medium for presentation of archived stories.

Thus the computer has called attention to itself as a medium, as have all media before it. The book was a storage and presentation device for medieval manuscripts before it gradually found itself its own genre: the novel, designed for mass production to a mass audience who were made literate by the very medium they held in their hands and who lost themselves in the novelists' worlds. Worlds writers like Dickens created.

Computer narrative has often been compared with film. The same awkward medium, highly technological, cranky and off-beat, laboriously capturing stage plays and images of trains arriving, suddenly finding itself, as in a seven-minute film called "The Great Train Robbery," made by Edwin S. Porter in 1903 out of different images spliced together to tell a story. Then came D. W. Griffith and the feature film, close-ups, tracking shots, complex narrative . . . . Hypertext is a tool, brought to the personal computer, that offers the beginnings of a technical grammar for the medium: not shots and cuts, but buttons and links . . . . The medium itself begins to coalesce, find form, find its true nature. And the true nature of the medium is not to recreate the novel, nor to disguise narrative as a game, nor to pretend it is cinema or television, but to be itself, its own graphic, textual, sonic, interactive self.

Meanwhile, the computer helps writers with the old media. It makes writing and rewriting a seamless process, because the text is fluid. Typos seem to correct themselves without thought. The thesaurus is on-line and readily available (convenient, close, near, nearby). The spell-checker catches many left-over typos. The outliner lets me move chapters, flowchart programs let me plot out both novels and computer games graphically and test their elements. My screenwriting software automatically does all the secretarial work, from inserting "continueds" to automatically numbering the scenes. Of course, anyone who has written on a computer is familiar with the computer editing glitches—those tiny sentence fragments that seem to hang around after the rewrite, making nonsense of the best intentions. An algorithm that checked for these little gremlins would be nice. Someday it will happen: the dialog box will pop up and ask if you really want to say, "The the dog cat is no longer in this room chamber."

My destop is green, like a billiard table. My icons have colors that I created, and when my CPU spits out a disk, it moos like a cow. My start-up screen is colorful computer graphics and ancient Greek music plays as the computer goes through its warmups. I've recently started using a track-ball for word processing (though not for drawing), and my home accounting package will give me random bits of financial wisdom if I ask it. My checkbook never did that.

I still have a wastebasket beside my desk as well as one on my desktop. I have real pencils, and real file folders, a real calculator (I never use that one), and real Post-it™ notes, Scotch™ tape, and paper clips. I even scratch illegible notes on little bits of paper that I cannot read when I need them. But for my writing, real writing, for which I am rewarded, I use the computer, and its metaphorical desktop has faded from my awareness, almost as if it were a genuine continuation of the horizontal surface of the desk itself, instead of some electronic window on a virtual world that ceases to exist when I turn the computer off.

That is the danger, that the metaphor has faded. Only for now does the Macintosh impose formal limits on the nature of my fiction, all our fiction. Unless we pause from time to time to consider how these metaphors work to create boundaries, and how they shift into new media, they will control us without our knowledge. Or our permission.

Building User-centered On-line Help

INTERACTING DAILY with a computer usually presents us with no complicated problems or unpleasant surprises. We use certain applications with functions we understand for a small, familiar set of tasks. But ask us to try to accomplish an unfamiliar task (like make an index for a document), or ask us to use a different word processor, or even to write the document on a different kind of computer, and the experience is quite different. Now our goals are less clear, we probably have a poorer understanding of the interface, and we have difficulty interpreting the response of the system to our actions.

We need help. But, even if there is on-line help available, the unfortunate fact is that most help systems tend to exacerbate users' problems. Finding the simplest piece of information can turn into a complicated exercise. Forget about looking up something quickly, the information will probably be buried deep in the recesses of the help database. If and when we find what we need, it will probably take a long time to get back to the task we were working on, if we can even remember what it was. The process is time-consuming and effortful, and is apt to leave us feeling ineffective and frustrated.

As a consequence, some people do not even try to use the help provided: in our laboratory, we notice that even when help is available, subjects frequently do not use it. People prefer to flounder around in their work

Abigail Sellen

University of California at San Diego
Summer Intern, Apple Computer, Inc.

Anne Nicol

Advanced Technology Group
Apple Computer, Inc.

environment, or better yet turn to an in-house expert, rather than use the on-line help provided by the system.

Why Do Users Avoid Using Help?

Researchers have addressed this question by studying use of various on-line help systems [See Borenstein, 1985, and Hysell, 1986, for example]. It turns out that users have several common complaints:

- Difficulty in finding information
- Failure to deliver relevant information
- Difficulty of switching between help and the working context
- The complexity of the help interface
- The quality and layout of help information

In this chapter, we discuss major issues that arise in the design of help systems to address user needs and complaints; we describe the research approach we took, some results of that research, and some of our prototype solutions and guidelines. Finally, we speculate on future directions for on-line help. Although our discussion and examples are based on a specific project (described below), we have found that the issues and guidelines apply generally to interface design decisions for on-line help.

How Can We Design Help That's Useful and Easy to Use?

This question is the focus for an ongoing research and development effort at Apple. For the past two years, engineers, writers, and researchers from several departments have collaborated in the design of interfaces to on-line help that will meet users' needs across a variety of applications. The project is "user-centered" in that users are involved throughout the design process. The process begins by observing the way that users naturally do something (such as asking for help). Users provide feedback on the interface at each stage in its evolution. (See the chapters by Norman and Gomoll in this volume for expansion on both of these points.) The aim of the project is not only to produce prototypes of on-line help interfaces, but also to explore and extend the range of possibilities for help and to construct guidelines for the design of help.

WHAT MAKES MANY HELP SYSTEMS DIFFICULT TO USE?

An analysis of common users' complaints (above) and of our own experiences sheds some light on this issue. For example, consider the problem I (Abi) had in trying to find out how to put a box around text in Microsoft Word 3.02 (although we use Microsoft Word Help as a negative example here, the system in fact has many excellent features and has been mentioned by numerous developers as a model help system).

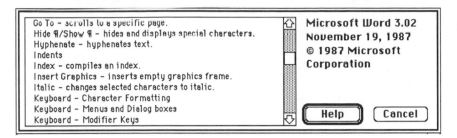

| Go To - scrolls to a specific page. |
| Hide ¶/Show ¶ - hides and displays special characters. |
| Hyphenate - hyphenates text. |
| Indents |
| Index - compiles an index. |
| Insert Graphics - inserts empty graphics frame. |
| Italic - changes selected characters to italic. |
| Keyboard - Character Formatting |
| Keyboard - Menus and Dialog boxes |
| Keyboard - Modifier Keys |

Microsoft Word 3.02
November 19, 1987
© 1987 Microsoft
Corporation

[Help] [Cancel]

Figure 1: Part of the list of help topics for Microsoft Word 3.02.

Although I had a specific task in mind, nothing in the list of topics in the on-line help seemed to be remotely related to what I wanted to do. By pure chance, and after much frustration, I found the information I needed under the heading *Paragraph-changes paragraph formatting*. Why did I have so much difficulty in finding it? There are at least two reasons:

- Not having had much experience with the program, I lacked the necessary knowledge to relate my problem, one of drawing a box around text, to a problem of paragraph formatting.

  Lesson: The conception of the problem that the user has may be very different from the conception of the expert, and people who design on-line help tend to be experts.

- My question was a question in terms of a task. Very few help topics laid out in Microsoft Word Help are organized in terms of tasks (see figure 1). In fact, there seems to be no consistent criterion used to designate how the help entries are presented. They are a combination of task-oriented topics (for example, Keyboard and Character Formatting), menu commands that often list the commands just as they appear in the menus (for example, Insert Graphics), and general definitions (for example, Indents).

  Lesson: Search time could have been greatly reduced if the form of the help topic corresponded to the kind of question I was asking.

This second point is also related to the problem of help not delivering the relevant information. It is not surprising that a user who wants to be presented with procedures will have difficulty when presented with definitions and descriptions. Similarly, a database that is task-oriented will tend to deliver information that is inappropriate for a user who wants a short description. In my example, the fact that I was asking a question in terms of a task meant that I needed a procedure. *The point is that the kind of question asked often determines the type of information required.*

Following the initiative of O'Malley [1986], we argue that one way of building an effective on-line help system is to start by noting the kinds of questions users ask when they need help. Each kind of question has important implications for the design of help in the interface.

Question Type	Canonical Form of the Question
1. **Goal-oriented**	What kinds of things can I do with this program?
2. **Descriptive**	What is this? What does this do?
3. **Procedural**	How do I do this?
4. **Interpretive**	Why did that happen? What does this mean?
5. **Navigational**	Where am I?

DIFFERENT HELP FOR DIFFERENT QUESTIONS

As a first step in designing the interface, a series of studies was conducted in order to discover what questions users ask. Pairs of users were given a set of tasks to complete using unfamiliar Macintosh software with no on-line help provided. Instead, the users were encouraged to ask questions when they needed help, either of one another or of the experimenters. We then recorded and classified the questions, resulting in the five categories presented in figure 2.

DESIGN IMPLICATIONS

The first implication for on-line help design is that *the kind of information delivered should be different depending on the question asked.* If the information is separated according to the kind of question, the amount of search time needed can be significantly reduced while the relevance of the information delivered is increased.

The second implication is that *the way in which information is accessed and presented should depend on the question asked.* A beginner faced with the Macintosh desktop for the first time might point to the trash can and ask, "What is this thing?" Descriptive questions are nicely served by a help system in which pointing accesses information. Contrast this with the novice who wants to know, "How do I remove a file?" The ability to point to something on the screen is not an integral part of the question-asking. The interface for procedural help should therefore look and function quite differently from the interface for descriptive help.

DIFFERENT INTERFACES FOR DIFFERENT KINDS OF HELP

Here is a more specific look at how help for each kind of question might be approached:

Goal-oriented Questions: "What Can I Do with This Program?" In order to interpret the interface of an application, the user must first have some idea of the different kinds of tasks it supports. Further, the user must have in mind a goal appropriate to the software before successfully embarking on a task. Most people are familiar with the purpose of the software they

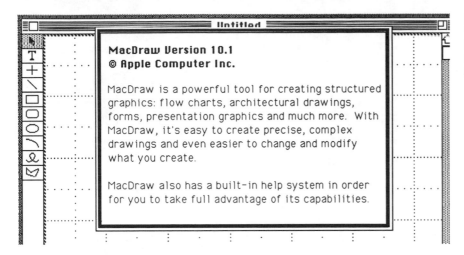

Figure 3: Answering the question, "What can I do with this program?" Users find it helpful to know the range of capabilities of a program, as well as its special features.

use, but occasionally users we observed asked that it be stated explicitly. Other times, users were not aware of the full range of functionality of a program. Two characteristics define this kind of help: 1) people who need it are unfamiliar with the interface; and 2) the information needs to be delivered only once or twice at most.

What are the implications for design?

• Introduce the information such that it will be easily accessible and highly visible to the novice user, without worrying whether it can be accessed quickly.

• Provide information that informs the user about the range of capabilities of a program, especially pointing out uses and functionality that users would not normally discover.

An example of how this kind of information might look for MacDraw is shown in figure 3.

Descriptive Questions: "What Is This? What Is It for?" Descriptive questions arose in a number of different situations, from trying to discover the name of an icon to finding out about the functional details of a menu item. There were essentially two behavioral modes in which users wanted definitions and descriptions of parts of the interface. The first was an exploratory mode in which users wanted to be able to point to objects on the screen or to menu items and ask for a description. The second was a task-specific mode in which the course of carrying out a task, some object or term needed to be defined.

The implications are that users should be able to ask for a definition both by pointing to items (especially important in graphical interfaces) and by asking in terms of a verbal label. Figure 4 shows how short descriptions might be delivered by pointing. In this case, the user might be new to the

Figure 4: Answering the question: "What is . . . ?" Pointing and clicking gives the user a short description of graphical objects in the Finder. More detailed information could be accessed through a glossary.

Macintosh and exploring the Finder. The interface should support browsing as well as quick access to definitions for particular terms relevant to the task being performed. With regard to browsing, it seems important to support exploration of the current working context in addition to providing a glossary for terms and concepts that users otherwise may not know exist. A keyword search would be one solution to serving task-specific descriptive questions.

Procedural Questions: "How Do I Do This?"   In our observations, procedural questions outnumbered any other kind of question. The form ranged from the very abstract in terms of high-level goals ("How do I start?") to the very specific in terms of executing particular actions ("How do I make this button disappear?"). The problem the user faces is that of translating intentions into the "language" of the interface. One possible solution is to provide access to procedural help through a menu so that users can recognize their questions rather than being forced to generate them. Further, recognition of the kind of question they want to ask can be facilitated by exploiting users' language rather than designers' language. That is, the vocabulary and formulation of tasks generated by users can be used to determine the structure of the procedural help menu.

Procedural questions are usually framed in terms of tasks users want to do. The options should therefore be articulated in task-oriented language. Further, research by O'Malley et al. [1983] shows that people looking for task-specific help tend to try to discover it through functionally related groups of commands. We found that the information was best presented in list form, with heavy use of graphics.

Finally, it is critical that this kind of help information be presented without obscuring or deactivating the working context, because procedures may be long and may need to be referred to while working. Figure 5 shows how information on how to change the size of a window might be presented in the Finder.

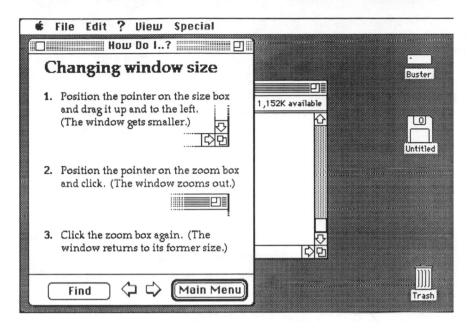

Figure 5: Answering the question, "How do I change the size of a window?" in the Finder.

Interpretive Questions: "Why Did That Happen?" Interpretive questions arise when the system responds in an unexpected way. An error message is one obvious time at which a user may be faced with an unexpected situation. But there are many situations in which the user might not understand the system response, whether or not an error message is displayed. The Macintosh environment, for example, is one in which very few actions are actually "illegal."

From the designer's point of view, it is an easier task to offer an explanation of what went wrong at the same time that an error message is presented rather than forcing the user to inquire. Consider the problem, though, of telling the user why the system responded as it did when no obvious error was committed. The computer must either infer what the user's true intention was (infer what task the user was trying to accomplish) or provide a way for the user to diagnose the problem by providing the necessary tools.

Inferring the user's intention is a difficult problem, and in part depends on the "intelligence" and tracking capabilities of the computer. Even if the computer is able to track a user's activities and store templates of procedures for typical tasks, many tasks can be performed in a number of different ways and thus may look nothing like the stored prescriptions. Another complication is that users may carry out multiple activities that overlap [see Miyata and Norman, 1986]. Further, users may have a completely different intention in mind than their actions would suggest as a result of incomplete or faulty knowledge about the interface. Users may not be aware of their own intentions. Thus the task of inferring intention is complex and bound to be error-prone.

One approach might be for the computer to offer an interpretation of the user's task that the user can then critique, perhaps by referring to a menu of alternative interpretations. Once the user agrees with the computer's interpretation, help could be provided in the form of a diagnosis of the problem. This kind of help could also be supplemented by providing tools with which users could carry out their own diagnoses. One example would be providing users with a way of viewing a history of their past actions. This would be useful in cases where the user committed a minor, undetected error (unintentionally selecting the wrong menu item, for example). Another useful diagnostic tool might be a list of common errors committed during the task at hand.

Navigational Questions: "Where Am I?"   The number of questions concerning navigation is very much application-dependent. Typically they arise most frequently with applications that are structurally complex and that contain a large amount of information. Hypertext-based software is one obvious example; hierarchically structured systems are another. Users tend to make heavy use of spatial metaphors: they report feeling "lost," speak of going "up" and "down" between levels or going "in" and "out" of situations.

Users often spontaneously construct spatial mental models or mental "maps" in order to move easily from one context to another. This has obvious implications for design. Reducing the memory load on the user is one benefit of making these mental "maps" explicit. Users can refer to the map instead of trying to retrieve information from memory to tell them "where they are." Another benefit is that a map can form the basis of a mental model on which the user relies to infer how to get from point A to point B without having to keep in mind a set of procedures for navigation. Thus, by exploiting spatial metaphors and allowing the user to make the inference, designers can help users avoid having to ask the question, "How do I get from point A to point B?"

Conceptual maps of this sort could take many different forms. These can be modeled after road maps, for example, or "You are here" maps like those found in department stores and subways. For a hierarchically based system (such as UNIX), a picture of the hierarchy that is updated automatically as the user creates and removes directories is another example of a solution to "navigating" around files. Obviously, the nature of the map will depend on the structure of the application.

ANSWERS INSTEAD OF QUESTIONS?

We have focused so far on users' questions as the basis for providing help. But sometimes, users don't know what questions would give them useful information. David Owen [1986] constructed a help facility for UNIX called "Did You Know?" to help users execute commands more quickly and efficiently and to use the full range of capabilities of the system. In response to the user's typing "DYK," the system provides useful pieces of information and suggestions that are characteristic of the kind of information that experts or "power users" tend to possess. For example, it might offer information of the form "Did you know that there is an easier way to clear the clipboard?" or "Did you know you could have four windows open at once?" We see this approach as a complementary, perhaps even a necessary, part of a complete help system along with the kind of question-asking facility suggested here.

HELP DESIGN AS A FUNCTION OF ITS MEDIUM

Just as it is critical for a help system to be tailored to user needs, it must also be designed for the medium that conveys it. Many on-line help systems are really electronic manuals, obeying the conventions and constraints of physical manuals. One point in favor of this approach is that the new user knows what to expect: the documentation will have book conventions like a table of contents and an index. But electronic manuals lack other desirable features of physical manuals: the ease of browsing or thumbing through the information; the immediate sense of knowing where one is in the book; the ability easily to shift one's attention back and forth between the physical manual and the screen; and the added confidence that, because the manual is a separate object, referring to help can't possibly have unexpected or irrevocable effects on the electronic working context.

What are the advantages of help delivered on-line? On-line help is not subject to the physical constraints of a book: it can be interactive and action-dependent. It can be dependent on the user's working context or on the history of a user's actions, and can take account of a user's skill level. On-line help can also be dynamic. Instead of having users read pages of printed text, help information can be presented using animation, even with voice overlay. Other features that can be incorporated into on-line help, impossible to deliver from a manual, are the ability to do keyword searches, and the ability to cut information directly out of the help text and paste it into the working environment. Finally, on-line help is more portable—an important consideration in light of the recent trend toward lap-top computers.

IMPLICIT VERSUS EXPLICIT HELP

The distinction between on-line help and the user interface is not necessarily clear-cut. In a sense, any actions that the interface either affords or constrains constitute help for the user. What menus are available and what options are on those menus inform the user (theoretically at least) of the range of possibilities for performing a task. Any sort of feedback that may be given to the user, whether as a prompt to the next action in a series of actions or in the form of an error message, could also be considered on-line help. This kind of help is *implicit* help provided by the interface. Usually, however, we use the term "on-line help" to refer to supplemental aid provided on-line once the design of the interface has been established. This is *explicit* help.

One understandable concern is that good explicit help may become an excuse for a bad interface. Help systems might be viewed as a way to "patch up" poor interface design. The other side of the same coin is that a well-designed interface should not need a help system. The aim should be to provide simple, self-explanatory interfaces. Although the ideal is commendable, reaching it seems unrealistic at the moment, especially considering the imbalance between the power and flexibility that much contemporary software affords and the state of the art in intelligent interfaces.

Future Directions

As interfaces become more adaptive and supportive, the need for explicit, self-contained help systems will diminish. The more truly context-sensitive we are able to make help, the less obtrusive it will be for users. But this will require more than a superficial understanding of context. For example, there will be times when the help you want is either unrelated to your current context or should *not* be related to your current context. For example, you may be between tasks and need help initiating a new one. It then becomes tedious to have to make sure to return to a different context in order to get the help you need. Alternatively, you may be in your current context in error. Any restriction on the help options available or any context-dependent information is likely to confuse you further. A human tutor would know when to ignore the context, or when to point out an error that caused you to be in the wrong context. Context-dependent help must either incorporate such inferential capabilities or provide a means for the user to carry on a dialogue with the computer.

Suggesting that future help will be more fully integrated into the interface implies that help may be more active. Now people usually have to ask for help, but more intelligent systems could anticipate user needs. This would be particularly useful for situations in which users may recognize the need for help but not know how to ask for it. Truly intelligent, active help would reinterpret the actions according to users' intentions. At the very least, help could complete commands, or prompt for the next action. More advanced systems would not only tell you how to carry out a task but actually perform it for you.

Active help systems may present their own special problems and obstacles, however. First, as discussed previously, there is the difficulty of designing a system that can interpret users' intentions. In the absence of this capability, the system is prone to develop wrong interpretations, leading to diagnoses and advice that may be entirely inappropriate, further confusing the user. Another pitfall discussed by Norman [1986] is that of the computer taking too much control from the user, leaving the user feeling like a bystander. The user is put in the position of being a passive observer rather than an active participant. Computer-initiated help in the form of unsolicited advice is potentially intrusive and irritating, just as a person looking over your shoulder offering advice can be.

Do we need to wait for advanced inference capabilities to provide more adaptive and supportive help? We don't think so. Using both the interactivity of the situation and users' intelligence, we can design help that "nudges" users towards making appropriate decisions and choices. And we can use advances in other arenas to make help more accessible. Different modes of access for help should be considered, for example. Voice activation is one obvious possibility; gesture is another (see Hulteen and Kurtenbach's chapter in this volume).

With regard to the method of presentation of information, animation deserves further exploration. In their chapter in this volume, Baecker and Small discuss ways in which motion can effectively add a whole new dimension to the way information is conveyed. Many of these ideas can be applied to the domain of helpful interfaces. The use of animation to present a history of a user's past actions is one example. Animation is already used in "guided tour" tutorials for the computer. This idea could be extended to become more interactive and integrated into the interface.

One of our objectives in the project at Apple has been to provide guidelines for developers based on our research and discussions. This will be a continuing effort as the work progresses, and the guidelines will become increasingly specific as we build an interface model. But the general philosophy for the design will remain the same. It is expressed in the following five principles:[1]

- On-line help should never be a substitute for good interface design.
- Help should be context-sensitive; it should not take the user away from the task at hand.
- Help systems should assist users in framing their questions and provide different help for different questions.
- Help systems should be dynamic and responsive.
- Users shouldn't need help to get help.

---

[1] These principles are listed in a document titled, "Guidelines for the Design of On-line Help," published by the Human Interface Group, Apple Computer, Inc., 1988.

Managing the Mundane

IT IS A TRUISM that computers are good at routine, repetitive tasks, and that they liberate people to perform the more complex, creative activities. Unfortunately, a computer can perform routine tasks only if a programmer has told it how to do so. When most computer users come upon a routine task, they are forced to do it themselves, for lack of a way of telling the computer what to do.

Allen Cypher

Advanced Technology Group
Apple Computer, Inc.

- When my department decided to have weekly meetings, I had to mindlessly paste *1:00–2:00 Dept. meeting* into my calendar for the next 20 Mondays.
- When I wanted to add my HyperCard stack of personal phone numbers to my stack of business phone numbers, I had to copy and paste the cards one at a time.
- Whenever I start a new paper in my word processor, I have to set the margins, font, and indentation.
- Whenever my Macintosh desktop gets messy, I have to shrink the windows one by one.
- When I decided to use bullets (•) instead of numbers to delineate this list, I had to replace each number by hand.

One could argue that if you don't like the way your computer operates, you can change it. (Quit complaining, roll up your sleeves, and write a

155

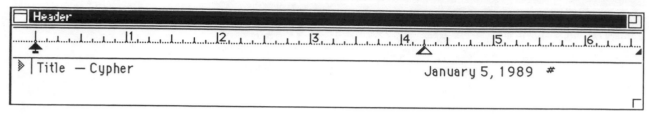

> Title — Cypher   January 5, 1989 #

Figure 1

program!) But insurance agents and journalists should not have to know how to program. And even though I know how to program, I am not about to take a two-day digression from writing this chapter to add a *number-to-bullet converter* to my word processor.

Programming is wonderful. It lets you do most anything imaginable. But users often want to do something simple, much less dramatic than "anything imaginable." To liberate users from the mundane, we need simple, accessible techniques for telling the computer what we want it to do.

Macros

One approach to telling the computer what to do is to use a *macro*. A macro is a sequence of user commands that can be replayed. You may record a macro by telling the computer to watch while you perform the commands.

For instance, I can tell the computer to watch while I turn the page in my HyperCard datebook, click on Monday, and then paste in *1:00–2:00 Dept. meeting*. Each time I tell the computer to replay my macro, it will add this meeting to the following week.

Another macro that I use sets up a heading for a paper in my word processor: It scrolls to the top of the document, selects the *Heading* command, adds a ruler, sets a tab stop at 4.25 inches, changes to left-justified text, sets 10-point font, types in "Title - Cypher," and selects menu items to insert the current date and page number, as shown in figure 1.

The power of macros is that you can get the computer to repeat anything that you as a user can do on your computer. There are a variety of macro tools currently available for the Macintosh—Tempo™, AutoMac™, QuickKeys™, and MacroMaker™, for instance—which allow users to automate tasks of this sort.

Alternatives to Macros—Scripts and Features

SCRIPTS

Scripting languages offer another means for users to gain control over the mundane. The idea here is for an application program to provide its own special-purpose language. Macintosh users are now familiar with the HyperTalk scripting language for HyperCard, and DOS and UNIX users have had "batch files" and "shell scripts" for quite a while. A special-purpose language can be simpler than a general-purpose one; its objects are the objects of the application, and its commands are precisely the actions that one wants to perform on those objects. For instance, the location of the HyperCard message box is specified by *the location of message box* in HyperTalk, and by *GlobalToLocal(messageWindow^.portBits.bounds.top Left)* in Pascal.

Scripting is a bit awkward in the Macintosh world, because the Mac features visual, direct manipulation interfaces. In this environment, scripting languages provide written equivalents for commands that a user typically invokes by clicking with a mouse. Dragging a corner of a rectangle in a Draw program would have a corresponding "Reshape Rectangle (58, 102)" command in the scripting language. A written command language affords a convenient way to describe commands for later use, enables programming features like variables, iteration, and conditional behavior, and allows the user to inspect and modify a sequence of commands.

The fundamental drawback to this approach is that it is a return to the written command-line interfaces that direct manipulation graphical interfaces have so effectively replaced. The advantage is that the user can learn a simple language instead of learning a complete, complex language like C or Pascal. But a user must potentially learn a different special-purpose language for each application, each with its own idiosyncrasies, and these languages typically have limited, unexpressive syntaxes for iteration and conditionals.

HyperTalk is an exciting development in scripting languages because HyperCard so effectively allows users to modify their environment. Most scripting languages just piece together conventional behavior, resulting in automatic but prosaic actions. HyperCard, on the other hand, shines at allowing users to change the appearance and behavior of their interface by adding buttons and animated objects. This additional degree of user power and control may give users the needed incentive to learn a special-purpose written language.

FEATURES

Another way for users to acquire the power and control that they need is through the addition of new features to an application. Programs for word processing, graphic design, and the like are continually evolving, and I am often struck by the frequency with which new features supersede macros that I have written (or wished I could have written!). For instance, the latest MultiFinder contains a *Set Aside* command that solves my problem of having to shrink all of the windows on the desktop when it gets cluttered. And there is a word processor that has a *Styles* command that replaces my macro for setting up the margins and font when I start a new paper.

Perhaps HyperCard will eventually have an *Append Stack* command, which would make it easy for me to add my personal phone numbers to my business numbers. And I would not be surprised to find a *weekly* command added to my datebook, so that weekly meetings would be easy to schedule. Incidentally, I have a similar problem with my VCR: it does have a special *daily* command that conveniently lets me record Dan Rather every day at 7:00, but, alas, there is no *weekly* command, so it takes a lot of work to record "**thirty**something" every Tuesday.

But program designers can never anticipate the desires of all users, and even if they could, the resulting program, which allowed users to change everything by clicking on the right box somewhere, would be hopelessly complex. I find it difficult enough that word processors now want me to know about gutters, kerns, and widows. As Don Norman's chapter shows, the more flexible a machine or program is, the more difficult it will be to perform individual tasks. You can play games and edit papers on the Apple IIGS, but it is easier to play a game on a Nintendo.

The Future of User Control

New features will certainly improve user control in the future, and perhaps scripting languages will become pervasive enough that someone in the office will be able to write a script to help with your most persistent mundane activities. But the greatest potential for helping users gain control over their day-to-day interactions with the computer lies in improved macro tools.

RECOGNIZING SIMILAR OBJECTS

One of the biggest problems in getting macros to carry out a repetitive activity is in specifying the set of objects on which the activity is to be performed. To the user, the objects are clearly similar, but it is hard for the user to describe this similarity to the macro tool. When I shrink all of the windows on the desktop, I am considering the windows to be a set of similar objects. When I add a meeting to every Monday, I am considering all of the Monday text fields to be similar objects. When I change the numbers *1. 2. 3. 4.* and *5.* into bullets at the start of five consecutive paragraphs, I am considering those numbers to be similar objects.

Macro tools currently have problems with objects because applications have no means of making their objects known to the tools. Some spreadsheet programs (for example, Excel™) and telecommunication programs (for example, MicroPhone™ II) have achieved a certain degree of success in making objects accessible by integrating the macro tool into the application.

I wrote a demonstration program to show some of the capabilities of a macro tool that knows about objects. The program makes reasonable guesses about which objects the user considers to be similar and then carries

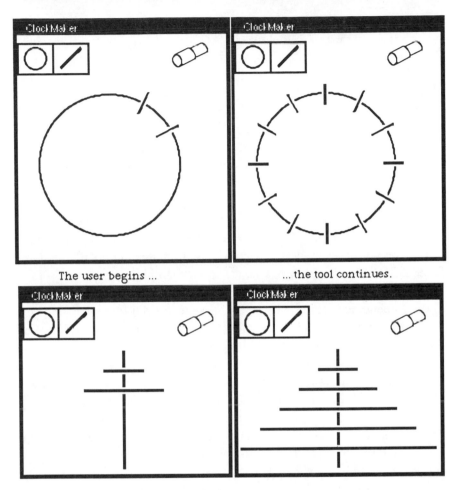

Figure 2

The user begins ...   ... the tool continues.

out iterations over these classes of objects. The inspiration for the program is the observation that when a user draws a clock face, it is fairly easy for a human observer to see that the 12 tick marks for the hours are similar. If a computer could detect the similarity, it could assist the user in making the drawing. I built into a Draw program a macro tool called ClockMaker, which has a *local frame of reference* feature—the clock tick marks, for instance, are drawn in the frame of reference of the circle that represents the clock face. The macro tool has access to all of the objects that the user draws. It compares the *features* of the objects (such as endpoints, line width) in order to detect similarities and patterns (see figure 2).

When it detects that the user is performing a regular, repetitive action on similar objects, it infers what the appropriate set of similar objects is and continues the user's action. In addition to drawing the clock face, the macro tool assisted with a Christmas tree, with graph axes, and other similar drawings. One notable feature of this approach is that the user never has to tell the macro tool to start recording—it is always on, watching for patterns.

HANDLING SPECIAL CASES

Another problem confronting macro tools is *special cases*. When I add my meeting on Mondays, what do I do for a Monday whose text field is already full? If I am cleaning my desktop by shrinking windows and arranging them in a row, what do I do when I get to the end of the row? If I teach my macro to replace digits with bullets, will it work properly when it gets to *10*, a two-digit number?

This problem is addressed by an area of research known as *programming by example* [see Smith, 1975 and 1976]. The basic approach is for the user to provide several examples, indicating how to handle different situations. Some systems detect a branch when a second example differs from the first. This can be effective, but it requires that the user repeat the common parts of the sequence identically, which may be quite difficult for lengthy macros.

To make this approach more robust, it is necessary to recognize when the user is employing a slightly different set of commands to achieve the same effect. Also, it would help if the system could recognize cases in which the user made a mistake and then repaired it. This is tantamount to identifying the user's *intent* in performing a sequence of commands. If applications supply an intelligent macro tool with information about the objects and actions in their domain, it should be possible to recognize enough of the user's intent to make programming by example effective for a considerable range of user activities. For instance, a basic knowledge of browsing in HyperCard would allow a tool to consider two sequences of browsing commands to be the same if they end up at the same card. A basic knowledge of *copy and paste* would allow a tool to notice that two *copy*s without an intervening *paste* indicate that the first *copy* was a mistake. The potential for applying programming by example to macros is great, because it promises to bring the power of programming to *all* users of computers.

An Environment For Collaboration

Collaborative Work

COLLABORATION TECHNOLOGY (CT) subsumes a group of technologies and behavioral science notions, the purpose of which is to facilitate and enhance the daily work and interactions of people and machines bound together under the umbrella of a common goal, project, or job. CT involves the study of problems in work patterns and flow cycles. At work, people express feelings like: *Things seem to take longer than they should. It's often difficult to accomplish even simple things. Why are things so expensive?* It became evident that to create technology to adequately support work, we had to take a much wider view of the user's world, to find the commonalities between professions and the modus operandi of daily work.

Key questions for people involved in business and industry are:

- What happens during one cycle of your industry?
- How do information and deliverables get passed from one to another and what types of information are utilized?
- What are the various jobs and who performs them?
- How is the project tracked?
- Where are the bottlenecks?
- What are common job frustrations in which technology may play a role?

Understanding the answers to such questions can guide the development of user- and process-based collaboration technologies. The goals of CT are

Harry Vertelney

Advanced Technology Group
Apple Computer, Inc.

to grease the skids of collective interaction, improve the qualitative daily experience for people, and improve the quantitative results for business and industry.

This chapter looks at how work on complex projects gets accomplished, emphasizing the key components of communication, cooperation, and co-ordination of dispersed people. A working environment is envisioned where database, communications, and user-interface technologies are sewn together to support the real activities of people involved in projects.

Project Characteristics

Consider industries and businesses whose purpose is to produce an artifact as a result of their work—that is, buildings, computers, toasters, aircraft, etc. General characteristics for projects produced in these types of businesses include:

- The projects are typically large and expensive. High degrees of interdependency based on requirements for information, adherence to deadlines, and the responsibility for large expenditures are inherent in such projects.
- The projects span amounts of time greater than a few months.
- The services of many professionals from different disciplines are required to perform the work, though a particular participant's involvement in the project may be only short-term or sporadic.
- Many of the participants are subcontractors or have their own businesses in their own locations.
- There is a need for ongoing communication between small, geographically dispersed working groups so that project components and information can be passed along to a downstream group in their most useful form.
- There is an additional need for at least one group to oversee and view the entire project from several different perspectives.
- Some parts of the business are heavily dependent upon computer-based systems and technologies, but there is little functionality parity and communication between the systems.

A Reference Model

Let's take a specific example—the architecture, engineering, and construction industry (AEC)—and see how these characteristics are manifested. A small project may involve dozens of people, whereas a large project can involve 10,000. A sampling of the types of workers includes: developers, brokers, architects, engineers, accountants, buyers, tradesmen, bankers, and more. Each of these people has a specific job to perform—deciding whether or not to build, finding property, acquiring financing, doing architecture and engineering, dealing with governing authorities, pounding nails, etc.—

DESIGN DEVELOPMENT: Phase I

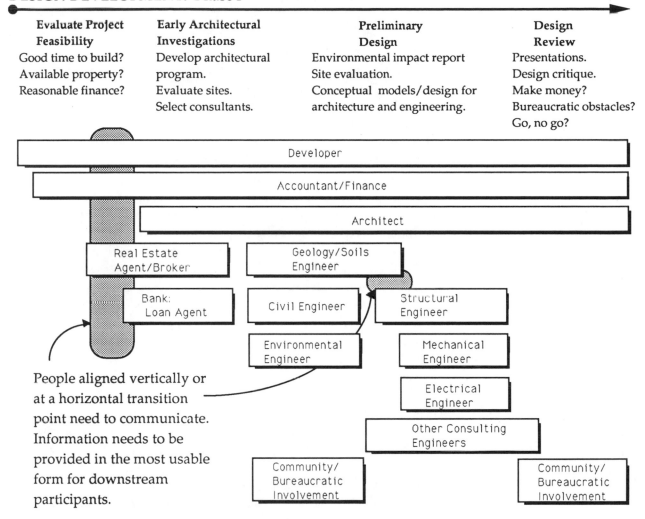

Evaluate Project Feasibility	Early Architectural Investigations	Preliminary Design	Design Review
Good time to build?	Develop architectural program.	Environmental impact report	Presentations.
Available property?	Evaluate sites.	Site evaluation.	Design critique.
Reasonable finance?	Select consultants.	Conceptual models/design for architecture and engineering.	Make money? Bureaucratic obstacles? Go, no go?

Developer

Accountant/Finance

Architect

Real Estate Agent/Broker

Geology/Soils Engineer

Bank: Loan Agent

Civil Engineer

Structural Engineer

Environmental Engineer

Mechanical Engineer

Electrical Engineer

Other Consulting Engineers

Community/ Bureaucratic Involvement

Community/ Bureaucratic Involvement

People aligned vertically or at a horizontal transition point need to communicate. Information needs to be provided in the most usable form for downstream participants.

and each has a set of tools (sometimes computer-based tools) that enables them to perform their work.

An AEC industry process model was generated for the purpose of visualizing the participants, information flow, types of tools and data required to do architecture.[1] Figure 1 shows a portion of that model.

The need to communicate and trade information regularly while completing their work is highest among the workers (represented by boxes) in vertical or adjacent columns. A majority of activities in a column needs to be completed before the collection of information can be utilized by the

Figure 1: AEC process and data flow.

---

[1] The model was shown to the American Institute of Architects, the Building Research Board of the National Academy of Science, and McGraw-Hill Publishers, the largest supplier of information to the AEC industry. All agreed this was a good general model, though its practical application would be slightly different on any given project.

next group, thus moving the project ahead. In practical terms, the project architect usually decides who should be involved to complete a particular phase, whom they should work with, who is responsible for supplying them with particular information, and how to present their work.

Consider the problems of two participants who need to work together: a soils engineer and a structural engineer. Part of the soils engineer's job is to analyze the soil bearing capacity so that the structural engineer can design a foundation that can support the building. One needs to be completed before the other can begin. Typically, the soils engineer works with drills, lab tools, maps, and computer tools, and the results of the work are recorded and transferred on maps and in a paper report describing the findings—pictures of information. The structural engineer uses a computer for designing the foundation, drawing its representation, and writing a specification report. The design calculations will require several of the results from the soils engineer's work, including the soil bearing capacity value. There is no nice way for the structural engineer's program to go into a database to identify and pull out the soil bearing capacity value. There is nothing resembling a project-wide database. The structural engineer will have to find and reenter the data or, if a data disk was included, find a data translator to make the results from one program usable by another. Translations and reentry of information result in information degradation and loss of productivity. This type of transaction—*here's some information, sorry it's not in a very usable form*—goes on constantly throughout the process, sometimes on a large scale, other times small.

At the same time, the participants need to communicate with one another to work together effectively. Studies show that office workers spend approximately 30 to 70 percent of their time in meetings [Panko, 1974]. *Let me check my calendar—how about the day after tomorrow?* The current situation requires the participants to find a convenient place and time, gather around a table, spread out some drawings, mark them up, make design and production decisions, then go back to their offices and somehow transcribe the meeting notes into their project work. A worse scenario involves the architect marking up his drawings, sending them out by crosstown messenger or an overnight mail service, and waiting for the recipient to make marks on the drawings and return the documents the same way, thereby linearizing the process. These delays result in project dead times—again, counterproductive and costly.

Characteristics of a Collaborative Environment

To provide technical support for a reference model that embodies many of the project characteristics described above, it became evident that a rich environment would be required where information could flow freely and people could collaborate and communicate with a minimal amount of interference and bureaucracy [for a comprehensive view of these issues, including reprints of four of Douglas Engelbart's papers, see Greif, 1988]. To accomplish this, technologies from three domains need to be sewn together: database, communications, and user interface.

DATABASE

In our environment, the database should provide for three main goals:

- **Act as the shared memory and project archive.** The database that contains all the original data, correspondence, CAD drawings, spreadsheets, specifications, voice mails, annotations, simulations, etc. should be available to provide the information to those who need it when they need it. An individual's involvement in a project is often shorter than the life expectancy of the artifacts produced by the project, so for posterity, there needs to be a place to look for information. *In 25 years, will anyone remember whether the building was engineered to support an additional two stories?*

- **Establish an audit trail for accountability purposes.** Each contribution to the project should be identified and time-stamped. Thus, we'll be able to learn more from our mistakes and our successes. *Whose fault was it the walkway fell down—engineer, materials acquisition, inspection?*

- **Minimize the impact of changes and redo's.** The nemesis of any large project is the impact of changes as they propagate through the system. Not knowing you're working with invalid information causes wasteful, costly effort. It is possible, though, to imagine an environment in which automatic notification of change and its subsequent evaluation is a commonplace occurrence. Applications can be written that understand information tolerances; that is, if the database notified you of a value change, the application would know whether the change is important enough to recompute and send out more notifications. *Recent heavy rains have caused unprecedented sliding near our building site; therefore, we recommend . . .*

Applications that deposit data into the project database also need to communicate with other databases [Building Research Board, 1986]. Applications may utilize a layer of functionality that helps link a need for information with the source of information. Consider the architect using a CAD program, working on a detail for door locksets. He usually draws the detail in the abstract, employing drawing notes and the written specification to clarify what the drawing really means. At the same time, there are industry catalogs in the office that contain the marketing and technical literature about prefabricated locksets. It should be a straightforward matter for the architect to direct his system to find the on-line industry information, copy the technical drawing and notes, and make the selection right

Figure 2: The project database.

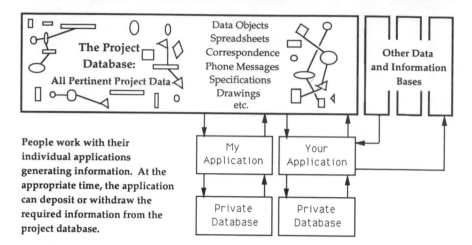

People work with their individual applications generating information. At the appropriate time, the application can deposit or withdraw the required information from the project database.

from the catalog to be included in his drawing. Checking the fire code would fall nicely into place here as a choice-verification activity.[2]

COMMUNICATIONS

Communications come in two flavors, synchronous and asynchronous. Participants in synchronous communication are connected to each other by technology or proximity, as in a telephone call or meeting, whereas in the asynchronous variety, communications are received sometime after they are sent. A robust collaborative environment must incorporate both types of communication.

Observations of synchronous communication situations (for example, the scenario of workers standing around the table full of drawings) show that progress and decisions at these meetings are made on the basis of availability of data, verbal communications, visual cues, and reactions of participants. It follows that, in order to approximate face-to-face meetings, a collaborative environment for participants not co-located requires multi-channeled communication—voice, sound, vision, and data. A studio is a good model for a collaborative environment; there are no major physical barriers between coworkers. When a question arises, one simply turns to the right person and asks it. In a moment or two, the knowledge is transferred and both people go back to their respective tasks. *Mini-meetings* are always occurring.

The studio environment could be approximated by leaving several channels of communication open while a group is working. Workers would enter their work spaces at their own locations and turn on their media connectors, which would stay open throughout the work day. A worker

---

[2] Architecture happens to be a particularly good choice for this model because the Construction Specification Institute has provided a numbering system for all building components to which all participants in the AEC industry adhere.

Figure 3: Dispersed group discussing a drawing.

could look up and ask a remote coworker a question, and both could make scribbles or notes on commonly observed screens. Without calendar-checking or formal meetings, all group members could have the option to collaborate on solving the problem at hand.

In the asynchronous domain, it's only a matter of time before an analyst will respond to a region on a spreadsheet by binding a voice mail message to that region. "Could you check these figures?—they seem a little low . . . ." Indeed, electronic mail (via text, voice, or video) is becoming so popular that technologies are being developed to organize, discard, and prioritize the large volume of mail, including junk e-mail, that is arriving at the e-mailbox daily [Malone et al., 1987]. Applications accessing the upstream results generated by another worker or group can be based upon similar processes and structures.

USER INTERFACE ISSUES

The user interfaces of today are designed primarily for individual users working alone. The interface represents a convergence of information and tools designed to help with the actual work a person is to perform on a project. User interfaces that can support diverse users and group-oriented activities must meet new criteria.

As Jonathan Grudin points out in his chapter, the introduction of collaboration technology has the potential to both enhance and disrupt the psychological and social dimensions of work situations. What happens when workers have the ability to project their presence onto the president's desktop? As we build higher and higher levels of connectivity among participants, both the physical and the hierarchical location of individuals will present less of a barrier to communication. As Grudin observes, considerable work will be required to identify both the benefits and the risks of such disturbances to the status quo and to build user interfaces that can minimize both the negative effects of and the natural resistance to change.

As the user interface continues to incorporate new channels of communication, new devices will appear in offices. How will computers, cameras, speakers, microphones, telephones, networks, large displays, video disk carousels, and VTRs be functionally and aesthetically integrated without the office becoming a technocable nightmare? **The user interface will have to provide the rules, processes, cognitive aids, and packaging necessary to make our environment rich but not bewilderingly complex, secure but not unfriendly, robust but not burdensome, and familiar but not invasive.**

The interactions of dispersed groups of people are changing. Teleconferencing environments that allow people in remote locations to communicate through voice, video, and graphics are being developed by various universities and telecommunications companies. How will these capabilities change work habits when such conversations can occur at the desktop? Media artists Kit Galloway and Sherrie Rabinowitz created an experience entitled *A Hole In Space*, which was a two-way video conference wall between Century City (L.A.) and Lincoln Center (N.Y.C.). The installation became a spontaneous forum for passers-by to engage in dispersed play and long-distance relationships that had previously been impossible [Tisch, 1988]. Media influence the course of a meeting because they interact strongly with participants' resources for communication and memory [Stefik and Foster, 1987]. Just having the communication windows and shared spaces will change the behavior of people.

Privacy, security, and network etiquette—the manner in which people conduct themselves through the network—are issues that will make or break the utility and acceptance of collaborative environments. We can look for guidance to areas of life where conventions already exist; for instance, most people know it's impolite to call someone on the telephone after 11:00 p.m. When a solicitor comes knocking, we know we don't have to answer the door unless we want to. We put locks on our doors to keep out intruders, and we also keep our rare and valuable items in safety deposit boxes. Similar conventions for collaborative environments will evolve as the technology becomes more ubiquitous.

Challenges

Substantial technical barriers in the areas of database technology, communications, and user-interface design prevent us all from having a useful collaborative environment now. Ongoing research in object-oriented databases, compound documents, and hypermedia promises to enable the kind of shared database required for serious projects. Compression technology advancements, along with high-speed, high-bandwidth networks capable of supporting meetings among remote workers with audio, video, and data channels, will help bring about the rich communications described above. Standards such as Broadband ISDN (Integrated Services Digital Network) will ensure that all of us will be able to play the game.

Improved design of user interfaces—including the physical work environment—will enhance collaboration, maintain consistency and ease of use, and guarantee our privacy. The user interface can transform the collection of diverse technologies required by collaborative work into an exciting, stimulating work environment that will support and enhance us in all our daily endeavors.

Groupware and Cooperative Work:
Problems and Prospects

COMPUTER APPLICATIONS THAT SUPPORT GROUPS are commonly known as *groupware*. Although electronic mail and bulletin boards are still the only widely known examples, considerable effort has gone into developing other groupware applications. As networks spread, we will see more voice applications, coauthoring tools, intelligent databases, group decision support systems, and other applications designed with the understanding that most work is carried out in a social context. However, progress may be slower than expected and may eventually lead us in unanticipated directions. In the first half of this chapter I describe problems that have led to expensive, repeated failures of groupware development efforts; in the second half, a groupware success story demonstrates the importance of focusing our analysis on the work setting and provides a basis for speculating about the future.

Problems in the Development of Groupware

Why is groupware more difficult than single-user applications to design and evaluate? First of all, because individuals interact with the groupware product, it has all of the usual interface design problems. What's worse, group members with different backgrounds, experiences, and preferences may all have to use the same groupware application. For example, different individuals may choose to use different word processors—or some may

Jonathan Grudin
Human Interface Laboratory
MCC

choose to write by hand—but two coauthors must agree to use the same coauthoring tool!

Another complication for groupware design is that within a group, individuals take on different roles. Thus, consider the differences within these pairs who might work together: author/editor, sender/recipient, speaker/listener, and supervisor/subordinate. Note that the same person can shift in role, being author at one moment and then, perhaps when reading a collaborator's contribution, editor. The software must support not only several people working together on a task, but also their different and potentially shifting roles.

A further complication is that once we enter the realm of group dynamics, various social, motivational, political, and economic factors come into the picture. These usually play little or no role in the design of single-user applications such as word processors or spreadsheets, but are central in the design of a system to support meeting management, for example.

Another obstacle is the difficulty of studying groups—group processes are often variable and context-sensitive, and usually unfold over a much longer time frame than individual activities. Days or weeks may be needed to observe the pattern of use of a group calendar or even an electronic mail system, with the further complication that the activity occurs in different locations. Organizational change that results from introducing the technology may take even longer to observe. And finally, after one *has* observed a group in action, it is hard to generalize to other groups—each group is different, and a group's experiences with an application are highly influenced by the conditions under which it is introduced.

In a recent paper [Grudin, 1989b], I examined several groupware applications that have failed to live up to their promise. In each case, my analysis was based on personal involvement in the design, evaluation, or use of the application as well as on the published literature. Five factors contributing to groupware failure were identified:

- Groupware applications often fail because they require that some people do additional work, and those people are *not* the ones who perceive a direct benefit from the use of the application.

- Groupware may lead to activity that violates social taboos, threatens existing political structures, or otherwise demotivates users who are crucial to its success.

- Groupware may fail if it does not allow for the wide range of exception handling and improvisation that characterizes much group activity.

- We fail to learn from experience because these complex applications introduce almost insurmountable obstacles to meaningful, generalizable analysis and evaluation.

- The groupware development process fails because our intuitions are especially poor for multiuser applications.

THE DISPARITY BETWEEN WHO DOES THE WORK AND WHO GETS THE BENEFIT

Given the different preferences, experience, roles, and tasks of members of a group, a new groupware application will never afford every member precisely the same benefit. When it is introduced, some people will have to adjust more than others. One can hope that the differences are not great—but often they are. There should be a collective benefit from using the application; ideally, everyone will also benefit individually, even if some benefit more than others. However, this ideal is rarely found; most groupware requires *additional* work for some users, who enter or process information that the application requires or produces.

Consider, for example, the automatic meeting scheduling feature that accompanies many electronic calendar systems. The underlying concept is simple: the person scheduling the meeting specifies a distribution list and the system checks each person's calendar, finding a time convenient for all. The immediate beneficiary is the manager or secretary who initiates a typical meeting, but for the feature to work efficiently, *everyone* in the group must maintain a personal calendar and be willing to let the computer schedule their free time. Ehrlich [1987a, 1987b] reports that electronic calendars are typically used as communication devices by managers. They are often not maintained by individual contributors. Thus, successful use of automatic meeting scheduling requires additional work for those group members who would not otherwise maintain electronic calendars. As a result, this groupware feature is rarely used.

Similarly, consider voice products, such as voice annotation to documents. The advantages of digitized voice over handwritten or typed input are almost all advantages for the speaker: speech is faster to produce, conveys emotion and nuance easily, and may be available without access to a computer terminal. The disadvantages to digitized voice, however, are overwhelmingly problems for the listener. It is harder to understand than typed or written material, slower to take in, not easily scanned or reviewed, more likely to contain errors, and more difficult to manipulate—for example, proposed edits to a document will have to be typed in by the listener anyway. This disparity may contribute to the repeated failure of voice products to meet sales projections [Aucella, 1987]. When is it acceptable for speakers to thus burden listeners? Possibly when users are speakers and listeners in equal measure, or where there is no alternative, as when use of hands or a keyboard is not possible. A disparity may also be accepted when the speaker is of higher status than the listener, as with dictation machines, where an executive's time is deemed valuable enough to warrant the arduous transcription effort.

As a third example, consider a project management application on a distributed system, covering the scheduling and chronicling of activities, the creation and evaluation of plans and schedules, the management of product versions and changes, and the monitoring of resources and responsibilities. Such applications are being developed [Sathi et al., 1986]. Clearly, the primary beneficiary is the project leader or manager; equally evident is that successful use will require other group members to enter considerable information that is typically not kept on-line. This may be resisted. For example, one ten-year project culminated in a "computer-assisted management system" installed on an aircraft carrier, "its primary purpose to help the Commanding Officer and his department heads administer the ship" [McCracken and Akscyn, 1984]. One factor contributing to its eventual replacement by a system that lacked management features was the difficulty of getting everyone to use it [Kling, 1987].

SOCIAL, POLITICAL, AND MOTIVATIONAL FACTORS

Groupware may be resisted if it interferes with the subtle and complex social dynamics that are common to groups. The computer is happiest in the world of explicit, concrete information. Central to group activity, however, are social, motivational, political, and economic factors that are rarely explicit or stable. Often unconsciously, our actions are guided by social conventions and by our knowledge of the personalities of people around us. It will be difficult to make such conventions, knowledge, and personal agendas available to the computer—a secretary's implicit knowledge of a manager's priorities may be difficult to impart to an on-line calendar. For example, secretaries know that managers' unscheduled time is rarely really free; unauthorized scheduling of a manager's apparently open time can lead to total rejection of automatic meeting scheduling [Ehrlich, 1987a]. Even trying to make social knowledge explicit may be a problem—we often tactfully keep our motivations and agendas (and our opinions of other people) to ourselves. Yet unless such information is made explicit, groupware will be insensitive to it.

With one work management system, any employee who identified and reported a priority problem began getting system-generated requests for progress reports to be forwarded to the Chief Executive Officer—a blatant example of a design that ignores the sensitivity of certain communications. So employees stopped reporting problems. The vigilant system noted that employees had stopped using it and alerted the administrator. The employees dealt with the resulting complaints by writing programs that periodically opened files and changed dates, which satisfied the watchful, automatic monitor. Thus "sabotaged," the work management system was of little use and was eventually quietly withdrawn.

Another active groupware development area that has failed to meet expectations is meeting management or group decision support systems [Kraemer and King, 1988]. The appeal of improving the efficiency of meetings is clear, but the decision-making process is often complex and subtle, with participants holding partially hidden agendas, relying on knowledge of the personalities of the others involved, and showing sensitivity to social customs and motivational concerns. Because such factors are never represented explicitly in a support system, the computer participates at a great disadvantage. In one case, a group considered using an issue-based information system in which arguments, counter-arguments, and decisions are entered by participants, creating a record of the decision-making process that can be used for subsequent review and exploration of alternatives. The plan to use the system was abandoned when it was recognized that the manager wanted the group to project a strong impression of consensus; the explicit record of opposing positions that the system would immortalize was politically unacceptable.

EXCEPTION HANDLING IN WORKGROUPS

Software may be designed to support group activities or procedures as they are "supposed to" happen, but descriptions of "typical" procedures can be misleading. Suchman [1983] argues persuasively that a wide range of error, exception handling, and improvisation are characteristic of human activity. Group activity may be particularly variable—strict adherence to a standard procedure may often be more the exception than the rule. But given the overall difficulty of developing software to support group activity, the desire to build the design around specific work procedures may be especially strong.

The problems that can result are illustrated in a case study by Rowe [1985, 1987]. Computerized stock control and sales order processing systems were introduced at a chocolate factory that is part of a large food company. Severe problems arose when the computer services division of the food company installed the systems in the chocolate factory:

> (People in) computer services refer to a "production mentality" where (chocolate factory) staff respond to problems as and when they arise, are eager to keep production operating and are loathe to indulge in long-term planning and adopt specific procedures. Most important, they expect others to adjust to them, and resist the discipline the computer imposes . . . . Moreover, not only did management fail to impose set procedures, but further ad hoc arrangements were positively encouraged by the sales department, as in the case of one customer who was assured that they could amend their Friday order up to 1:00 p.m. on a Monday. No doubt it believed it was working in

the best interests of the company, but its actions created considerable problems for those trying to operate the computer.

In some areas, the manual system continued to be used out of necessity. At one point, the general manager "became convinced that someone was sabotaging the system."

Here Suchman's observation is critical: if more human activity is ad hoc problem solving than we realize, if descriptions of "standard process" are often post hoc rationalizations, the workers' behavior that seemed pathological to the computer services division may well have been an optimal response to the work environment. For example, catering to the needs of specific customers is often considered good, when it can be done.

The general manager recommended that the system be withdrawn, but "he was overruled by group head office, who were not prepared to lose face over the installation." By hiring new personnel and taking other expensive measures, the management made the system work. This points out another problem facing groupware. The system described by Rowe was a large, expensive system: upper management was prepared to do a lot to make it succeed. But a typical groupware application or feature, such as meeting scheduling or voice annotation or even meeting support, will rarely have the same degree of visibility and backing—and thus would fail under similar circumstances.

THE UNDERESTIMATED DIFFICULTY OF EVALUATING GROUPWARE

Task analysis, design, and evaluation are never easy, but they are far more difficult for multiuser applications than for single-user applications. An individual's success with a particular spreadsheet or word processor is unlikely to be affected by differing backgrounds or by the personalities of other group members, so single users can be tested in a lab on the perceptual, cognitive, and motor variables that have been the focus for single-user applications. But it is difficult to create a lab situation that accurately reflects the social, motivational, economic, and political dynamics that are quite likely to affect the use of groupware.

Thus, evaluation of groupware requires a different approach, based on the methodologies of social psychology and anthropology. These skills are absent in most development environments, where human factors engineers and cognitive psychologists are only starting to be accepted. These methods are more time-consuming. Much of a person's use of a spreadsheet might be observed in a single hour, for example, but group interactions typically unfold over days or weeks. Furthermore, the methods are less precise. Evaluating groupware "in the field" is remarkably complex because of the number of people to observe at each site, the wide variability of group composition, and the range of environmental factors that play roles in determining acceptance, such as user training, management buy-in, and vendor follow-through. Given these interacting influences, evaluation may require a full implementation. Even then, establishing success or failure will be easier than establishing which underlying factors brought it about.

Finally, the difficulty of evaluation is increased dramatically by the complexity of an application that provides features and interfaces that vary according to users' jobs, backgrounds, and preferences. A single-user application may be adopted if it appeals to a reasonable fraction of the members of a group. Groupware often will have to appeal to all group members.

The Breakdown of Intuitive Decision-making

Thousands of developer-years and hundreds of millions of dollars have been committed to various application areas that could be termed groupware, despite little or no return [Grudin, 1989b]. Often, the same mistakes are made over and over. How does this happen?

Decision-makers in a position to commit resources to development projects rely heavily on intuition. The experience and track record of a development manager considering a groupware application is generally based on single-user applications. Intuition is likely to be a far more reliable guide to single-user applications than to multiuser applications. A manager with good intuition may quickly get a feel for the user's experience with a word processor or spreadsheet, for example, but fail to appreciate the intricate requirements of a groupware application that requires participation by a range of user types.

Not surprisingly, decision-makers are often drawn to applications that selectively benefit one subset of the user population: managers. Consider the active groupware development areas: group decision support systems primarily benefit decision-makers; project management applications primarily benefit project managers; automatic meeting schedulers benefit those who convene meetings; digitized voice products appeal to those who rely on speech (remember the dictation machine). Similarly, managers may see themselves as prospective casual users of features such as a natural language interface and may support their development, without recognizing either their limited utility for heavy users or their development cost [Grudin, 1989b].

This bias is understandable—each of us has ideas about what will help us do our job. But managers tend to underestimate the down side, the unwelcome extra work required of other users to maintain such an application, a burden that often leads to neglect or resistance. For example, a group decision support system or work management application may require many people to learn the system and then enter data, may record information that participants would prefer not to have widely disseminated, and may block other means to influence decision-making, such as private lobbying. Also, as described above, managers may fail to appreciate the difficulty of developing and evaluating good groupware. Finally, they may not recognize that because systems and applications are getting cheaper and thus less visible to management, users will less often be forced to do additional work to ensure an application's success. For example, an expensive voice messaging system failed initially at one site, but succeeded when top management insisted on its use and removed the alternatives; however, no such push is likely for a much less visible voice annotation feature.

Of course, managers are not alone in having poor intuition for multiuser applications. As researchers, designers, implementers, users, evaluators, or managers, our computer experience is generally based on single-user applications. This history determined the skills we acquired, the intuitions we developed, and the way we view our work. For example, human factors engineers are trained to apply techniques based on perceptual, cognitive, and motor psychology to study phenomena of brief duration, but are unfamiliar with the techniques of social psychology or anthropology needed to study group dynamics over time.

In particular, we are not trained to think deeply about the disparity between the benefit obtained by and the work required of different user categories, beyond distinctions among novice, casual, and heavy users. We may rely on feedback from a few "typical users," often the target audience, the principal beneficiaries of the application. For groupware, this leads us to focus on managers. For example, the greatest user interface challenge for an intelligent project management application will be to minimize the information entry effort required of each worker. But instead, attention is directed toward information display, toward the user interface for the principle beneficiary, the manager. "Managers must know what information is needed, where to locate it, and how to interpret and use it. Equally important is that they be able to do so without great effort" [Sathi et al., 1986]. This may appeal to the manager sponsoring the project, but *exclusive* focus on improving the system for its principal beneficiary is not wise.

The converse may also occur: a decision-maker may not recognize the value of an application that primarily benefits nonmanagers, even when it would provide a collective benefit to the organization. This is particularly true for applications that might create additional work for the manager. The second half of this paper addresses this point in the context of electronic mail, a groupware success story.

Computer Supported Cooperative Work: A Shift in Perspective

Computer support, even of individuals, is already changing the way groups and organizations function. But the problems described above suggest that the technology-driven approach to progress that works relatively well with single-user applications is failing with multiuser targets. We need to understand more about how groups and organizations function and evolve, as well as more about individual differences. This has long been pointed out by visionaries such as Douglas Engelbart, but it is easier to recognize the problem than to truly escape the technology orientation that is reflected in the term *groupware* itself. Research and development methodologies that truly focus on users' work and workplaces are only starting to appear [for example, see Bjerknes et al., 1987; Bodker et al., 1988; Whiteside et al., 1988].

The term *computer supported cooperative work,* adopted by a number of researchers and developers, explicitly identifies "work" as the central concern. Even with that emphasis, many members manifest a technology-driven focus. [See Greif, 1988, for an overview; Grudin, 1989a, reviews a recent collection of research papers.] Successful proponents of a work-centered approach include a number of Scandinavian researchers who stress the importance of "workplace democracy"—engaging the users or workers meaningfully in the design process, a slow mutual education process that results in users becoming true members of the design team [Bjerknes et al., 1987; Bodker et al., 1988].

This time-consuming, labor-intensive approach may not be equally appropriate for all development projects. It is still evolving but has already taken the tremendously important step of bringing computer scientists into meaningful contact with labor unions, historians, and economic theorists. Advances in computer support for group activity will require sensitivity to issues such as the balance of work and benefit, social conventions within organizations, and political and motivational concerns—issues that have long interested unions, economists, management or organizational design specialists, and others. The knowledge and approaches of these fields must now be joined with computer science.

Electronic Mail: Viewing a Groupware Success from an Organizational Perspective

The potential for electronic mail to augment group activity was foreseen thirty years ago; today, a variety of related computer-mediated communication forms establish it as the clearest groupware success story. How has electronic mail, broadly defined to include distributed communications such as electronic bulletin boards, avoided the pitfalls into which most groupware stumbles? Is electronic mail a potential model for groupware? In the remainder of this chapter, I analyze electronic mail in the organizational context, describe the effect this medium is beginning to have on the structure of work, and speculate on emerging changes in industry and academia.

How does electronic mail fare with the five obstacles to groupware described above?

- Who does the work and who benefits? Insofar as the sender/recipient distinction is concerned, electronic mail provides an equitable balance. The person with a message to communicate does a little more work to type it, while the receiver can read it easily and whenever convenient; thus, the primary beneficiary typically does a little more work.

- Compatibility with social practices: The essentially conversational format of electronic mail allows us to apply existing social conventions. However, there are differences, which lead to clearly identified problems such as "flaming" and "junk e-mail," and to more subtle but crucial problems described below.

- Exception-handling: the asynchronous, informal nature of most electronic mail makes it flexible, although mail applications have been developed that impose more structure—and that may suffer accordingly [see the discussion of The Coordinator in Grudin, 1989a].

- Difficulty of evaluation: As with all groupware, the overall costs and benefits of electronic mail are difficult to assess.

- Poor intuitions for groupware: Our intuitions concerning electronic mail may be improving as its use spreads.

To summarize, electronic mail avoids most of the problems that hamper other groupware. Its use within organizations is spreading, although not with explosive speed. Its progress has been anomalous: less through the normal product development and marketing processes than by spreading from academic and public sources. Understanding why this is true may be the key to understanding the future of groupware and the impact of information technology on organizations.

The key user distinction for electronic mail in most organizations is not that of sender and receiver, it is that of manager and subordinate. In fact, this is likely to be the key distinction for any groupware application, not because the technology itself recognizes the supervisor-subordinate distinction, but because that distinction is so critical in the workplace itself. The reception of technology in an organization is determined by the distinctions found in the workplace; to understand this, we must free ourselves from a bias to focus on the distinctions designed into the technology.

In hierarchic organizations, the types of work done by managers and by workers are quite different—as are the rewards. In the United States in particular, we tend to downplay these differences. We often aim for collaboration between labor and management. But some tension exists in organizations large enough to support and profit from electronic mail, and even where tension isn't evident, the roles of manager and subordinate differ.

Unlike the other groupware applications discussed, electronic mail does not selectively benefit managers or decision-makers. In fact, the contrary is probably true. The asynchronous nature of electronic mail may bother managers whose time is tightly budgeted: "Mostly, a lot of times, I won't respond. I'll print the message and stick it in their file and wait until their weekly meeting," one manager noted in an interview. The ability for anyone to disseminate information rapidly can create new and not always welcome challenges for managers, whose jobs often involve filtering and routing information. In a classic bureaucracy, lateral communication is minimized—information flows up and down through the hierarchy. Managers are aware of everything entering or leaving their groups. The resulting inflexibility can lead to inefficiency; rigid bureaucracies, from the Soviet Union to the U.S. Navy, abound with tales of undercover exchange systems devised to cope with this inefficiency. Electronic mail, like the telephone on each worker's desk, supports more efficient lateral communication—but it is threatening to the bureaucratic organization and creates difficulties for managers who rely on the hierarchical organizational model.

For example, one managerial responsibility is to absorb information from higher levels and tailor its presentation to subordinates to maximize their understanding or obtain a desired response. If a manager receives such information electronically, it is easier to forward it without such tailoring. In fact, editing may be counterproductive, because other electronic versions of the message may exist and may be forwarded laterally into the group, immediately revealing any tampering. This places the manager in a no-win situation. Similarly, the ability of anyone to send a message instantly to everyone in an organization creates a volatility that management must cope with.

In a powerful essay based on field studies, Constance Perin [1988] makes a convincing case that "these electronic social formations represent new sources of industrial conflict . . . they are seen as subverting legitimated organizational structures." While noting the collective value of electronic communication to large organizations, Perin describes how it comes into conflict with traditional organizational practice. For example, "the very 'invisibility' of electronic social fields, which may be cultivated bureaucratically because they are believed to enhance productivity, also delegitimates them and becomes the source of managerial negativism and suspicion." A case study by Fanning and Raphael [1986], cited by Perin, concludes that electronic mail "is simply not a management tool, if by management we mean those above the level of project leader . . . . a medium which allows widely separated people to aggregate their needs is, in fact, quite frightening. Some managers correctly foresee that such a system can be most upsetting to the current established order, and do not participate in it as a result."

Where does this leave electronic mail and the groupware that builds on it? Although Perin describes cases of individual managers discouraging or terminating its use, many large organizations have assumed an overall benefit and have successfully introduced electronic mail. Many students and professionals are growing accustomed to it. Thus, the forces Perin describes are likely to play themselves out over time, eroding management control and changing the nature of organizations. Some organizations were designed according to notions of efficiency and control that are quickly becoming outmoded; finding new organizational forms, and minimizing the cost of shifting to them, are challenges for the near future.

Implications for Organizational Change

In summary, by enhancing communication, worker-centered groupware will tend to undermine the authority structure of those hierarchic organizations with relatively incomplete standardization of work processes. Furthermore, the resulting decentralization of control will *further reduce* the prospects for success of groupware that selectively benefits management—which includes most groupware being developed today. Management that has lost some of its ability to control events may find it more difficult to mandate the use of applications that benefit management at the expense of other workers. Thus, successful groupware products may be those whose use clearly benefits subordinates; one example is a group decision support system that is used as part of a *process* that is designed to ensure benefits to all participants, in particular to those usually disadvantaged in meetings [e.g., McGoff, cited in Grudin, 1989a]. In particular, there is promise for groupware that builds on electronic mail, such as the Object Lens system [Lai and Malone, 1988], whose users can fill in message templates and other forms to filter or share information in varied, flexible ways.

The changes in organizations and societies that are eventually traced to technological innovation have rarely been predicted; the effects of groupware will surely follow that pattern. However, we can look for signs of specific changes that may occur. The two examples below suggest how the success of electronic mail may lead to the reorganization of work processes and the birth of new organizational forms.

FROM HACKER CONSULTING TO PURE ADHOCRACY

In *Hackers,* Steven Levy [1984] describes the birth and death in the 1960s and 1970s of the "hacker ethic," central to which was the view that "all information should be free"—including the engineering designs, product plans, and software that were at one time freely exchanged in computer laboratories and clubs. The book charts the erosion of this ethic as one after another of these forms of information became commercially important.

Although different kinds of information are now involved, today's electronic bulletin boards and mail networks support extensive consulting activity. For many users, access is free or inexpensive. By 1985, the capability for using such networks to guide research, development, and even marketing had been noted [Perlman, 1985]. The flow of information through them is reminiscent of the hacker ethic—one can pose a question and get free advice, some of it of high quality.

The commercial potential increases as networks rapidly expand and interconnect. Following the precedents described by Levy, network "hacking" may yield to commercial exploitation—to network-based consulting organizations that go well beyond existing on-line newsletters, extending the electronic market concept [Malone et al., 1987]. A central service may screen consultants, route requests for services, possibly oversee contracts, and monitor problems. An exchange could lead to an individual contract or to the assembly of a team for specific work, drawn from available and qualified individuals on the net. A project might rely on electronic mediation or might bring participants together for a limited time. An early example is Photosource International, a business run from a farmhouse. Photosource International brings together professional photographers and their customers, primarily publishers of newspapers, magazines, and books. Initially a paper newsletter, it now uses networks to reach about 40 percent of its customers. Photo buyers submit descriptions of photos or assignments to one of three distribution lists, based on price range. In addition to providing the forum, Photosource International uses feedback from photo sellers to rate photo buyer performance and requests evidence of professional history from sellers who wish to appear on the highest-level distribution list. Ultimately, specialized network-based services of this type may consolidate, enabling multidisciplinary teams to be assembled electronically.

This generalization of a consulting company is an extreme form of "adhocracy," an organizational structure that "is able to fuse experts drawn from different specialties into smoothly functioning project teams," [Mintzberg, 1984]. Adhocracies include present-day consulting, advertising, and film companies. They are highly decentralized organizations of professionals deployed in small teams in response to changing conditions in dynamic, complex environments. The adhocracy is the organizational type that least adheres to traditional management principles, relying on constant contact to coordinate among teams. Electronic mail should increase the efficiency of an adhocracy, rather than threatening it as it threatens the hierarchic, bureaucratic organization.

THE IVORY TOWER GETS A SILICON FINISH

A good place to look for portents of change is the research university, where some departments have pioneered the use of electronic mail. There are suggestions that a significant transformation in research and higher education is underway. The forces at work have parallels in other technologies, so first consider some better-understood influences of several advances that preceded the computer.

Technologies—transportation, print, film, telephone, radio, television—have eroded traditional social and cultural barriers, as captured in McLuhan's concept of the global village. For example, as a college freshman twenty years ago, I shared a dormitory with students from many regions of the United States. We discovered a large common experience that transcended geography and even social class; specific television programming was the most easily recognized factor, with wide-scale product distribution and other influences also evident. This revolution continues as the technological infrastructure spreads over the globe. The Vietnam War was brought into the American home two decades ago; China's recent embrace of travel and electronic media shaped the 1989 student strike.

However, a counteracting tendency works against homogenization. Telephones allow corporate headquarters to be geographically removed from manufacturing plants, automobiles allow social restratification into urban-suburban groupings, and with cable and the relaxation of government monopolies in television, greater choice again allows people to regroup or diverge. Electronic mail and bulletin boards provide almost unlimited specialization according to personal interests, thus contributing to this reorganization.

Campuses have been to some extent communities apart, "ivory towers" focused on research and learning, distanced from local influences. As a result, to produce peers with whom to discuss ideas and collaborate, research faculty have had to take the time to explain the foundation of their own work to students and colleagues, including those with different specialties or from different departments. Building a common understanding, a mutual set of interests, was an effortful but necessary part of being a community of scholars. No longer is this true. A researcher with access to electronic mail (plus more journals, more conferences, FAX, and lower telephone costs) can contact a large number of researchers at other institutions who already have very closely matched interests. One can easily obtain high-quality feedback on ideas without investing the time to educate students or colleagues.

Geographic proximity is still an important factor in full-fledged scientific collaboration [Kraut et al., 1988], but electronic mail and broader bandwidth groupware successors may change that. Two-party exchanges between colleagues with an established common purpose and active electronic group discussions are widespread, especially in computer science departments. The resulting efficiency of communication, which is likely to spread quickly through the academic world, can accelerate research progress tremendously. One drawback is that interdisciplinary cross-fertilization may be reduced as this capability for specialization is utilized and extended. Another likely consequence is a dramatically increased polarization of research and teaching functions, with advanced instruction itself occurring more through electronic exchange and with a new approach to basic instruction that has yet to evolve.

Acknowledgments

My understanding of the significance of electronic mail was greatly abetted by Constance Perin and my need to keep working on it was patiently pointed out by Liam Bannon. Don Norman, Jim Hollan, Steve Poltrock, Will Hill, and Wayne Wilner commented usefully on an early draft.

Sermons
Introduction

OUR PROFESSION, ALTHOUGH YOUNG, has its share of celebrities. **Brenda Laurel**
At our authors' conference at Asilomar, we made a collaborative timeline
that showed the things in each author's life that most influenced his or her
ideas and career in interface design. Some were events—the moon landing
(or for some of us "senior citizens," the first manned spaceflight), the
introduction of the Atari VCS, or the film *2001*. Some were places—Xerox
PARC, SRI, the Media Lab, Atari Research. On almost everyone's list were
the names of a few people with whom the author's first encounter—reading
a paper or meeting the individual in person—had a profound effect: "Interface heroes" like Vannevar Bush, Douglas Engelbart, Alan Kay, Don
Norman, Ted Nelson, Larry Tesler, Ivan Sutherland, or Nicholas Negroponte.

The seven chapters in this section are the voices of people whose work
and points of view have deeply influenced some or all of us in the way that
we think about human-computer interaction. The views and styles represented in this section are diverse and often contradictory. We include them
here as a way of sharing ideas and perspectives that can encourage thought,
argument, and inspiration.

About the Contributors

"Father of the personal computer" is a title Alan Kay disclaims, but many
acknowledge that it was his ideas that succeeded in getting industry's

Alan Kay

Donald A. Norman

attention for the concept. It was at the Xerox Palo Alto Research Center (PARC) that Kay conceived of Dynabook, the powerful lap-sized personal computer of the 1980s to come that would allow people to draw and write anywhere. Dynabook was the inspiration for Alto, the forerunner of Macintosh. Another particularly celebrated contribution was Smalltalk, a very high-level object-oriented programming language used by nonprogrammers. Kay pioneered the use of icons instead of typed words for telling computers what to do next. Kay received his Ph.D. in 1969 from the University of Utah. He joined the artificial intelligence project at Stanford and in 1970 became a founding principal at PARC, where he remained for ten years. Since Xerox, he has worked at Atari, where he was chief scientist, and at Apple Computer, where he is currently an Apple Fellow, one of a few select scientists who have an independent charter to pursue far-out ideas for Apple's future. Beyond computers, music is Kay's special passion. He has been a professional jazz musician, composer, and has built several musical instruments.

Donald A. Norman is Professor and Chair of the Department of Cognitive Science at the University of California, San Diego. The theoretical scope of his work is broad, aimed at developing strong foundations for the study of mind. His applied work focuses on what he calls "cognitive engineering," which studies how best to make systems and devices understandable and usable by a wide range of people. Norman's current research examines the design of cognitive artifacts that extend human cognitive capabilities and allow people to perform activities where the knowledge and skills required for a task are distributed among people and machines and across time and space. He has authored eight books, including *User-Centered System Design* (which he edited with Steve Draper) and *The Psychology of Everyday Things* (the paperback version is entitled *The Design of Everyday Things*).

Ben Shneiderman

Ben Shneiderman is Head of the Human-Computer Interaction Laboratory, Professor of Computer Science, and Member of the Institute Advanced Computer Studies, all at the University of Maryland, College Park. He is the co-author, with Greg Kearsley, of the recently published hyper-book/disk *Hypertext Hands-On!* and author of *Designing the User Interface* and *Software Psychology*. Dr. Shneiderman is editor of the Ablex Publishers series on Human-Computer Interaction, author of 120 technical papers, and creator of the Hyperties hypertext system. He is an international lecturer and consultant for many organizations, including Apple, AT&T, IBM, Library of Congress, and NASA.

Jean-Louis Gassée, former president, Apple Products, joined Apple Computer, Inc., in February, 1981. He was responsible for managing all of Apple's product functions globally, including product marketing, worldwide manufacturing, and research and development. Under his leadership as founding general manager, Apple France became Apple's largest international subsidiary. Before joining Apple, Gassée was president and general manager of the French subsidiary of Exxon Office Systems. He also has held several management positions with Data General. During his six years at Hewlett-Packard, Gassée was responsible for overseeing the launching the company's first desktop scientific computer and the development of its sales organization in Europe. A graduate of the Faculty of Sciences, a math and physics university in Orsay, France, Gassée holds a master's of science degree.

Jean-Louis Gassée

Dr. Timothy Leary is one of the most accomplished and influential liars of the 20th century. During the 1950s he managed to invent and publish inflammatory fabrications about inner potential, self-help, interpersonal relations, and linguistic determinism. In the 60s he circulated subversive concoctions about consciousness alteration, self-directed brain change, and personal reality construction. In the 70s his seditious misstatements led to his being exiled and imprisoned for seven years. In spite of this correctional rehabilitation, he published six books that touted treasonous inventions about reimprinting, neuropolitics, and the neurogenetics of personal migration. In the 80s he broadcast extravagant fictions about the personal computer as an appliance for consciousness change and interpersonal communication. All of these lies, creations, and fabrications were allegedly designed to encourage individuals to think for themselves and question authority. He is, it must be granted, not alone in these disreputable and disrespectful activities.

Theodor Holm Nelson is a philosopher, filmmaker, author, and designer of interactive systems for personal computers. Nelson coined the terms *hypertext* and *hypermedia* in the early 1960s. He has worked in dolphin research, publishing, and in various university departments. His principal work since 1960 has been concerned with the design and development of open hypertext publishing and the Xanadu™ information server. His classic

Dr. Timothy Leary.
Photo: Alice Springs

Theodor Holm Nelson

Nicholas Negroponte

books, including *Computer Lib/Dream Machines, Literary Machines,* and *The Home Computer Revolution,* continue to provide conversion experiences for their readers. Nelson holds a B.A. in philosophy from Swarthmore and an M.A. in sociology from Harvard. He is presently a Distinguished Fellow at Autodesk, Inc., in Sausalito, California.

Nicholas Negroponte is Professor of Media Technology and Director of the Media Laboratory at the Massachusetts Institute of Technology. Negroponte, along with Jerome Wiesner, President Emeritus of MIT, founded the Media Laboratory in 1985. Before founding the laboratory, Negroponte had been an MIT Professor of Computer Graphics and was the founder and director of MIT's Architecture Machine Group, working on computer-aided design and videodisc technologies. Negroponte has been with MIT as an instructor, assistant professor, and professor since 1966. His other academic affiliations include visiting professorships at the University of California at Berkeley, the University of Michigan, and Yale University. He served as the executive director of the World Center for Personal Computation and Human Development in Paris, and was the Chairman of Computers in Everyday Life with the International Federation of Information Procuring Societies in Amsterdam. Among the books he has authored are the award-winning *The Architecture Machine,* as well as *Soft Architecture Machines, Computer Aids to Design and Architecture,* and *Human Interface* (published in Japanese only).

User Interface:
A Personal View

WHEN I WAS ASKED to write this chapter, my first reaction was "A book on user interface design—does that mean it's now a real subject?" Well, as of 1989, it's still yes and no. User interface has certainly been a hot topic for discussion since the advent of the Macintosh. Everyone seems to want user interface but they are not sure whether they should order it by the yard or by the ton. Many are just now discovering that user interface is not a sandwich spread—applying the Macintosh style to poorly designed applications and machines is like trying to put Béarnaise sauce on a hotdog!

Of course the practice of user interface design has been around at least since humans invented tools. The unknown designer who first put a haft on a hand axe was trying not just to increase leverage but also to make it an extension of the *arm*, not just the fist. The evolutionary designer whom Richard Dawkins calls the Blind Watchmaker [Dawkins, 1986] has been at it much longer; all of life's startling interfitness is the result. A more recent byproduct of the industrial revolution called *ergonomics* in Europe and *human factors* in the U.S. has studied how the human body uses senses and limbs to work with tools. From the earliest use of interactive computing in the fifties—mostly for air traffic control and defense—there have been attempts at user interface design and application of ergonomic principles. Many familiar components of modern user interface design appeared in the fifties and early sixties, including pointing devices, windows, menus, icons, gesture recognition, hypermedia, the first personal computer, and

Alan Kay

Apple Fellow
Apple Computer, Inc.

more. There was even a beautifully designed user interface for an end-user system in JOSS—but its significance was appreciated only by its designer and users.

Therefore, let me argue that the actual dawn of user interface design first happened when computer designers finally noticed, not just that end users had functioning minds, but that a better understanding of how those minds worked would completely shift the paradigm of interaction.

This enormous change in point of view happened to many computerists in the late sixties, especially in the ARPA research community. Everyone had their own catalyst. For me it was the FLEX machine, an early desktop personal computer of the late sixties designed by Ed Cheadle and myself.

Based on much previous work by others, it had a tablet as a pointing device, a high-resolution display for text and animated graphics, and multiple windows, and it directly executed a high-level object-oriented end-user simulation language. And of course it had a "user interface," but one that repelled end users instead of drawing them closer to the hearth. I recently revisited the FLEX machine design and was surprised to find how modern its components were—even a use of icon-like structures to access previous work.

But the combination of ingredients didn't gel. It was like trying to bake a pie from random ingredients in a kitchen: baloney instead of apples, ground-up Cheerios instead of flour, etc.

Then, starting in the summer of 1968, I got hit on the head randomly but repeatedly by some really nifty work. The first was just a little piece of glass at the University of Illinois. But the glass had tiny glowing dots that showed text characters. It was the first flat-screen display. I and several other grad students wondered when the surface could become large and inexpensive enough to be a useful display. We also wondered when the FLEX machine silicon could become small enough to fit on the back of the display. The answer to both seemed to be the late seventies or early eighties. Then we could all have an inexpensive powerful notebook computer—I called it a "personal computer" then, but I was thinking *intimacy*.

I read McLuhan's *Understanding Media* [1964] and understood that the most important thing about any communications medium is that message receipt is really message recovery; anyone who wishes to receive a message embedded in a medium must first have internalized the medium so it can be "subtracted" out to leave the message behind. When he said "the medium is the message" he meant that you have to *become* the medium if you use it.

That's pretty scary. It means that even though humans are the animals that shape tools, it is in the nature of tools and man that learning to use tools reshapes us. So the "message" of the printed book is, first, its availability to individuals, hence, its potential detachment from extant social processes; second, the uniformity, even coldness of noniconic type, which detaches readers from the vividness of the now and the slavery of commonsense thought to propel them into a far more abstract realm in which ideas that don't have easy visualizations can be treated.

McLuhan's claim that the printing press was the dominant force that transformed the hermeneutic Middle Ages into our scientific society should not be taken too lightly—especially because the main point is that the press didn't do it just by making books more available, it did it by changing the thought patterns of those who learned to read.

Though much of what McLuhan wrote was obscure and arguable, the sum total to me was a shock that reverberates even now. The computer is a medium! I had always thought of it as a tool, perhaps a vehicle—a much weaker conception. What McLuhan was saying is that if the personal computer is a truly new medium then the very use of it would actually change the thought patterns of an entire civilization. He had certainly been right about the effects of the electronic stained-glass window that was television—a remedievalizing tribal influence at best. The intensely interactive and involving nature of the personal computer seemed an antiparticle that could annihilate the passive boredom invoked by television. But it also promised to surpass the book to bring about a new kind of renaissance by going beyond static representations to dynamic simulation. What kind of a thinker would you become if you grew up with an active simulator connected, not just to one point of view, but to all the points of view of the ages represented so they could be dynamically tried out and compared? I named the notebook-sized computer idea the Dynabook to capture McLuhan's metaphor in the silicon to come.

Shortly after reading McLuhan, I visited Wally Feurzeig, Seymour Papert, and Cynthia Solomon at one of the earliest LOGO tests within a school. I was amazed to see children writing programs (often recursive) that generated poetry, created arithmetic environments, and translated English into Pig Latin. And they were just starting to work with the new wastepaper-basket-sized turtle that roamed over sheets of butcher paper making drawings with its pen.

I was possessed by the analogy between print literacy and LOGO. While designing the FLEX machine I had believed that end users needed to be able to program before the computer could become truly theirs—but here was a real demonstration, and with children! The ability to "read" a medium means you can *access* materials and tools created by others. The ability to "write" in a medium means you can *generate* materials and tools for others. You must have both to be literate. In print writing, the tools you generate are rhetorical; they demonstrate and convince. In computer writing, the tools you generate are processes; they simulate and decide.

If the computer is only a vehicle, perhaps you can wait until high school to give "driver's ed" on it—but if it's a medium, then it must be extended all the way into the world of the child. How to do it? Of course it has to be done on the intimate notebook-sized Dynabook! But how would anyone "read" the Dynabook, let alone "write" on it?

LOGO showed that a special language designed with the end user's characteristics in mind could be more successful than a random hack. How had Papert learned about the nature of children's thought? From Jean Piaget, the doyen of European cognitive psychologists [see Piaget, 1926, 1928, and 1952]. One of his most important contributions is the idea that children go through several distinctive intellectual stages as they develop from birth to maturity. Much can be accomplished if the nature of the stages is heeded and much grief to the child can be caused if the stages are ignored. Piaget noticed a kinesthetic stage, a visual stage, and a symbolic stage. An example is that children in the visual stage, when shown a squat glass of water poured into a tall thin one, will say there is more water in the tall thin one even though the pouring was done in front of their eyes.

One of the ways Papert used Piaget's ideas was to realize that young children are not well equiped to do "standard" symbolic mathematics until the age of 11 or 12, but that even very young children can do other kinds of math, even advanced math such as topology and differential geometry, when it is presented in a form that is well matched to their current thinking processes. The LOGO turtle with its local coordinate system (like the child, it is always at the center of its universe) became a highly successful "microworld" for exploring ideas in differential geometry.

This approach made a big impression on me and got me to read many more psychology books. Most (including Piaget's) were not very useful, but then I discovered Jerome Bruner's *Towards a Theory of Instruction* [1966]. He had repeated and verified many of Piaget's results, and in the process came up with a different and much more powerful way to interpret what Piaget had seen. For example, in the water-pouring experiment, after the child asserted there was more water in the tall thin glass, Bruner covered it up with a card and asked again. This time the child said, "There must be the same because where would the water go?" When Bruner took away the card to again reveal the tall thin glass, the child immediately changed back to saying there was more water.

When the cardboard was again interposed the child changed yet again. It was as though one set of processes was doing the reasoning when the child could see the situation, and another set was employed when the child could not see. Bruner's interpretation of experiments like these is one of the most important foundations for human-related design. Our mentalium seems to be made up of multiple separate mentalities with very different characteristics. They reason differently, have different skills, and often are in conflict. Bruner identified a separate mentality with each of Piaget's stages: he called them *enactive, iconic, symbolic*. While not ignoring the existence of other mentalities, he concentrated on these three to come up with what are still some of the strongest ideas for creating learning-rich environments.

The work of Papert convinced me that whatever user interface design might be, it was solidly intertwined with learning. Bruner convinced me that learning takes place best environmentally and roughly in stage order—it is best to learn something kinesthetically, then iconically, and finally the intuitive knowledge will be in place that will allow the more powerful but less vivid symbolic processes to work at their strongest. This led me over the years to the pioneers of environmental learning: Montessori Method, Suzuki Violin [Suzuki, 1969], and Tim Gallwey's *Inner Game of Tennis* [1974], to name just a few.

My point here is that as soon as I was ready to look deeply at the human element, and especially after being convinced that the heart of the matter lay with Bruner's multiple mentality model, I found the knowledge landscape positively festooned with already accomplished useful work. It was like the man in Moliere's *Bourgeois Gentilhomme* who discovered that all his life he had been speaking prose! I suddenly remembered McLuhan: "I don't know who discovered water but it wasn't a fish." Because it is in part the duty of consciousness to represent ourselves to ourselves as simply as possible, we should sorely distrust our commonsense self view. It is likely that this mirrors-within-mirrors problem in which we run into a misleading commonsense notion about ourselves at every turn is what forced psychology to be one of the most recent sciences—if indeed it yet is.

Now, if we agree with the evidence that the human cognitive facilities are made up of a *doing* mentality, an *image* mentality, and a *symbolic* mentality, then any user interface we construct should at least cater to the mechanisms that seem to be there. But how? One approach is to realize that no single mentality offers a complete answer to the entire range of thinking and problem solving. User interface design should integrate them at least as well as Bruner did in his spiral curriculum ideas.

One of the implications of the Piaget-Bruner decomposition is that the mentalities originated at very different evolutionary times and there is little probability that they can intercommunicate and synergize in more than the most rudimentary fashion. In fact, the mentalities are more likely to interfere with each other as they compete for control. The study by Hadamard on math and science creativity [1945] and others on music and the arts indicate strongly that creativity in these areas is not at all linked to the symbolic mentality (as most theories of teaching suppose), but that the important work in creative areas is done in the the initial two mentalities—most in the iconic (or figurative) and quite a bit in the enactive. The groundbreaking work by Tim Gallwey on the "inner game" [1974] showed what could be done if interference were removed (mentalities not relevant to the learning were distracted) and attention was facilitated (the mentalities that could actually do the learning were focused more strongly on the environment).

Finally, in the 60s a number of studies showed just how modeful was a mentality that had "seized control"—particularly the analytical-problem-solving one (which identifies most strongly with the Bruner symbolic mentality). For example, after working on five analytic tasks in a row, if a problem was given that was trivial to solve figuratively, the solver could be blocked for hours trying to solve it symbolically. This makes quite a bit of sense when you consider that the main jobs of the three mentalities are:

enactive   know where you are, manipulate
iconic   recognize, compare, configure, concrete
symbolic   tie together long chains of reasoning, abstract

The visual system's main job is to be interested in everything in a scene, to dart over it as one does with a bulletin board, to change context. The symbolic system's main job is to stay with a context and to make indirect connections. Imagine what it would be like if it were reversed. If the visual system looked at the object it first saw in the morning for five hours straight! Or if the symbolic system couldn't hold a thought for more than a few seconds at a time!

It is easy to see that one of the main reasons that the figurative system is so creative is that it tends not to get blocked because of the constant flitting and darting. The chance of finding an interesting pattern is very high. It is not surprising, either, that many people who are "figurative" have extreme difficulty getting anything finished—there is always something new and interesting that pops up to distract. Conversely, the "symbolic" person is good at getting things done, because of the long focus on single contexts, but has a hard time being creative, or even being a good problem solver, because of the extreme tendency to get blocked. In other words, because none of the mentalities is supremely useful to the exclusion of the others, the best strategy would be to try to gently force synergy between them in the user interface design.

Out of all this came the main slogan I coined to express this goal:

Doing with Images makes Symbols

The slogan also implies—as did Bruner—that one should start with—be grounded in—the concrete "Doing with Images," and be carried into the more abstract "makes Symbols."

All the ingredients were already around. We were ready to notice what the theoretrical frameworks from other fields of Bruner, Gallwey, and others were trying to tell us. What is surprising to me is just how long it took to put it all together. After Xerox PARC provided the opportunity to turn these ideas into reality, it still took our group about five years and experiments with hundreds of users to come up with the first practical design that was in accord with Bruner's model and really worked.

DOING with	mouse	*enactive*	know where you are, manipulate
IMAGES	icons, windows	*iconic*	recognize, compare, configure, concrete
makes **SYMBOLS**	Smalltalk	*symbolic*	tie together long chains of reasoning, abstract

Part of the reason perhaps was that the theory was much better at confirming that an idea was good than at actually generating the ideas. In fact, in certain areas like "iconic programming," it actually held back progress, for example, the simple use of icons as signs, because the siren's song of trying to do symbolic thinking iconically was just too strong.

Some of the smaller areas were obvious and found their place in the framework immediately. Probably the most intuitive was the idea of multiple overlapping windows. NLS had multiple panes, FLEX had multiple windows, and the bit-map display that we thought was too small, but that was made from individual pixels, led quickly to the idea that windows could appear to overlap. The contrastive ideas of Bruner suggested that there should always be a way to compare. The flitting-about nature of the iconic mentality suggested that having as many resources showing on the screen as possible would be a good way to encourage creativity and problem solving and prevent blockage. An *intuitive* way to use the windows was to activate the window that the mouse was in and bring it to the "top." This interaction was *modeless* in a special sense of the word. The active window constituted a mode to be sure—one window might hold a painting kit, another might hold text—but one could get to the next window to do something in *without any special termination*. This is what *modeless* came to mean for me—the user could always get to the next thing desired without any backing out. The contrast of the nice modeless interactions of windows with the clumsy command syntax of most previous systems directly suggested that everything should be made modeless. Thus began a campaign to "get rid of modes."

The object-oriented nature of Smalltalk was very suggestive. For example, *object-oriented* means that the object knows what it can do. In the abstract symbolic arena, it means we should first write the object's name (or whatever will fetch it) and then follow with a message it can understand that asks it to do something. In the concrete user-interface arena, it suggests that we should select the object first. It can then furnish us with a menu of what it is willing to do. In both cases we have the *object* first and the *desire* second. This unifies the concrete with the abstract in a highly satisfying way.

The most difficult area to get to be modeless was a very tiny one, that of elementary text editing. How to get rid of "insert" and "replace" modes that had plagued a decade of editors? Several people arrived at the solution simultaneously. My route came as the result of several beginning programmer adults who were having trouble building a paragraph editor in Smalltalk, a problem I thought should be easy. Over a weekend I built a sample paragraph editor whose main simplification was that it eliminated the distinction between insert, replace, and delete by allowing selections to extend *between* the characters. Thus, there could be a zero-width selection, and thus every operation could be a replace. "Insert" meant replace the zero-width selection. "Delete" meant replace the selection with a zero-width string of characters. I got the tiny one-page program running in Smalltalk and came in crowing over the victory. Larry Tesler thought it was great and showed me the idea, already working in his new Gypsy editor (which he implemented on the basis of a suggestion from Peter Deutsch). So much for creativity and invention when ideas are in the air. As Goethe noted, the most important thing is to enjoy the thrill of discovery rather than to make vain attempts to claim priority!

Quo Userus Interfacus?

Or, now that the Mac way of doing things has taken hold, will we ever be able to get rid of it? If the IBM 3270/PC way of doing things is "machine code," doesn't that make the Mac the COBOL of user interface designs?

One way to look at the prospects for improvement in the future is to consider user interface as just another ripple in the main current of human extension over the past several hundred thousand years. As I see it, we humans have extended ourselves in two main ways. The first to leap to anyone's mind is the creation of *tools*—physical tools like hammers and wheels and figurative mental tools like language and mathematics. To me, these are all extensions of gesture and grasp. Even mathematics, which is sometimes thought of as forbiddingly vague, is actually a way to take notions that are too abstract for our senses and make them into little symbols that we can move around. The M-word for tools is *manipulation*. The second way we have extended ourselves is more subtle. Lewis Mumford points out that for most of our history the most complicated machines constructed by humans have mostly had humans as moving parts [Mumford, 1934 and 1967–70]. In other words, we are creatures who both like to convince others to work on our goals and are willing to be convinced in turn to work on the goals of others. Mumford calls these structures megamachines; I call the process goal cloning. The M-word here is *management*. We manipulate tools but manage people.

Both of these ideas were applied early to computer-user interface designs. So far in this chapter we have been discussing tool-based ideas, because the Macintosh is the most well known of all tool-based interfaces. Yes, there is still considerable life in the computer-based tool that is manipulated, but it is starting to drown in incremental "enhancements." It took Hercules a considerable time to clean the Augean stables, and it may take just as long to get the next real step in tool-based design. As always, the key is to forget the vividness of the present and to get back to basic principles that are centered directly on the human condition. As is often the case, it is not how well we can learn but how well we can *unlearn* that will make the difference. We have to discard fondly held notions that have sneakily become myths while we weren't watching. An old adage is that no biological organism can live in its own waste products—and that seems just as true for computer designs. If things continue as they are now going, we will soon be able to see the original Lisa and Mac as an improvement on their successors!

One of the most compelling snares is the use of the term *metaphor* to describe a correspondence between what the users see on the screen and how they should think about what they are manipulating. My main complaint is that *metaphor* is a poor metaphor for what needs to be done. At PARC we coined the phrase *user illusion* to describe what we were about when designing user interface. There are clear connotations to the stage, theatrics, and magic—all of which give much stronger hints as to the direction to be followed. For example, the screen as "paper to be marked on" is a metaphor that suggests pencils, brushes, and typewriting. Fine, as far as it goes. But it is the magic—understandable magic—that really counts. Should we transfer the paper metaphor so perfectly that the screen is as hard as paper to erase and change? Clearly not. If it is to be like magical paper, then it is the *magical* part that is all important and that must be most strongly attended to in the user interface design.

While the magic is being designed, the very idea of a paper "metaphor" should be scrutinized mercilessly. One of the most wonderful properties of a computer is that no matter how many dimensions one's information has, a computer representation can always supply at least one more. One result is that any seeming distance between items in our world of limited dimension can be competely "disappeared."

This is something that Vannevar Bush and his chief prophet Doug Englebart noticed immediately, and hypermedia was born. In a world of Dynabooks, information will not be printed—it would destroy most of the useful associations—and something much more than superpaper will emerge. The notion of hypermedia is much more a "user illusion" than a "metaphor."

Let me attack a few more sacred cows. For example, the desktop "metaphor." I don't want a screen that is much like my physical desk. It just gets messy—yet I hate to clean up while in the middle of a project. And I'm usually working on lots of different projects at the same time. At PARC they used to accuse me of filling up a desk until it was uselessly tangled and then abandoning it for another one! One solution to this is "project views" as originally implemented by Dan Ingalls in Smalltalk-76. Again, this is more of a user illusion than a metaphor. Each area holds all the tools and materials for a particular project and is automatically suspended when you leave it. A bit like multiple desks—but it is the magic that is truly important. Here the magic is that every change to the system that is made while in a project area—no matter how deeply made to the system (even changing the meaning of integer "+"!)—is logged locally to the project area. Yet each of the project areas are parallel processes that can communicate with one another. This is a user illusion that is easy to understand yet doesn't map well to the physical world.

How about the folder? One of my longstanding pet hates is to have them behave anything like their physical counterparts. For example, as they existed in Officetalk, Star, Lisa, and Mac—like real folders—there is only one icon for a document or application and it can be in only one folder. This drives me crazy, because the probability of *not* finding what you are looking for by browsing has just been maximized! It is trivial to have as many icon instances for a given doc or app in as many folders as one wishes. They should be near any place where they might be useful. (Dragging a singleton out on the desktop is not a solution to this problem!) But even if that were fixed we have to ask: why a folder? Instead of passive containers, why not have active retrievers that are constantly trying to capture icon instances that are relevant to them? Let's call them *bins*. Imagine having a "memos" bin that, whenever and wherever you make up a memo, captures a copy of the doc icon. You might have a "memos to boss" bin that automatically captures only those icons of docs sent to your boss. Folders kill browsing. Bins extend its useful range.

That wonderful system, HyperCard, in spite of its great ideas, has some "metaphors" that set my teeth on edge. Four of them are "stack," "card," "field," and "button." In "stack" we find grievously unnecessary limitations, not the least of which is the strange notion that only one stack can be in front of us at a time.[1] This is not just imitating paper with a vengeance—it is building in a limitation not imposed by the physical world. Thus, when we need to get "help" we are forced away from the very image we need help with in order to delve into the help stack—and this on the very machine that first successfully introduced multiple windows to the commercial world!

Again, to echo a previous complaint about folders and icons, we can't

---

[1] This is no longer true in HyperCard version 2.0.

directly have a card in more than one stack—this is partly because stacks serve some of the purpose of a class in an object-oriented language. However, this confounds the use of a stack as a set or collection of useful items. Being able to copy a card into a new stack doesn't count, because it is dynamic fidelity we are interested in most of the time.

Finally, in spite of their obvious similarities, stacks, cards, buttons, fields, and values are all quite separate entities. So a card can't contain a stack. A variable can't contain a stack, card, field, or button (or anything but a string value). You can paint on a card but you can't paint on a button. You can make a button or field a different size and move it around but you can't do this with a card. And so forth.

Here the metaphors have almost completely sunk the magic.

Why not just have one kind of object that can contain objects? The objects can be contained sequentially (relative to their before-after objects) or randomly (relative to their containing object). All the objects are sensitive to the mouse and messages, and are scripted. "Stacks" and "fields" are just objects as sequential containers. "Cards" are objects as random containers, themselves contained in a sequential "stack" container. "Buttons" are just small painted cards. And so on. Often design is best done not by adding features but by consolidating them into a more unitary concept.

Perhaps even more frustrating is the metaphor as a siren's song. The one that has led me the farthest without satisfying results has been the attempt to use icons for generative literacy—end-user programming. By the late sixties, the use of icons as signs in computer graphics had been in practice for years. Informally, they seemed to work much better than labels. Semiotics provided one explanation. In semiotic theory a sign is not a word but actually constitutes an entire sentence. Thus, to the extent that the sign could be recognized, it was a very efficient way of saying something. The work by Haber [1970] suggested that it was easy for humans to learn iconic signs and that the image mentality was efficient in finding a given one from a bulletin-board-like collection. Several interactive systems were built using this idea. An early one in Smalltalk was the Shazam animation system in which all interaction was controlled by icons.

The difficulty—perhaps the snare—of icons lies in trying to go beyond their obvious efficiency as signifiers. I was probably the worst offender because I believed then (and still do) that the nirvana of personal computing comes when the end users can change their tools and build new ones without having to become professional-level programmers. I believed then (and still do) that the key is to find a context in which most of the things they want to do are as obvious as, say, moving furniture around in a house. And much of the key has to be iconic because it is the only system in which the end user doesn't have to remember dozens of facts and processes.

Almost everything to the iconic mentality is "before-after," like a bird building a nest. The current state of things suggests what to do next. Extensive top-down planning is not required—just squish things around until you like the total effect. Of course, in a playpen like that, plans do come to mind and can be useful. But major things have to be accomplished by bottom-up exploration with obvious ingredients or end-user programming will not come to pass.

Well, I still believe all this. The question is whether it can all be done iconically. Is it possible to perform one of those nifty Brunerian feats in which an entire cognitive area—the symbolic—is shifted to another—the iconic—to permit long chains of abstract construction to be carried out in a concrete world? I certainly thought so, and I have to admit still feel a great yearning as I write down the old dream. All I can say is that we and others came up with many interesting approaches over the years but none have successfully crossed the threshold to the end user.

One of the problems is how to get concrete signs to be more abstract without simply evoking the kinds of symbols used by the symbolic mentality. More difficult is how to introduce context in a domain whose great trait is its modeless context-freeness. In most iconic languages, it is much easier to write the patterns than it is to read them. One of the most interesting puzzles in iconic programming (and iconic communication in general) is why there is such a disparity between how understandable images are while they are actively being constructed and how obscure even one's own constructions can appear even the next day. I believe that the major reasons for this can be accounted for as a consequence of *semantic focus*—analogous to that of foveal vision, but having to do with the amount of meaning and connectivity that can be solved by looking at a diagram. A suggestive explanation is found in Minsky's and Papert's book *Perceptrons* [1969], where they show that certain diagrams are beyond the level of complexity that a perceptron of a given aperture can solve.

It is likely that our biological structures have similar limitations at the iconic syntax level. Two other factors also are at work. The first is a "semantic fovea"—an area limitation of content understanding quite analogous to the "perceptron" limitations having to do with simple connectivity. The second factor is a property of images in general—their unsortedness. In other words, unlike paragraphs and lists of words, images have no *a priori* order in which they should be understood. This means that someone coming onto an image from the outside has no strategy for solving it. Painters throughout history have built partial solutions into the paintings themselves, by organizing the compositions to move the viewer's eye about without their being consciously aware of the movement.

One learns strategies for certain types of images. In circuit diagram reading, for example, one often starts with the power supply or with certain obvious "subdiagrams" (such as an amplifier) and starts to ask and answer questions about the surrounding components.

It is obvious why constructing a diagram is much less difficult than trying to read one. During construction, one is controlling focus by looking only at the parts that seem relevant at the time. The general strategy of the diagram is already part of the context and doesn't have to be ferreted out. The analogy to writing prose is quite clear, but prose has the advantage that a writer can employ considerable foreshadowing and building up of context before getting to the main point. The scene can be set at will. Except for a few stereotypes, this is extremely difficult to do with an image. What does this imply for iconic communication?

First, that there are severe limitations on the complexity of the image that can be solved by the visual system. An image of any complexity must therefore be one that has already been learned—essentially as a single symbol—regardless of the apparent complexity of its parts. An image that consists of two or more already learned images cannot have much more than "an association" with its sibling images. Connections between the subimages are likely not to be interpreted correctly. It would not be surprising if the visual system were less able in this area than the mechanisms that solve noun phrases for natural language.

Although it is not fair to say that "iconic languages can't work" just because no one has been able to design a good one, it is likely that the above explanation is close to the truth. If so, a major new direction that should be taken is toward a *rhetoric* for programs expressed as something more like essays—or more accurately, in the hypermedia equivalent of an essay. In the T_EX books, Knuth has furnished us with several examples of a master programmer and writer in conjunction with WEB, a rhetorical program formatter, to produce outstandingly readable programs. The challenge would be to produce a language in which the *act* of programming produces within it an understandable explanation.

There is surely much more to be said about tool-based interfaces—it is clear that the few small ideas in the Mac have scarcely scratched the range of expression in our hundred-thousand-year odyssey of tool design. *Manipulation* is still vibrantly alive, not exhausted. But it is now time to consider *management* of intelligent computer processes as an inevitable partner to tool-based work and play. I trace the modern origin of this idea back to John McCarthy's *Advice Taker* of the late fifties, in which he points out that we will soon be living inside vast networked "information utilities" and will require an intelligent assistant to find resources useful to us. A retrieval "tool" won't do because no one wants to spend hours looking through hundreds of networks with trillions of potentially useful items. This is a job for intelligent background processes that can successfully clone their users' goals and then carry them out. Here we want to *indirectly manage agents*, not directly manipulate objects.

The technological forum for this paradigm shift in the 90s is easy to imagine. Intimate computers (ICs) will be commonplace—Dynabook-like and even smaller. The clumsy analog cellular telephone of today will quickly be replaced by digital cellular packet-switching in which all media can be equally well represented, and this mechanism will be an obligatory component of one's IC. The most dreary projections ensure at least 100 MIPS per user and it will likely be much more, some in the form of special "beyond the curve" MIPS for special tasks such as real-time 3-D graphics and speech recognition.

The only stumbling place for this onrushing braver new world is that all of its marvels will be very difficult to communicate with, because, as always, the user interface design that could make it all simple lags far, far behind. If *communication* is the watchword, then what do we communicate with and how do we do it? We communicate with:

- Our selves
- Our tools
- Our colleagues and others
- Our agents

Until now, personal computing has concentrated mostly on the first two. Let us now extend everything we do to be part of a *grand collaboration*—with one's self, one's tools, other humans, and increasingly, with *agents*: computer processes that act as guide, as coach, and as amanuensis. The user interface design will be the critical factor in the success of this new way to work and play on the computer. One of the implications is that the "network" will not be seen at all, but rather "felt" as a shift in capacity and range from that experienced via one's own hard disk.

Another less obvious implication is that electronic mail will eventually be a very secondary medium of communication—used primarily when schedules don't mesh, for general dissemination of information, and for those situations in which independent thinking is required, particularly at the onset of projects. Network services may very well start with e-mail, but their strategy will be of much wider scope, so that several years further on, e-mail will simply be seen as a seamless part of a much wider way to amplify the user's endeavors.

Another critical strategic element is to design the services as a testbed for future technologies. This is particularly important given the lack of developed precursor technologies. As an example, it will be some years before English understanding (via typing, let alone via speech) will be at a level to sustain general conversations and understand general commands as one would give to an assistant. But much can be done now with limited English understanding in the medium of electronic mail where real-time replies are not expected and the context is restricted: registering complaints, answering requests for information about products, and so forth.

Because we design and control the user interface we can set up situations in which the system can seem much more capable than it really is without having to say: "Ignore that man behind the curtain."

Why agents at all? Well, for the same reasons that humans have used each other for agents since social interaction through communication became one of the main human traits. There are simply many areas where manipulative tools don't apply or take too long. An example is *NewsPeek*, a system I and others designed at MIT almost a decade ago. As later perfected, *NewsPeek* stays up all night looking for the newspaper you would most like to read at breakfast. It logs into a half dozen information systems including NEXUS, AP, *The New York Times*, etc., looking primarily for topics of interest to you, but also those that are especially interesting to humans in general. It reads the articles to the best of its ability—when it comes across a famous name, like "Mitterand," it finds his picture on a video disk that has 45,000 pictures of famous people—it finds maps of places mentioned on another video disk. It redefines the meaning of news—the major headline might be "Your 3:00 Meeting Is Cancelled Today" because one of its sources is your own electronic mail and it wants to bring important things it finds there to your attention. A sidebar might read "Your Children Slept Well Last Night."

Manipulative tools are simply not up to these and similar tasks—they require an agent. Another example is the situation in a large repository of information such as the Library of Congress in which there are many tools—such as the card index (the size of your home town library!) and various computer systems—but in which all transactions are carried out by human agents they supply to you when you walk in the door. The human agents are experts in not just the content of the Library, but also *the strategies of the library*. It is in these two main areas—tasks that can and should be done while you are doing something else, and tasks that require considerable strategy and expertise—that agents will gain ascendancy over tools.

The Mac already has a simple agent—it's the alarm clock desk accessory that gives a "bong" at the desired time. Simple and safe. What if we could get the alarm clock to trim the size of our hard disks periodically by deleting files? It could be done easily with HyperCard. It would still be simple to state the requirements, but we now have a very different perspective on safety. We would not like to give any current end-user programming system such a task—even if it could carry it out—without there being considerably more mechanism to explain, to make back-ups, to check and recheck. In short, we quickly want agents to have much of the common sense we would expect from a person, and to be able to learn more. It will not be an agent's manipulative skills, or even its learning abilities, that will get it accepted, but instead, its safety and ability to explain itself in critical situations.

Thus, agent development will move in two directions and later will be reconciled. Much of end-user programming in the near term will be agent-based, but only in domains in which well-meant screw-ups are not disastrous. In a serious operating system in which "delete" means simply "put this name on a list for archiving," and "undelete" is easy, these "manipulative" agents can be allowed considerable freedom. Still, there is a limit to how much remaking of a world any user wants to go through, and these agents are really not meant to be pervasive.

The second direction will move more slowly, as it has to take care of two major situations: those in which undo is hard or impossible, and those in which the user's problems are difficult to solve. The first category includes not just problems of deletions and the like, but also more personal interactions. It would not do for an agent to randomly insult clients with whom it is trying to make appointments. It is indeed hard to undo an insult!

My point here is not so much that agents are the next big direction in user interface design—that has been clear for a decade—but that this next step from the manipulated tool to the managed process will necessarily be much larger than that of the "glass teletype" to the Mac. One reason tools are easier is because they are like amplifying mirrors—they reflect and increase the user's own intelligence. An ocean vessel a mile long can be run by one tiny person because it has been designed as a continuation of the pilot's extensions into the universe. The creation of autonomous processes that can be successfully communicated with and managed is a qualitative jump from the tool—yet one that must be made. And user interface design can help the transition.

At the most basic level the thing we most want to know about an agent is not how powerful it can be, but how trustable it is. In other words, the agent must be able to explain itself well so that we have confidence that it will be working on our behalf as a goal sharer rather than as a demented genie recently escaped from *The Arabian Nights*. A really well done explanation facility will be needed regardless of whether the agent is instructed in rules, gestures, or English; whether it is anthropomorphic or tabular. This is an important and long-standing area of user interface design with disappointingly few workers.

Well, there are so many more new issues that must be explored as well. I say thank goodness for that. How do we navigate in once-again uncharted waters? I have always believed that of all the ways to approach the future, the vehicle that gets you to the most interesting places is Romance. The notion of tool has always been a romantic idea to humankind—from swords to musical instruments to personal computers, it has been easy to say: "The best way to predict the future is to invent it!" The romantic dream of "how nice it would be if . . . " often has the power to bring the vision to life. Though the notion of management of complex processes has less cachet than that of the hero singlehandedly wielding a sword, the real romance of management is nothing less than the creation of civilization itself. What a strange and interesting frontier to investigate. As always, the strongest weapon we have to explore this new world is the one between our ears—providing it's loaded!

Why Interfaces Don't Work

WHAT IS THE GOOD NEWS about computers and their interfaces? Alan Kay is reported to have said that "the Macintosh has the first interface good enough to be criticized." That is supposed to be the good news? Sorry folks, things are seriously wrong in interface land, despite all the rhetoric about how good things are.

What is there to criticize? As the good poet once said, "Let me count the ways." Why do we insist on using the computer? True, it lets us do things we could not do before. And many of our normal tasks can now be done faster, better, more accurately. I use a computer by choice—to write this paper, for example. But the technology is awfully primitive. And the system is driven by the technology, not by what the person needs or wants. There is an amazing tendency to use these beasts in places that are completely inappropriate.

The Macintosh is indeed worthy of being criticized. It is my computer of choice, for I find it the easiest to learn and to remember of the score of computers and operating systems I have used. The emphasis on graphics has allowed me to see my intended product and to manipulate that product more directly than with other systems. And the development of the internal toolbox has caused developers to be consistent in their use of screen, mouse, and keyboard, even when their natural tendencies would have led them elsewhere. As a result, most new programs can be used immediately, with

Donald A. Norman

Director, Institute for Cognitive Science
University of California, San Diego

little or no study, often without even opening the manual. The same cannot be said for other systems.

These virtues lead to the problems. When consistency is common, it is taken for granted and the user comes to rely upon it. But when things we have learned to rely on suddenly become unavailable, it can be worse than if they never existed at all.

Consistency indeed: One of the powers of the Macintosh is within the ready availability of four very important commands: undo, cut, copy, and paste—the list of four, we can call them. The list of four is supposed to appear on every edit menu. It is available from the keyboard as four secret key combinations. The list is even printed neatly below four keys on the super-sized keyboard I am using. So what is wrong with the list of four? I could start a critique of the failure of limited "undo," or the problems with only a single buffer for the contents of a "cut" or "copy" and the lack of visibility of the contents of the cut/copy buffer, but a more serious problem is that the magical four commands aren't always available, neither in all commercial programs nor in all standard Apple systems (for example, dialog boxes and HyperCard).[1]

I have a long list of complaints with interfaces. With the Macintosh, the Apple II, the IBM PC, the Sun, the Vax: you name it, I can criticize it. I can write long articles and books about these complaints. In fact, I have. What bothers me so much? **The real problem with the interface is that it is an interface. Interfaces get in the way. I don't want to focus my energies on an interface. I want to focus on the job.** My tool should be just something that aids, something that does not get in the way, and above all, something that does not attract attention and energy to itself. When I use my computer, it is in order to get a job done: I don't want to think of myself as using a computer, I want to think of myself as doing my job.

Two tales that illustrate the perversity of computers, and that doing things with them can be harder than doing without

TALE 1: NINTENDO VERSUS THE APPLE IIGS COMPUTER

I bought a game (*California Games*, Epyx, Inc.) for my son's Nintendo machine. He unwrapped the package, popped the game into the game slot on the Nintendo, and started playing. Time to get the game running—a few seconds.

I purchased the same game, *California Games*, for my son to use on our

---

[1] My pet peeves include things like Borland's Sidekick™ address and phone book and the DayTimer™ address book. Microsoft Word™ doesn't let you paste material into the find or replace boxes—most definitely counterproductive. Worst of all, Apple's own HyperCard™. There are lots more examples I won't bother to enumerate: by now, you should have gotten the point.

To play a game with Nintendo, one simply inserts the cartridge into the slot, pushes the "on" button, and starts playing. Specialized devices make for simplified operation.

Apple IIGS computer. My son and I tried to start the game, but we couldn't get it going. We had to go into the control panel of the Apple IIGS (by typing Command-Control-Escape, of course), then selecting "control panel," and then moving up and down the options with the arrow keys on the keyboard. We had to decide whether we wanted 40- or 80-character display, whether fast or slow speed should be used, whether the alternate display mode should be on or off, and whether the start-up slot should be 5, 6, 7, or scan (and whether slot 6 should be "your card" or "disc"). We had to start the game over so that we could try it out, and then continually repeat the entire operation until we got all those settings right. Time to get the game running—5 minutes.

Why is Nintendo, the game machine, so superior to the more powerful and flexible computer? Nintendo is also a computer, simply disguised as a game. The users just want to play a game, and Nintendo lets them do that simply, directly.

Nintendo is specialized for its purpose. It therefore can be tailored to work directly upon insertion of the game cartridge. Users don't know that Nintendo is a computer, don't need to know, and don't want to know. The users just want to play games. Nintendo is superior because it addresses the users' needs directly. It lacks the power of the general computer: it would make a lousy word processor. But by specializing, it can do its intended job better and more efficiently than can more powerful, general-purpose machines, as least from the viewpoint of the user. But that is what this business should be all about: the viewpoint of the user.

Nintendo also takes advantage of specialized input devices. Computer users tend to use the keyboard for everything, but as usual, specialization is superior.

But, you say, Nintendo is too specialized, it can't do all that a general-purpose machine can do. True. But maybe there is a trade-off here: generality and power versus specialization and ease of use. If so, we ought to examine this carefully. Maybe we need fewer general devices, more specialized ones. More on this later.

TALE 2: DAY-TIMER POCKET ORGANIZER™ VERSUS FOCAL POINT™ ON THE MACINTOSH

I purchased a Pocket Day-Timer set for organizing my activities. It came with a set of monthly calendars (which specifies activities on a half-hour basis), a 6-year calendar (which specifies activities on a daily basis for the next 19 months, then on a monthly basis for 4 1/2 years after that), a phone and address book, a notepad, a daily expense account, and all sorts of specialized pads and forms. It even came with an "archive storage chest," a small box with monthly file folders in which to keep both the unused monthly calendars and the old, used ones (to keep for such things as IRS inquisitions?). I read the instruction booklet (a thin manual) and the "work

The Apple IIGS computer. On the surface, it is the same as Nintendo: insert the game disk into the slot. But with Nintendo, that is all there is; with the IIGS, the work has just begun.

organizer booklet." Then I assembled the specialized items I cared about into the leather case that I had also ordered, copied phone numbers into the phone and address book, copied over my commitments and conference schedule for the next 6 years and entered my detailed plans for the next 6 months. Many of the Day-Timer's specialized forms and booklets didn't fit

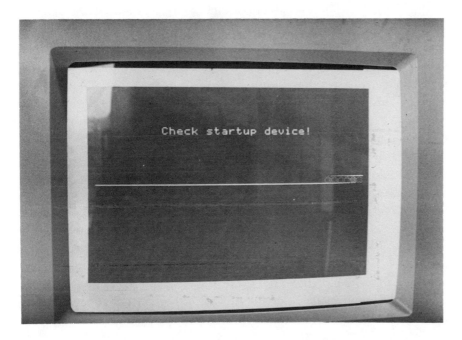

A familiar sight to Apple IIGS users. Nintendo, as far as I can tell, has no error messages at all. More important, it has no need for them.

The Day-Timer pocket calendar system. Direct, simple, powerful.

my needs, so I simply ignored them and didn't put them into the leather case.

Total time to get going—less than an hour.

I also bought Focal Point, the highly touted time management and calendar scheme for the Macintosh, which runs under Hypercard. First, I had to transfer five disks' worth of material onto my computer system and then I had to "install" the program with a rather unique procedure that put a new "button" onto my Hypercard Home Stack. Next, I had to tell it the period for which I wanted the program's calendar, daily schedule, and "to do" schedule to be set up. I decided I needed it to be set up for the next 18 months (in fact, I usually need at least the next 24 months—the Day-Timer provides 6 years—but the manual warned that this would take too long). This set-up took 45 minutes to an hour (I lost track). Then I had to transfer address information from my other files, which involved modifying a HyperCard script, politely provided by the company. Then I had to set up my schedules and learn how to operate the program. Finally, I had to customize the program, going in and tinkering with the scripts (that is, the programs) for the (sigh) fields, buttons, cards, stacks, and backgrounds, and then I had to redraw some of the background patterns.

Why did I have to do all this? Because Focal Point was set up for a different sort of person than me: it had all sorts of specialized charging schemes: almost anything you did ended up computing charges to bill the client by the hour. And messages resulting from outgoing calls were separate from those for incoming calls, which were stored separately from messages for "clients," or messages called "notes" (and notes could be scattered

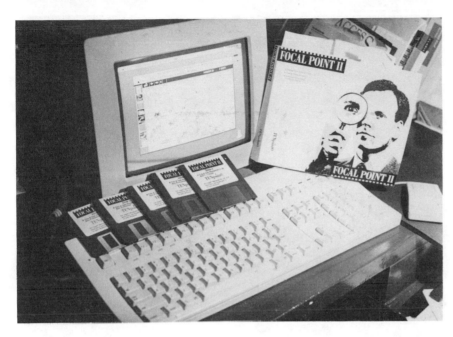

Focal Point for the Macintosh requires five diskettes and a big instruction manual. Plus, of course, a computer.

about in dozens of different places). I soon discovered that I couldn't remember in which note-place I had put any particular comment, so I removed all those extraneous spots and stuck to one location (not unlike the reason Apple got rid of those extra mice keys and stuck to one: with only one key or one place, you know where to find the thing and what it means).

Focal Point came with a 330-page manual, and a lot of work that had to be done to get it started. Total time to get it organized in a satisfactory manner—6 hours.

COMPUTERS CAN BE SUPERIOR—SO WHY SO MUCH DIFFICULTY?

These tales make it sound as if I oppose the computer. Not at all. After all, why do I keep using it? Why do I keep buying calendar programs, and the Day-Timer's computer address book, and systems like Focal Point? Because they offer significant advantages over other systems. I use Focal Point daily—always running on either my home or office computer. I like the fact that I can type legibly rather than scrawl illegibly. I like the fact that I can search for things. When am I giving that talk in Detroit? I go to my calendar and execute the command *find "detroit"* and the calendar for March 30 appears. That certainly beats skimming pages of handwritten calendar sheets. But these virtues come at a severe price. The calendar program, along with all the others, has had to sacrifice convenience and ease of use for the constraints imposed upon them by "the computer system." The computer system that seems to have put technology first, convenience and practicality last.

Compare Focal Point (on the left) with the Day-Timer system on the right. Which is better? Well, each has its place, which is why I use both of them.

Computer programs are difficult to set up and get running: the set-up is umpteen-times harder than that for the paper-and-pencil versions. Worst of all, they aren't there when you need them most: in the streets, on the bus, at the breakfast table, or on the toilet. And even when computers are available, it is difficult to keep remotely distant systems in synchrony. To use my calendar program in both my home and office, I must always carry the latest files with me on floppy disks (and hope I don't get confused and "update" one of the systems with out-of-date information).

Computer systems have the potential to offer significant advantages to the user, but at the moment, those advantages come at a high price. We need to combine the power of the general-purpose computer with the simplicity of Nintendo and the virtues of portable, paper-based systems. I should be able to purchase a calendar/address book and be using it in minutes. I shouldn't have to read or follow complex instructions: insert it into the computer and get to work—just like Nintendo.

What Are Computers For?

Much effort is devoted to the production of interfaces for computer systems—and some resulting efforts are actually quite good. Nonetheless, I believe that on the whole, putting the emphasis on the interfaces is wrong.

An interface is an obstacle: it stands between a person and the system being used. Aha, "stands between"—that is the difficulty. How can anything be optimal if it is in the way, if it stands between the person and what needs to be done?

If I were to have my way, we would not see computer interfaces. In fact, we would not see computers: both the interface and the computer would be invisible, subservient to the task the person was attempting to accomplish. It is the task that would be visible, the task and the tools being used to accomplish that task. The question posed today is in the form "How should we design the interface?" I would replace that question with quite a different one. I would ask "What tools should be provided for the task?"

What are computers for? The user, that's what—making life easier for the user. So that should be the starting point. Yes, the rules of interface design are critical, but they are of secondary importance to getting the task right, to aiding the user. Good design starts by asking what the user needs, what the program can do for the user.

Keep the Technologists Out of Sight

On the one hand, modern technology has worked wonders, providing many advances in communications and computation. On the other hand, technology dominates too much: we find ourselves catering to the needs of the technology instead of having the technology cater to us.

My home and office are filled with the blessings of modern technology, but the result is that I spent an ever-increasing amount of time trying to learn the new frills and options, and ever-increasing amounts of time "updating" the computer system, doing preventive maintenance, or taking the stuff to the repair shop. Who is in charge, anyway?

Keep the technologists busy. Keep them inventing and creating. But make them keep their hands off of product design. Product design should start off by getting the priorities right:

1. The user—what does the person really need to have accomplished?
2. The task—analyze the task. How best can the job be done?, taking into account the whole setting in which it is embedded, including the other tasks to be accomplished, the social setting, the people, and the organization.
3. As much as possible, make the task dominate; make the tools invisible.
4. Then, get the interaction right, making the right things visible, exploiting affordances and constraints, providing the proper mental models, and so on—the rules of good design for the user, written about many, many times in many, many places.

Am I naive? Did I ignore market considerations, marketability, manufacturing costs, time schedules, the established customer base? Yes, these must be considered and often must be given critical weight, but unless the first four points are addressed, the whole market may collapse: if customers become frustrated with the lack of usability of products, they respond by rejecting the whole technology.

We need to aid the task, not the interface to the task. The computer of the future should be invisible. There will certainly not be separate applications and documents (programs and files). Why do we need programs and files anyway? These are artifacts of the requirements of hardware. Think about what you must do today to use computers for some task. How much is forced upon you by the technology; how little is directly relevant to the task you are trying to accomplish?

Reflections

Why are we where we are? Where do we go from here?

We are here, in part, because this is probably the best we can do with today's technology and, in part, because of historical accident. The accident is that we have adapted a general-purpose technology to very specialized tasks while still using general tools. Keyboards, simple pointing devices, and video displays are not the most appropriate ways to interact with many of the tasks we do today, but they are all the computer provides.

A real office uses specialized, idealized tools. The interaction with hand or desk calculators is superior to the interaction with the one displayed on the screen. The same with the writing or drawing or computing or composing tools.

And the generality of the machine means we must "set it up" specially for each task, with the set-up changing each time the task changes, or the hardware changes, or something else happens. But I never have to set up my specialized tools: they come set up, and they stay that way.

In *The Psychology of Everyday Things* [Norman, 1988], I emphasized the fact that it is the tasks that are central, not the tools. There, I talked about doorknobs and light switches, water faucets and doors. I did this to emphasize that all technology has its foibles and difficulties, not just the computer. And that it is the task that is critical. A door has an interface—the doorknob and other hardware—but we should not have to think of ourselves as using the interface to the door: we simply think of ourselves as going through the doorway, or closing or opening the door.

The computer really is special. It is not just another mechanical device: it really has the power to simplify lives, to give us powerful tools that aid us in our bidding. But the same lessons still apply: focus on the tasks, not the tools. Today the focus is still on the computer itself, to the detriment of all of us.

Why doesn't the interface work? Because we still think of using the interface, because we talk of designing the interface, because we talk of improving the interface. Sure, the interface needs improving, but the improvement should follow naturally when the focus of design becomes the tasks to be done, the needs of the person, and the jobs to be accomplished. Then the interface will work, not because it doesn't exist, but because it blends so seamlessly with the task to be done that it disappears from consciousness.

Do not let the criticisms in this paper take away from the accomplishments: we truly now do have computer systems worthy of criticism! Great strides have been made in the attention paid to the user. The programs of today are immensely superior to those of yesteryear—they are more powerful, easier to use, more responsive to users and their needs. But the battle is not over—we have come far, but there is still a long way to go. There are great opportunities and great challenges ahead.

Acknowledgments

This paper benefited by comments of the many and vocal reviewers at the conference of contributing authors at Asilomar. Jonathan Grudin provided helpful comments and suggested the concluding paragraph.

My research is supported by grants from Apple Computer, Inc. and Digital Equipment Corporation to Affiliates of Cognitive Science at UCSD and by a grant from the Nippon Telegraph and Telephone Company.

The following products are discussed or mentioned: Nintendo, a children's computer game: Nintendo and Nintendo Entertainment System are trademarks of Nintendo of America, Inc. California Games is a product of Epyx, Inc. The Macintosh and the Apple IIGS are manufactured by Apple Computer, Inc., as is HyperCard. Focal Point is copyrighted by Danny Goodman and marketed by Activision. The Pocket Day-Timer is made by Day-Timers, Inc. Microsoft Word is produced by Microsoft Corporation.

User Interface Races:

Sporting Competition for Power Users

COMPETITION CAN BE A POWERFUL STIMULANT to high performance. Car or boat races, rodeos, tennis matches, and chess tournaments
are lively sporting events that encourage high levels of skill, training, mas-
tery, and accomplishment. Marathons and 100-yard dashes focus on physical ability, and chess tournaments and spelling bees are intellectually oriented. Yacht racing or rodeo events combine intellectual, physical, and
technological challenges. In almost every field, there are acknowledged
masters who have won the admiration of their colleagues by facing the
competition and winning.

The computer field has its share of challenges in terms of marketing
competition and the race to build the fastest supercomputer. A more refined
contest is the Annual Computer Chess Championship sponsored by the
Association for Computing Machinery. Supporters assert that such contests
are good fun, good publicity, and even help advance research goals.

I propose user interface races for the same reasons: fun, publicity, and
the advancement of user interface research. I think that public user interface
races would be a nice addition to computer conferences and expos. The
media always like a good contest, the participants would have fun and win
prizes, and we would all learn a lot about what makes for successful user
interfaces. Although the focus of this idea is competition, we should be
aware of the need for balance between competition and cooperation. The

Ben Shneiderman

Head, Human-Computer Interaction
Laboratory
University of Maryland

spirit of cooperation might be engaged here by having individuals work together in teams.

I have tried a user interface race with my students in an advanced Computer Science Department seminar on user interface design at the University of Maryland. My simple word processor race had three timed parts:

1. Type in an 81-word quote from a textbook.
2. Put the words in alphabetical order with one word per line, except that duplicate words should be repeated on the same line.
3. Repeat part 2.

The times ranged from 1 minute 48 seconds to 6 minutes 56 seconds for part 1, basically demonstrating a moderate three-to-one ratio in typing speed. For part 2, there was an enormous range, from 3 minutes 8 seconds to 49 minutes 30 seconds, revealing a dramatic difference in tools and skill. Finally, for part 3, the range was from 2 minutes 30 seconds to 47 minutes 3 seconds, but more than half of the users cut their times by 40 percent.

This data was the basis for a lively discussion about which strategies and tools were most efficient, predictions of performance as a function of text length, guesses about the impact of using a mouse, arguments about which macro facilities would be best, and discussions about screen sizes, fonts, multiple windows, pointing devices, response times, display rates, function keys, keyboard design, etc. We had several conjectures about what facilities should be added to word processors to speed this task. The student with the fastest time for part 3 received a box of candies, and in a non-competitive spirit he offered to share it with the entire class. Students repeated the three parts once in a command environment and once in a WYSIWYG environment, but no clear winner emerged here. The fastest times were usually with facilities that permitted macro creation or that had some sorting capability.

It was a successful class exercise, but I would like to encourage user interface races in more public places with well-organized rules, serious prizes, and judges. Adherence to the rules would have to be checked, penalties would have to be applied for errors in the completed product or for violations in the rules, and there would have to be appeals processes. At the conclusion of the race, judges, contestants, and audience members could participate in a round-table discussion of the interface issues that had been revealed.

A Variety of Races

A good race should have a clear goal and an unambiguous way of rating performance. It should be complex enough to be engaging yet clear enough that participants understand all aspects. There should be no shortcuts that would make their discoverer the certain winner. A race should be short enough to keep participants and spectators involved, and it should admit of enough diversity in approaches to elicit cleverness and skill.

Let me suggest a few user interface races, recognizing that these can be refined and that others may come up with more satisfying challenges:

- *Directory handler descrambler*: Each participant receives a hierarchical directory with 26 files distributed throughout three levels. The files are named AA through ZZ and contain a single line with the name of a person beginning with A through Z (for example, AA contains Albert; ZZ contains Zelda). The goal is to print the full list of names in alphabetical order, one per line, in the shortest amount of time.

- *Graphic editor gambit*: Each participant starts with a blank screen and must draw a version of the word ONE from the back of the U.S. one dollar bill (complete with shading and drop shadow) in letters 2 inches high. (Other possible drawings might be the logo of a computer company, a famous picture such as Robert Indiana's LOVE, a state or city flag, or a technical drawing such as a circuit diagram or flowchart.) Each contestant gets five minutes and the judges rate the quality on a 1.0 to 6.0 point scale (similar to figure skating).

- *Spreadsheet superstar showdown*: Each participant starts with a blank spreadsheet and constructs a personal budget sheet for a 12-month year (labeled across the top with the full names of the months), with categories down the side for Income, Housing, Food, Entertainment, Transportation, and Savings. Housing is a constant cost of $800/month, food costs $16 times the number of days in the month, entertainment costs $150/month in the spring and fall and $240/month for other months, except August, when a vacation trip increases the amount to $800. Income is fixed at $2,000/month, so savings can be computed as the difference between expenses and income. Compute row and column sums. The winner is the first to compute the full spreadsheet.

- *Communications chain competition*: This is a form of team competition. Each team has an equal number of members, say six. The lead participant for each team sends a message with his or her name and the time of day on a single line. The next person adds his or her name and the time. The team passes the growing message around until all team members have added their names and the time. The winning team is the first to get the full message sent back to the lead participant.

- *Database query quiz*: Prepare a database with two columns and 1,000 rows. The first column should contain a randomly chosen letter (A–Z) and the second column should contain a randomly chosen number

(0–9). Participants must produce a three-column database with the first two columns indicating letter-number pairs that occur more than once and the third column containing the actual frequency.

- *Charting contest*: Produce a labeled bar chart showing yesterday's minimum, maximum, and average temperatures (three vertical bars) at six cities. The six city names must appear under each bar, the x-axis must be labeled, and there must be a title, "Yesterday's Temperatures."

Of course, organizers can create their own races, just as golf course designers create their own challenges to attract players. We all have to learn about what makes for a good or bad user interface race.

Future Fantasy

Who knows—maybe someday you'll turn on the television and hear: "This is Howard Cosell broadcasting from beautiful College Park, Maryland, where today we will witness the finals at the International Word Processing and Spreadsheet Olympics . . . ."

The Evolution of Thinking Tools

In the popular mythology the computer is a mathematics machine: it is designed to do numerical calculations. Yet it is really a language machine: its fundamental power lies in its ability to manipulate linguistic tokens—symbols to which meaning has been assigned.— Terry Winograd [1984]

The protean nature of the computer is such that it can act like a machine or like a language to be shaped and exploited. It is a medium that can dynamically simulate the details of any other medium, including media that cannot exist physically. It is not a tool, although it can act like many tools. It is the first metamedium, and as such it has degrees of freedom for representation and expression never before encountered and as yet barely investigated.—Alan Kay [1984]

WE HUMANS ARE IN LOVE WITH OUR TOOLS because they help us become more than we are, to overcome our limitations and extend the boundaries of what it is possible to do with our brains and bodies. We can conceive of physical and mental challenges for which our natural endowment is inadequate, and we have a knack for inventing tools to help us overcome those limitations in pursuit of our goals. As Henri Bergson put it, "Intelligence, considered in what seems to be its original feature, is the faculty of manufacturing artificial objects, especially tools for making tools" [Bergson, 1911].

Logic and languages, symbols and semantic systems, are the thinking tools for making thinking tools that shifted human evolution into overdrive. Symbols got us from the primeval savannah to the surface of the moon in an astonishingly short period of time, evolutionarily speaking [Levine and Rheingold, 1987]. The personal computer has the potential to propel us even farther, even faster, in the coming decades.

Our species has been in its present physical form for around a hundred thousand years. Somewhere along the way, probably not long after our primate antecedents descended from the retreating forests and started to hunt in packs, the spoken word was born. About twenty thousand years ago, information was encoded on cave walls. Six thousand years ago, hieroglyphics carried messages to the underworld and to the future. And the alphabet that encodes this sentence evolved from the symbols intro-

Jean-Louis Gassée
Former President, Apple Products Apple Computer, Inc.

with
Howard Rheingold

duced by Phoenician seafarers a relatively recent three thousand years ago. Logic and mathematics, a scant few thousand years old themselves, were the toolmaking tools that made science possible—the ultimate toolmaking tool of the past three centuries.

It has been an exhilarating ride from alphabets to astronauts. Why shouldn't humans love these tools that enable us to overcome the limitations of nature, to find better and better ways to express our highest potential? We love symbols, don't we? Symbols save our thinking processes from needless mechanical toil—as do computers. Symbols and computers also have the potential to become something more than labor-saving devices. They are vehicles for creating that which has never been created before. "Language serves not only to express thoughts, but to make possible thoughts which could not exist without it," is how Bertrand Russell put it [Russell, 1948].

If you want to think about the future of the human-computer interface, think about the history and future of symbolic systems. The true antecedents of tomorrow's computers were not calculating machines or electronic circuits, but alphabets, natural and formal languages, and the symbolic language known as science. What good does it do if you can invent a lever or a way of life, if you have no way of telling someone about it? And how can you build an understanding of the world without the model-building tools of language and number, logic and science? The future evolution of the personal computer interface is the next step in the story of symbolic thinking tools.

The power of computation lies in precisely the protean character celebrated by Alan Kay in the words quoted at the beginning of this article. Computers are hierarchies of abstractions built upon electronic instantiations of Turing machines. This is a new and startling leap in a fairly long intellectual quest. Symbol systems and thought have coevolved ever since humankind boosted its collective intelligence by creating and communicating more powerful mental representations. The convergence of mathematics and technology that made computers possible was the genesis of a new phase in intellectual coevolution. The interface is the cognitive locus of human-computer interaction, and it also evolves rather rapidly. In that sense, the evolution of the human-computer interface is beginning to drive the evolution of intelligence.

Computers are simulation engines—powerful tools for mental-model building. We are only beginning to see them as such. All of our thinking tools, from language to logic, involve an acquired skill at constructing mental models and communicating them. And the power of these mental models is that they give the whole species a platform for thinking and expressing ourselves more effectively, for communicating and collaborating and building the next higher level of symbolic thought. The tool for building that next level is the computer, and as we learn to use it better, we are going to change the way we see the world, for such is the nature of powerful intellectual instruments.

Interface builders, you are building more than control panels for computing machines. You are bringing into existence different angles on reality. You are firing up simulation engines. You are changing the way we look at the world.

The Interpersonal, Interactive, Interdimensional Interface

INTERFACE WIZARDS OF SILICON VALLEY, you know a great deal about the pathways electrons weave through solid-state circuits, and you are beginning to envision how to use software to build cathedrals of abstractions, and more of you are taking the trouble to learn something about human perceptual and cognitive systems. I'd like to suggest that it would be wise to anticipate what happens when you unlock a whole new dimension of consciousness for millions of people, a profession I've been practicing for some 35 years.

Today, like you, I am learning how to expand consciousness and raise intelligence by means of computer software. Together with a team of programmers, artists, and thinkers, I'm designing new kinds of hardware, thoughtware, and courseware for people who use personal computers. Recently, it has become clear to me that the state of human-computer interface design in 1989 mirrors the state of psychology in 1959, when my colleagues and I started using neurotransmitters to activate and reprogram the human brain.

Just as Professor Richard Alpert and I studied the mind-transforming properties of LSD by booting-up divinity students, artists, prison inmates, and ourselves, today's human interface designers are about to unleash equally undreamed-of changes in the consciousness of people all over the world by giving them a tool for expanding the power of their minds.

The changes that tomorrow's computer interfaces are going to cause in

Timothy Leary

the minds of millions of people are good and necessary, considering the fact that we are entering the home stretch in our race against extinction. Personal computers that evolve from contraptions to companions in less than one human lifespan are part of an overall acceleration of the biosphere's systems for becoming conscious enough to take control. The cellular circuit resonates with the neural circuit, the communication circuit, the computation circuit, and the whole planet waking up to itself in the nick of time.

I can tell you from experience that the cultural acceleration associated with unlocking that much consciousness is intense. Those two heavy hitters of human nature—denial and resistance—come into play whenever people are challenged to change the foundations of their reality. A lot of energy is released very quickly when a psychedelic or a cybernetic interface to hyperspace activates such a fundamental change. It helps to be prepared for that.

I predict that if interfaces are designed with the notion of interpersonal communication in mind, the information technologies of the next ten years are going to link amplified individual minds into a global groupmind. Interactivity is interpersonal. When the computer hardware and multimedia storage and display technology and communication networks of the near future reach critical mass, we're all going to have to relate to our computers, ourselves, and others, in a whole new way. The personal computer is in the process of becoming the interpersonal computer.

In a similar way, psychologists had to look at their field in a whole new way when my own research propelled the evolution of psychotherapy into an unexpected new dimension. To most people, the events that started in Harvard's psychology department in the early 1960s are part of a more exciting cultural history about the beginning of the awakening of our species. What computer interface designers might not know is that those events also constituted a turning point in psychotherapeutic theory. The evolution of the notion of *interactive*, as it is used by computer interface designers, parallels the evolution of the notion of *interpersonal* in the field of psychology. Both concepts are related to very wide and deep and irrevocable changes in the way people relate to the world.

When I started exploring new directions in the science of psychology in the 1950s, a whole new direction of evolution for scientific thought was just beginning to become evident. The history of the psychotherapeutic process in particular had undergone revolutionary changes since the time of Freud, especially in terms of the relationship between the therapist and the patient. The classic Freudian psychoanalyst sits behind the analysand, who lies on a special kind of couch that psychoanalysts like to use, and the analysand does all the talking.

My earliest intuitions were that the future lay in a new way of perceiving the system that included the subject/patient, the observer/therapist, their environment, and even their worldviews. I knew that the gestalt movement in psychology modeled human perceptions and relations in terms of a kind of field. And I was aware of the implications of Heisenberg's Uncertainty Principle: scientists can no longer consider our observations to be strictly neutral in regard to the systems we are observing. A physicist shoots atoms down a linear accelerator and crashes them into other atoms. An anthropologist enters a village. A psychotherapist sits down and listens to a patient. But the atom, culture, or personality that is observed is not precisely the same as one that is not observed. The parts of the system that observe the system also change the system by their act of observation.

In the field of psychotherapy, the implications of this are that the therapist and patient, analyst and analysand, are part of a total field. The shocking idea that the patient can change the therapist becomes not only valid but vital to understanding the transactions that take place in psychotherapy.

In the 1940s, Harry Stack Sullivan at the Washington School of Psychiatry noted that while doctors think they are diagnosing or treating the patient, they are acting within a field, the nature of which is determined to a tremendous extent by the thought and behavior of the patient. My Ph.D. thesis at Berkeley in 1950, later published as a book, was called *Interpersonal Diagnosis of Personality*, in which I extended Sullivan's model.

I was hired by Harvard in part because of a manuscript I had written called *The Existential Transaction*. Professor David McClelland, then the director of the Harvard Center for Personality Research, wanted to know what the title meant. I explained that by *existential* I meant that psychologists should work with people in real-life situations, like a naturalist in the field. We should treat people as they actually are and not impose the medical model or any other model on them. I explained that I used the word *transaction* to suggest that psychologists shouldn't remain detached from their subjects. They should get involved, engaged in the events they're studying. They should enter each experiment prepared to change as much or more than the subjects being studied. So he hired me.

My quest led me beyond the walls of Harvard and the boundaries of academic psychology. But some of my original hypotheses continue to intrigue me. And I think the interpersonal approach to human minds and human relations is going to emerge as a human interface tool of great importance in the future. It took me thirty-five years after I wrote my thesis to find the right technology to actually see these interpersonal interactive fields I first theorized at Berkeley. The computer interfaces that are being designed today for the computers of tomorrow are going to bring the issue to the forefront again.

When the printing press made it possible for people outside the elites to become literate, the alphabet became a liberating force. But the original uses of every language, from alphabets to computer languages, seem to be as tools for an elite who wish to prevent the wider population from enjoying such freedom. The Phoenician alphabet was invented as a way of hiding information from Greek traders and other rivals. Whenever I see that alphabet on a keyboard, I see a phalanx of Phoenician soldiers facing me. You can see the look of triumph on the face of a DOS wizard when his fingers rapidly tap in some long string of alphabetic commands. These DOS wizards often smile, secretly, because they are demonstrating their arcane power to manage the secret commands. The mouse is a guerilla device, an end-run around the Phoenician guardians of the code. Nonprogrammers can approach the holy of holies that was originally created for the exclusive use of the programming priesthood. And the screen itself has become the key battleground in the revolutionary liberation of human minds that accompanies the revolution in computer interface design.

The screen is where the interpersonal, interactive consciousness of the worldmind is emerging. The screen is where the perceptual wetware groks the informational output of the cyberware. The screen is where minds of tomorrow will mirror themselves, meet each other, enter the universe of information and knowledge. The screen is the window onto the info-worlds that are already evolving into the hyperweb conceptualized by Ted Nelson [1974], the Matrix predicted by cyberpunk bard William Gibson [1984].

We know there will be technological breakthroughs soon in what we see on screens and the way we interact with those screens: Fiber-optic cables that deliver billions of bytes of information per second, high-definition television, global interactive multimedia computer conferencing, storage media that will enable you to carry the Library of Congress in your pocket, wristwatch supercomputers, head-mounted displays, and virtual realities are coming down the pike at high velocity.

One of these days, the screens that most people face all day will be big enough and quick enough and high-res enough to engage our attention more powerfully than the boob tube already does. More important, when we talk to these new screens, they will talk back. The systems now in place for processing data and communications are a bit more interactive than they used to be, but not as interactive as they are going to get—and that difference won't be incremental, it will be paradigm-busting. An airline reservations clerk can easily connect with the mainframe, read data, and enter data to make your travel arrangements. *But he or she isn't able to connect with his or her own mind, or with a virtual community of other minds.* In various corners of the scene, however, people are building mind-tools and cyberspace communities that are harbingers of the kind of interactivity the whole population is going to experience over the next twenty years.

The computer screen is a device for finding out how to use the power of our minds. It is also a means of making contact with other minds. It is both interactive and interpersonal. It is a tool for amplifying the consciousness of individuals and for facilitating the interpersonal relationships among human beings. Up until now, our communication technologies have been "dumb" because they could only pass specified information back and forth. Soon, software agents and intelligent networks will help us find out who we want to communicate with, filtering and hunting through the terabytes of data for those that interest each one of us in our own idiosyncratic ways.

The Macintosh interface was the first one to deal the nonprogrammer into the mind-amplifier game. Now we have to join together in a bigger system that connects all the amplified minds together in the right way. Software of the future, and the interfaces between individuals and the Matrix, will be designed for people to interact with their own minds and with one another. And these systems will have to be designed to change and evolve as the systems and the minds teach one another. More and more people will be interacting with one another through screens in the next few years. The technologies have been waiting in the wings for a long time. Doug Engelbart's laboratory used shared screens (and screens that combined video with computer displays) in the 1960s. Xerox PARC's COLAB was a step toward using shared control of a screen to create a place where minds could interact. Computer conferencing, electronic mail, and BBSs already constitute a communication subculture—hundreds of thousands of people already use computer screens as portals to other minds. It is good that interface designers are including cognitive psychologists in their enterprise, but I believe it would be much better if interface designers were to tap the resource of social psychology as well. The personal computer interface is based on the way individual people deal with ideas and information; the interpersonal computer interface will be based on how people communicate with one another. Realizing the full potential of the human-to-human model (as advocated in this book by Negroponte, Brennan, Buxton, and others) will require a strong new interpersonal perspective.

Interscreening could be a way to repersonalize the relationships that have been depersonalized by dumb technologies like the boob tube. There's a tremendous opportunity for cultural leverage here. The right kind of interface design can take advantage of the world's evolving communications web and turn our screens into windows on one another's minds.

The Right Way to Think About Software Design

Theodor Holm Nelson

*Distinguished Fellow
Autodesk, Inc.*

WHAT IS WRONG with people's imaginations? Writing in 1989, after designing interactive software for over twenty-five years, I am dismayed at the dreariness of the interactive software that people today think is liberating and forward-looking. Compared to what it should and will be, today's interactive software is wooden, obtuse, clumsy, and confused. The pervasive lack of imagination and good design is appalling.

I explicitly include the Macintosh in this critique, because many naive people treat that machine (especially its system software and conventions) as some important step in civilization. The premise of the Macintosh and the Macalikes is fine. We want ease of use and clear visualization of our work. But the execution and control structure are slow and drab.

To see tomorrow's computer systems, go to the video game parlors! Go to the military flight simulators! Look there to see true responsiveness, true interaction. Compare these with the dreary, pedestrian office software we see everywhere, the heavy manuals and Help Screens and Telephone Support. The world of work at computer screens is still a benighted world. And even when individual programs are tolerable, the task of making combinations of programs fit together is hopelessly arcane.

A lot of programmers and committees are creating a lot of bad designs, and the ways they are thinking about it and going about it assure that design will stay bad for a long time to come. Perhaps worse is that almost no one seems to be able to recognize *good* design—except users, and that only sometimes.

I would like to say some things about bad design, then talk about the principles of design in general.

Elements of Bad Design

MISTAKE 1: FEATURITIS AND CLUTTER

"Featuritis" is a principal and well-known disease of software. In the older days, featuritis meant having to remember (and correctly arrange and type) numerous keyboard options. Today, however, the blight of featuritis is taking on new forms. In the popular iconic world, it becomes a new style of screen clutter.

You face a screen littered with cryptic junk: the frying pan, the yo-yo, the bird's nest, the high-button shoe. Or whatever. You must learn the nonobvious aspects of a lot of poorly designed screen furniture and visual toys: what they actually do, rather than what they suggest. You must explore the details of each until you understand what it "really" means. In the old days, you tried to understand the various input commands and their maze of options. Today, you try to understand what the icon means. Instead of "you don't understand computers," it's now "you don't understand the metaphor."

Featuritis doesn't mean that a program aspires to do too much; there need be no limit on how many distinguishable things a program can do. The disease of featuritis is the unclarity and confusion that results from *having too many separate, unrelated things to know and understand*. The relationship between *power and flexibility for the user* and *simplicity at the interface* need not be inverse. Ultimately, the best software design assimilates all its functions to a few clear and simple principles.

MISTAKE 2: METAPHORICS

A tedious array of icons is supported by the new Metaphoric Ideology, deeply a part of the Apple-oriented world. A metaphor is an implicit comparison, or in the more ethereal versions of the doctrine, it is a free-floating idea with a handle (such as a picture or catchword).

I would like to venture that this "metaphor" business has gone too far. Slogans and catchphrases are all very well, and these things have their uses for people who are going to learn software by *approximating* rather than *understanding*.

Let us consider the "desktop metaphor," that opening screen jumble that is widely thought at the present time to be useful. First developed at Xerox PARC, it is now seen (in different styles) on the Mac, the Amiga, the Sun, the NeXT, and the infamous Microsoft Windows. Though "look and feel" details may vary, the underlying concept is the same, and the concept is where the weaknesses lie.

Why is this curious clutter called a desktop? It doesn't *look* like a desktop; we have to tell the beginner *how* it looks like a desktop, because it doesn't (it might as easily properly be called the Tablecloth or the Graffiti Wall).

The user is shown a gray or colored area with little pictures on it. The pictures represent files, programs, and disk directories that are almost exactly like those for the IBM PC, but that are now represented as in a rebus. These pictures may be moved around in this area, although if a file or program picture is put on top of a directory picture it may disappear, being thus moved to the directory. Partially covered pictures, when clicked once, become themselves covering, and partially cover what was over them before.

We are told to believe that this is a "metaphor" for a "desktop." But I have never personally seen a desktop where pointing at a lower piece of paper makes it jump to the top, or where placing a sheet of paper on top of a file folder causes the folder to gobble it up. I do not believe such desks exist; and I do not think I would want one if it did.

Now, I am not criticizing the idea of having mnemonics, or of creating useful visualizations in order to present ideas. In no way do I advocate the old typed command line. What I object to is severalfold: first, these mnemonic gimmicks are not very useful for presenting the ideas in the first place; second, their resemblance to any real objects in the world is so tenuous that it gets in the way more than it helps; and third, which is by far most important, *the metaphor becomes a dead weight*. Once the metaphor is instituted, *every related function has to become a part of it*.

The visualizations become locked to some sort of continuing relation to the mnemonic. It becomes like a lie or a large government project: more and more things have to be added to it, and they have to be in some way, possibly some obscure way, consistent. (A hideous failure of consistency is the garbage can on the Macintosh, which means either "destroy this" or "eject it for safekeeping.")

Here is the problem with metaphors: you want to be able to design things that are *not* like physical objects, and the details of whose behavior may float free, not being tied to any details of some introductory model. Metaphors are like WYSIWYG: useful in limited contexts, but ultimately a drag, a dead anchor [See Nelson, 1989].

The alternative to metaphorics is *the construction of well-thought-out unifying ideas*, embodied in richer graphic expressions that are not chained to silly comparisons. These will be found by overall virtuality design (below), and not by metaphors, which I consider to be using old half-ideas as crutches.

MISTAKE 3: ADD KETCHUP

Some people think software will be improved by making it conversational and populating it with crypto-social entities—perky or sassy personalities full of greetings and apologies, that respond to, and in, some sort of English. (It is proposed in Apple's "Knowledge Navigator" film that they should even have animated faces, like Max Headroom.) I think it should be otherwise. We do not need gratuitous social interaction, but rather clear, sensible models of the working domain.

A *globe* is my model of a proper information system. A globe does not say "good morning"; it does not bother you with menus, icons, or prompts. You turn it and move your head to the most useful position for overview or detail, that's all. These crypto-social models have created a false trail of design directions, and are wasting effort and misdirecting hopes. Applying artificial intelligence to dandify bad designs is like putting on ketchup to dandify a bad meal.

Toward Virtuality Design

THE MOVIE ANALOGY

It should be noted that the mistakes just listed all have to do with psychological and visual effects of screen events on the user. And in what field have the psychological and visual effects of screens been widely experimented with, and come to great prominence? Why, movies, of course.

Many people have now noticed that interactive software is in some ways like movies, and that the process of making software is in some interesting ways like movie-making.[1] Here are the central parts of the analogy:

- Making software is like making movies because both are about *how moving presentations affect the mind and feelings of the viewer*. The talented software designer subtly calculates the overall structure and how it will affect the viewer or user; not merely putting parts together. Technical concerns are merely preliminary, the substratum; what counts are the artistic planning, execution, and the reunified tuning of all the parts.

- The parts are subjected to a unified tuning process after they have been formally joined. We do not merely put them together, but trim, balance, time, subtract, and even reorganize them on new principles (see below).

- Special talents are required that have nothing to do with the technicalities. The greatest of these is the ability to conceive and realize a unifying vision.

I would like to consider software and movies both as parts of the same field, which I call *virtuality*.

---

[1] I first published this comparison in 1967 in an article called "Getting It Out of Our System" in Schechter, *Information Retrieval: A Critical View,* Thompson Books, 1967.

WHAT IS VIRTUALITY?

There are many ways of thinking about the responding computer screen. Perhaps it is just a technical device, the readout of a new form of calculator. Or perhaps it is just a new form of movie screen, where the lessons (and talents) of movie-making need to be applied.

I believe that movies and the computer screen are both best understood in still larger terms. It is for this I propose the term *virtuality* (as distinct from such terms as *artificial reality* and *virtual reality*, both oxymorons). The virtuality of a thing is what it *seems* to be, rather than its reality, the technical or physical underpinnings on which it rests.

Virtuality has two aspects: *conceptual structure*—the ideas of the thing—and *feel*—its qualitative and sensory particulars. In a movie, the conceptual structure consists of the plot and the characters, and the feel consists of atmosphere, suspense, and style. In architecture, the conceptual structure is the idea of a building and the sense of where things are, and the feel is the sweep and style and detailing. In a video game, the conceptual structure includes the rules and strategies, and the feel includes the tuning, spirit, motion characteristics, colors, and other sensory aspects.

The objectives of a designer will vary depending on the purposes of the virtuality. In almost all forms of design, we are concerned with conceptual structure: we want people to understand the result, and for it to be clear and useful to them. And in almost all forms of design, we are concerned with feel: we want the details of the finished work to be welcoming, pleasing, and easy for those who will see and use it.

Virtuality Design

THE DESIGN OF PRINCIPLES

In the metaphorical approach, the metaphor becomes the central concept—the principle, if you will, to which all other aspects of the design must adhere. The problem, as we have seen, is that slavish adherence to a metaphor prevents the emergence of *things that are genuinely new*.

What I call the design of principles is the more sweeping, serious alternative to metaphorics. In metaphorics, we begin with a familiar image or idea and try to pack into it, and tack onto it, some coherent set of functions that are constrained to be related to that metaphor. Freely designed *principles*, on the other hand, do not have to stay attached to any image. (This is why "metaphor" talk is counterproductive: it makes us try to stay within some clumsy concept such as "desktop metaphor" rather than reaching by the design of principles toward a new conceptual organization that has not previously existed.)

By a principle I mean an idea that other ideas are going to fit into or under. If you understand the principle clearly, the details follow from it.

Principles, unlike metaphorical correspondences, are plastic and redefinable. It is possible to fit ideas under the same set of principles in many different ways; conversely, the same ideas can be fit under many different principles.

THE JINGLING-IDEAS METHOD

The design of principles consists of the detailed working-out of structures and ideas: we take a set of possible principles and endeavor to assign to them all the functions we want to include; then rework and rework, reassigning, redefining the principles and their visualizations until we get the best overall fit. The reciprocal nature of this process is the source of its strength: it avoids the unidirectionality of metaphorics (top-down) and featuritis (bottom-up) as design techniques.

I describe this process as the jingling-ideas method. When you hold a bunch of coins in your hand, they start as just a heap. However, if you shake them for a little while, in the right sort of way, they tend to assemble into a stack. This same method works in the process of design. If you think about all the things you want a design to do, and at first they don't fit together, the thing to do is *jingle them in your mind* until they stack up together. The result will be the gradual organization of these desiderata into a usable set of principles, aligning in some new fashion. Probably they won't include all the things you wanted, but you'll probably get most of what you wanted—in a clean design. (The more you can divorce your thinking from previous designs, the more likely you are to discover powerful new integrative principles.)

COMBINING THE OLD AND THE NEW

Today there are only a few organizing principles in interactive software: spreadsheets, databases, treating individual items as searchable, menus (in various styles, such as pull-down and Lotus), and windows, for example. Each of these involves an idea and a related visualization for it which together have a virtuality—conceptual structure and feel. Some of the principles derive from "old" (metaphorical) models; in the case of spreadsheets, it is the two-dimensional piece of paper; in the case of databases (including HyperCard), it is the three-dimensional stack of cards.

But some of the principles are also genuinely new. VisiCalc™, the first spreadsheet program, was a remarkable achievement: not only did it take the business concept of a paper spreadsheet and give it automatic calculation, but its whole structure was a tour de force in the design and balancing of principle. VisiCalc's REPLICATE feature is an excellent example of the abstract nature of the design of principle. To replicate a column *and its formulas* corresponds to nothing that was on earth previously; and when metaphoric thinking was dismissed, it could be designed cleanly with no reference to anything that had come before.[2]

Tomorrow's new principles will involve both old concepts and new, fitting under new principles of visualization. These new principles must and will be *lucid*, *vivid*, and *obvious*, once you have seen them. They will be spatial because a screen is spatial, indicating multiple connection and multidimensional connection.

Representing Interconnected Information: An Example of Conceptual Structure Design

Once we leave behind "two-dimensionality" (virtual paper) and even "three-dimensionality" (virtual stacks), we step off the edge into another world, into the representation of *the true structure and interconnectedness of information*. To represent this true structure, we need to indicate multidimensional connection and multiple connections between entities.

We can think of the new connective structures as being basically of two different types.

- *Multidimensional connections*: Uniform or systematic spaces. The data on a globe is a nice example of a systematic space.
- *Discrete connectedness*: Mapping individual and disparate interconnections, as in hypertext, hypermedia, etc.

Tomorrow's file servers, such as the Xanadu™ electronic storage and publishing system, will maintain various types of connections among files or documents. But that is just the technical mechanism for holding the connections. How will we actually see and use them? Working on this problem has led to the emergence of two new principles. The principle of *connected windows* combines two "old" principles to form a new one. The principle of *wormholes* (out of which information may be enticed) is a "new" principle created to provide a visualization for unseen parts, continuities from the seen to the unseen.[3]

Designing the Feel and Fine-Tuning

Virtuality is to some extent designed as a whole (as in the movie script), to some extent evolves as the parts are made, and to some extent is fine-tuned (as on the movie set and in the cutting and mix).

Consideration of feel comes generally, if ever, after the conceptual structure. Sometimes it is something that can actually be carefully planned and

---

[2] For a fuller discussion, see pp. DM 69–71 in T. Nelson, *Computer Lib*, 2nd edition, Microsoft Press, 1987.

[3] Some children's books published earlier in the century had illustrations with die-cut doors you could look behind; so did *Flair* magazine, a publication of the late 1940s. These should be an inspiration.

The contents of one screen window are never related to those of any other, and of course it is not necessary to indicate their connections in any way. Even if they were related, indirect ways of showing the relationships would be quite sufficient.

WHO SAYS THEY'RE NOT RELATED? Information is connected every whichway!

Why should we have to settle for indirect connections, when the real ones can be shown in a direct and immediate fashion by lines linking two windows?

WHAT IS, IS; AND IT IS THE COMPUTER'S DUTY TO SHOW IT! Any forms of interconnection should be a part of the overall envir-

LINKED WINDOWS

engineered, like the handling of a car (which in today's automotive world involves calculation as to steering, the distribution of weight, shock absorption, the angles of struts, etc.). But the feel more usually comes in the rework and fine tuning.

Beginning with the overall virtuality that is wanted—the conceptual structure and feel—the designer then works back to design the particulars. If it is a movie, the director takes the script down into the details of each scene and atmospheric nuance. If it is a program, the designer works on the particulars of every feature and tries to configure each so that it fits seamlessly into the whole.

When most of the separate parts have been completed, the tuning phase begins. Like film editing, the process consists of intercomparison decisions about fragments already in hand. In the tuning phase, we work to get the feel just right (and usually modify the conceptual structure to a lesser extent,

WORMHOLES

USER POINTS AT "WORMHOLE" SYMBOL, CONNECTED TEXT IS EMITTED

The quick brow

sometimes throwing parts out and sometimes assimilating them to new or revised generalities).

ON ARTISTRY

Historical accident has kept programmers in control of a field in which most of them have no aptitude: the artistic integration of the mechanisms they work with. It is nice that engineers and programmers and software executives have found a new form of creativity in which to find a sense of personal fulfillment. It is just unfortunate that they have to inflict the results on users.

Learning to program has no more to do with designing interactive software than learning to touch-type has to do with writing poetry. The design of interactivity is scarcely taught in programming school. What we need in software is what people are taught in film school, at least to whatever degree it can be taught. Designing for the little screen on the desktop has the most in common with designing for the Big Screen (directing theatrical films). Interactive software needs the talents of a Disney, a Griffith, a Welles, a Hitchcock, a Capra, a Bob Abel. The integration of software cannot be achieved by committee, where everyone has to put in their own addition (featuritis again). It must be controlled by dictatorial artists with full say on the final cut.

As computer hardware improves, tomorrow's production values should go up and up. Tomorrow's systems will be high-performance, full-flavored, profoundly rich. The difference between tomorrow's software and today's will be, to use Mark Twain's telling phrase, the difference between the lightning and the lightning bug.

The Noticeable Difference

Nicholas Negroponte

Professor of Media Technology
Director, Media Laboratory
Massachusetts Institute of Technology

WHEN I WAS A LITTLE BOY, my mother had a linen closet, the back of which had a "secret wall." The secret was no big deal. It was a collection of pencil lines that we periodically and carefully made to mark my height. Each pencil line was dutifully dated, and some were close together due to frequency and others were more spread apart because, for example, we had been away for the summer. Using two closets did not seem to make sense.

This scale was a private matter, and I guess in some way measured my intake of milk, spinach, and other good things.

By contrast, growth has a more dramatic face. A rarely seen uncle might comment: "How much you have grown, Nicky" (since I saw you two years ago, we suppose). But I could not really see that. All I could see were the little lines in the linen closet.

In many regards, I look upon the human factors community as experts in drawing those little lines and measuring the distances between them. I suppose the good part of this view is that the field, like the body, does grow. What is disappointing is a lack of lust for big changes that will be so obvious, if not visceral.

I recall an abundance of theory about the "just noticeable difference" (the JND) and was always puzzled by the fact that, if it was "just noticeable," why was it so important. I still wonder today (1989).

I am increasingly convinced that the human interface with computers needs such big differences, that they will be (a) noticeable, and (b) unnecessary to measure (unless you have a certain flavor of NSF grant).

I am reminded of some recent work at the Media Lab's experimental grammar school, the Hennigan. The field of education is replete with measurement systems (few as debilitating as the SATs). The pressure to measure is even larger in that field than in ours. But when I learned that truancy at Hennigan dropped from 50 percent to almost 0, I was convinced that here too there are noticeable differences that tell us a great deal more about our achievements than a part of a percentage point, which must be as affected by a Saturday stomachache as by anything else.

I remember "scholarly" papers (circa 1972) that argued against color in displays. They were filled with tables, control groups, and the like, proving that color could be confusing. Today, I hear of similar studies that suggest that speech and natural language are not appropriate channels of communication between people and computers in many, if not most, applications. I am further puzzled.

I certainly understand that I don't want the pilot of a 747 to land an airplane by singing songs or a doctor to perform open heart surgery by humming to his apparati. But I can't fathom any cause to avoid richness in communication, especially as computers become ubiquitous and are part of the quality of our daily lives. This comes from a belief (not shared by all, I know) that computers should be more like people.

When this happens, we'll see the difference, as if staring in a mirror of time. We'll see what my uncle saw, versus the little lines in the closet.

Technique and Technology
Introduction

PEOPLE OFTEN ASK what is a good interface design. Because a computer system product is the user interface [Heckel, 1984], the answer is that a good interface design is one that the user continues to use. VisiCalc™ is often considered as having one of the first interface designs that was transparent enough that the "ordinary" user could use it irrespective of its technical functionality. It has been iterated upon and new capabilities added. The Swiss Army knife, designed about a hundred years ago, is still being used. The basic functionality and interface have not changed much at all. In fact, "newer" designs periodically have added "special" features, but the basic design seems to stand the test of time. This seems to be a good design for users.

Computers, on the other hand, have changed a great deal from ENIAC to Mac, and so too have their interfaces. Today's personal computers hardly seem like the same sort of machines as their not-so-distant ancestors. Will the Macintosh interface, for instance, be able to stand the test of time? The main user operations and style of the Mac have not changed for several years, yet it does have some expanded functionality. In the computer business, lasting for seven years is a good beginning, but the goal is that, a few decades from now, the Macintosh will still be used as a benchmark for new, improved interfaces.

Principles of design are hard to articulate: the more you state and use them, the more exceptions there seem to be. Nevertheless, many user tasks/

S. Joy Mountford

operations follow the same sorts of basic behaviors and can be modeled in similar fashions. Much of our everyday activity is involved with searching, retrieving, editing, and sharing information with others. The computational details of how something is edited are mercifully invisible to the user. However, in comparison to the way we actually just "do" these tasks in the real world, we still have to learn a relatively complex set of procedures to perform editing and retrieval tasks. The art and science of interface design depends largely on making the transactions with computers as transparent as possible in order to minimize the burden on the user. This section illustrates some of the new technologies that are most likely to change the user's experience with the computer, in an effort to make users' tasks more natural to perform.

One of the interesting things to note about the technologies described in this section is that many of them have their roots in a variety of other engineering professions and are just beginning to have a presence within the computer world. More particularly, they are having their first real application and use within the interface in an effort to add some interface functionality or meaning. We suspect that many of the expectations and styles of user interaction may change based upon a much richer set of interface technologies. Ways of expression and qualities that have hitherto been viewed as exclusively "human" can now start to become part of our computer systems. We may soon be able to converse with our computers by speaking and gesturing, to control dynamic multimedia objects with our own two hands, and to perceive the status of a system at a glance through such means as color and animated visualizations of internal processes. These sorts of capabilities will substantially change the ways we can use computers and also what we will begin to expect from them. The more successful we are at interface design the more likely it is that we can achieve seamless and transparent interaction between users and their entire technological environment.

The problem with a lot of technological innovations (for example, stereographics) is that they seem to be dandy in a demo situation, but it is not clear what the technology will provide for the user. In other words, they seem to be technologies in search of a problem. It is the job of engineers to invent new technological capabilities and to demonstrate them, but it is the job of an interface designer to see a problem that a user may have or to consider a new, better way that a user's task can be accomplished. Sometimes technologies can help; sometimes redesign without any technological innovation may be the solution. On the other hand, it has been hard to evaluate all the benefits of some technologies. Years after color in computer displays was introduced, its effects and uses are still being explored. We do know that color is attractive and better simulates the real world; the issue before us, though, is how to best to apply it in some meaningful fashion at the interface (see Salomon's chapter).

Our current interface styles have been accused of being designed for use by a "deaf, mute Napoleonic person" (as Bill Buxton says), because both hands are rarely used except in typing, and sound is used hardly at all. The ability to have multiple I/O devices and to configure your world as you wish would enhance individual control, permit user customization, and enable user preference (see the chapter by Chen and Leahy). Currently, when we use a mouse to point, the *movement* of the mouse has limited "meaning"; for example, selecting individual items, grouping objects together with the "lasso," or performing drag-and-move activities. Having the ability to use the actual motion to express gestural-like "meanings," such as those we indicate with beckoning or throwing gestures, promises to increase the range of expression at the interface (see the chapter by Kurtenbach and Hulteen).

The film industry has long used different media effects dynamically over time. However, until recently, this kind of information has been too costly and slow to provide in any meaningful fashion across a range of applications. This limitation is quickly changing, and in their chapter, Baecker and Small discuss some of the ways in which animation could be used successfully at the interface. Another byproduct of the power of animation is the ability to provide a visualization of information that has not been amenable to presentation before, such as ways of representing program execution through animation.

As the user's interface style becomes more powerful interactively through the use of more expressive motor activities, the desire to converse becomes stronger. Richness in one modality (motor) needs to be enhanced with provision for the other naturally concomitant skills (verbal). The ability to build upon certain natural characteristics of human behavior can increase the responsiveness and conversationality of the computer (see Schmandt's chapter). As the potentially available number of communication methods for control of the user's environment increases, so too does the need to provide new methods of richer information display. New data types and media will enable presentations of a much richer and varied bandwidth of communication. It seems as if sound may be one of the information channels that historically has been underutilized (see the chapter by Mountford and Gaver) and that could substantially enhance the task environment when coupled with an associated rich interface environment.

Interface designers caution against buying systems based on their added functionality or extra widgetry. Users should consider whether the extra features actually contribute anything in terms of usability—often extra features buy more trouble for the user. One of the most popular areas of interface growth is in the development of hypertext and multimedia systems. Even the press is beginning to demand to know what such systems are for, and furthermore for whom they are best suited. Gygi's piece in this section describes some of the symptoms and solutions for the problem of designing usable hypertext. As we add features to support natural, individual, and expressive user communication, the so-called standard and consistent interface may be in danger of becoming fragmented. This would seriously undermine all the great strides forward in interface expressiveness. During this transitional phase of interface development, "hybrid systems" can serve as good examples for interface designers—in his chapter, Blake suggests that the hybrid systems of today may become the standard systems of tomorrow.

Perhaps the metaphor of filmmaker, not desktop publisher, is a more apt one for the creators and viewers of tomorrow's technologies. The use of this section's expressive, truly interactive technologies will continue only to the extent that their interfaces are adequate, enabling, and engaging to users. This can be achieved successfully only by approaching the task-technology match from the user's point of view. The papers in this section are not just about adding new technologies to the interface—all of them examine the nature of the user's tasks/problems and explore ways in which technologies can be adapted and applied to facilitate and enhance users' performance.

These chapters provide a glimpse of some new technology trends that promise some exciting changes in users' power and the types of activities they will be able to engage in with their computers. The most interesting part of these potential changes to the interface will come from the integration of new technologies in different combinations for different tasks. A richer sensory environment will enable a greater range of expression, making computers more powerful extensions of our natural capabilities and goals.

Animation at the Interface

DESPITE MANY YEARS OF ADVANCES in computer graphics hardware and software, and in human interface technologies, designs, and styles, our user interfaces are still primarily static. The purpose of this chapter is to review ways in which dynamic imagery and animation have been used in interfaces to date, and to sketch some ways in which they could be used to enrich the interfaces of the future. Our thesis is that current uses of animation at the interface have barely scratched the surface of what is possible and interesting.

Ronald Baecker
Ian Small

Dynamic Graphics Project
Computer Systems Research Institute
and Department of Computer Science
University of Toronto

What Is Animation?

Animation is not the art of *DRAWINGS-that-move* but the art of *MOVE-MENTS-that-are-drawn*. What happens between each frame is more important than what exists on each frame. Animation is therefore the art of manipulating the invisible interstices that lie between frames. The interstices are the bones, flesh, and blood of the movie, what is on each frame, merely the clothing. [Norman McLaren, 1968, as quoted in Baecker (1969)]

Animation is "the graphic art which occurs in time" [Martin, 1969]. It is a dynamic visual statement, form and structure evolving through movement over time.

The Saturday morning cartoons with which we are all familiar barely scratch the surface of the possibilities of animation. Yes, animation can be used for entertainment and for storytelling, but it can also be used to establish a feeling or a mood, as a diversion, for drama, as identification, for selling or persuasion, and for explanation and teaching.

Inanimate objects can be energized with feeling and emotion [*Luxo Jr.*, Lasseter, Reeves, et al., 1986; *Red's Dream*, Lasseter, Reeves, et al., 1987]. Orders of magnitude of time and space can be compressed and made accessible [*Cosmic Zoom*, Verrall, 1968; *Powers of Ten*, Eames, 1971]. Time and space can be combined in innovative ways [*Pas de Deux*, Mc-Laren, 1967].

It is also important to realize that there are numerous animation techniques [Laybourne, 1979] with which one can produce effective dynamic imagery that are far simpler than the full motion of two-dimensional or three-dimensional character animation. Thus, we should look to the language of cinema for models of how our interfaces could behave. This suggests that we include, as global changes to the entire screen, the *cut*, the *fade in (fade out)*, the *dissolve*, the *wipe*, the *overlay*, and the *multiple exposure*. Locally, within a region of the screen, interfaces should allow the *pop on (pop off)*, the *pull down (pull up)*, the *flip*, and the *spin*. Finally, they should allow, as either global or local phenomena, *reverse video, color changes, scrolling, panning, zooming in (zooming out)*, and *close-ups*. We shall see below how such effects can make an interface more memorable and vivid, more captivating and enjoyable to use.

How Is Computer Animation Produced?

Animation in all forms and media, whether based on traditional painted cels, clay models, or computer-generated imagery, whether rendered in flipbooks, recorded on videotape, or displayed on a computer screen, is composed of sequences of static images changing rapidly enough to create the illusion of a continuously changing picture.

Animation depends on the fact that images formed on the human retina persist for some time after the source of the image has disappeared. Because of this, a set of images rapidly displayed in succession appear to blend together into a continuum. The speed at which images must be displayed in order to achieve apparently continuous imagery depends on the persistence time. For example, standard film speed is 24 frames (distinct static images) per second, and the NTSC video standard specifies 30 frames per second (which is actually produced as 60 fields per second, a field being either all the even or all the odd scan lines of the image). Animated sequences presented at 15 frames per second will be perceived by the average viewer as being jerky.

Animation produced on modern computers is fettered by the discrete nature of the computer's display. A modern display is composed of a set of colored or monochrome pixels arranged in a rectangular array called a raster. The contents of the raster are stored in a hardware device called a frame buffer. Images are created by setting each individual pixel in the raster to an appropriate color; when viewed as a whole, the collection of densely packed pixels can appear to represent a continuous image. Although this concept sounds crude in comparison to high-grade film stock, surprisingly good results can be obtained if care is taken in the way images are created, especially when a series of images is used to create an animated sequence.

While the pixel and the raster are the basic tools for displaying computer imagery, the step from a set of static images to an animated display is not a simple one. Effective animation on a computer display generally depends on some degree of hardware support, a number of software tricks, or a combination of both. Although hardware support can speed up the rate at which animation can be produced, the clever use of software techniques can also accelerate and improve a given platform's animation potential. These techniques include the use of *double buffering* [Baecker, 1979], *color map animation* [Shoup, 1979], and the use of *incremental updates* to redraw only those portions of a frame which have changed, a technique pioneered by the programmers of early videogames.

Animations can be specified in any number of ways (they can even be described in words, although they lose most of their magic in the telling), and computers can generate animation using a variety of techniques. *Picture-driven animation* [Baecker, 1969] creates dynamic sequences through the appropriate selection and positioning in each frame of one animation cel chosen from a family of similar cels. *Keyframing* [Burtnyk and Wein, 1971] relies on the specification of static images at a number of particular frames (keyframes). Based on the surrounding keyframes, the computer can then interpolate all the frames lying in between, a process called in-betweening. Both of these processes actually have their roots in traditional cel animation production. *Procedural animation* [Reynolds, 1982] is generated automatically from a procedural description of the animation; often the procedure will take a set of parameters, allowing it to produce an entire family of similar animation sequences, the particulars of which depend on the precise values of the parameters.

Each of these techniques has a particular application to and impact on the production of computer animation. The exact mix of hardware support and software availability determines to a significant degree the type, quality, and volume of computer animation that a particular environment can support. But in deciding what kinds of images we actually want to produce, hardware and software considerations are secondary to the *purpose* of the image and the *user's tasks and goals*. How can we employ animation to create more engaging, useful, and usable interfaces? We will examine three roles for animation: to reveal structure, process, and function. For each role, several subroles will be illustrated by scenarios.

Animation of Structure: Exploring Complex Environments

The field of real-time three-dimensional computer graphics has revolutionized design, simulation, and testing. The automotive design team of today can create a complete model of a hypothetical car and animate it in real time on their workstations, placing it in different environments and viewing it from different angles. Only ten years ago, a similar process would have required the construction of a scale or life-size mock-up, a much more expensive and time-consuming process. Our new capabilities accelerate and cheapen the design process, and encourage more alternatives to be explored in greater detail than was previously feasible.

SCENARIO, ANIMATION OF VIEWPOINT: EXPLORE VIEWPOINTS TO DETERMINE THE RELATIONSHIP BETWEEN AN ENTITY AND ITS ENVIRONMENT.

Consider the creation of new entities for which spatial considerations are important. The appearance of a hypothetical object from multiple viewpoints, whether the object is considered independently or in relationship to a surrounding environment, is of prime importance to its design. Significant questions include:

• What can be seen and how does it look from a particular viewpoint?
• Are there viewpoints from which the object is particularly unappealing or from which the object clashes with its environment?
• What is the overall impact that the new object has on its environment as one moves through that environment?

These questions can best be answered using animated walkthroughs or flybys. Numerous applications for the animation of viewpoint may be found in CAD systems and CAD applications.

A simple example of the use of animation viewpoints is provided by John Danahy's study of the impact of a proposed building project in the Ottawa Parliamentary Precinct [Danahy, 1988]. Figure A in the color insert illustrates Ottawa's Parliament Hill shown with and without a proposed new building, and also from two different perspectives. The street-level view makes it clear that the proposed new building will block pedestrian sightlines to existing key buildings. The ability to animate the viewpoint is crucial to achieving such insights.

SCENARIO, ANIMATION OF APPEARANCE: VISUALIZE HOW AN OBJECT, STRUCTURE, OR SYSTEM WOULD LOOK UNDER VARIOUS CONDITIONS OF LIGHT AND SHADE.

Consider the computer simulation of any complex object or structure. Depending on the nature of the object, the user may need to know the following:

- What does the object look like under different lighting conditions?
- How does the object interact with its surroundings under different lighting conditions?

Animating the appearance of the object will help to answer both of these questions. By animating the addition, movement, change of spectral qualities, and removal of different lights, we can simulate the object under different lighting conditions and in transition between those conditions.

Figure B in the color insert shows a computer model of the downtown core of Toronto at two different times of the day, producing radically different configurations of light and shadow.

SCENARIO, ANIMATION OF ALTERNATIVE FUTURES: EXAMINE ALTERNATIVE FUTURES TO EXPERIENCE HYPOTHETICAL ENVIRONMENTS VISUALLY OR TO SIMULATE ACTIVITIES TOO DANGEROUS OR DIFFICULT TO VIEW DIRECTLY.

Consider a situation that can evolve in a number of different ways. It is valuable to be able to simulate and visualize these possible futures in order to determine which is most desirable. Questions prompting the simulation and visualization include:

- What are the potential futures and their associated costs and benefits?
- What is the visual impact of each?
- What elements do each of the potential futures have in common?

Questions such as these can be addressed by animating each of the alternative futures. In essence, such animation is the visual equivalent to asking "What if ?" questions of a spreadsheet.

John Danahy has made extensive use of the animation of alternative futures in considering various planting schemes for softening the visual impact of power lines on the surrounding environment [Danahy, 1988]. Figure C in the color insert presents four images from a study prepared for the Ontario Hydroelectric Commission in which the effects of different kinds of vegetation were simulated over the entire growth cycle.

Of the three areas we discuss, animation of structure and its use in applications represents by far the most mature and widespread use of computer animation. It has been spurred for the past decade by the introduction and development of sophisticated hardware accelerators for assisting in the production of real-time animation. This highly specialized field has been embraced by the scientific and engineering communities, who view the use of this technology as a natural and logical extension of their work.

Animation of Process: Visualizing Algorithms and Programs

Another role for animation is in revealing or explaining complex processes such as computer programs. This is part of an activity that we call *program visualization* [Baecker, 1986].

A program is a computation that executes and unfolds over time, so it is natural to use animation as a method of portrayal. Our goal could be to explain the process, to simplify it to make it accessible, or perhaps to reveal its full complexity gradually and in a layered manner.

SCENARIO, ANIMATION OF ALGORITHMS: SIMULATE AND VISUALIZE A CLASS OF ALGORITHMS.

To understand how a particular algorithm or class of algorithms works, it often helps to construct a visual model of what happens when the program executes. Often, these models can be useful in comparing several algorithms that are similar but slightly different. These visual models are designed to address some of the questions frequently asked about algorithms:

- What are the basic characteristics of the algorithm?
- How exactly does the algorithm achieve its goal?
- Is the algorithm implemented recursively, as a loop, or in some other manner?
- What type of data structures does the algorithm use?
- How fast does the algorithm run with respect to other algorithms in the same class?

Each of these questions will be of particular interest depending on the programmer's requirements. Answers will be provided compellingly and convincingly by a successful animation of the algorithm, which can reveal an algorithm's traits, basic strategy, and overall performance characteristics.

In the film Sorting Out Sorting *[Baecker, 1981], a number of different sorting algorithms are animated and compared. The dynamic visual representations of the executing algorithms convey their basic structure in an extremely effective manner, as shown in figure D in the color insert. This figure presents six still images from the algorithm "race" held at the end of the movie, in which the nine algorithms race against each other on identical data, compellingly illustrating the performance differences between the algorithms.*

Another visual experiment included in Sorting Out Sorting *proved instructive. At the end of the film, we included as a recapitulation a 12-times speeded-up version of the entire movie. Animation sequences literally whiz by, but, because we've seen them before in slow motion, they are meaningful even at high speed. They become, in a sense, dynamic pictograms, animated icons representing the algorithms.*

Figure A: Ottawa's Parliament Hill
shown from two different
perspectives. Images courtesy of the
Centre for Landscape Research,
University of Toronto.

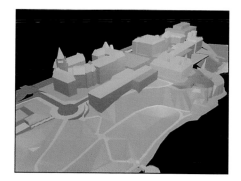

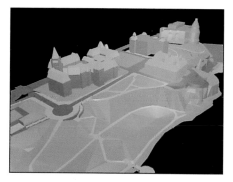

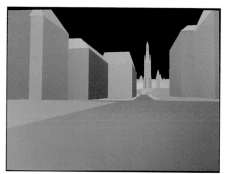

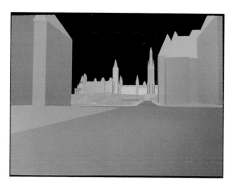

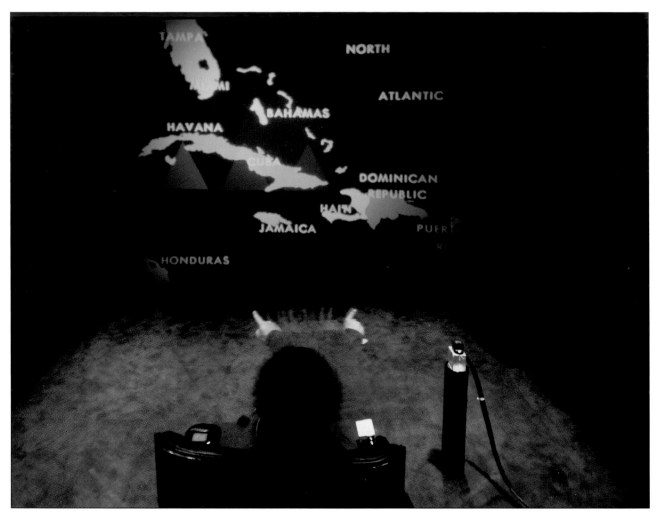

Figure K: Put That There. A time-lapse photograph shows a user "dragging" a triangle across a map of the Caribbean.

Figure A: Ottawa's Parliament Hill shown from two different perspectives. Images courtesy of the Centre for Landscape Research, University of Toronto.

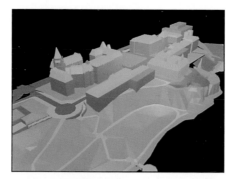

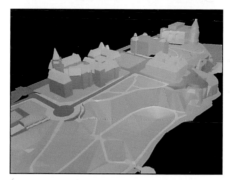

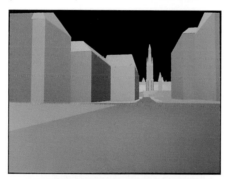

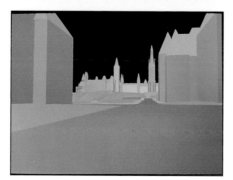

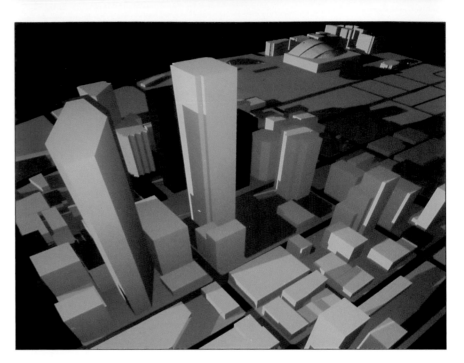

Figure B: A model of the downtown core of Toronto. B1 (top) shows the long shadows characteristic of the early morning, and B2 (bottom) represents the city at noon. Images courtesy of the Centre for Landscape Research, University of Toronto.

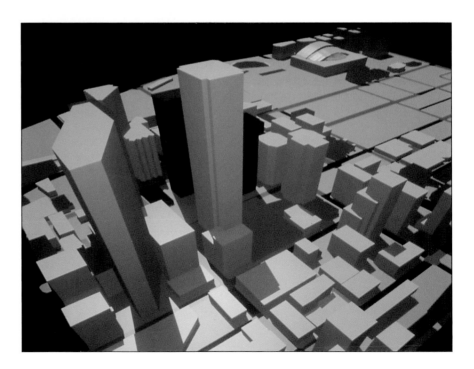

Figure C: An illustration of how a proposed planting scheme will help screen a person's view of an electric transmission line over a 15-year period as the vegetation matures. The images (read top to bottom) show a view before planting, after planting, after five years, and after fifteen years. Images courtesy of the Centre for Landscape Research, University of Toronto.

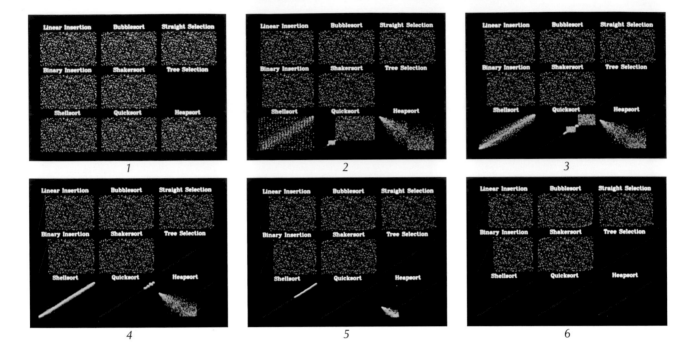

Figure D: An illustration of how interesting features of nine different sorting algorithms are vividly portrayed by their animations. For example:

- *The movement of data is depicted by the movement of dots. A color change (from yellow to red) denotes when an item reaches its ultimate "sorted" position.*
- *The recursive behavior of the quicksort and its use of partitioning are clearly visible (D2–D4).*
- *The property of shellsort in which, through multiple passes, it pushes all of the data closer and closer to the "sorted" state is apparent (D2–D5).*
- *The paradoxical tendency of heapsort to move large items closer and closer to the front before switching them to their correct position toward the back of the data is vividly shown (D2–D5).*
- *The five "n squared" algorithms are immediately distinguishable from the four that are "n log n" (D3–D6).*

Frames are excerpted from Sorting Out Sorting, produced and directed by Ronald Baecker, Dynamic Graphics Project, Computer Systems Research Institute, University of Toronto, 1981. Distributed by Morgan Kaufmann, Publishers.

Figure E: Color appearances change based on their relationship to other colors. Each "X" appears to be the color of the opposite background, however, both "X's" are the same color. Reprinted courtesy of Yale University Press.

Figure F: The small brown squares appear to be two distinct colors, but they are identical. Once again, placement and relationships with other colors affect interpretation. Reprinted courtesy of Yale University Press.

Figure G: When any color is added or changed in a design, the overall effect must be reconsidered. By altering only one color in this pattern (black changes to white), the entire character of the pattern is transformed. Reprinted courtesy of Yale University Press.

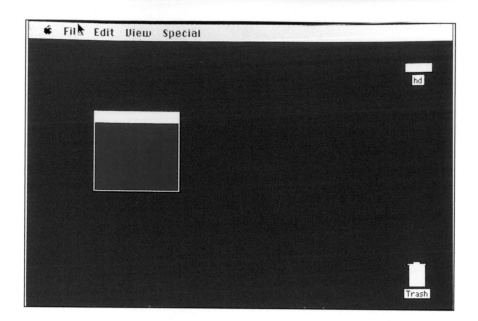

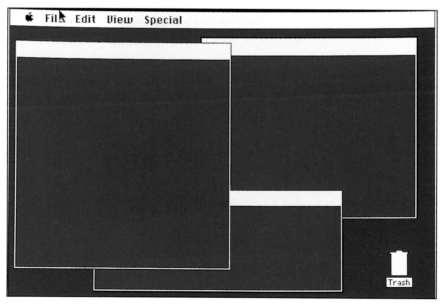

Figure H: How should colors be chosen for dynamically changing displays? When the size and placement of elements are altered, the overall color effect can change. This figure shows two abstracted Macintosh desktops. A user might select colors while looking at the window configuration of H1 (top), only to find these colors have a different effect in the H2 layout (bottom). The opening of several windows changes the apparent saturation of both the red in the background and the blue in the window interiors. Also, note that the user's work environment changes from primarily red to blue.

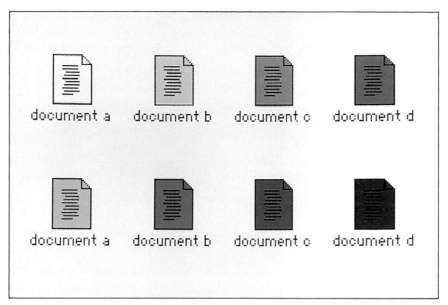

Figure I: Which document is oldest? In each row, color coding is used to indicate that age proceeds from the left to right—"document a" is the newest, "document d" is the oldest.

In the top row, the code shows age through "yellowing." Document a is the newest because it is a crisp white icon, while document d is the oldest because it has yellowed most. The strong contrast created in document d by the combination of deep yellow and a black outline is undesirable. The user's eye is quickly drawn to document d, while he would probably prefer his attention drawn to the newest documents.

In the bottom row, the coding uses degree of "dullness" to indicate age; the newest documents are brightest and most visually salient, while older documents become progressively duller. This coding more closely supports users' needs.

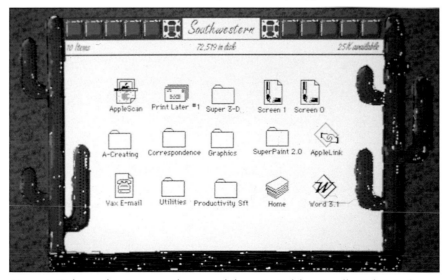

Figure J: Color and texture greatly expand the potential for visually rich interfaces; they can help provide users with compelling computing environments. As this playful example created by Kristee Kreitman shows, color and texture assist the creation of a "thematic" desktop. What new interface metaphors are possible when color and texture are available as design elements?

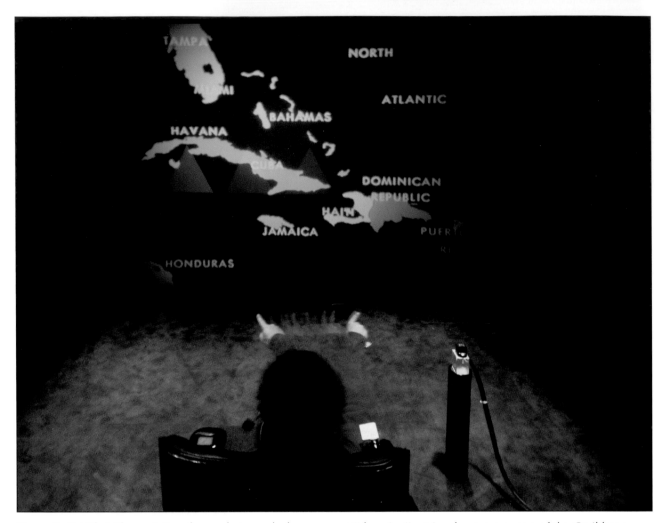

Figure K: Put That There. A time-lapse photograph shows a user "dragging" a triangle across a map of the Caribbean.

Figure L: The DataGlove™ (© VPL Research, Inc., 1988). Image courtesy of VPL Research.

Figure M: VIDEOPLACE Telecommunications. A teacher and student in different locations discuss a homework assignment. Each sees a composite image of the teacher's and student's hands pointing to relevant information (© Myron W. Krueger).

Figure N: A one-finger drawing produced by a user standing in the middle of the room.

Figure O: CRITTER, a computer-generated playmate.

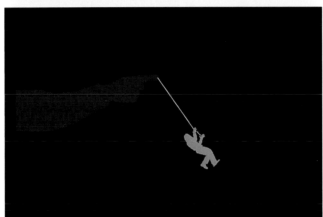

Figure P: Users interact via telecommunications at VIDEOPLACE.

Figure Q: A user can create a spline curve using thumbs and forefingers with VIDEODESK.

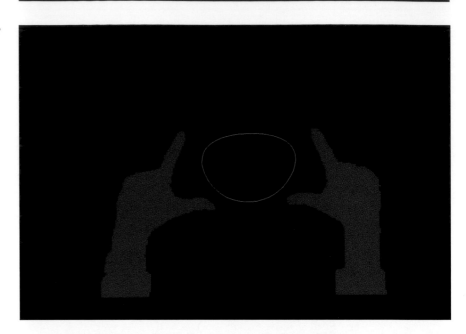

Figure R: Three-dimensional solids can be easily created "by hand" with VIDEODESK.

*Figure S: The VPL DataGlove™
Model 2 (© VPL Research 1989).*

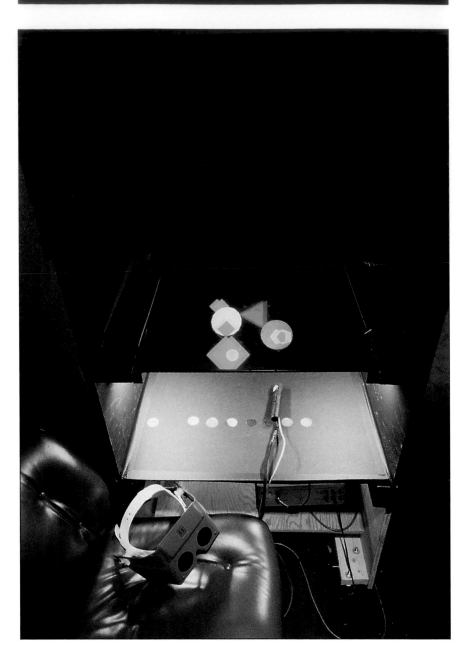

Figure T: Workstation prototype, developed at the MIT Architecture Machine Group, for three-dimensional drawing and manipulating virtual objects in a limited virtual environment (© Scott Fisher 1982).

Sorting Out Sorting was produced laboriously, by constructing and tailoring programs to visualize each specific algorithm to be animated. Other investigators have attempted to build tools to aid the process of program animation—for example, Balsa-II [Brown, 1988] and Movie and Stills [Bentley and Kernighan, 1987]. We also have looked at this problem. The result was LOGOmotion [Baecker and Buchanan, submitted for publication], a prototype system for the graceful and unobtrusive animation of algorithms. To use LOGOmotion, we merely indicate which procedures and data structures we want to observe, and LOGOmotion constructs a default animation of the execution of a LOGO program. If the default animation is not satisfactory, we describe how to improve it by writing additional code in LOGO.

Movies such as *Sorting Out Sorting* and systems such as Balsa-II and LOGOmotion are important because they encourage the use of animation as a vehicle for visualizing and aiding the comprehension of complex programs. How can we understand the behavior of distributed computing systems operating in dozens of sites, multiprocessor systems consisting of hundreds of integrated processors and memories, or expert systems operating with thousands of rules? Perhaps, once we learn how to define and construct animations of such systems, we will be better able to master their complexity.

Animation of Function: Making Interfaces More Comprehensible

Even if the computations underlying a program are simple, the interface to it may appear to be complex. Animation can help cut through the complexity of an interface. Animation can:

- Review what has been done
- Show what can be done
- Show what cannot be done
- Guide a user as to what to do
- Guide a user as to what not to do

In other words, animation can help us review the past, understand the present, and describe the future. It can help us answer the questions: "How did I get here?", "Where am I?", and "Where am I going?". We shall describe eight uses of animation—animation as:

Identification:	What is this?
Transition:	From where have I come, to where have I gone?
Choice:	What can I do now?
Demonstration:	What can I do with this?
Explanation:	How do I do this?

Feedback: What is happening?

History: What have I done?

Guidance: What should I do now?

SCENARIO, ANIMATION AS IDENTIFICATION: IDENTIFY AN APPLICATION QUICKLY AND VIVIDLY WHEN IT IS INVOKED.

Consider a user starting an application with which he is unfamiliar: the user is unsure of whether he has selected the correct application, and of whether the application does what he wants. Furthermore, he may have to wait while the application is loaded and initialized before finding out. Many home computer games have made use of this waiting period, which is an excellent time for:

- Identifying which application has been started
- Marketing and calling attention to the manufacturer's name
- Conveying to the user a sense of what the application does

These tasks can be accomplished effectively with animation. Although the application name and manufacturer can be identified by static type, an attractive animated presentation is more likely to be remembered. Although text and static pictures can inform the user of the application's function, an animation can convey information more vividly and more rapidly.

A typical example of this use of animation occurs in the Robotropolis Preview in the computer game Robot Odyssey 1 [The Learning Company, 1984]. The user is treated to a one-minute animated preview of highlights from the game, is introduced to the game's portrayal of him and his three robot companions, and is introduced to the task of ascending upwards through the five levels of Robotropolis with the help of the robots.

This type of animation is already in occasional use, particularly in video games, but it is not yet pervasive in any particular environment.

SCENARIO, ANIMATION AS TRANSITION: ORIENT THE USER DURING TRANSITIONS FROM ONE PROCESS TO ANOTHER.

Animation can be used successfully to portray and clarify transitions in the state of both the working environment and individual processes. In such cases, animation attempts to:

- Keep the user aware of changes to the working environment
- Locate and identify newly created entities within the environment
- Cue the user to new or old areas of interest.

These goals can all be achieved by simple animation effects.

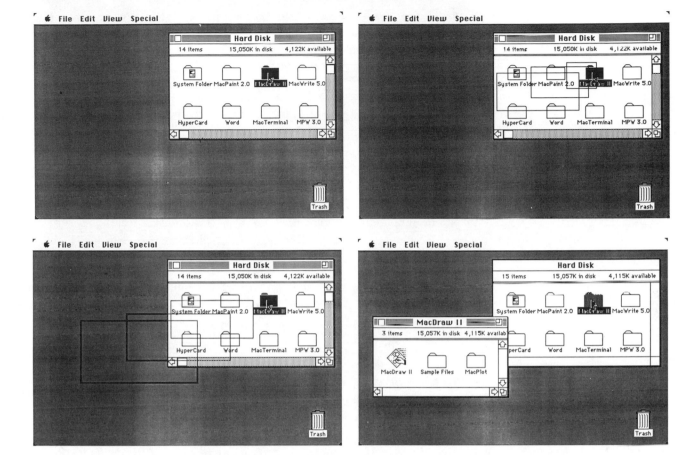

A good illustration is the zoom used in the Macintosh desktop environment (figure 1). The outline zoom that accompanies the opening (and closing) of an icon orients the user to the location and origin of the new window that appears on the desktop. This is particularly helpful in a crowded environment. If the new window were to appear without the opening zoom, it would be more difficult for the user to determine that he had indeed opened the correct icon. The closing zoom assists in informing the user where he was working before he started the process that has just been completed.

Figure 1: Transition to a new folder on the Macintosh Desktop (read right to left).

This type of animation is already in widespread use on the Macintosh, perhaps because of its relative ease of implementation and uncontroversial nature. In fact, HyperCard provides users with a variety of special visual effects to highlight transitions, including zooms, wipes, and dissolves.

SCENARIO, ANIMATION AS CHOICE: PROVIDE AN OVERVIEW OF COMPLEX MENUS.

Typical pull-down and pop-up menus occupy a fair amount of screen space, especially on personal computers, with their relatively small displays. This can result in a loss of context, as the information that relates to the user's menu choice ends up being hidden behind the menu. Furthermore, complex hierarchies of menus require large numbers of menu selections in order to arrive at the desired menu choice. Animated menus represent one potential solution to these problems.

The basic idea is simple. Instead of the menu and its choices being displayed statically, different sets of choices, submenus, and other items can be animated by displaying them in succession using techniques such as paging, flipping, cycling, scrolling, or three-dimensional rotation. The benefits that can result from such techniques include:

- Reducing the screen space required by the menu and the degree to which the menu obscures other material on the screen
- Allowing rapid display of the entire menu set and of the relationships between menu items

Consider, for example, a desktop publishing system in which there are large numbers of combinations of typeface, weight, slant, and point size. Conventionally, we could make a set of independent selections, not knowing if the combination is valid, or use a hierarchic set of menus designed to allow only valid choices. An alternative is to animate the set of all valid combinations (figure 2).

Animations of this kind are possible with current technology; research is required to determine if they are effective.

SCENARIO, ANIMATION AS DEMONSTRATION: IMPROVE THE INFORMATION CONTENT OF ICONS OR SYMBOLS USED TO PERFORM ACTIONS.

Although desktop environments often make use of icons to represent actions that can be performed, the static nature of these icons limits their information content. Instead, imagine the possibilities of using dynamically changing pictograms—animated icons. Such use of animation could:

- Increase the amount of information that is contained in the iconic representation
- Clarify the function of the icon through the use of animated rather than static symbols

Both of these items are best achieved through the use of carefully scripted animation that is tailored to the particular icon. The animation of an application icon allows more information about the application to be con-

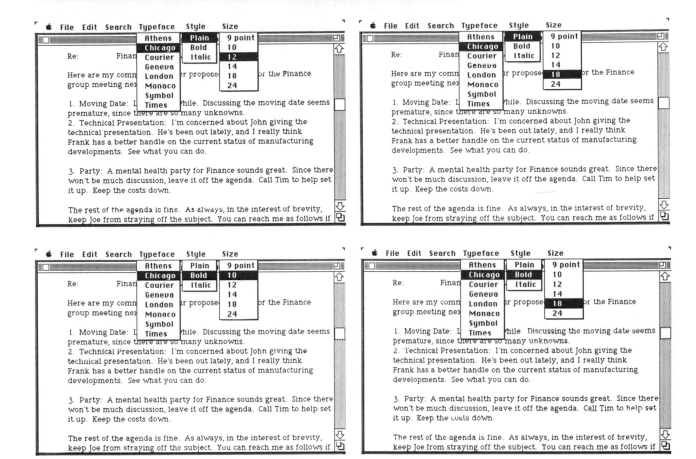

Figure 2: An animated menu set describing valid typographic choices (read right to left).

veyed to the user at an earlier stage; the concepts are similar to those described in the section entitled "Animation as Identification." The animation of action icons is more radical, however.

In many paint programs, most of the icons are self-evident, but some are not. Obscure icons include the Paint Can, the Spray Can, and the Eraser. Even more problematic is the trio of the Paint Brush, the Pencil, and the Closed Curve. It is not at all obvious from their icons how the attributes of brush shape, line thickness, and fill texture affect these three drawing operations. A great deal of trial-and-error may be required to understand what is going on. Animation can clarify underlying relationships and introduce functionality (see figure 3).

This type of complex animation requires significant computing power and some degree of operating system support, particularly if animation of a number of different icons is to exist concurrently. Again, research is required to determine the perceptual and cognitive implications of such animation.

Figure 3: An animated icon describing the Eraser in a paint program.

SCENARIO, ANIMATION AS EXPLANATION: PROVIDE MORE INTERESTING, UNDERSTANDABLE, AND COMMUNICATIVE TUTORIALS AND EXPLANATIONS.

Animation is a compelling communications medium, comparing favorably with the more commonly used static media involving text and pictures. As a result, a natural application of animation is for tutorials and explanations, such as the "Guided Tours" that are distributed with some Apple products. Whereas animation as demonstration provides only a superficial introduction to function, animation as explanation presents a detailed tutorial illustrating technique. These tutorials differ from error and help messages (see below) in that the situations they portray are purely hypothetical and are used only for purposes of illustration. Animated tutorials can:

- Depict complex sequences of steps and evolving situations more realistically and convincingly than textual explanations
- Maintain the user's interest by being lively and enjoyable

Consider the processes of Copy and Paste in the Macintosh. An animated tutorial such as that shown in figure 4 could communicate very effectively the concept that the Clipboard holds only the result of the most recent Cut or Copy operation, highlighted in figures 4a and 4c by the dashed line, and not also the result of a preceding action.

Such animations must be designed well in order to be effective, the large investment of time required usually precluding their use. Tools for accelerating the authoring of these animations must therefore be developed.

SCENARIO, ANIMATION AS FEEDBACK: PROVIDE CURRENT INFORMATION CONCERNING THE STATUS OF A SYSTEM OR ITS BACKGROUND PROCESSES.

A considerable amount of information about processes running in the background can be conveyed to the user through an iconic representation of each process. This approach was advocated by Myers [1984] in his design of the Sapphire windowing system for the Perq workstation operating environment. Figure 5 shows a Sapphire icon at four stages in the execution of a C compiler processing the file foo. The upper horizontal bar is a percent-done process indicator [Myers, 1985] showing the progress of the compiler on a set of files. The three stars indicate that the window associated with the icon is not displayed; as can be seen from figure 5d, the window was brought on to the screen after the keyboard input request signaled in figure 5c. In addition, the exclamation mark in figure 5d indicates that the process needs attention.

We can extend these ideas and adapt them to create a more animated interface. Animated icons associated with processes could convey such information as:

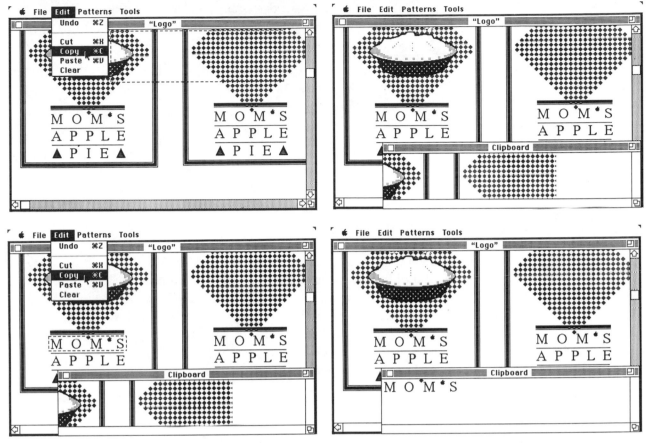

Figure 4: An animated tutorial: only the last Copy appears in the Clipboard (read top left, top right, bottom left, bottom right).

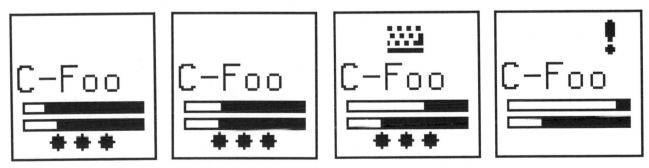

Figure 5: An animated icon giving feedback to Sapphire users. This figure is taken from Brad Myers' article, "The User Interface of Sapphire," IEEE Computer Graphics and Applications, Volume 4, Number 12 (December 1984), © 1984 IEEE.

- Whether the process is active at any given instant in time
- What portion of the computer's time is being devoted to the process
- What balance of other computer resources is required by the process
- How close the process is to completion, as is done, for example, with file copying in the Macintosh Finder and with pagination and file saving in Microsoft Word

Simple animation can communicate such information to the user, using scaling, transparency, color animation, and bar graphs similar to Myers's. Imagine an icon that needs attention changing color to become progressively more red as it is ignored for an increasingly long period of time. Indeed, color could also be used to convey the balance of resources required by the process, with a process that is totally compute-bound being blue, a process totally I/O-bound being yellow, and more balanced processes having a color in between. Similarly, an icon's size could be used to convey an idea of how much compute power the process is consuming.

Obviously, attempting to communicate all this information for each process would lead to both a pulsating display and a riot of information that the user would not be able to assimilate easily. Thus, good design is essential. Given sufficient compute power and operating system support, such animation could be provided easily.

SCENARIO, ANIMATION AS HISTORY: PROVIDE ACCESS TO INTERACTION HISTORY AND TO HISTORICAL CONTEXT.

Users frequently get lost in applications. All of a sudden, they realize that they have no idea where they are or how they got there. The availability of history is important to the user in these situations, for it can:

- Show exactly what steps were taken to get to the current state
- Demonstrate the precise results of specific actions recently undertaken
- Provide rapid overviews of general trends in the user's recent activities

Consider the process of copying a portion of a graphic document into a word processing document using Cut and Paste. An animated history such as that shown in figure 6 could allow the user to review how a picture was included in the document and from where it came.

Animated historical overviews can be produced easily by supplying a history of the user's actions to a procedural animation package that interprets the transactions in the historical log to produce descriptive animation specific to the actual application or environment being used. These *animated histories* are almost exact playbacks of the user's recent (or not so recent) activities. Of interest is the ability to play these histories backwards or forwards, to concentrate on specific segments, and to play them at

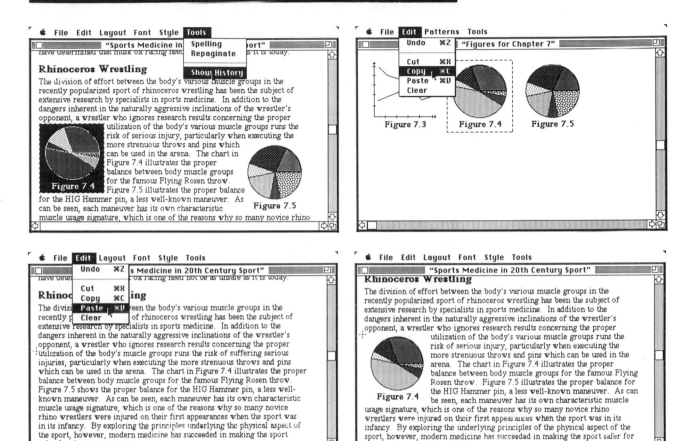

Figure 6: An animated history showing a Copy and Paste sequence (read right to left).

arbitrary speeds. This latter ability allows the user to compress a great deal of history into a short period of time, which is useful for refreshing familiar material or scanning for general trends. More abstract historical animation is more complex to produce but can rely on similar strategies [Kurlander and Feiner, 1988; Sukaviriya, 1988].

Although simple, this approach requires extensive disk space for storing the transaction logs, which makes it infeasible for current floppy-disk-based home computer applications. For scientific workstations, however, animated histories are closer to becoming a reality.

SCENARIO, ANIMATION AS GUIDANCE: IMPROVE THE DELIVERY OF ERROR MESSAGES AND HELP AND THEREBY ACCELERATE THE CORRECTION OF MISTAKES.

Computers, even those with what are considered user-friendly environments, tend to produce error messages that are abrupt, unhelpful, or cryptic. The careful use of animation in these messages can aid in making them appear less intimidating, can convey more information, and can help users determine how to correct mistakes more quickly. Such animation can:

```
a
Now is the time for all
excellent dudes to come the
aid of the party!
1,$p

—
```

```
a
Now is the time for all
excellent dudes to come the
aid of the party!
1,$p
p
.p

—
```

```
a
Now is the time for all
excellent dudes to come the
aid of the party!
1,$p
p
.p
?
help

—
```

```
a
text ...
more text ...
still more text ...
.
next editor command
```

Figure 7: Animated guidance in response to a UNIX mode error.

- Indicate the set of steps that produced the error
- Show what happened as a result of these incorrect actions
- Show what would have happened had the user followed various similar courses of action
- Provide exact instruction demonstrating the steps required to achieve a desired result

The first two stages can be achieved easily using the techniques described earlier for producing animated histories. The third and fourth stages require the application to be able to determine possible courses of action, but these steps can use the same animation capability. In this case, the application produces alternative future histories that can then be displayed using the animated history mechanism, thus producing animated futures.

Even providing only the first two stages would be valuable. A common experience when one is confused and stuck is to describe the problem to someone else. Often, the other person doesn't even get a chance to respond, because in the very act of articulating what has been done, one often realizes the mistake that has been made.

Consider, as an example, the common append mode problem of the UNIX editor ed (figure 7). The user is typing text, but fails to realize that he has neglected to exit from append mode (7a). He becomes confused because the system appears mute (7b), and asks for help. The system then reviews his recent actions (7c), notes that he is in append mode (that is, executing an append command), and plays an animation showing typical uses of append (7d). "Aha!" says the user, immediately seeing the mistake.

The automatic generation of such guidance requires a system to "understand" what a user is trying to do, what has gone wrong, and what the user should do to fix it. This will likely require the application of artificial intelligence techniques.

The examples of *animation of function* appear simple. Yet appearances can be deceptive. There are difficult problems in the design of appropriate, effective animation. There are also difficult problems in implementation. Unlike *animation of structure* and *animation of process*, where we expect to require significant resources and where we are willing to wait for suitable effects, these new examples must execute instantaneously. If response is sluggish, users will retreat to the fast, safe world of static text and static pictures.

Conclusions

We have described a variety of roles for animation at the interface. *Animation of structure* and *animation of process* are relatively conventional roles that emerge out of several decades of work in interactive three-dimensional computer graphics and in program visualization. Far newer and therefore in a sense much more exciting, however, is *animation of function*. Here we are not only using animation at the interface but also animation in and of the interface.

But many questions remain. How do we design such animations so that they are clear and comprehensible, attractive and appealing? How do we prevent animation from becoming too complex to be effective? It must not become too busy and too distracting, either spatially—in that too much is going on in parallel—or temporally—in that too much is changing too quickly. Such questions can be answered only through the extensive development of prototypes and through user testing.

Can we develop tools to enable the automatic or semi-automatic construction of interface animations? Or is this premature—need we focus all our energies for the moment on developing the art of describing algorithms and interfaces visually, on advancing the art of *program illustration*?

If we can answer some of these questions and further explore the ideas developed in this paper, *program illustrators* of the future, both human and automated, will be able to employ animation, along with other media such as audio and video, to make interfaces to computer systems more enjoyable and more comprehensible.

Acknowledgments

Support from the Natural Sciences and Engineering Research Council of Canada, from the Information Technology Research Centre of the Province of Ontario, and from Apple Computer is gratefully acknowledged. Work on this paper was begun at the University of Toronto and was completed while the authors were visiting the Human Interface Group of Apple Computer.

New Uses for Color

COLOR IS USED in a variety of ways in everyday life, yet it is seriously neglected in the human-computer interface today. Successful application of color is difficult, and this is surely one reason for its underuse. Also, computers haven't been capable of displaying color for very long. Undoubtedly, many of the best uses for color on the computer are still to be uncovered, designed, and tested.

This work offers a collection of new interface ideas to explore. Some of the discussion describes work undertaken at Apple by myself and others—the problems we encountered and the solutions we considered. What you read here will likely raise more questions than it will provide answers. I do not spell out any concrete color "rules" to follow. Rather, I provide ideas to think about, take issue with, and hopefully be inspired by.

The relevant literature on color is overwhelming. It draws on many disciplines, including physics, art, physiology and psychology. Details on specific aspects such as color reproduction, color models, monitor calibration, and human eye physiology are not covered here. References are given to some sources for this information.

Why Is Color Application So Difficult?

There are a number of reasons why it is difficult to design with color. Most of these problems are not unique to computer environments. A brief look at some of the issues will aid further discussion.

Gitta Salomon
Advanced Technology Group
Apple Computer

COLOR INTERACTS WITH ITS ENVIRONMENT

The appearance of a color depends on the colors in the environment that surrounds it. Any color is influenced by its location, its placement, and the size and shape of the area it fills. Many illustrations of these phenomena are given in Josef Albers' book *The Interaction of Color* (see figures E, F, and G in the color insert).

The implication to interface designers: we need to take a great deal of care in applying color. We cannot choose colors in isolation; they must be chosen in context. Our color "compositions" may need refinement and alteration with the addition of every color. If a specific color scheme is important, we have to protect it from colors that could alter its appearance. For instance, Shell Oil Company placed its yellow shell-shaped logo on a controlled red background. They realized the logo's impact could be severely reduced by leaving the background to chance [Claus and Claus, 1971].

Computer color design has a unique problem. How should colors be selected for dynamically changing displays? In the real world, artists carefully pick colors to fit static environments; living rooms and car interiors aren't easily reconfigured. But the Macintosh Desktop can change (see figure H in the color insert). Windows can change in size, shape, or number. A user might choose colors for the Desktop interface elements that look fine in the context in which they were chosen, but as soon as the user opens ten windows, the desired visual effect may be lost.

CHANGING EXTERNAL CONDITIONS AFFECT PERCEPTION

Ambient lighting, whether it is fluorescent, incandescent, or daylight, also affects the appearances of colors. Just as articles of clothing that match in the department store may not match in daylight, the environment a computer monitor finds itself in can alter color appearances. In my own office, I have to contend with the constantly changing illumination coming in through the windows combined with fluorescent lights overhead. Although I always recognize a single "orange" as "orange" on the screen, specific color schemes sometimes appear distinctly different as a result of the illumination.

Furthermore, computer monitors vary in their calibration. There is no guarantee that a particular color combination on one screen will look exactly the same or have the same effect on another screen.

PHYSIOLOGICAL AND CULTURAL DIFFERENCES AMONG INDIVIDUALS

The challenge of good color interface design is still more complex. Our user population is made up of individuals with diverse color perception capabilities. A few factors to keep in mind [De Grandis, 1986, and Murch, 1985] are:

- Older people are less sensitive to color and often need higher brightness levels. They also lose ability to discern blue hues.
- Eight percent of the male and 0.5 percent of the female population have color deficient vision. The most common deficiency is the inability to distinguish red from green.
- Cultural differences can affect the number and categories of colors individuals recognize. Common color names can refer to different ranges of hues in dissimilar cultures. Even occupational differences can create variations in color perception. Some people can discern subtle color distinctions where others cannot.

To compensate for some of these problems, color can be used in combination with other cues such as shape, pattern, or location. And colors that avoid discriminating against specific audiences can be chosen. For example, maps can be designed that are easily distinguished by people who are red/green color deficient.

What *Can* Be Done with Color?

Instead of despairing over the seemingly insurmountable obstacles discussed in the last section, I think the whole thing is rather intriguing. Color is a genuine challenge. Just as we wouldn't easily give up color in the world around us because it's too problematic to use, we shouldn't abandon trying to use color on the computer. What can we really do with color on the computer? What are the interface issues we can actually attempt to tackle? Basically, the way I see it, there are two distinct domains:

- We can design *interfaces that use color to impart information* to the user. That is, we can create interfaces where color either provides the user with information not available otherwise, or where color redundantly reinforces information imparted through another medium, such as text or shape.
- We can design *interfaces that allow users to choose colors* for their own devices, be they paint programs or presentation slides.

I want to make a couple of general points about each of these domains, and then I'd like to discuss some concrete examples from each arena.

INTERFACES THAT USE COLOR TO IMPART INFORMATION

The definition of information I assume here is rather broad. It includes the type of factual information imparted through "color coding"; for example, a map uses color coding to indicate climate zones by showing deserts in yellow and tropical rain forests in green. The definition also includes "aesthetic" information; that is, color that creates an *environment* for the user on the screen is also informational color.

When we furnish interfaces that use color to provide information, we set an example of how to apply color to computer displays. Therefore, skilled color designers should be involved throughout the design process. We recently observed Macintosh color monitor users [Wagner and Salomon, 1987] informally at Apple. What we saw reminded us of the way people applied multiple fonts at the Macintosh's introduction. People were inclined to overuse the capability to the point that visual clarity was actually degraded. In the case of fonts, many individuals learned to use them effectively after exposure to good examples. Similarly, we need to provide good examples of color use to achieve the same effect.

INTERFACES THAT ALLOW USERS TO CHOOSE COLORS

These interfaces take the form of various color selection tools and can run the gamut (no pun intended) from simple *pick-one-color-out-of-ten* tools to *RGB color model based* tools to *intelligent advisors* that help users select entire palettes of colors.

Sorting: An Example of Color Coding

IMPLEMENTATION OF A COLOR-CODING SCHEME

Recently, we constructed a prototype that color-codes icons in the Macintosh Finder to indicate attributes such as the age or size of a file. We faced several design decisions. Should hue, saturation, or value change to indicate different characteristics? Are there real-world metaphors that could facilitate the coding?

Choosing the Color Code   We selected saturation and value because we felt a hue-based code in this case is not intuitive. Our culture has no obvious codes or conventions of hue ordering to indicate attributes such as old, older, oldest or small, smaller, smallest. The visible spectrum has been suggested as an ordinary scheme, but many people do not remember the order that the colors follow. Literature supported our decision. In cartography, gradient color schemes are found to be easier to read than hue-based schemes [Keates, 1962]. Also, hue-based codes are mainly associated with qualitative rather than quantitative changes [Olson, 1981].

Using Real-world Metaphors   The first scheme we tried for "age of document" coding was based on a real-world metaphor—documents fade to yellow over time. Recent items were depicted as icons filled with white, older items were depicted as progressively more saturated yellows. It turned out that these color choices didn't work. The oldest items (deep yellow with a black outline) seemed to leap out of the screen, giving them disproportionate visual importance. The more interesting current items appeared white, completely negating their coding. Currently, we are applying a scheme that progresses from yellow through several gradually duller shades of brown (see figure I in the color insert). This scheme preserves the fading metaphor.

FINDING THE RIGHT CODING SCHEME

Finding a suitable coding scheme can be difficult. Several sources [such as DeGrandis, 1986, and Marcus, 1986] recommend specific color codes to use. Most agree that red elicits the strongest reaction from individuals. Many suggest that because of red's association with stop lights, it should be restricted to representing danger. In our informal survey [Wagner and Salomon, 1988], we found red to be one of the colors most frequently used by people devising their own coding schemes. It was used for a number of different reasons, none of which were inherently tied to danger. It seems a mistake to attribute any single meaning to a specific color.

Often, our instincts can lead to good codes. The fact that red or purple is never used for water features in maps, whereas blues and greens are often used, suggests we intuitively can recognize some effective color codes [Keates, 1962].

Providing a legend, as many maps do, may be a good alternative when less intuitive codes are used. Additionally, codes can be learned over time. Through cultural conditioning, we've developed quite a few strong color associations. For example, black and orange are linked to Halloween; pink and gray recall the 1950s. People connect certain colors with the schools they attended. Every athletic team is associated with distinctive colors. Spectators immediately know whether a team is "home" or "visiting" by the way colors are applied to the uniforms (light on dark or dark on light) A brief user test should quickly indicate if a code contradicts common belief.

Using Redundant Color—Two Cues Are Better Than One

Color can be used to give a user the intimation of reality. It can improve a user's understanding of the situation and support immediate comprehension. For example, when the technique of colored "hillshading" is applied to maps to show land surfaces such as mountains and valleys, readers react positively [Keates, 1962]. Similarly, military cockpit displays often provide environmental information through color; the sky may be shown in blue, brick buildings in red. Using color in this way may aid search time [Reising and Artez, 1987].

These examples suggest that color can help users understand interface metaphors. The original Macintosh Desktop metaphor was restricted by a design that only allowed black and white. How would its appearance have differed if the designers had used color? Could it have included more functionality if the designers had had unlimited access to shape, color, and texture to support the metaphor? With the ability to quickly render full-color scenes on the computer, we can simulate three-dimensionality and provide richer, more effective, and easier-to-understand metaphorical interfaces.

What new kinds of metaphors could we support with the addition of color? A creative example of an alternate "desktop" is shown in figure J in the color insert. The figure illustrates the potential for creating personal "artificial realities" using a combination of texture and color. It suggests a way to provide a visually rich environment that users might find aesthetically pleasing. Color provides the opportunity to express things that could not be as effectively or attractively represented in black and white.

It's commonly recognized that environmental color can influence state of mind and mood. For this reason, school and hospital rooms are often painted specific colors. As computer displays grow in size, we can use color to create more complete user environments that support the activities to be undertaken. In the development of an experimental cooperative work environment, Capture Lab, environmental color was applied to make the surrounds more conducive to group work [Mantei, 1988]. Specific color combinations were used to give the appearance that visual distance between participants was less than it actually was. We can take this type of use of color one step farther, and bring it into the screen itself to help support the activities underway.

COLOR AS A MNEMONIC

When presented in conjunction with certain shapes and locations, color can create strong associations. Why is it likely that the strongest association you have when I mention the term "Pepto-Bismol" is pink—and a very specific pink at that? Likewise, the yellow boxes at the film counter are immediately recognized as Kodak, the yellow-rimmed magazine in the mailbox is obviously the *National Geographic*. People can recall the color of a magazine advertisement and the part of the page it appeared on, but little else. It seems possible that we could use distinctive colors similarly within computer programs—colors that appear in certain contexts could aid recognition and recall. Why not give people the ability to attach colors to parts of documents and provide color "bird's-eye views" that quickly lead users to certain locations? Searching within large documents could become much easier.

Interface Possibilities for Color-selection Tools

COLOR-SELECTION TOOLS BASED ON REAL-WORLD MODELS

Most color-selection interfaces in use today are based on "color spaces"—conceptual models that provide a way to describe color. These models often lead to simple calculations, and programmers can work with them easily. However, users unfamiliar with how the spaces are defined can find them confusing. For example, users confronted with the commonly used "RGB space" have no intuitive basis for choosing the numbers to input for the red, green, and blue parameters. Some selection interfaces try to visually depict the color model in use. Because color models use three dimensions to describe color, they can be difficult to represent on a two-dimensional computer monitor.

But what are the tasks typical users are trying to accomplish? Rather than provide tools that try to represent the actual spaces, we can take advantage of the color knowledge users bring to the program to help them select colors. For example, in paint programs designed for skilled painters, color picking tools that let the user "mix" paints as they do in the real world would make sense (see Blake's chapter in this volume). If a program's purpose is to simulate lighting design, why not replicate the same procedures lighting designers use with real physical gels and lights? Most people can easily choose colors from displays of the available choices, such as crayon boxes or paint chip racks in hardware stores. In the same way, selection interfaces can present the basic choices "up front." We can use relevance feedback—the user indicates how close the current color is to the desired color—to refine choices and arrive at the "right" color.

HELPING USERS SELECT MORE THAN ONE COLOR AT A TIME

Sometimes users have to select more than a single color at a time. The task they have at hand involves selecting a set of colors that work together. Nonexpert color users could benefit from a program that would provide a dynamic, interactive way to examine numerous color combinations. The program could be fashioned after the existing consumer software product, *Jam Session* (Brøderbund, 1987). *Jam Session* lets users "play along" with songs regardless of their musical ability. By using the computer's keyboard, the most unmusical user can indicate when they want to make a change, thus indirectly affecting what is played without ever hitting a wrong note. In the same way, "Color Jam Session" could let users indicate where they wish to make a color change and the program would provide suggestions for what the color change might be. The user could veto suggestions and request other possibilities.

Programs that provide assistance to the user in color-related tasks could be tailored to various application domains. It's often easiest to provide assistance when the domain is well-known, as described in the next section.

PROVIDING COLOR-SELECTION ASSISTANCE

PowerPoint (Microsoft, 1988), a program for making presentation slides, provides an interesting tool for creating color schemes. A user selects a slide background color from a large set of choices. The program responds with several foreground color possibilities. Once a foreground color is selected, the program displays sets of "accent colors." Every time the user makes a selection, the screen displays what the final slide will look like. The program spares the user from constructing an entire color set from scratch, but the user maintains an important role by choosing between options. In addition, *PowerPoint* permits the user to override any of the colors in the suggested schemes. After exposure to many examples, users might learn some of the "rules" necessary to construct quality slides.

USING NEURAL NETWORKS TO PROVIDE ASSISTANCE

Color-selection "assistants" for users can be a powerful interface tool. In limited domains, such as presentation slide design, rules for color design can be formulated. In general, though, it seems that artists and designers are often intuitive and don't rely on concrete color rules in their work; therefore, defining rules for a color expert system could be difficult.

Last summer, I had a hunch color composition could be approximated by the type of "pattern matching" neural networks support. By training a network with color examples, we might be able to teach it successful color combinations. We set out to create a neural net-based "assistant."

We explored the problem of selecting colors for the Macintosh desktop interface elements, such as the scroll bars and window titles [Salomon and Chen, 1989]. A group of designers created "good" color sets, and these sets were used to train a network. Once trained, the network was embedded in a color-selection program. Users were able to select as few (or as many) colors as they desired and at any time could request the program to complete the set. Users often liked the network's suggestion, but objected to one or two colors. Those colors could be easily changed—a much simpler task than picking the entire color set from scratch. Users were also exposed to color solutions they might not have thought of themselves.

Not everyone who tried the neural net program was satisfied with the results. One person always preferred random color choices better than the network's suggestions, because she disliked its bias toward pastels. This raised some interesting questions. Because color is often an issue of taste and no two designers handle it in exactly the same way, it might be worthwhile to train the network in several distinct styles. For example, one training session could be based only on high-tech color sets, another on colors Matisse painted with, and another on a specific culture's color preferences. A user could select a preferred "genre," and the appropriate training results would be swapped in. The network might also adapt to an individual's taste. Preferences could be inferred by the color selections a specific user made over time.

Using Color to Visualize Data and Processes

SUCCESSES IN VISUALIZING LARGE DATA SETS

Color can be used to help people extract useful information from seemingly uninterpretable volumes of data. By assigning different shades of the hues red, green, and blue to different levels of blood flow, researchers have been able to analyze changes in blood flow to the human cerebral cortex [Lassen, 1979]. In order to visualize a complex simulation model of a particular pest infestation, color computer graphics were successfully applied [Cox, 1988]. A total of seven dimensions of data were capable of depiction in the resulting simulation "movie." Three of those dimensions were represented with color; three more were encoded on each of the three spatial axes. The seventh dimension, time, was embodied in the frame-by-frame nature of the movie itself.

The effectiveness of this use of color relies more on human pattern recognition than on the ability of individuals to recognize specific colors. For instance, two viewers of a simulation movie need not have complete agreement on the hues of the colors shown. They both can still recognize movement and patterns. Even those with color-deficient vision can see "clusterings" in the data. Therefore, using color for data visualization gets around many of the problems with color described earlier.

A certain level of complexity is involved with selecting how colors should be mapped onto data sets to aid visualization. Color assignments that make for interesting-looking images may be meaningless from a scientific standpoint. Even worse, color may be applied in such a way that it causes false interpretation.

USING DYNAMIC COLOR CHANGES FOR NOT-SO-LARGE DATA SETS, TOO

We're accustomed to color providing us with temporal cues. As seasons change, colors in our environment change. By looking at the color of the leaves on trees, we can roughly estimate the time of year. Similarly, the color of the sky indicates the time of day. Where extreme precision is unnecessary, color can subtly furnish information. It can depict the extent of completion of a computer process, or the relative CPU load that a particular process requires (for an example, see the Baecker and Small chapter).

Color changes can also camouflage or, alternatively, call attention to structures. In Sunnyvale, California, a formerly sky-colored water tank was recently repainted green. Several residents noticed it for the first time. Similarly, as a user moves through complex environments, the computer could hide or reveal items that meet certain criteria. Using image processing and color theory techniques, some items could be visually amplified, other items could fade into the background. Unimportant items could literally be hidden in the shadows. Techniques used by fine artists offer still other possibilities. Spatial metaphors could be supported by desaturating colors and defocusing shapes to imply distance.

Conclusions

We've covered a lot of material in the last few pages. Much of the discussion has focused on the complexity of bringing color into the interface, and it's easy to become overwhelmed. However, it's just as easy to create a program such as "Color Jam Session," examine the issues it raises, and proceed, step by step, based on the findings. In tackling color, this is the approach we should take.

Through experimentation we can learn about people's expectations—what works and what doesn't. For example, by trying to provide users with "good" color sets, we discovered just how subjective "good" is when it comes to color. If we move forward by small increments, we can learn where certain techniques are appropriate and if and how they are extensible. As we gain familiarity with the domain, guidelines and rules may indeed emerge.

How should we continue? As I've pointed out, the world around us contains numerous examples of color use. Take another look at that piece of "op art" hanging on the wall. Much of op art combines vivid colors to produce the illusion of movement along boundaries [Barrett, 1971]. Can we apply similar kinetic effects to the computer screen to draw the eye quickly to certain areas? As screen size continues to grow, we'll need to use such effects. Even that dish of cellophane-wrapped candies on the coffee table can be inspirational. Why not try visually bundling similar datatypes in semitransparent, color-coded wrappers? At this early stage in our explorations, any intriguing idea may be worthy of investigation.

Figures E, F, and G were selected with the guidance of Sonya Haferkorn. Penny Bauersfeld assisted with the creation of the images shown in figure H.

Recognizing the Symptoms of Hypertext . . . and What to Do About It

Kathleen Gygi

Interactive Telecommunications Program
New York University
Summer Intern, Apple Computer, Inc.

HYPERTEXT IS BECOMING EPIDEMIC, or so it seems. It used to be that computer illiteracy was the problem. Then hypertext came along, making bold promises about a more natural way of representing information, leading to greater ease of use. But sometimes the cure can be worse than the disease. Hypertext, like any new medium, comes with its own set of unique problems.

Ostensibly mimicking the way the brain stores and retrieves information, hypertext's aim is to permit fast and easy access to vast quantities of information by establishing multidimensional links among related items. But even when hypertext is used only as a presentation medium, users are prone to develop hypertext-related symptoms—spatial and conceptual disorientation, for instance—if designers have not guarded against them.

Until building hypertext systems becomes a mature art, many of these symptoms will persist—but conscientious designers can mitigate them simply by applying some design rules and common sense. The first step is to recognize the early warning signs. The following diagnostics are for both hypertext designers and those who are sure they are immune to hypertext. Today, many programs have hypertext-like characteristics, whether or not their designers choose to label them "hyper."

The checklist can be used to answer such questions as: "How do I know I have hypertext?", "When does multimedia become hypermedia?", and "Where am I?" If you are a hypertext or hypermedia designer and your users exhibit recognizable symptoms, you should take immediate action to relieve them. If you are an opponent of hypertext, the following preventive measures and remedies can apply to common nonhyper interface problems as well. Following the checklist is a clinical discussion of the etiology of hypertext pathology and some suggestions for a cure.

HYPERTEXT SYMPTOM CHECKLIST

1. Name

Do you call your software:

[ ] Hypertext
[ ] Hypermedia

2. Interface

Does your software interface feature:

[ ] Buttons
[ ] Cards
[ ] Frames
[ ] Links
[ ] Network(s)
[ ] Nodes
[ ] Webs

3. Organization

Is information in your software characterized by:

[ ] Chunks (bite-sized pieces)
[ ] Dynamic structures
[ ] Loosely structured information
[ ] Multiple information spaces
[ ] Multiple levels
[ ] Multiple modes
[ ] Sequencing or temporality

---

1. Name

If you call your product hypermedia or hypertext, make sure that you have carefully considered the use of remedial devices. If you don't, read on anyway. Even if you are *sure* you don't have a hyper-product, if you've checked any of the boxes on the checklist, you still might have a problem.

2. Interface

If you checked any of these items, you're talking hypertext lingo. For the uninitiated: a *link* is any electronic connection between two different pieces of information. Links generally connect something that is currently on the screen with something that isn't. They define the relationships between different pieces of information. Nodes, cards, or frames are the atomic information units. One chunk of information is generally displayed per window/card/frame. Full-blown hypertext is often considered to be a network of nodes connected by links. Links in these systems may be typed and/or have attributes. The user accesses information in the nodes by navigating the links. Links can be executable; i.e., they invoke some action or process. In some programs, links are triggered by clicking on the appropriate button/anchor (an iconically represented hot spot); in others, they are triggered by pulldown menus. Paths are default routes through the network. Analogous to *networks of nodes* are *stacks of cards* or *framesets of frames*, all connected by links.

Networks

Networks can exist on two levels: networks of information nodes, and networks of users. The oft-heralded network nation may be at hand. On the other hand, this may be just the telephone companies' agenda. The notion of semantic networks is prevalent in cognitive science and AI. Also note, the network is a dominant metaphor of postmodernism. Ted Nelson transcends this telementality by renaming the Big Network as the *docuverse*.

3. Organization

In conventional documents, physical structure and logical structure are closely related [Smith and Weiss, 1988]. Both are usually linear. The organizational structure and cross-references are fixed at printing time. In hypertext, links and nodes are presumably dynamic (unlike the predetermined branching in older generations of software). In traditional textual forms, the attempt to suggest multiple paths or branches is limited mainly to devices such as footnotes and cross references. Hypertext content is not bound by such organization.

Chunk Size

In hypertext, information is chunked in small pieces. A node is supposed to represent a single concept or idea. Some people feel that HyperCard is not really hypertext because the chunk size is too big (and you can link only between cards). This might get you off the hook if you feared you had hypertext for real. A nice hypertext slogan is: "One interface object per database object!" This is an attempt to make the abstract concrete by having ideas correspond to perceptual objects (the user manipulates ideas and their relationships by directly manipulating windows and icons) [Conklin, 1987]. It is also symptomatic of the move towards modularity and object-oriented computing environments.

Multiple Information Spaces

A document/dataspace can have multiple information spaces and each information space can be multileveled. If the difference eludes you, imagine a library. Each book is a different information space with a distinctive look and feel. You can quickly see the multiple levels within each book by looking at the table of contents. Try diagramming your document or dataspace. Do you need to draw lots of crisscrossing arrows to explain the connections between objects and levels of information? Do you quickly run over the edge of the paper? Do you need more than two dimensions? Transitions between dataspaces can be disorienting for the user, especially if they entail context switching.

4. Tasks

Any of these tasks might be an indicator of hypertext or a cofactor. They all are related to hypertext in its information-creation and -management strain, as opposed to mere information presentation. Hypertext can mimic software intended for these applications, because they all share common interface features. Programs are not technically considered to be hypertext if they lack some key feature. Window systems, for example, do not have the single underlying database; outline processors do not support references between outline entries; and database management systems lack the single coherent interface [Conklin, 1987]. But they, too, can exhibit hypertext symptoms.

5. Interaction

All of these are characteristic interactions in hypertext systems. They are the modes in which users peruse and manipulate information. Annotation, collaboration, linking, and versioning, like networks of users and dynamically changing content and structure, are features of extensible media.

Browsing and Navigation

Information is not brought to the user; rather, the user has to go to different places in the dataspace to get information. Cast as explorer, the user goes searching for information in an unconstrained manner. Less aimless than browsing, navigation is a metaphor used to impart some sense of intentionality as well as spatiality; however, the explorer's docuverse potentially encompasses all information that has been or can be recorded—a fairly awesome vista.

HYPERTEXT SYMPTOM CHECKLIST
Continued

4. Tasks

Is your software intended to be used for:

[ ] Authoring
[ ] Collaboration
[ ] Idea processing
[ ] Note taking
[ ] Outlining

5. Interaction

Does your software allow:

[ ] Annotation
[ ] Browsing
[ ] Linking
[ ] Navigation
[ ] Versioning

6. Multimedia

Does your software support or include:

[ ] Animation
[ ] Graphics
[ ] Numerical data
[ ] Sound
[ ] Text
[ ] Video sequences

7. User behavior

Do users of your software exhibit or produce:

[ ] Associative clutter
[ ] Cognitive or physical disorientation
[ ] Erratic or random choices
[ ] Overload of short term memory

8. Remedial devices

Does your interface feature:

[ ] Contextual webs, filters, interest neighborhoods
[ ] Goal pilots, goal trees
[ ] Graphical browsers
[ ] Guided or marked paths, trails
[ ] History lists, history trees
[ ] On-line help
[ ] Maps, global and local
[ ] Preview or retrace features

---

6. Multimedia

If you checked more than one of these, you have multimedia. Some people seem to think that multimedia representations constitute the dynamic element in hypertext. Not so. Hyper*media* requires the hyper-representation of nontextual information; that is, it is a network of linked nodes that contain multimedia information. The so-called dynamism in hypermedia results from the user's ability to alter the medium, not from a dynamic presentation. A caution: dynamic presentation does not guarantee a dynamic user. Educators learned this the hard way, but people persist in believing that multimedia is *inherently* motivating.

7. User Behavior

Do users frequently ask what they are supposed to be doing? Do they exhibit confusion, frustration, erratic or aberrant behavior? These symptoms are typical of being lost in hyperspace or overwhelmed by too much information and too many choices. They usually result from users' unfamiliarity with a domain and lack of good models of the information space. At-risk groups include: students, readers of the popular trade press, users of public information kiosks, and purchasers of personal productivity tools. The confused, the inattentive, those whose associative powers are weak, may link at random or compulsively. The severity of "linkitis" [Van Dam, 1988] is variable. Linking everything with everything is the electronic version of a bad acid trip. Watch out for link addicts! Associative clutter can manifest itself both on the screen and in the user's aching head.

8. Remedial Devices

If you checked any of these boxes, you are way ahead of the game. Nine out of ten barefoot doctors recommend graphical browsers as a preventive measure. This may be necessary but not sufficient. If you didn't check any of these boxes, consider this: Very few people memorize the page they are on when they put down a book. We need bookmarks—nothing fancy, any piece of paper will do. Try diagramming a path through your network. If you need bookmarks—or worse, yellow Post-its™ with GOTOs scribbled on them—you need help.

Discussion

WHAT'S IN A NAME?

Vannevar Bush, science advisor to FDR, is credited with the notion of a medium permitting linking by association rather than indexing [Bush, 1945]. Ted Nelson is usually credited with the moniker *hypertext*. In this case, *hyper-* used as a prefix does not mean *excessive*, but rather *above* or *beyond*. (*Meta-* used to be used to indicate going to a higher level, but *hyper-* is catchier). Semantic snags abound. For lack of a better term, we call hypertext structures *documents*. HyperCard stacks, for example, are hypermedia structures, but are they really documents?

Definitions of hypertext can be similarly confusing. They can be grouped into two types, broad-spectrum (Group I) and the more clinical variety (Group II). Group I definitions are commonly found in the popular press and in advertising and marketing literature. Group II definitions are found in technical journals and characterize research efforts at developing computer-supported hypertext systems. Consider the following examples.

Group I

- Hypertext works by association rather than indexing.
- Hypertext is a format for nonsequential representation of ideas.
- Hypertext is the abolition of the traditional, linear approach to information display and processing.
- Hypertext is nonlinear and dynamic.
- In hypertext, content is not bound by structure or organization.

Some of these are statements of resolve rather than definitions. They range from the vague to the seemingly specific. Hypertext as nonsequential or nonlinear text is something of a red herring. Even though printed text may be linear in physical form, there is nothing to say it is *logically* such: witness stream-of-consciousness fiction, poetry, letters, or notes to ourselves. Before there was electronic hypertext there was manual hypertext. The real problem is that text-based artifacts are used primarily to communicate the end products of human thinking rather than the intermediate stages. They do not generally portray the thought processes that produced them. People view writing as a way of communicating with others rather than a way of helping themselves think.

Group II

- Hypermedia is a style of building systems for information representation and management around a network of nodes connected together by typed links [Halasz, 1988].
- Hypertext is: 1) a form of electronic document; 2) an approach to infor-

mation management in which data is stored in a network of nodes and links. It is viewed through interactive browsers and manipulated through a structure editor [Smith and Weiss, 1988].

- Hypertext connotes a technique for organizing textual information in a complex, nonlinear way to facilitate the rapid exploration of large bodies of knowledge. Conceptually, a hypertext database may be thought of as a directed graph, where each node of the graph is a (usually short) chunk of text, and where the edges of the graph connect each text chunk to other related text chunks. An interface is provided to permit the user to view the text in such a database, traversing links as desired to explore new areas of interest as they arise, check background information, and so forth [Weiland and Shneiderman, 1988].

- Windows on the screen are associated with objects in a database, and links are provided between these objects, both graphically (as labeled tokens) and in the database (as pointers) [Conklin, 1987].

These are more rigorous attempts at definition, but no one seems to agree on the necessary features of hypertext. The crux of Group II definitions is the presence of computer-supported links. Another agreed-upon feature is that hypertext systems (ideally) allow the user to follow links quickly. An interesting characterization of hypertext is that it is a tool for manipulating information that is intermediate between word processors, which deal with information on the character or sentence level, and file managers, which deal with higher-level aggregates [Conklin, 1987]. Presumably, this intermediate level is appropriate for "idea processing."

Hypertext can come in several forms. Some systems are primarily devices for information presentation. Such systems incorporate only the front-end features of hypertext, to the end of providing a uniform interface. The hypertext back-end entails database creation and manipulation features. Computer-supported hypertext documents are extensible and editable. The user can add new links, add new nodes, or change the contents of existing nodes, while maintaining the integrity of different versions of the document. Collaborative-work applications must possess the ability to represent changes in the structure of information as group work progresses over time.

Hypertext as a presentation medium or as an interface for exploratory browsing is becoming increasingly popular with educators and developers of public displays—for example, for museums and information kiosks. Even though these systems don't have to deal with many of the technical problems associated with the back-end, they are not immune to the "lost in hyperspace" complaint. Many other programs share interface features with hypertext, including window systems, electronic mail, and teleconferencing applications [Conklin, 1987]. Although they may lack one or more of hypertext's characteristic features, they may still manifest hypertext-related symptoms.

Etiology

The major problem facing hypertext and hypermedia systems has to do with managing complexity—how not to overwhelm users with vast amounts of information. The authors of conventional documents spend considerable time organizing their presentations to that end. Hypertext documents sacrifice traditional discourse cues, both semantic and physical. Besides blurring the traditional roles assigned to author and reader, dynamic, extensible media impose a high cognitive load on users. The effort and concentration needed to maintain several tasks or trails at the same time can be overwhelming. Both author and reader must be more aware of process than they are in traditional documents [Conklin, 1987].

Lack of cognitive control structures can lead to cognitive entropy: users forget what they were supposed to be doing, are confused as to which links they did or didn't follow, etc. [Pea, 1988]. The major problem for first-time users of any complex computer system, especially if they are entering new knowledge domains, is lack of guidance. Large homogeneous dataspaces that are intended for browsing, hypertext or not, can be a special problem for novices. How are they to decide which questions to ask, which associations to make, which hypermedia links to follow? Whereas experts may require total freedom in navigating though information spaces, novices may quickly get lost or disoriented. Their only strategy may be random choice. It also takes considerable time to follow all possible trails. This is not solely a hypermedia problem; it is a version of the familiar system-design problem of how to accommodate both the novice's need for structure and the expert's need for flexibility.

If your system is very large, has multiple layers of information, or involves complex relationships among pieces of information, you will face similar problems, whether the information is presented in sequential or nonlinear fashion. It's even worse if it's extensible. People can get lost in any dataspace, particularly if they're novices. In complex information spaces, users need a sense of the entire domain that accommodates the limitations of short-term memory. It is particularly difficult to keep the user's model of the dataspace simple in a network-based navigational system. Unfortunately, there is no natural topology for an information space [Conklin, 1987]. Ted Nelson's discussion of "virtualities" provides an alternative to the simple metaphors of today's interfaces for addressing this problem (see Nelson's chapter in this volume).

New concepts or conventions can cause considerable problems for users. Icons may not convey their intended meanings. The source and target of any given link may not be apparent to the user, especially if entities can be either pieces of text or nontextual information. The notion of executable links may need some explaining. People have difficulty following references backwards in conventional documents, and hypertext introduces bidirectional linking. Hypertext users cannot rely on common database-searching and querying techniques. What will prevent users from always taking the wrong link? And what about the path not taken?

Some Prescriptions

Here are some presecriptions for hypertext designers. Careful consideration should be given to conventions for representing nodes, links, and other important information [see Weiland and Shneiderman, 1988]. The selectable items must be readily apparent. Typed nodes should be distinguishable so that a user can tell at a glance what class of node is being represented [Conklin, 1987]. Link and button taxonomies should be developed. Because transitions between dataspaces can be disorienting as well as time-consuming, some kind of preview device is needed. A retrace mechanism could serve as the electronic equivalent of bread crumbs. Hypertext systems should employ well-marked paths, noting through-routes, cul-de-sacs, dead ends, and detours. And we need to support "link-blazers" as well as link-followers [Van Dam, 1988].

Mainstream computer science remedies for hypertext symptoms rely on spatio-visual devices. Visual highlighting and iconic representation is used to convey important information. Graphical browsers can help to prevent disorientation. So can system maps, global and local. There are well-known spatial data navigation techniques to help people find information in large electronic databases. Other techniques for managing complexity entail filtering or eliding information, suppressing levels of detail, or providing only information relevant to the current context. Filtering can entail incremental as well as partial disclosure. Other techniques for providing orienting cues to users are suggested in this volume; for example, storytelling and narrative techniques might be used to arrange content into meaningful patterns (see Abbe Don's chapter). Animation or filmmaking techniques could be used to orient users through transitions between dataspaces, and animated overviews could provide access to historical context (see Baecker and Small's chapter).

Hypermedia can require extensive metalevel decision-making and thinking skills on the part of users. The notion of cognitive management tools is relatively unexplored. For example, we might provide "goal pilots" or "goal trees" for the purposes of cognitive navigation [Pea, 1988]. Authoring poses another set of problems. Protocols governing link creation need to be formulated. Authors also need guidance and support to properly chunk information into discrete units consisting of single concepts or ideas, whether creating new information or converting existing text into hypertext.

BEYOND THE ELECTRONIC SLIDE SHOW

Hypermedia has many potential strengths. Multiple perspectives and alternate representations provide varied access paths to knowledge, reinforcing and enhancing knowledge acquisition. Multiple modalities permit a better match of underlying concept, representation, and interaction methods. Dynamic media can present information that otherwise might be inaccessible in time, fashion, or physical implementation. For example, dynamic media create the potential for learning through process, a form of computer-based apprenticeship [Pea, 1988]. Computer replays can show how a decision was reached or an article constructed. Video segments or animations might teach expert skills or evaluate performances.

Hypermedia has weaknesses as well. Users can be distracted from goal-directed activities by multimedia stimulation [Pea, 1988]. More important, correspondences between different kinds of representational forms and different kinds of information are poorly understood, as is the nature of multimedia literacy.

Although humans have highly developed visual and aural perceptual skills, it is not clear that our abilities to understand and manipulate non-text-based representations are similarly well developed. At a low level, there is the problem of ambiguity, pictorial and perceptual, in graphical interfaces. For example, icons do not necessarily convey the desired meaning, especially when used to represent complex objects or processes [see Gittens, 1986]. Consider the following two icons used in HyperCard stacks:

The icon on the left, the Previous Arrow, causes the user to go back (as opposed to forward) one card in a linear sequence of cards. In most cases, the icon on the right, the Return Arrow, is used to pop the stack. This can have unanticipated results. In practice, this icon can mean that the user is taken back either to the immediately preceding branching/launch point or to some higher level in the information hierarchy, which the user may have visited many moons ago. In other words, the user cannot be sure of where the arrow leads. To interpret these icons properly requires not only familiarity with convention but also a good model of the data structure and the developer's intentions.

As mentioned above, techniques developed for existing dynamic media bear examination—particularly storytelling, filmmaking, and animation. We need to identify those composition and comprehension skills that are necessary in order to manipulate multimedia systems and dynamic-event-processing tasks.

As Oren and Hakansson both observe in this volume, new media will lead to new forms of literacy. Whether that new literacy will be an insurmountable hurdle or the kind of breakthrough in human augmentation that Engelbart and others have prophesied will depend in no small part on the skill and care of the designers of hypermedia interfaces.

Adventures with Hybrid Systems:

Integrating the Macintosh Interface with External Devices

The Macintosh and Hybrid Systems

THE MACINTOSH WAS ORIGINALLY CONCEIVED as a totally self-contained personal computer. In fact, early publicity releases likened it to an "appliance" whose operation would be as simple and intuitive as that of a toaster: plug it in, turn it on, and it works. Soon after its introduction, however, it became clear that the same attributes that distinguished the Macintosh as a personal computer were also attractive to system developers looking for a "user-friendly" front end for complex systems. This integration of a standard, mass-produced product with specialized or custom components results in what can be termed a *hybrid system*. Despite Apple's portrayal of the Macintosh as a machine intended to "fly solo," system designers lost little time in making the Macintosh a popular user interface for hybrid systems.

The implications of adapting the Macintosh, as opposed to a more conventional PC, to customized systems were complex. Unlike its predecessors, the Macintosh had a set of user interface conventions that cut across specific applications. These attributes were associated with the machine's overall "environment," not with a particular program. Although neither perfect nor comprehensive, these conventions did comprise a considered system for presenting Macintosh user interfaces. Users soon began to expect standard ways of manipulating windows, selecting from menus, and so on. But hybrid systems typically required the inclusion of additional interface features to control the additional system components. The intro-

Tyler Blake

Human Factors Graduate Program
California State University, Northridge
and
President, Intuitive Software & Interactive
Systems, Inc.

duction of these foreign elements into the Macintosh universe often violated assumptions of the basic interface design. In the process, some substantially altered (and occasionally bizarre) user interfaces were produced.

What are the issues confronting the designers of interfaces for hybrid systems? How do we achieve seamless integration of "standard" and "non-standard" components? A review of selected Macintosh-based systems may help to illustrate some common pitfalls in complex UI development. First, many UI designs are fragile and can be seriously distorted by relatively small changes in the system design. Second, a few key aspects of the UI design warrant particular attention when extending an existing interface to accomodate additional components: the user conceptual model, the inter-action techniques, and the user's overall task flow. Third, some simple principles of human factors analysis can be helpful in anticipating the impact of user interface modifications on the overall effectiveness of the hybrid system. Finally, the study of current hybrid systems may help antic-ipate the interface challenges of tomorrow's conventional systems.

Accommodating User Models in Hybrid Systems

User perceptions of hybrid systems hinge principally on two factors: (1) whether the users are primarily "task-" or "system-" oriented and (2) the user's prior experience with the individual system components. Task-oriented users approach the system as a specific tool used to get something done; system-oriented users approach the system as a general tool that can be used for multiple purposes. In task-oriented systems, metaphors are convenient means of portraying system attributes and operational tools in a way that does not require technical knowledge and that takes advantage of the user's prior knowledge. Because hybrid systems typically are dedi-cated to vertical applications, most users will be task-oriented and should be given task-related tools consistent with user-relevant metaphors. But to be effective, these tools and associated metaphors may also need to be flexible. Have you ever used the handle of a screwdriver as a hammer? If so, you have something in common with millions of people who freely "adapt" tools for purposes not envisioned by their designers. The usefulness of a metaphor isn't judged by whether it is literally "true," but rather by how well it allows people to understand and to predict system behavior. Thus, a system metaphor that is inconsistent with the real world can be effective if the inconsistencies are either (1) consciously known to the user, or (2) of no consequence to the user's activity.

An example of the first case is found in the development of an integrated drawing/paint package for fine arts users. As is common with total novice populations, resistance to computerization ran high. One specific objection also surfaced in talking to users: most of the artists were experts on color mixing in the "hard copy" world, a process that is based on subtractive principles of color combination. The computer-video system (which is based on additive principles) was perceived as foreign and confusing, and reduced the "experts" to novices. To address these concerns, a "subtractive" mode of operation was added to the user interface. When this option was selected, the system would approximate the color combinations that would result from a subtractive color mixing (that is, "off-line" using hard copy media). The results were notable for two reasons. First, the subtractive mode was extremely successful in breaking down resistance because the users could predict the results almost immediately. Second, the subtractive mode was quickly abandoned after users got comfortable on the system; that is, they easily replaced the "incorrect" model after using it as a transition aid.

The second case, when metaphorical inconsistencies are irrelevant to user activities, can be illustrated by the electronic pencil tool commonly used in paint programs for free-hand sketching. Most artists will turn a "real" pencil at various angles in order to get different line widths and/or shading effects. With the electronic variety, this activity is superfluous because the "pencil" can be assigned a near-infinite variety of width and shading characteristics. Any computer-based attempt to simulate turning a two-dimensional pencil on an angle would likely be awkward and confusing; fortunately, it is also unnecessary.

Input Devices and User Controls

Perhaps the most distinctive aspect of the Macintosh in 1984 was its use of the mouse as a primary input device. Like all controls, the mouse is better suited to some operations than others; further, as one component in an integrated system, its effectiveness will be largely determined by how well the design of the mouse interface is coordinated with other factors (for example, the screen design, the sequence of activities).

One critical parameter affecting mouse operation in hybrid systems is the control-display ("c/d") ratio between mouse movement and cursor movement. The simplest form of c/d ratio considers only the distance the user moves the mouse to determine appropriate distance for cursor travel. Given a c/d ratio of 1:1, a one-inch movement of the cursor will result in a one-inch travel of the cursor on screen. A more complex type of calculation also considers the *velocity* of the mouse movement. In the case of the Macintosh, a velocity above a critical threshold would result in a doubling of the cursor position formula. For example, if I move the mouse two inches "quickly" (that is, more quickly than the specified threshold), the c/d ratio will double to 2:1 from 1:1, and the screen cursor will travel four inches instead of two.

Different user operations require different c/d ratios to make them easy to perform. For example, selecting from a pull-down menu requires a fairly high c/d ratio (so that small hand movements don't result in the user selecting an menu item adjacent to the one desired. But that same c/d ratio would require users to move the mouse large distances in order to move from one side of the screen to the other. The velocity-modified c/d ratio provides a compromise. Thus, I can quickly traverse the width of the screen with a rapid movement and still have an adequately high c/d ratio for making more careful, deliberate movements. Or can I?

One prototype system that used the Macintosh for manipulating medical images used 19-inch monitors in place of the 9-inch native screen. As users viewed the six 19-inch monitors arranged in two rows of three before them, the amount of screen real estate was now approximately 2,500 percent greater than the native Macintosh screen for which the c/d ratios were intended. With only the two user-selectable c/d ratios available, users had two undesirable choices: (1) optimize ease of use for detailed movements like menu selection, and suffer when performing gross actions like moving windows (which could require lateral movements of up to two feet!) or (2) provide speedy response for gross actions and endure the frustration and quasiparalysis of the hand that resulted from trying to make slight movements.

Interestingly, most users blamed the Macintosh (and specifically the mouse) for their difficulties rather than the software. Although this is a little like blaming a screwdriver handle for performing poorly as a hammer, the real source of operational problems in hybrid systems is often invisible to the end users.

In any event, two features were developed to improve the situation: (1) a "speed key" was assigned to the keyboard that radically increased the c/d ration when depressed (users could also obtain a more predictable increase by holding down any of the numbers 1–9 and moving the mouse; the c/d ratio was multiplied by that factor) and (2) a graphic representation of the six monitors was added to the top of each screen; each monitor in this representation contained an "instant travel" button that allowed the user to directly select that monitor as the active screen. (This graphic also served as a status indicator showing which monitor was active, and it was later extended to allow users to "swap images" by relocating the individual monitor icons.) Most users relied on the graphic "hyper buttons," but a minority of hard-core speed-key devotees were also in evidence.

Response Time and User Pacing

Among the crucial aspects of good user interfaces is the principle of consistency of response time. In fact, producing consistency of response time is sometimes more important than optimizing absolute response time.

To understand why this is true, consider the issue of work pace. It is far easier for people to set the pace of an activity themselves than to be "paced" by the system. In fact, for any repetitive activity we develop a "self-paced" rate that is neither too fast nor too slow for our taste. Walking is the prototypical example. The way we walk (for example, the length and speed of our steps, the uniqueness of our gait) is so individualized that we can often identify people very far away just by their walk.

Nothing is tougher than trying to perform a self-paced activity at an imposed pace. Try walking 10 percent more quickly or slowly—not just for a few minutes but *all the time*. It's a lot harder because you have to *think* about walking, whereas self-paced walking is reflexive. When response time is predictable, we can adopt a consistent, self-paced rate of interaction that requires a minimum of mental effort. Where response time is variable, we are forced to routinely monitor the system status. Result: our concentration on the task is broken, and the interface becomes intrusive.

Hybrid systems, with their need for communication among "separate" devices, often have very different response times for actions that *seem* identical to the users but that may actually require highly varied amounts of processing. Thus, response time can vary in ways that can be unfathomable to the user. One hybrid application plagued by this lack of uniformity is a university database retrieval system used to support the design of a hypothetical space station community of 10,000 people. Because of the interdisciplinary nature of the topic, this system involved a variety of information sources and storage media, including optical disks, videotape, CD-ROM, on-line databases, networked storage devices, and local hard disk storage. As you might guess, these sources had widely varying retrieval times.

To further complicate the matter, the Macintosh had been equipped with a large amount of RAM dedicated to a cache memory system. So files that had been previously retrieved during a search might be accessed almost immediately *if* they were still resident in the RAM cache—or it could take up to twenty minutes! (The actual contents of the RAM cache were known only to the system, and it wasn't talking.) In a misguided attempt to achieve interface consistency, the designers presented all data sources to the user in a common iconic fashion, as is often done on the Macintosh desktop. In doing so, they also obscured the source of the information until **after** a request for retrieval had been made! Needless to say, users who assumed they were requesting locally stored information were often horrified to discover that they would have to wait up to eighty times longer than expected. To the extent that a user's need for predictability is ignored, hybrid systems will fail to provide a key attribute of good interface design.

User Expectations in Hybrid Systems

Although we tend to discuss consistency of user interfaces as though it represented universal goodness, motherhood, and apple pie, reality is sometimes different. After all, another way of saying "consistent" is "rigid" or "inflexible." Thus, the goal of consistency should at times be compromised in the interest of ease of use, accuracy, or other such user-interface criteria. Inconsistencies would be expected to arise in third-party application programs, but the Macintosh has several "conscious inconsistencies" built into the basic interface. For example, files thrown in the trash are gone forever if they are not retrieved before the machine is shut down, but disks dragged into the trash are removed from the system only temporarily, with their files intact. As with any design, one can always argue that there is a better way, but this intentional inconsistency does provide an effective means of disk management. Sometimes deviations from established conventions are justified in order to significantly enhance usability.

A major challenge, however, is to make it clear to the user which attributes are generic "Macintosh" features and which are application features. Many pioneering users familiar only with MacPaint were ultimately surprised (and sometimes hysterical) to find that the "UNDO" function was not universal but was available only in some programs. Even then, it may not *always* be available, as evidenced by the periodic and mysterious replacement of "UNDO" with "Can't UNDO" in the Edit menu. To produce an effective interface for a hybrid system, designers must assess user expectations based both on the Macintosh and on the external, application-specific components.

Integrating User Expectations

Studying user expectations from both the system and application domains can yield creative as well as technical improvements. For example, a voice analysis and display system was developed to test the premise that people could better learn the proper pronunciation of words if they could hear those words pronounced "in their own voice." Consider, for example, the case of children learning a foreign language. Frequently their voice model may be an opposite gender, adult voice which they must first "translate" into their own registers in order to correctly mimic the words. What if you could hear the word "correctly" in a voice similar or identical to your own?

Here's how it worked. A user attempted to pronounce a word into a speech digitizer. The instructor played back the word sound and adjusted the frequency, timing, and other sound parameters as needed to improve the accuracy of the pronunciation. In order to do this, a number of sound display and adjustment control methods were researched based both on a task analysis and on subjective data collected from relevant professionals. Prototype displays and controls were presented to three groups: (1) a group familiar with linguistics but not the Macintosh, (2) a group familiar with the Macintosh but not linguistics, and (3) a group familiar with both. Of interest were the expectations that each group had of how the interfaces would work, and how they might like to see them work.

Several creative control and display concepts were applied to the interface by those unfamiliar with the application requirements but familiar with *what a Macintosh II should be able to do*. For example, a subject familiar with CAD systems suggested that instead of tediously connecting data points with line segments, instructors could draw approximate voice curve segments free-hand; then the system could generate a series of straight line segments and vertices along that path (that is, implement a curve-fitting procedure) to provide specific editing points. Several similar functions, not initially identified by the domain experts, were received enthusiastically by the speech professionals. Early data also point to specific and large performance improvements.

User Expectations Based on External Components

Because hybrid systems contain a mix of familiar and unfamiliar components, it would not be unusual for users to have strong preconceived models about some parts of a system and little or no conceptual model for other system components. In the case of unfamiliar components for which the user has no preconceived model, the user interface designer's task is to present a clear model of operation and usage *appropriate for the end user*. All too often, however, the model presented represents the designer's view of the world.

A common user control technique is to construct a "soft" version (that is, a screen-based graphic) of the component machine that the user operates via direct mouse operations. A common major mistake: trying to represent the external component literally in order to make the simulation "accurate." The result is often simulated machines that are overly complex for the user's task, awkward to operate, and inconsistent with the Macintosh environment. An example can be found in one of the first Macintosh-based hybrid systems built: a patented system for the color-conversion of black-and-white videotape to color. The system required operators to "colorize" the image by assigning color values to replace the gray-scale values in the black-and-white images. The color scheme used had to conform to NTSC broadcast standards for color television. Output signals for television are typically analyzed by a machine called a vectorscope that represents color via a "color wheel" of frequencies representing five primary colors on the axes. The hue of a signal is represented by the position on the circumference of the circle; the intensity is represented by the distance from the center (intensity increases with distance from the circle center).

Although the physical vectorscope is a display-only device designed to show signal composition, its basic format was adopted for both the display *and the control* of color settings. The failure to consider the separate requirements of control and display tasks is a common failure in hybrid systems. As a result, altering the color composition required the user to move the five small display boxes (each representing different regions of gray scale from very dark to very light) around a "color wheel." (Note: this choice reflected the conceptual model of the system architects; that is, this is the way **video engineers** think about color.)

A number of human factors problems resulted from this procedure. First, because both the hue and the intensity scales are nonlinear, the visual impact of moving the control boxes a specific distance varied widely depending on the color wheel location. Second, the system required the users to manipulate two dimensions (hue and intensity) simultaneously with the same control box; thus, an attempt to change hue often resulted in inadvertent shifts in intensity, and vice versa. Third, the control-display ratio often required precise movements with the mouse, producing both fatigue and position errors. Finally, the entire conceptual model of the vectorscope proved to be a difficult one for the nontechnical and artistically oriented operators to grasp.

Several prototypes for redesigned controls that conformed more closely with Macintosh conventions were configured and tested. The revised control mechanisms addressed several problems. First, the scales used to adjust hue and saturation could be adjusted separately or together as desired for different types of adjustments. Second, the scales were perceptually based rather than linear to provide a more even result of repositioning the control boxes across the entire scale. Third, three different methods for control settings were available: (1) a direct manipulation of the control boxes with the mouse, permitting approximate initial settings to be rapidly configured, (2) indirect movement of the control boxes via intuitive arrow controls, which facilitated finer adjustments, and (3) numerical entry of exact values into the box displaying the current setting that allowed precise matching to a reference source. The result was a control mechanism that had little in common with the physical vectorscope but that resulted in significantly improved performance for the task at hand.

Direct modeling of *familiar* components can pose other problems. Although the concept of operation may be clear, different operational characteristics between the actual and simulated devices can sometimes provide the worst of both worlds. For example, a system was developed to facilitate the analysis of videotaped records of user interaction with computers. Operators needed to control two VCRs, so a series of soft controls modeled after the VCR's physical controls were provided. Because VCRs are a common consumer device, there seemed to be little danger of user confusion in creating analogous soft controls.

However, there are two major discrepancies between the operating characteristics in the "soft" and "hard" environments. Although few problems were encountered with the discrete controls (for example, play, stop, fast forward, rewind), variable controls such as "shuttle" and "jog" proved to be awkward and unusable. Although conceptually similar, the soft controls lacked the tactile and auditory cues available to users of physical controls. Interestingly, some of the most useful of these cues were not even part of the machine's design; for example, the whirs and clicks of the tape transport mechanisms (see the chapter by Mountford and Gaver). If crucial aspects of the "hard" devices can't be provided to the user, the designers of soft controls may need to discard physical device models in favor of alternative constructs that are optimized for "soft" operation.

Interim Conclusions

Most user interface designers in the near future will have to consider many of the issues that currently challenge (and sometimes vanquish) today's designers of hybrid systems. In fact, as the integration of multiple media (for example, voice, graphics, video, optical media) becomes more commonplace, the "hybrid" of today may become the standard system of tomorrow. The systematic study of hybrid systems can provide a rich source of insight, inspiration, and research agendas for the interface design community. For developers like Apple, such systems stand as testimony to the unmet needs of users who require transparent integration between personal computers and the wide range of devices and systems that will support thousands of *whole* user tasks. Systems that allow these components to be used simultaneously and seamlessly will be a critical next step in the evolution of user interface design.

A Design for Supporting New Input Devices

Knives and forks are the basic eating utensils.
But half of the people in the world use chopsticks.

Michael Chen
Advanced Technology Group
Apple Computer, Inc.

Frank Leahy
Product Engineering
Apple Computer, Inc.

You can get to work in 30 minutes.
But I can get there in 20 by taking this shortcut.

A person can't lift a Volkswagen.
But you can lift a Cadillac by using a set of pulleys.

Just deal with the situations one at a time.
But try working the clutch and accelerator of your car separately.

In the beginning there was the keyboard; then came the mouse. Today we can choose among dozens of different input devices. Some input devices provide identical functionality but with a different interface; for example, a trackball can be used instead of the mouse. Other devices supply new functionality; for example, a pressure tablet supplies pressure as well as position information. The four point-counterpoints given at the start of this chapter remind us that it is often possible to use a new tool (or in our case a new input device), or to use several tools in concert, to achieve a given goal more easily and quickly. The same is true with the computer—different input devices provide different interface capabilities, giving the user additional tools to accomplish a particular task.

A significant problem with computers today is that it is impossible to attach new input devices simply and transparently. The goal of this paper is to describe a strategy for application-input device communication that simplifies the connection of new devices, allows new devices to be used with existing applications, and supports the simultaneous use of two or more input devices.

Let's look a little more closely at the above four point-counterpoints to see what they mean to us as computer users.

- *Alternate ways of performing the same task*
  Just as culture and efficiency often designate the eating utensil of choice, some Macintosh applications use the Tab, Return, and arrow keys for cursor-like movement. It is also possible to purchase other pointing devices, such as trackballs, to control the pointer. This means the user has at least three different ways to position the pointer. Having these alternatives means that users are free to select the most suitable device for themselves and for the situation at hand.

- *Shortcuts that make a task easier to perform*
  Just as driving a different route can have a dramatic effect on how long it takes to get home, using the Command key equivalents of menu commands on the Macintosh can dramatically speed up commonly used commands.

- *Additional tools that make a task possible or easier to perform*
  With a pulley it is possible to lift a weight that is either difficult or impossible to lift without it. The ability to input positional information quickly and easily with the mouse makes the direct manipulation interface possible. Of course, one can input positional information from the keyboard, but doing so is as inappropriate as trying to input keystrokes with the mouse.

- *Multiple devices working together to make a task possible or easier to perform*
  The simultaneous use of the accelerator and the clutch makes it infinitely easier to get a car with manual transmission underway. Similarly, the use

of an electric piano keyboard connected to the computer, along with the computer keyboard and mouse, allows musicians to write, correct, and replay compositions much more quickly than can be done with a computer keyboard alone.

In real life, people deal with many different tools. In the kitchen we use one set of tools—knives, spoons, egg beater, frying pans. In the bathroom we use an entirely different set of tools—toothbrushes, combs, hairdryers. These tools have evolved and lasted because they efficiently meet the needs of the job. On the computer, two input devices—the keyboard and mouse—are typically used for all of our tasks; unfortunately, they are not always the right tools for the job at hand. As computers start to deal with a wider set of tasks, a larger set of input devices will be needed. Even today, many new input devices are being introduced in the market.

People also deal with multiple tools simultaneously. When we talk to another person, we use multiple modes of communication such as speech, hand gestures, eye contact, and touch. When we work with pottery, we may use a foot treadle to turn the pot and both hands to shape the clay. Some of the confusion and frustration that people feel with the computer may be caused by the fact that they are forced to use the same input device for all tasks. Multimodal input can be more expressive, and it can provide a level of redundancy that helps a program to interpret ambiguous situations. Moreover, the simultaneous use of input devices can provide a synergy that makes the *whole* interface more efficient and expressive than the sum of its parts.

Adding new input devices to computers, as well as adding the capability to support multiple input devices, increases the communication bandwidth between the user and the computer. Unfortunately, however, most existing computer systems support only the two most common input devices: keyboard and mouse. People who want to use new input devices must buy software that has been specifically written to use them.

The logical connection of new input devices can be simplified, even while the complexity of these devices increases. The rest of this paper is devoted to describing situations in which new and multiple input devices are useful, and then presenting our model for attaching and communicating with input devices.

Why Support Multiple Input Devices?

There are many uses for new or multiple input devices. This section describes only a small number of such devices within a large universe of possibilities. Refer to the chapters in this book by Buxton, Kurtenbach and Hulteen, and Mountford and Gaver—as well as to the literature and to your imagination—for additional examples.

The universe of contexts in which new and multiple devices can be used

Figure 1: Universe of possible users and devices.

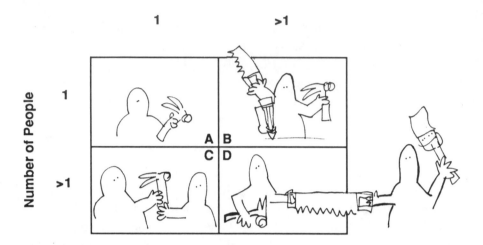

Number of Devices

can be broken down into four parts, as shown in figure 1. First is the single user controlling a single input device (box A), second is the single user controlling multiple devices simultaneously (box B), third is multiple users sharing a single device (box C), and fourth is multiple users controlling multiple devices simultaneously (box D). In the following discussion, it does not matter whether the people and devices are physically separated.

BOX A: SINGLE USER, SINGLE DEVICE

This box includes many new input devices that have been constructed to solve specific problems. One such device is the VPL DataGlove™ (see the chapter by Fisher and that by Kurtenbach and Hulteen). It is a device based on a glove worn by the user that reports its location and orientation in space as well as the articulation of joints. The user can use the DataGlove to execute computer commands through gestures or to interact with virtual three-dimensional objects in a manner similar to that used for interacting with real objects. Another such device is a voice recognizer that allows for speech input (see Mountford and Gaver's chapter for more details).

A significant interface problem is using these devices in situations where their specificity is not needed. How does one change from the task of manipulating objects in a virtual 3-D world to the task of text entry if all that is available is a DataGlove? Or how does one "point" using a voice recognizer? Because of such difficulties, these specialized input devices are usually used in conjunction with other more conventional devices.

BOX B: SINGLE USER, MULTIPLE DEVICES

Many tasks are inherently performed in parallel. Imagine cooking, drawing, or arranging music with one hand tied behind your back. The same is true of tasks performed on the computer. The input devices used in a multiple-device system need not be complicated; the current Macintosh interface provides several facilities for using multiple inputs using just the mouse and keyboard. For example, holding down the Shift key with one hand while clicking the mouse button with the other hand provides a grouping mechanism to select multiple objects. Using command key equivalents with one hand while manipulating the mouse with the other allows operations to be performed on objects quickly.

Consider several possible new input devices that would allow for simple multiple-device scenarios. A simple and effective technique for scrolling a text document would be to provide the user with a thumbwheel next to the keyboard that can be rotated to scroll a text document up and down.[1] Or, two thumbwheels could be used as alternatives to the vertical and horizontal scroll bars in a window. Another possibility would be to use a trackball to scroll the frontmost window in any direction.

There are many other examples of situations in which we would like to be able to use two hands to perform tasks on the computer. Consider sizing and positioning a rectangle in a drawing program, or using a painting program in which one hand is used to paint while the other selects colors or scrolls the window. Buxton and Myers [Buxton, 1986] showed that scrolling-selection and sizing-positioning tasks could be done more efficiently with two hands. Moreover, most subjects tested adopted the strategy of using both hands simultaneously without being instructed to do so. This result is not surprising, because people use both hands at the same time for many noncomputer tasks.

For certain tasks, a large number of input devices can be useful. Brooks [Brooks, 1988] pointed out that one of their three-dimensional molecular modeling systems uses 15 different input devices. Each device is dedicated to perform a specific function, and thus each device can be customized to provide excellent compatibility between the input and the resulting output. The use of dedicated input devices also takes advantage of muscle memory; one can quickly learn to associate the functionality of a device with its physical location and kinetic properties. You are probably able to reach for and shut off the alarm clock in the morning with your eyes closed. The caveat is that this will work only in your home, not in a hotel room. The same caution also applies to providing *too* many input devices.

---

[1] A similar technique was employed by Engelbart and his team in the NLS system with the mouse plus a five-key set. Larry Tesler's Gypsy system, developed at Xerox PARC in 1975, used three keys on the "left" hand to scroll up and down.

Box C: Multiple Users, Single Input Device

A simple example of a situation in which multiuser single input device sharing is needed is an educational activity in which the teacher and student(s) are separated. *SideBand*™ [Nexus, 1989] is a Macintosh program designed to support just this type of collaboration. It was originally designed to allow teachers in the Australian outback to interact with university professors in Sydney, using the Macintosh to augment televised lectures as well as to provide a shared workspace for all participants. This shared workspace is a networked version of the common whiteboard. In a group meeting an individual can step up to the whiteboard and control the session by taking control of the marker. Similarly, in *SideBand* one person at a time can control the host cursor and thereby control the networked collaboration.

This type of application has other possible uses. For example, a teacher can be a guest to each student's machine, which allows the teacher to monitor students' progress and give direction if necessary. There are other examples of multiuser collaboration in the literature. Mantei [Mantei, 1988] and Stefik [Stefik, 1987] describe systems in which individuals in a meeting can, through their own machines, cooperatively create presentation outlines in a shared computer file. Collaborative products such as *SideBand* raise interesting questions about how to accept, maintain, and relinquish control of the host cursor, as well as how to let everybody know who currently has control.

Box D: Multiple Users, Multiple Input Devices

All three of the works referenced above (*SideBand* and the systems described by Mantei and Stefik) actually allow the use of both the keyboard and mouse. These two input devices are so fundamental to the environments in which these three systems operate that none of the systems would be particularly interesting if they did not support both devices. The more interesting case of multiuser, multidevice collaboration would involve other input devices. Not much is known about collaborative sharing of input devices other than the keyboard and mouse. We can imagine, though, extending any of these three systems to support multiuser, multi-input collaborations, admittedly with some effort.

Current Device Models

The use of new and multiple input devices can create exciting opportunities for human-computer interaction. The problem is that few, if any, systems make it easy for either the user or the programmer to use new input devices. At the lowest level, incompatible connectors and incompatible bus (electrical) signals can make it impossible to attach a particular device. For example, an RS-422 input device cannot be used on a machine with only a SCSI port, even if a mating connector is available. Assuming connector and bus compatibility, the next problem is writing a device driver. Every operating system has its own driver format, requiring device manufacturers to write a separate driver for every computer to which the device is to be attached. Today, many companies do support different busses and device drivers. What is lacking, however, is a coherent, high-level model for application-input device interaction.

The next three sections briefly describe three different input device interaction models in use today. What we hope to gain from reviewing these three models is an understanding of where they fail to meet our goal, which is to provide a model of application-input device interaction that supports new devices and encourages the use of multiple devices.

THE MACINTOSH MODEL

The Macintosh event model [Apple, 1985] is similar to that used by many event-driven computer systems today. The Macintosh event model supports two input devices, the keyboard and mouse, and can generate and distribute only five events from these devices—mouse down, mouse up, key down, key up, and auto key. It is not possible to send other events from these two devices—for example, gestures from the mouse or tunes from the keyboard.

Programs that want to use other types of devices—for example, a pressure tablet or a 3-D input device—must bypass the event system and talk to the device directly. Consider a paint program that would like to be able to work with all of the pressure tablets on the market. Unfortunately, because a Macintosh event does not contain pressure information, the paint program must communicate with the tablet directly rather than through the event system. Supporting new tablets requires that the paint program be updated for each new tablet. In addition to the programmer's burden, users are locked into whatever hardware is supported by the programs they use; they cannot choose the best from among a set of similar devices.

THE GKS MODEL

The GKS model [ISO, 1983] classifies events into one of six logical devices. The specification of logical devices makes it possible for graphics packages to be independent of the particular piece of hardware used to generate the event. For example, a text string could be typed at the keyboard, picked from a list, or even spoken into a microphone. The program doesn't care as long as the text string is delivered from a logical string device.

The six logical devices are:

Locator	A device for specifying a coordinate position (x,y)
Stroke	A device for specifying a series of coordinate positions

String	A device for specifying text input
Valuator	A device for specifying scalar values
Choice	A device for selecting menu options
Pick	A device for selecting picture components

The problem with this model is that the six logical devices cover a very limited range of input devices; however, the idea of classification of physical devices into logical devices has merit. Users, programmers, and manufacturers all would benefit from such a classification. Manufacturers would benefit because there would be standard logical device specifications to meet, and their products would be interchangeable with other products that met the same specifications. Programmers would benefit because they could program to a logical device, no longer having to deal directly with the input device hardware. And users would benefit because they could purchase the best from among the various devices that supported the *logical* device in which they were interested.

THE NeWS MODEL

NeWS™ uses a different model for defining and managing events [Sun, 1988]. Events can be names such as "MouseUp" and "MouseDown." Because names can be any legal PostScript™ object, the event name space is unbounded. This is a nice model because it allows complete flexibility in defining new events for new input devices.

Unfortunately, there is a drawback to an unbounded name space, namely the difficulty in managing the name space. If new input devices are allowed to arbitrarily assign event names, it is possible to wind up with two *different* events with the *same* name. Similarly, it is possible for two different devices that produce the *same* event to give those events *different* names.

A New High-Level Device Interaction Model

Our device interaction model has two parts: 1) an extensible and semi-structured name space, and 2) event transmogrification [Watterson, 1988].

With an *extended name space*, such as is used by the NeWS model, it is possible to define event names for any new device that might be introduced. The name space must be structured; otherwise, as was pointed out in the discussion of the NeWS model, event-naming problems can result. Yet, if the name space is *too* structured, the restrictions could inhibit the building of higher-level or more complicated events such as gestures. The GKS model of logical devices provides a good base for structuring the name space. Devices are classified according to logical capabilities, and event names are defined that support those logical capabilities. A physical device that supports a logical device is required to support at least the events produced by that logical device.

Logical device classifications provide for a *minimum* level of functionality. Any physical device that supports a given logical device is interchangeable with any other such physical device. Physical devices are not limited to supporting the events for one logical device. A complicated physical device such as the DataGlove could choose to support many logical devices: a position device, a force-sensitive device, a 3-D device, a 6-D device, or even a joystick-type device.

The second part of our model, *event transmogrification*, allows one physical device to mimic several logical devices. This mimicking can be done in a way that is transparent to both the user and the programmer, given the proper system support. When a physical device generates an event that is not understood by an application, the application sends the event back to the device for transmogrification. The device is given a prioritized list of input devices that the application understands. The physical device compares that prioritized list to all of the logical devices that it is capable of mimicking, picks the highest priority device, repackages the original event for this highest priority logical device, and sends the event back to the application. The existence of logical devices provides an organized way for a physical device to determine which logical devices it can/wants to emulate.

Here is a real-world example that will help the reader visualize the interaction between an application program and an input device that results from our model. Imagine a person wearing a DataGlove. The person is using three programs: a 3-D modeling program, a color paint program, and a word processor. The 3-D modeling program understands DataGlove events and responds to the DataGlove input without the need for transmogrification. The color paint program does not understand DataGlove events, but does understand both a pressure-sensitive tablet and a mouse, preferring to get pressure-sensitive tablet information. Because the DataGlove has been programmed to mimic both the pressure-sensitive tablet and the mouse, the DataGlove transmogrifies its events into pressure-sensitive tablet events. The word processor, on the other hand, accepts only keyboard and mouse input, preferring keyboard events. Unfortunately, the DataGlove has not been programmed to transmogrify its events to keyboard events, being unable to recognize sign language gestures or virtual typing, but it has been programmed to mimic a mouse and so transmogrifies its events to mouse events for the word processor.

Summary

As computers become faster and capable of handling increasing complexity, people will want to attach new, presumably more capable, input devices. They will also want to be able use several devices simultaneously, whether physically connected or controlled over a network. We have described what we think are the two primary features of this model: an extensible event name space and event transmogrification. Only through the adoption of a coherent high-level model of interaction between input devices and applications can both users and programmers benefit from using new input devices, or from using two or more input devices simultaneously.

Gestures in Human-Computer Communication

EVERY DAY, PEOPLE USE GESTURES to communicate with other people, to communicate with their dogs and cats, with their colleagues, with their friends, with their loved ones, with everyone; they use gestures when they can't say what they want, when they don't want other people to hear them say it, when they want to touch, when they'd rather not touch; they gesture to emphasize their ideas, to express their feelings, to make themselves understood by many people at once, to demonstrate what they mean . . . . Gestures are so much a part of human communication that we seldom notice them.

Imagine human communication without gestures—people saying good-bye without waving, giving directions without pointing, conducting a hundred musicians in a symphony by sending messages to each of their music stands.

We sit down in front of our computers today and gestures stop. The vast majority of us peck at arrays of buttons (called keyboards) and push little boxes (called mice or pucks) around on desks, pads, or panels. Some people don't even get the little boxes. A few get to speak, write with a pen, or touch a display screen. Essentially no one waves good-bye to their computer at the end of the day (at least with the expectation that the computer will understand the gesture and do anything because of it).

Without computers that can understand gestures, there can be no such things as computer augmentation of dance, recognition of expression

Gordon Kurtenbach

University of Toronto
Summer Intern, Apple Computer, Inc.

Eric A. Hulteen

Advanced Technology Group
Apple Computer, Inc.

through movement, drawing in space, imaginary musical instruments, or systems that allow users to conduct computer music. All of these activities must wait until a computer system is developed that recognizes gestures that a two-year-old child understands.

The bottom line is that gesture is an extremely effective element of communication. A computer's inability to understand gesture makes certain interactions difficult and the computing experience as a whole less fulfilling. Computers are impoverished and that neglected domain, gestures, is an opportunity for enriching human-computer communication.

Definition

A gesture is a motion of the body that contains information.

Waving good-bye is a gesture. Pressing a key on a keyboard is not a gesture because the motion of a finger on its way to hitting the key is neither observed nor significant. All that matters is which key was pressed.

Using your hand to show the motion of a falling leaf is a gesture. A teenager flailing at a video game joystick is not gesturing but rather is operating a controller that senses in which of eight possible directions a stick is being pushed.

Beckoning with your index finger is a gesture. Handwriting is not a gesture because the motion of the hand expresses nothing; it is only the resultant words that convey the information. The same words could have been typed—the hand motion would not be the same but the meaning conveyed would be.

Sign languages are made up of gestures.

Directing traffic is a gesture language.

Why Use Gestures as Computer Input?

If all computers interfaces were easy to use, effective, and satisfying, we probably wouldn't be advocating gesture as computer input. But the reality is that interfaces exist that are hard to use, ineffective, and unsatisfying, and gesture input could solve some of those problems. Essentially, gesture input provides two advantages. First, in certain interface tasks, gesture input outperforms other input techniques; that is, using a gesture, as opposed to selecting from a menu or clicking a button, may be a faster or a more intuitive interface technique. Second, gesture input may provide the user with more functionality—in other words, there are tasks that cannot be done without gesture input. There are many tasks for which these advantages can be exploited.

ORIENTATION

If you've ever used a 3-D graphics program, you have probably been frustrated trying to place objects in a scene. Some programs only allow you to type in the coordinates of the object's location and various rotations and scalings to get the object where you want. Other programs are somewhat better—they let you use the mouse to drag the object to the place you want it, switch modes so you can rotate the object with the mouse, and switch modes again so you can scale the object. There are variations on this "mode-switching" theme, but essentially you are limited to a series of transformations of the object.

At times when using a 3-D graphics program, I have become extremely frustrated trying to manipulate objects into place. My reaction was, "If I could just reach into the screen, grab the object, put it in the place I want it to be, and squeeze it down to size, I would be happy." That's what gesture can do. How? Gestures in 3-D space provide a direct mapping between gesture and the manipulated object. In addition, the hand can be used to specify rotation and scaling—you can rotate the hand to rotate the object or open and close the hand to scale an object up and down.

CONNECTION

Making connections between objects is a fairly generic interface task. You can type in a command something like "connect A to B" or, in a graphical representation, select A, then B and then select the command "connect." Both these techniques work well, but consider what happens if the "path" of the connection must be specified as well (a very typical requirement in circuit layout applications). A gesture, consisting of pointing to the first object and then tracing the path to the second object, gets the job done in one motion.

POINTING/GROUPING

The first time I decided I wanted to throw several files into the trash on my Macintosh at the same time I ran into the multiple selection problem. Previously, I had been pointing at individual files to indicate which file I wanted to throw away. This worked fine, but now I wanted to point to several files at once. If I was indicating to someone else which files these were, I would point and say, "this one, this one . . . " or, better, I'd just make a circle gesture around the group of them. Sadly, I couldn't do this on my Macintosh. Eventually I consulted the manual to determine how to "extend my selection." Later I learned I could drag out a rectangle to select a group. In fact, gesture provides a more intuitive and natural alternative to ad hoc selection/grouping methods.

FUNCTION

Gestures increase function by virtue of their expressiveness. That is, a gesture may control multiple parameters at the same time, thus allowing a user to manipulate data in a manner not possible by modifying each parameter individually. For example, a conductor simultaneously controls both tempo and volume of the music by gesture. The rhythm of the gesture controls tempo and the size of the gesture controls volume. This allows an efficient communication not possible by adjusting the tempo and volume independently.

PHYSICALITY

The physicality of gesture input has a value in itself, and in some applications, such as computer music, sculpture, and simulation, this is important. Compare conducting music with textually specifying tempo changes and emphasis. The physicality of the interaction contributes to the creativity, effectiveness, and satisfaction of the conductor. Ask any chord-slashing rock guitarist or sculptor—getting your body involved is essential.

In each of the above tasks, gestures allow the many subtasks involved to be chunked or compounded into a single interaction or motion. This, coupled with the intuitive nature of gesture, is the reason why gestures as computer input are powerful and exciting.

Uses of Gestures as Computer Input

There is a continuum of uses of gestures as computer input. The continuum maps onto the degree of multimodality in the interface. At one end of the continuum, gestures are used to augment information that is carried by one or more other channels of communication—the gestural input may be redundant. For example, computer lip-reading has been used to assist a computer speech recognition system [Petajan and Bodoff, 1988]. When the speech recognition system fails to recognize an utterance, the lip-reading recognition system is invoked. Information about the movement of lips provides additional information to help the speech recognition system.

In the middle of the continuum, gestures carry essential information that is not redundant on other channels (which carry other, essential, information). For example, in the case of pointing at an object in a display and saying "that one," the gesture indicates which one and the speech input indicates when to observe the gesture. Neither input channel alone is sufficient to carry the whole message.

At the far end of the continuum is the case where gesture is the primary channel of input. Computer systems designed to support communication with disabled persons may use gestures as the only input channel—no keyboard, mouse, or speech recognizer. Another example is the case of using gestures to describe objects. For most people it is easier to draw a curve with their hand than to figure out the polynomial equation that describes it.

Aspects of Gesture-tracking Technology

Some technology is required to capture gestures for computer input. This technology constrains the user, as well as the gestures that can be captured, to varying degrees.

Gestures drawn with a stylus onto a tablet are constrained to a two-dimensional space—such a technology is said to have two degrees of freedom. If the position of a sensor can be determined in space, the technology has three degrees of freedom. If both the position in space and the orientation of the sensor (pitch, yaw, and roll) can be determined, it has six degrees of freedom. If the speed and acceleration of the sensor can be determined, then you've reached eight degrees of freedom.

The technology to capture gesture has varying degrees of intrusiveness. Most people do not feel too intruded upon by having a video camera pointed at them while they carry out some task. On the other hand, most people would feel constrained by having to put on a full body-suit (like a space-suit) before they could use their computer.

In addition to an input device that is used to track the user's motion, software must be used to recognize gestures. The complexity (and hence the effectiveness) of gesture recognition depends on many factors: the number of degrees of freedom, the number of gestures to be recognized, and whether gestures are input in a discrete or continuous fashion. Some gestures are static—like a "peace sign" or "victory sign." Other gestures are dynamic—as in "waving good-bye." Dynamic gestures are harder to recognize than static gestures because they involve the additional dimension of time.

Examples of Gesture in Real Systems

Many experimental systems that employ gesture have been built, too many to describe here. We would like to describe a few systems and explain what makes them exciting.

VirtualStudio

VirtualStudio [Kurtenbach, 1988] demonstrates how fluid, error-free interactions can be achieved by using gesture as opposed to other interaction techniques. A command and all its parameters can be expressed in one gesture. VirtualStudio is a graphical interface to control connections among audio devices. Audio devices are represented by icons and the connections among the devices are represented by arcs. By using a combination of gesture and direct manipulation commands, a user can edit the configuration of the devices. "Paper-and-pen" types of gestures are used to move, copy, delete, connect, and encapsulate icons and arcs (figure 1).

Figure 1: Moving a group of icons in VirtualStudio.

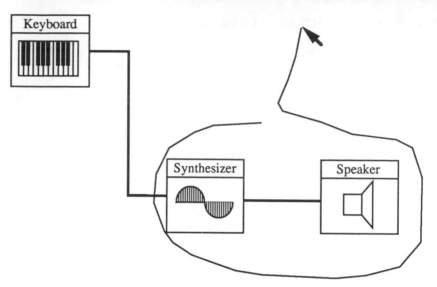

Before: The user gestures the icons to be moved and their destination.

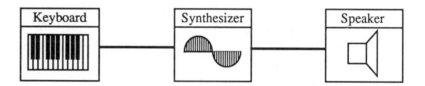

After: The system responds by erasing the gesture and moving the icons.

PUT THAT THERE

Gesture is effective in disambiguating other input technologies [Mountford et al., 1984; Schmandt and Hulteen, 1982; Bolt, 1980]. For example, *Put That There* was an interface developed by Hulteen and Schmandt at MIT using both voice and gesture input. The user sat in front of a wall-sized display, wearing a microphone and a gesture-tracking device on the wrist (see figure K in the color insert). Through a combination of pointing and spoken commands, objects were created, named, moved, copied, and erased. A user could move objects by pointing to an object, uttering "put that . . . ", and then pointing to a new location and uttering "there"—gesture disambiguated the meaning of "there."

The input device used to track gestures in *Put That There* had six degrees of freedom. The sensor was a cube small enough to be embedded in jewelry or worn on the wrist. A small cord ran from the sensor to additional hardware.

Although the *Put That There* interface did not actually use the motion of a user's hand (only pointing was recognized), it captured the essence of gestural interfaces. Positions were input to the system using the same gestures we use in everyday life; we gesture by pointing to objects and locations.

DATAGLOVE™

Gesture is extremely effective for specifying the position, size, and orientation of 3-D objects, and a device called the DataGlove™ is an example of a hand tracking input device that permits this [Zimmerman et al., 1987]. This device is a glove that the user wears. Analog flex sensors in the glove measure finger bending (see figure L in the color insert). The position and orientation of the hand is tracked by a Polhemus sensor. The glove has a wire that connects it to additional hardware.

The DataGlove has been used for many applications: as a controller for a 3-D hand model, an interface to a visual programming language, a music and sound synthesis controller, a finger-spelling interpreter, and a computer-generated object manipulator. Its most obvious use has been for 3-D object manipulation. By using the DataGlove, the user can interact with virtual objects in a manner similar to interaction with real objects. A user sees virtual objects in 3-D and manipulates them by hand. The virtual objects can be grabbed, twisted, squeezed, thrown, and set down. The gestures that a user makes in manipulating real objects are mapped directly from gesture commands in the virtual world. A virtual environment of this type has been developed at NASA Ames Research Center [Fisher 1986], using a head-mounted 3-D display [Sutherland 1968] and a DataGlove.

VIDEODESK

The systems described above have all used input devices that the user wears or holds. What is exciting about a system called VideoDesk [Krueger, 1983] is that the user is freed from wearing or handling an input device. In this system, a user sits at a white desk while an overhead video camera observes the motion of his hands over the desk. Behind the desk is a display in which the user can see the digitized video camera view of his hands. The video image is analyzed by gesture recognition software (see figure M in the color insert).

Several applications have been developed to demonstrate the system. One such application allows users to "finger paint" on the display. Not only are gestures used to spread the paint, but special gestures are used to pop up and select commands from menus. Another application allows users to produce virtual 3-D sculptures on the display in the same manner as a potter using a potter's wheel. Using two hands, a sculptor makes the same motions as a potter: by moving her hands up and down, expanding and contracting, she creates various levels of the "pot."

Another compelling aspect of this system occurs when several users in separate locations, each with his or her own VideoDesk, share the same video image. In other words, users see their own hands and the other users' hands on their screen. In this situation, natural hand gestures can be used to communicate among the users. For example, one user might indicate to another user that an object should be erased by making a cross gesture over it. The developer of VideoDesk is just beginning to explore this cooperative work technique.

Why Haven't Gestures Been Used More?

One of the factors hindering the acceptance of gesture input devices is the cost of devices to track gestures. Historically, computers came equipped only with keyboards. In order to use gestures, an additional input device was required. Today most computers are sold with some sort of pointing device. Kurtenbach has shown how gestures can be used to manipulate a 2-D icon-based interface using a mouse [Kurtenbach, 1988]. Nevertheless, other "gesture capable" input devices, especially the 3-D variety, are still expensive.

Another factor inhibiting the use of gestures is the lack of more robust gesture-recognition techniques. Only recently have we finally begun to see complete, user-independent character recognition systems [Suen et al., 1980], and gesture recognition is in many cases a more complex process than character recognition. This is especially true for dynamic, 3-D gestures, suggesting that further research and development in gesture-recognition techniques is required.

Gesture input has been competing with other effective forms of input in many applications. For example, although prototype gesture-based graphics editors have been implemented, they've had to compete with an established base of production-quality, full-featured graphics editors that use command-line or menu-based interfaces. The benefit of using gestures in these interfaces has been outweighed by the value of the user's familiarity with the more established forms of input.

Fundamentally, the problem for gesture input has been that new interface paradigms can't be introduced in a piecemeal fashion. Like the mice that came before them, gestures await a full interface based on them to become established in the marketplace. Once a whole interface has been designed, implemented, and introduced, gestures will begin to compete effectively with other input techniques.

The Future

Where can gestures find their niche in the computer world? We don't believe in the future that we will be "waving" at files to close them or using sign language instead of typing. We *do* believe the physicality of gestures has a value in itself and that there are applications, like computer music, sculpture, and simulation, in which this is important.

Users will be able to get more physically involved with their computers. For example, interactions with computer music composition/performance programs of today are only as physical as a key click. Even an input device as simple as a mouse could be used to input conducting gestures. It's time we stopped thinking about computers as glorified typewriters and thought about them as expressive instruments. In a similar fashion, computer sculpting might consist of a system through which a sculptor could sweep out virtual 3-D sculptures using gestures. Gestures could also be used in simulation applications. Imagine simulating throwing a ball in 3-D space where a user can input the velocity and the spin of the ball by "gesturing" the throw. The point is that in these applications, spontaneity, creativity, and realism are enhanced through an efficient, expressive input technique.

Many other challenging research issues surround the use of gesture. How can gesture be used to assist other input technologies? For example, a user's gestures could assist speech recognition/natural language systems; a video camera could track the user's movements and take these gestures into account when trying to determine what the user is trying to do. What happens when gesture commands and other interaction techniques, such as direct manipulation and menu-driven commands, are combined?

How can we exploit the parallel input potential of gestures? Parallel input is defined as simultaneous user input from several devices. It has been demonstrated that, for certain tasks, the speed of performing the task is strongly correlated to the degrees of parallelism employed [Buxton, 1986]. Nonintrusive gesture input technology, such as video camera observation, lends itself to parallel input. A gesture-tracking system could track both the user's hands at the same time. Systems like Krueger's VideoDesk have already begun to exploit this potential.

Recognition of gestures is still a major problem in itself, but gesture can also be used within some computer applications independent of recognition. For example, some collaborative work systems allow users to view each other's hands on their computer screen [Ehrlich et al., 1989]. One user can gesture to another such things as "remove this" or "look at this." The computer does no gesture recognition at all.

Just as in real life, in computer use there are applications in which gesture is the natural form for expression and there are applications in which gesture provides additional information or an alternate method of expression. Human-computer interfaces that recognize and respond to gestures will increase the range of applications for computers, improve ease-of-use by increasing the diversity of choices of input, and make our lives with computers richer and more satisfying.

Talking and Listening to Computers

SCIENCE FICTION MOVIES and books have long depicted the use of spoken dialogues to assist people working with electronic systems. It seems that we have been waiting a long time for talking and listening to become part of everyday user-machine transactions. How much longer must we wait before we can have spoken conversations with computers?

It is obvious that we all talk to animate objects, and sometimes in frustration even to inanimate ones (such as computers). Similarly, if less noticeably, most of us routinely listen to nonspeech sounds to discover what is happening in the world. We listen to the pitch of our automobile engines to judge when to shift gears, to the gurgle of pouring liquid to know if a container is almost full, and to traffic sounds to judge the danger of crossing a street. Moreover, many users listen to the sounds of their printers, modems, and disk drives to help assess the state of their systems. Computer programmers sometimes used to debug their systems by wiring tone generators to their computers, or by tuning a nearby radio to listen to their machines [Norman, personal communication, 1988]. How can the natural tendency to talk and listen to the everyday world be further exploited in computers? How can we design speech and audio interfaces that enable users to listen to the model world of the computer?

The strength of interactive computing still resides largely with the visual power of graphics, while alternate sensory modes of input and output are often ignored. This chapter examines ways that the audio channel can be

S. Joy Mountford

S. Joy Mountford

Human Interface Group
Apple Computer, Inc.

William W. Gaver

Rank Xerox EuroPARC
Summer Intern, Apple Computer, Inc.

used effectively to extend the power of graphical interfaces. In particular, we address speech input, an application for sound that is familiar if seldom realized, and nonspeech auditory output, an application that has only recently been explored.

We will describe some of the ways that talking and listening to computers can enhance user performance. We are not attempting to describe all the possible forms of speech and sound input and output. Summaries of state-of-the-art technology and voice I/O applications are described in the annual proceedings of such conferences as the American Voice Input and Output Society (AVIOS), and there are also good references for the use of nonspeech audio in interfaces (see, for instance, *Human-Computer Interaction*, vol. 4, no. 1, an issue that is devoted to this topic). What we hope to show in this chapter is that interface designers can use speech and sound in a variety of ways to improve interfaces.

The Appeal of Auditory Interfaces

The perfect interface environment is one in which the interface is transparent to users, with nothing between them and their tasks [Norman, 1987]. Although there have been remarkable advances in various techniques for interacting with computers, they are almost entirely visual in nature. Perhaps the best examples of this are direct manipulation systems. These systems present a model world to users, employing graphical representations of the objects in that world that may be manipulated. Direct manipulation interfaces are powerful for a number of reasons [Hutchins et al., 1986]. However, with the increased freedom from textual I/O comes an increased dependence on manual input and graphical output. In many situations, users simply have too much to do or see. Auditory I/O is a natural, available, and systematically underutilized channel for enhancing user-computer communication.

THE VALUE OF SPEECH RECOGNITION

Most of us find speech a well-learned, rich, and efficient medium for sharing information and meaning. While speaking, a person can obtain visual information and perform manual skills at the same time, thus overcoming the more limited bandwidth implied by today's graphic/pointing systems. Speech is most powerful when used in highly time-shared activities, typical of the visual and manual worlds in which we all exist. Furthermore, speech input can be used to communicate with computers from remote locations—for example, by telephone.

Input to direct manipulation systems typically is performed by manipulating objects within the interface. This is conceptually a natural way to interact with systems, but users must frequently move their hands from the keyboard to the mouse and back again. With the use of larger and multiple screens, as well as multilayered hierarchical menus, the time taken to move back and forth between the two input devices becomes more significant. Adding the ability to recognize users' speech output would be a natural complement to the use of mouse and keyboard [Firman, 1988]. In such a system, the user could "direct" using voice commands, especially to access hidden functionality; for example, selecting Chooser items by uttering such words as "Select Printer X." Users would be able to keep their hands and eyes on the task with minimal task interference.

It is rare to perform any task without having to time-share between two or more activities, and speech could be used to trade off between tasks efficiently. Although speaking can interfere with some tasks (for example, one can't very well speak and hear at the same time), many other tasks can be performed while speaking (for example, one can more easily speak and sort papers at the same time). Analyzing different types of tasks in terms of their incoming and outgoing stimuli types and modalities is critical in understanding the total number of tasks a user can perform at one time. Wickens, Mountford, and Schreiner [1981] proposed a performance model to assess the different effects of modality on dual task performance. This model, and others like it, suggests that speech technology can be used to enable task time-sharing and to facilitate the performance of some activities, especially when the user's hands and eyes are busy.

Speech can be used independently of manual input, or the two modalities can work together. An essential part of normal conversation is centered around the use of nonverbal communication, particularly eye contact and hand gestures (see the chapter by Kurtenbach and Hulteen). Very few speech application interfaces have integrated verbal and nonverbal forms of communication, but this is a promising area of future research. Another potentially powerful feature of speech is its ability to be used for remote communications, even with very limited vocabulary speech recognizers. Such ideas have already been successfully explored within such domains as banking [Brooks, 1988], on-line sales reporting [DEC, 1985] and inquiries about stock availability, price, and delivery [Witten and Madams, 1977].

THE VALUE OF NONSPEECH AUDIO

Sound is a familiar and natural medium for conveying information that we use in our everyday lives. The following examples help illustrate the important kinds of information that sounds can communicate:

- Information about **physical** events:
  We can hear whether a dropped glass has bounced or shattered.

- Information about **invisible** structures:
  Tapping on a wall is useful in finding where to hang a heavy picture.

- Information about **dynamic** change:
  As we fill a glass we can hear when the liquid has reached the top.

- Information about **abnormal** structures:
  A malfunctioning engine sounds different from a healthy one.

- Information about events in **space**:
  Footsteps warn us of the approach of another person.

Using nonspeech sounds to provide system information is appealing for several reasons. First, by adding sound to the interface the bandwidth of communication can be significantly increased. Second, the information conveyed by sound is complementary to that available visually, and thus sound can provide a means for displaying information that is difficult to visualize, especially with limited screen real estate.

Just as we risk overburdening our manual capabilities by relying on gestural input, so do we risk overburdening our visual systems by depending on graphical displays for everything. System information is traditionally displayed via graphical feedback that remains on the screen, although it may be obsolete or irrelevant soon after it is shown. The result is often crowded, incomprehensible displays. In addition, there are numerous situations in which the metaphor used to create a computer's model world does not lend itself to the display of certain kinds of information (for example, the status of a hidden process).

Sound and vision are complementary modes of information. Whereas sound exists in time and over space, vision exists in space and over time. Graphical displays exist in space at a location, so that many visual messages can be displayed at once, and they are usually available for a second glance. But one has to look in the appropriate direction to see a visual object, whereas one need not face a source of sound to listen to it. In addition, sounds are relatively transient in nature and thus are well suited for conveying changes in system state and for presenting discrete messages. A sound can be heard in many locations at a certain time, whereas a visual object may be seen in a certain location at many times.

Imagine, for instance, how useful an audio monitor for background printing could be. As you start the job, a low, steady sound informs you that it is being processed. While you continue with other work, the sound is modified to tell you how much is done, the speed of printing, perhaps even how close the printer is to running out of paper. Finally, when the job is completed, the sound stops, perhaps ending with a slightly more noticeable sound to emphasize that the printing is done. Using sound in this way can provide information about many processes without cluttering the screen.

Informative sounds like these need not be particularly noticeable or interfering to users. There are already many everyday sounds present in a typical work environment, from the background whir of a ventilator to the small shuffles, taps, and scrapes of books, papers, staplers, and so on. Well-designed auditory interfaces should form a natural extension of existing auditory environments, employing sounds that are distinguishable without being surprising or distracting.

In summary, sound can be used to display the status of processes in multitasking environments. It can be used to convey information about discrete events in the computer, such as the arrival of mail or the acquisition of a target. Sound can enable remote access to machines and access by the visually disabled. Just as speech can reduce the need for manual input, so can sound reduce the need for graphical output.

Examples of Successful Audio Interfaces

In the preceding section, we described why speech and audio might enhance the interface. Now we will illustrate with some examples of successful uses of these technologies. It is in this section that the relative ages of work on speech input and audio output become most obvious. Although we discuss several applications that use speech, we address only one audio interface. This is partly because this is one with which we are most familiar, but even more because there simply aren't many existing examples. Although we feel nonspeech audio output has great potential, there can be no denying that most of that potential has yet to be realized.

SPEECH RECOGNITION

Many of the most successful uses of speech recognition involve situations in which users' hands and eyes are occupied simultaneously. Speech recognizers were first used by the Chicago Mail Depots to inventory parcels while sorting them. Similar applications are illustrated by Love [1988] for dispatching personnel, and by North, Mountford, and Kruger [1982] in a printed circuit board kitting task. The latter study involved installing an isolated-phrase speech recognizer with a computer to assist in entering part numbers during factory kit assembly and inspection tasks. The correct parts were logged in by voice for eventual printed circuit board construction. In this eyes-hands busy task, operators increased their task efficiency by about 70 percent, calculated from recordings of both speed and accuracy. This high increase in efficiency is typical of such efforts. Improved performance was also due to the users' ability to tailor their vocabularies: using familiar names to correspond to the parts in the kit assembly increased efficiency by making part names more memorable.

Many different application areas have implemented speech recognition systems successfully for a range of users' tasks. Recently, medical science has been applying speech aggressively to such situations as voice data capture and recording in complex user settings. Speech recording capabilities have also been enhanced by adding speech recognition; for example, in a computerized dental examination system [Baumgarten and Schiavone,

1988] and in a voice-controlled microscope facilitating microsurgery procedures [Liang and Narayanan, 1988]. Attempts are also being made to facilitate speech therapy by using computer-animated speech processing of the speech-recognized utterances [Hutchins, 1988]. In the area of instruction, voice recognition has been used to enhance learning in a classroom [Sprouls, 1988] and in interactive video-based training applications [Rao and Lieff, 1988].

Airborne applications are another eyes-hands busy task domain that has benefitted for some time from applications of speech recognition [for example, Mountford and Schwartz, 1983; Bernabe, 1988; North and Lea, 1984]. Pilots work in highly time-critical environments in which they are frequently overloaded with "essential" tasks to complete. Voice commands can be used to prepare or check data while performing other continuous manual tasks, such as flying.

An interesting project called Put That There was conducted at MIT in the mid-70s by Schmandt and Hulteen. The basic innovation of this system was in helping to disambiguate a recognized speech utterance by using pointing to provide additional information about users' intentions. A wall display was presented to users, who wore a Polhemus position-sensing device on their wrist and spoke into a head-mounted microphone connected to a speech recognizer. Users indicated the area of the map they wanted to change by pointing in the appropriate direction, and then stated verbally what they wanted to change in that area. The use of these two technologies together was critical to the overall success of the users' spoken and gestured command utterances. Neither technology could have successfully performed the task in isolation, but used together, they helped disambiguate the data from each source and increased the success rate and ease of use of this system. In addition, the pairing of these two technologies formed a very natural coupling from the users' point of view; we often gesture while speaking to clarify meaning.

Unfortunately, this apparently natural coupling of technology seems not to have been pursued much further since the design of Put That There. Mountford et al. [1984] conducted a similar study in which subjects performed one task using either pointing and speech or pointing and manual command input, while simultaneously performing a continuous manual tracking task. The preliminary results from this study indicated that performance of the speech and pointing task was superior to that using pointing with a manual command, while a manual continuous task was performed simultaneously. The natural pairing of these speech and gesturing technologies seems to offer much promise for the introduction of new styles of human-computer communication, particularly because the technologies are now becoming much more compact, accurate, and affordable.

Most of us are familiar with using telephone answering machines to leave messages for one another, so even now we don't have to talk in

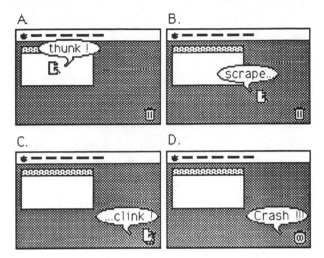

Figure 1: A typical interaction with the SonicFinder.

person to make plans. An exciting development from answering machines is the possibility of integrating the telecommunications system with other electronic devices, so that the phone system has access to computer systems. Phone Slave [Schmandt and Arons, 1985] is an intriguing combination of both audio and graphics in an interface used to access a series of telecommunications capabilities (see Schmandt's chapter). This system creates the illusion of a conversational answering machine, supports voice or text electronic mail access, and provides on-line telephone directory assistance. It demonstrates that a combination of voice and gesture on a touch screen can enhance a diverse range of telecommunication tasks.

Nonspeech Audio Output: The SonicFinder

The SonicFinder is an audio interface in which information is conveyed using auditory icons as well as standard graphical feedback [Gaver, 1989]. The SonicFinder (also known as Finder Sounds) modifies the original Apple Finder by extending the visual desktop metaphor into the auditory dimension. The information that is available in the existing interface is used to trigger and control the playback of sounds sampled from recordings of everyday sound-producing events. In the SonicFinder, events in the interface such as selecting a file are mapped to sound-producing events such as tapping an object.

Figure 1 shows a typical interaction with the SonicFinder, in which a user selects a file, drags it over the desktop to the trash can, and drops it (thus deleting the file). In the SonicFinder, these events are accompanied by auditory icons meant to convey complex information in intuitive ways. For instance, selecting a file sounds like tapping an object whose size is proportional to that of the file. Dragging the file makes a scraping sound that changes as the file is moved over windows and the desktop and stops when it is moved onto a container into which it may be dropped. Finally, dropping the file into the trash can produces a crashing sound that provides confirmation that the file has indeed been deleted.

The SonicFinder is a prototype that has been distributed internally within Apple Computer. We have been soliciting users' feedback through questionnaires and informal interviews for more than two years. Several strengths of the SonicFinder have become clear in this process. First, the SonicFinder enhances confirmation of users' actions. For example, many Macintosh users have played the frustrating game of "chase the trash can," in which one drops an object over the Trash icon but not into it (because a true hit depends on the cursor's position, not the overlap between object and trash icons). Although visual confirmation of a hit is given by highlighting the trashcan icon, this seems to be less effective in confirming the action than the knocking sound heard when using the SonicFinder. This use of sound is a natural accompaniment to the physical and visual act, reflecting the ways sounds are used in everyday life.

The SonicFinder also offers potentially increased flexibility of interaction to users. The auditory icon that accompanies copying is a good illustration. When an object or group of objects is copied, the sound of pouring water accompanies the event. The frequency of the sound is continuously increased to indicate progress by analogy with the sound a container makes as it is being filled. The copying sound presents information that is completely redundant with the visual feedback, but the graphic indicator currently used requires users to attend to the screen, whereas the sound does not. During lengthy copy operations (as, for instance, when many files are copied), the advantage of using an auditory icon to display progress is obvious and pronounced.

Finally, the addition of auditory icons increases feelings of direct engagement with the model world of the computer [Laurel, 1986]. Hearing as well as seeing the objects and events of the computer world makes that world much more tangible. Once a user has become accustomed to the SonicFinder, using quiet Finders is comparable to wearing earplugs in everyday life. Direct engagement as a quality is difficult to specify, and probably even more difficult to reveal through user testing. Experience with the SonicFinder, however, has convinced us that direct engagement is an important aspect of the user's experience.

Gains in direct engagement, confirmation, and flexibility make the SonicFinder an appealing interface example. Still, the SonicFinder only hints at the potential role of nonspeech audio in the interface. It is probably best to think of the SonicFinder as a demonstration that:

• Sound can be incorporated naturally into the interface.

• Sound can provide redundant information that is potentially useful.

- Sound can provide information that is not graphically displayed.
- Sound can present some kinds of information better than graphics can.

A number of people have used the SonicFinder as their standard interface for more than two years at the time of this writing. For these users, a telling piece of evidence in favor of the addition of sound in their interfaces is that they complain of missing it when they use a quiet Finder. For some people, at least, the addition of sounds is valuable, and for this reason alone the SonicFinder can be counted a success.

On the other hand, critics complain of loud sounds simultaneously emanating from many users' work spaces. This is a difficult complaint to address. It must be remembered that volume levels should be set low in order for sounds to be used naturally and subtly. Furthermore, audio interfaces should used varied sounds subject to user control. The eventual goal is to modify the SonicFinder and release it as a Desk Accessory with a Control Panel to turn individual Finder sounds on or off, and to add new sounds based on individual user preferences. Providing user control should help address problems with the current implementation of the SonicFinder.

Design Implementation Issues for Auditory Information

A number of strategies for using speech input and sound output have been developed, both in terms of technologies and in terms of the ways they are used. In this section, we discuss these techniques for speech and sound in turn, and address both those methods we feel to be most useful and pitfalls to be aware of in developing auditory interfaces.

SPEECH RECOGNITION SYSTEMS

Speech recognizers are either speaker-dependent, trained by individual users to recognize isolated words or phrases, or speaker-independent, with a more limited vocabulary being recognized regardless of the speaker. The reliability of speech recognizers is much greater when they are trained to match the idiosyncrasies of each speaker, rather than being speaker-independent systems. Affordable speaker-dependent, isolated-phrase speech recognizers with vocabularies of up to about a thousand words are available and are being tried in a variety of vertical markets. The technology used to create speech recognizers varies considerably, and the costs of the products are equally varied. A quick look at *Speech Technology* magazine will give an overview of the available systems.

The progress expected to occur within automatic speech recognition (ASR) will come indirectly from improvements in VLSI technology, which is approximately doubling performance every year at constant cost. It is our belief that it is only a matter of time until the average personal computer has the computing power to perform continuous speech recognition for thousand-word vocabularies. Improvements in the theory of ASR are moving it away from the realm of heuristic programming to a more solid basis in the statistics of Markov processes. The Hidden Markov Model (HMM) is a theory that has produced substantial improvements in ASR in several major research centers in the U.S. It is being used to pursue continuous speech recognition for dictation (requiring 20,000 words or more) by Dragon Systems, Kurzweil, and IBM. It is also used for more task-specific applications such as Official Airline Guide queries by SRI, personnel record queries (Bolt, Bernanek, and Newman), controlling spreadsheets (Carnegie Mellon University), and dialing telephones with spoken digits (AT&T Bell Labs).

The HMM approach provides a systematic means for combining knowledge from different sources (semantics, syntactic, intonation, and acoustic analysis). This has transformed the task of building ASR systems to a task of digitizing and labeling speech samples. In terms of the real needs of building speech understanding systems, the HMM approach provides the best solution to date. It is expected that HMM, in combination with progress in VLSI, neural net computing, and other techniques, will accelerate progress in both price and performance for speech recognition over the next two to three years.

The most successful implementations of speech technology today use speaker-dependent, connected-word recognizers and mostly digitized speech output. These isolated word/phrase systems typically use syntactically-branched grammar structures to increase their operational success. This means that the structure of users' spoken communication must follow a rather limited format, often being verb-driven, followed by nouns and qualifiers, such as "Select" (verb) "X" (noun) "now" (qualifier), or "Enter" (verb) "256" (noun) "OK" (qualifier). Obviously this is not the way we normally converse, but it is typical of some jobs in which the niceties of conversation are eliminated for more efficient communication, such as in air traffic control, medical operations, and command situations.

We believe that ultimately users would like to communicate completely openly and reliably with a speech system that can understand and generate natural language. Nevertheless, efficient user-computer transactions do still occur using limited-sized vocabularies. Although people often choose recognizers based on the *number* of words they recognize, they should consider their actual *flexibility*. The utility of limited-vocabulary recognizers can be substantially enhanced by using task-oriented grammars and custom-designed vocabularies. It is important to remember that until vocabularies are unlimited, users have to learn and remember all the recognizable words and expected grammatical structures. The smaller the system set, the more easily and quickly users can learn. Furthermore, the larger the vocabulary offered, the greater the likelihood of machine confusion in the recognition of speech commands.

Selecting the best vocabulary/word items to be used is a critical feature that often does not get much attention during the design of specific applications. The word items should be chosen based on the current terms most familiar to prospective users of the system. However, after preliminary vocabulary selection, confusability studies should be run with word equivalents on the recognizer in pretests to find any frequently misunderstood or confused items. For example, certain speech recognizers have been shown to confuse the words *one* and *four,* words that seem quite distinct to users. Some recognizers have problems distinguishing spoken fricatives, so *one* and *four* or *a* and *eight* are confusable, especially when spoken quickly and indistinctly—which is the normal way of speaking.

It is also helpful to consider the environmental conditions in which the task will be conducted. Contrary to popular belief, overall noise level does not make recognition any more difficult, but sudden, loud noises do. Of course, in order to get the highest rate of recognition the voice system should be trained in the same environmental conditions as the real implementation. No special conditions should be enforced during training, because templates obtained in these conditions would be uncluttered or "clean" compared with those obtained in real environments.

Trained recognizers are often unable to understand users whose voices have changed due to illness or stress, and in fact must be retrained periodically to account for natural, longer-term changes in users' voices. This problem is currently being addressed by generating dynamic retraining algorithms designed for use in changing conditions. The amount that each particular utterance template shows a difference or drift away from a stored template is collected during all transactions with the speech system. This is considered as the amount that the speaker's template "drifts" over time, and it can then be used to prompt the user to update their stored templates. This sort of technique for accommodating the way in which a normal user speaks in the real world is likely to play an increasingly important role in helping to make speech technology more usable and thus more acceptable to users.

Additional factors have limited the overall success of voice technology. For example, the use of microphones is generally difficult. Wearing a microphone that is tethered to a communication system restricts the user's movement, which is a serious problem because speech systems are often used in mobile or remote situations. Head-mounted microphones usually ensure the best speech recognition performance because they are closest to the user's mouth and reduce external noise from the environment, but they are irritating to wear for long periods of time. In nonremote uses of speech, the exact placement of the fixed microphone is an important consideration to avoid accidental triggering. Future study needs to identify ways of embedding microphones systematically into other physical structures, so there is not just one dedicated microphone.

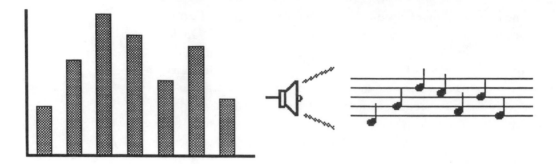

Figure 2: Sound graphs map data dimensions to parameters of sound. In this example, the data parameter indicated on the visual graph by height is mapped to pitch to construct an analogous sound graph.

Another particularly poorly designed feature on most speech recognition systems is the means of turning on the recognizer. Most systems require users to manually trip an activation switch to tell the system to be ready to receive spoken commands. This is a poor choice of initiation modality, since voice dialogs are usually employed when users have their hands busy, or want them free. A preferred way of initiating recognition would be to use a voice command to wake up the system. This could be set up so the system is listening at all times to wake up to a series of words like "wake up." Of course, this command could also be customizable (see Schmandt's chapter).

TECHNIQUES FOR USING AUDIO OUTPUT

Early work on audio messages focused on the development of sound graphs [Mansur et al., 1985] as tools to aid researchers exploring multidimensional data. Typically, each dimension of data is mapped to a dimension of sound (see figure 2), so that each multidimensional data point specifies a new sound, or the parameters of a continuous sound over time. Patterns in the data manifest as patterns in the sounds, so that, for instance, all high sounds might be loud and all low sounds soft. Using this strategy, Bly [1982] showed that subjects could reliably distinguish members of two multidimensional, normally distributed data sets after listening to exemplars of each; Mezrich et al. [1984] found that subjects could perceive correlation in many-dimensional data; and Morrison and Lunney [1985] showed that blind subjects could learn to recognize spectrographic data mapped to chords and series of chords.

An obvious application for auditory I/O is to give visually disabled people greater access to computers. Morrison and Lunney's [1985] spectrographic display system was aimed primarily at enabling visually disabled students to use sophisticated chemical analysis tools. Edwards [1989] developed an auditory interface to a modified direct-manipulation word processor that was usable by blind and visually impaired subjects. He used a combination of simple pitch encoding and speech to provide information about location in the system and results of menu selections. The wide

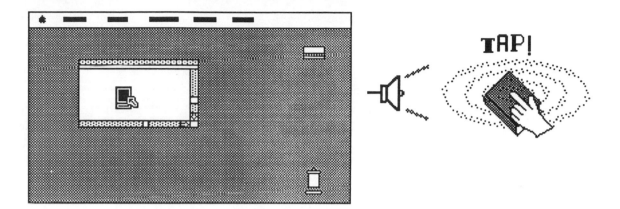

Figure 3: Auditory icons are everyday sounds meant to give information about events in the computer by analogy with everyday events.

relevance of such work is emphasized by Buxton's [1988] observation that we are all visually impaired when faced with a cluttered graphic display.

Nonspeech sounds can also be used to create audio monitors, which exploit the fact that listeners tend to ignore continuous, unchanging sounds, but are alerted by unusual variations. Audio monitors may be created by allowing streams of data to determine some parameter of a continuously present sound (for example, pitch, rhythm, or timbre). Such audio monitors can be designed to be unobtrusive except when the data varies outside of its normal or acceptable range, at which point the sound becomes more salient.

A newer strategy for using sound in the interface is to integrate informative natural sounds into the interface in the form of auditory icons [Gaver, 1989, 1988, 1986]. For instance, figure 3 shows a system in which selecting a file is represented by a sound like someone tapping on a book. Not only can the sound convey the kind of event naturally, but other parameters of the event (like the size of the file) can be communicated by changing parameters of the sound source (like the size of the book). Because auditory icons can provide information about several aspects of an event, they can convey organized multidimensional information. Auditory icons can be developed systematically so that similar sorts of events make similar sounds. In addition, they can be designed to be compatible with the graphic portion of the interface, and so are likely to make the world of the computer more engaging for users.

The ultimate success of auditory icons depends on the development of good analogies between events in the computer and sound-producing events in the world. When such analogies are hard to find, sounds can be given meaning by design. One way of doing this is to sparingly use motives—short musical phrases—to stand for system messages [Blattner et al., 1989]. A system of motives may be developed in which similar system messages are represented by variations of a single underlying theme. Such a system of motives is like a designed language in which the relations among motives and their meanings are not as intuitive as for auditory icons. Moreover, unless they are designed with great care, motives are likely to be dismissed as "bad" music. Nonetheless, motives may be useful for conveying information that is difficult to map to everyday sounds.

Poorly designed auditory interfaces can be extremely annoying. For example, such recent inventions as talking Coke machines,* speaking and responding dolls [Frantz, Reimer, and Wotiz, 1988], talking automobiles ("The door is a jar!"), and the buzzing tones used to remind drivers to fasten their seat-belts and turn off their headlights have frayed the patience of both users and innocent bystanders. Because we have no earlids, volume control at least is mandatory in any auditory interface. In addition, users working in noisy environments or those with hearing deficiencies may find it difficult to obtain information from sound, and the transient nature of audio messages can place an unacceptable memory load on users. Of course, earphones can help overcome the problems of annoying nearby people, and allow the use of sounds even in noisy environments. Many employees have already taken to wearing headphones in open office environments to avoid distractions. But sounds should be designed to be as unobtrusive as possible, so that earphones ideally are not necessary.

Several rules of thumb should be used in choosing sounds to reduce annoyance. The most important axiom is that familiarity breeds contempt. Repetitive audio messages of all types quickly become tiresome. Auditory messages should always be as varied as possible, either randomly along irrelevant dimensions or by representing as many dimensions of information as possible so that identical messages are relatively rare. Another heuristic is that musical sounds and phrases are more likely to distract and irritate people than everyday sounds. Auditory interfaces should form a natural extension of everyday auditory environments.

Memory-load problems and hearing disabilities are more difficult to surmount, but we should not forget that these problems have counterparts in visual displays. Too many sounds may be difficult to distinguish and remember, but so are cluttered graphical screens difficult to search. The ability to use auditory interfaces will be limited by hearing disabilities, but so is the ability to use visual displays limited by one's sight. In general, using both sound and graphics together and tailoring the output medium to suit the user and the situation will win over more restrictive strategies.

Where Next with Speech and Sound at the Interface?

So far we have outlined a number of successful implementations using speech recognition and nonspeech audio output, and examined some of the

---

* Ed. note—A talking Coke machine placed in the student cafeteria of a California college was so annoying that students circulated a petition to have it removed. When the authorities failed to respond, the machine was vandalized relentlessly until its "voice" was disabled.

interface issues encountered in designing both types of interface. Now we will describe some future directions and challenges.

THE NEED FOR BETTER TOOLS

Providing users with accessible means to enter speech and sound information will be an important design lever for gaining wider acceptance of speech recognition and audio messages. Digitizers such as MacRecorder and SoundCap have shown the tremendous possibilities of real-time speech recorders. Most of their uses are for fun, but they also make possible applications such as voice annotation and customized audio interfaces.

As the capability for adding sound to a data stream grows, so too does the need for efficient editing, synchronizing, and summarizing techniques for sounds. As yet the tools for editing sound at the interface are inadequate and nonintuitive: spectral analyses are hard to understand and interpret even for the most skilled. The ability to represent the audio channel in alternate forms and to create summaries of lengthy sounds will become necessary if we are to expand the user's bandwidth for communication. The presentation of data in multimedia forms can be used to enhance subsequent data analysis [see, for instance, Bly, 1982; Pickover, 1988; and Peterson, 1987]. As we begin to be able to store and play back more and more information, the ability to access different data sources efficiently, both as sounds and as pictures, will be more important. Such pioneering work is described in the "Intelligent Ear" paper by Schmandt [1981], showing an interactive graphical display to control nongraphical media. Such techniques could be used to provide quick visual summaries of soon-to-be frequent taped collaborative meetings, for instance. Sound sources could be visually categorized by speaker, type of occurrence, and time. Likewise, libraries of sounds could be visually categorized by source, date, or sound type.

PROMISING DIRECTIONS

The future for audio interfaces lies in designers' abilities to incorporate other modalities into rich expressive interfaces typical of what we expect today from graphical interfaces. Many of the most important design directions are best set by examining how people use speech and sound in their everyday lives. For instance, nonverbal channels such as gesture, paralinguistics, and facial expressions are critical for conversation, and this should be reflected in future speech applications. The verbal commands used by future operators may be disambiguated by accessing this information through a combination of other technologies such as automatic lip-reading systems [Petajan et al.,1988] or gesture/pointing recognition, as in Put That There.

Similarly, using parameters of nonspeech sound sources to encode information seems to reflect ways people already listen to the world. Auditory icons and other audio messages are likely to prove particularly effective in multitasking environments, in which users might hear when one process is completed rather than scan the screen for graphic feedback. They may also prove useful in collaborative systems to help users keep track of who is doing what and where. A better understanding of when it is best to use speech messages or sounds needs to be acquired. Indeed, understanding what kinds of useful information can be conveyed by sounds may change aspects of the model world used to give structure to interfaces.

Another promising application of speech technology is the capability to leave voice annotations or Post-it notes on electronic documents to serve as personal reminders or comments to others. Such applications decouple the use of voice from answering machines and extend its power to the computer interface.

The use of speech recognition and audio output in interfaces is likely to become particularly appealing with the ability to securely access remote information. We would like to call up our personal computers and ask them to send some files over to each other (particularly when the authors are on opposite sides of the Atlantic). Speech is already being used to open up new application arenas by enhancing phone answering machines, in the form of a phone-based ordering machine [ELTON, Corrick and Warren, 1988], product and service ordering systems [Butler-in-a-Box, Searey, 1988], banking [Brooks et al., 1988], and university registration [Eddy, 1988; Reed, 1988; Schuster, 1988].

Audio interfaces designed for the visually disabled suggest that non-speech audio can also support remote access to computers. For instance, confirmation that spoken commands have been carried out might be indicated by brief, unobtrusive sounds. Location in a file system might be encoded by a characteristic sound, and information about variables of the system state such as available memory and processing load might be provided by changing environmental modifiers of sound such as reverberation.

The use of speech and sound in interfaces is, in some ways, only in its infancy. But we feel that these technologies hold much promise for the future in reducing our dependence on manual and graphical I/O. Whether speech is used alone over the telephone, or with pointing and facial expression, whether sounds are used to provide continuous information about background processes or discrete messages about user-initiated events, and whether the aim is to expand the interface for all users or to provide access to visually impaired or remote users, auditory interfaces will prove a significant new addition to the designer's repertory.

Illusion in the Interface

ALTHOUGH INTELLIGENT AND INTERFACE are often used in the same sentence, few user interfaces really manifest much intelligence. This would require reasoned attempts to understand the user's requirements by paying attention to the implications of user actions rather than simply responding directly to those actions. To do so is difficult, of course, impinging on some of the unsolved problems in such domains as computational linguistics, artificial intelligence, and cognitive psychology. Some interfaces, however, may *appear* to be intelligent, from the perspective of the user, simply by making the right response at the right time. This appearance or *illusion* of intelligence aids user interaction by fostering a sense of confidence or reasonableness in the interface, and can add a powerful positive quality (provided, of course, that it does not raise user expectations to a level that cannot be realized).

This illusion of intelligence is decidedly *not* magic. Magic requires distraction, focusing the audience's attention on details visually removed from the location where the actual mechanics of the trick are to be performed. Interface illusion occurs directly at the focus of user attention. It succeeds only to the extent that it correctly models common human actions, and in particular to the extent that it can predict an expected response. This ability can be gained only by studying human-to-human interactions.

All the author's experience in this field is limited to speech interfaces, that is, dialog systems employing some forms of speech recognition and

Chris Schmandt

Media Laboratory
Massachusetts Institute of Technology

335

generation to accomplish a task. It may be hard to extend these claims to other media, as those new media (video screens, keyboards, mice) are new tools in our species' experience. They cannot yet be strongly tied to emulating any forms of human behavior other than that of the using a computer, exactly the domain we have to step back from to study human social interactions.

Speech as an interface is both rich and deceptively difficult. Speech recognition by computer is still in its infancy, and despite exaggerated claims by seekers of venture capital, high-performance recognition devices with any sizable vocabulary simply do not yet exist. Even the better experimental devises are fragile, and they work best when the talker attempts to speak extremely clearly and consistently, quite unlike the way one speaks in "natural" conversation. Anyone attempting to build a user interface with today's speech technologies is confronted with the need to detect and gracefully handle a large number of errors that are *beyond the user's control* (as opposed to, say, unexpected results due to sloppy mousing).

The richness of speech is, of course, the result of its necessary role as our primary medium of human communication. It is no coincidence that conversations are ripe with intonational gestures, significant pauses, opportunities for interruption offered and possibly accepted, and introduction of subtopics and parallel conversations. We have developed very robust methods of cueing and resolving poorly comprehended portions of a talker's speech even when talking to a stranger or when visual contact is missing, as over a telephone. We use voice all the time to affect the world, to cause other people to do or stop doing activities, and to attempt to change their views of ourselves and others. And we are very good at this.

The remainder of this chapter will describe three examples of speech interfaces that may be said to present illusory intelligence. All three exploit some insight into ordinary human conversational behavior to "do the right thing at the right time" based on triggering a small set of rules. Although very simple, each of these interfaces is powerful in small ways at implying a richness or appropriateness of human-computer interaction. These techniques may or may not be extensible; no major claims should be made in this matter yet. But under any circumstances, they should offer thoughts as to some exploratory directions in interface design, especially relevant to voice systems.

Conversing without Understanding

The *Phone Slave* is the first example. It was a conversational answering machine that played a series of prompts to callers and recorded their replies.

The basic dialog asked five questions:

- "Hello, Chris's telephone, who's calling, please?"
- "What's this in reference to?"

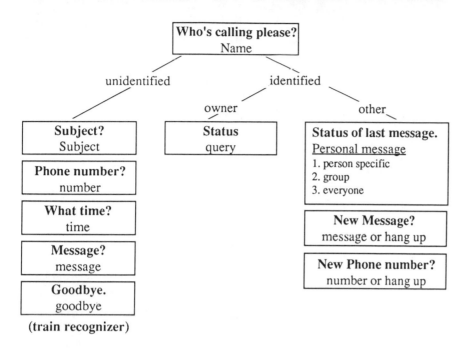

Figure 1: *Phone Slave conversation tree.*

"He's not available at the moment but he left this message . . . .
At what number can he reach you?"
- "When will you be there?"
- "Can I take a longer message for you?"

Between each of these prompts, callers' replies are recorded digitally, each into a separate sound file, for later retrieval by the owner [Schmandt and Arons, 1984, 1985].

Several other features of the system are worth describing for the sake of understanding the intended range of applications of Phone Slave, though none of these are key to the topic of the chapter. Phone Slave tried to go beyond normal answering machines and to act more like a personal voice mail system by identifying known callers using speech recognition (or touch tone sequences), and by playing them specific personal greetings and messages, as well as indicating whether recent messages had been received by the owner yet. It allowed the owner both local access (via a touch screen) and remote telephone access (via speech recognition or touch tone detection) to messages and other system functions. It unified voice and text messages into a single service, using text-to-speech synthesis to recite text messages for remote access. Finally, it provided a graphical user interface to a rolodex-type file with speed dialing, message recording, and selection among a number of prerecorded generic outgoing messages.

The key point for current discussion is the conversational mode of message taking: alternating playback of prompts and recording of responses. There were two motivations for this method. We desired to encourage callers to leave a message, and a complete message as well; this was relatively early in the "answering machine era" and resistance to automatic message-taking was much higher than it is now. Second, by breaking the response into separate components, random access by the owner was facilitated. One of the major problems of voice as data is that it is hard to scan and not yet possible to transcribe to text for keyword searches. Because Phone Slave could not turn speech into text, it couldn't really answer such questions as "Who left messages?", but it could make a very good approximation of an answer by playing back the recordings of each caller (presumably) identifying herself, in response to the "Who's calling, please?" question. The likelihood of this sound being what the owner wanted to hear (in this case, a caller reciting her name) depended on the effectiveness of the conversational model.

This is the place where the illusion needs to be maintained. The problem is, of course, that the computer can't *really* carry on an intelligent conversation, because it can't understand what the caller is saying without better speech recognition than is available. On closer examination, however, we realized that business telephone conversations with a receptionist are very ritualized. A caller is, in general, greeted with the called party's name or organization, asked to identify herself, and often queried as to the nature of the call. These initial exchanges show strong patterns—for example, with regard to their length and order [Kojima, Nishi, and Gomi, 1987].

Parts of this protocol remain well defined for other types of calls as well. Typically, the called party responds with something noncommittal, usually "hello," and the calling party then takes a conversational turn to identify herself. In other words, when the phone is answered and a voice asks who's calling, it is both natural and expected to respond appropriately, and it is this expectation that Phone Slave took advantage of. Having identified herself, the caller now seems much more committed to the interaction; it would be rude, or perhaps reflect poorly on the caller in other ways, to hang up at this point, and the conversation continues.

So far, though, all we've really seen was that Phone Slave made the correct initial conversational move. To carry through this promise, it needed to ask exactly the correct questions, and this required a fair amount of time listening to humans on the phone as well as refining the content of the five recorded outgoing prompts. Of course, there were a number of failure modes that might cause the computer to interrupt or request repetition, such as excessively long responses (the caller saying more than is desired) or the caller saying nothing out of confusion. Although no claim is made that this conversation is foolproof, these details would be a digression.

In the case of successful conversations, the caller may or may not realize she is talking to a computer. Although we were not trying to deliberately mislead the caller, an illusion of intelligence, either the assumption that one is talking to a human or that one is talking to a very clever machine, certainly aids the interaction. Several other factors contribute to Phone Slave's ability to generate this illusion relatively successfully.

The first is use of high-quality digitized speech for output. Although many telephone message systems use various speech compression schemes to save disk space, this degrades the speech and, if pushed, may even interfere with intelligibility. Phone Slave took the attitude that for the limited amount of disk space required for prompts, the extra storage was not significant (it used 64 kilobit/second linear PCM encoding), although compression might be applied to incoming messages, which only the owner would hear.

The second critical step is the pacing of the conversation. When you phone someone and get a machine, it is usually evident it is a machine before it says a single word, just from the timing (if it isn't evident from the initial timing, it quickly becomes so from the recording quality). To maintain the proper rhythm, Phone Slave employed an adaptive pause detection algorithm to determine when the caller was finished speaking and to play the next prompt. Rapid talkers (as measured by the maximum intra-sentence pause length) had short timeouts and faster response. Slower talkers had longer timeouts, to trade off responsiveness for not cutting a talker off in mid-sentence.

Phone Slave employed a number of factors for a smooth conversation: caller expectations, normal telephone protocol, high-quality digitization, and adaptive pause detection. In some of its recorded conversations, the caller did not realize she was interacting with a computer. Even when the illusion was only partial, it still contributed to recording an effective message.

Modeling User Attention

Phone Slave managed to have limited conversations without employing any speech recognition. A later project, the *Conversational Desktop*, [Schmandt, Arons, and Simmons, 1985; Schmandt and Arons, 1986], used recognition extensively in an office communication context. Voice was used to place and receive phone calls, to look up information in external databases such as airline schedules, and to maintain personal organization information such as a schedule and audio reminders. One small detail of the Desktop's implementation is of particular relevance to this discussion.

A problem with speech recognizers, at least in current incarnations, is that they are designed to determine *which* word in their vocabulary was spoken, and very poor at deciding *whether* the word is inside or outside the vocabulary set. This is largely a result of the flexibility allowed to the

Figure 2: System geometry of the conversational desktop.

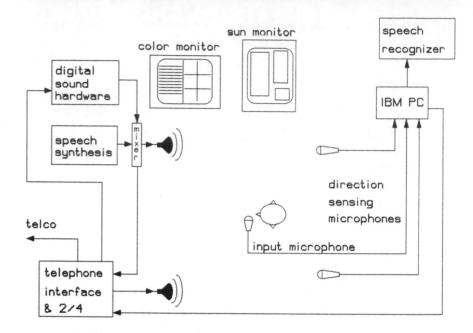

internal pattern-matching algorithm by use of dynamic time warping [Sakoe and Chiba, 1978], which can compensate for variations in speech rate.

As a result, one must be careful to speak to the recognizer only about those topics for which it is trained. This can be difficult, especially in an office environment, where voice is so heavily used and for so many asynchronous events (the phone rings, somebody sticks his head in the door). The obvious solutions are either a hardware switch on the audio line or use of a spoken command to ignore recognition results until some key phrase is heard (the later was done in an earlier project, Put That There, described in the chapter by Kurtenbach and Hulteen). Both of these require conscious activity on the part of the user, however, both on initiation of the "don't listen to me" state and also at its termination.

What is really needed is for the recognizer to know when it is spoken to. General recognition, particularly the ability to discriminate whether a word should be recognized at all, is not reliable enough to determine attentional state from semantics of the speech itself. An alternate method was invented, which gave the *illusion* of listening in waiting for orders. We chose the direction of speech as the trigger.

The idea is simpler than its implementation. When I speak to someone, with relatively few exceptions I look at them. This is often associated with direct eye contact, which is most comfortable face-on. If the office were arranged with the computer display against a wall and away from the door where visitors might appear, the computer could be assigned a unique direction. Users are already accustomed to looking at computer screens to see if anything is happening in response to commands, so it is natural to turn in their direction to talk. This is accentuated with another person in the office; the talker needs to look away from the other as a cue that the current utterance is not meant for him.

This cue can be taken advantage of by looking for changes in amplitude of the voice signal as the talker moves his head to face the screen. The radiational characteristics of the head are such that the directional decrease in amplitude is most easily measured behind the speaker and in a midrange of frequencies [Flanagan, 1960]. Because directionality is greatest behind the head, we placed a pair of microphones there, and, with a little bit of time averaging, compared their outputs to give a single bit of direction information.

Although this interface is somewhat difficult to set up and calibrate acoustically, in terms of the user interaction it is nearly flawless and extremely comfortable to use. The appearance is that the computer understands enough of the conversation to know when it is being spoken to, whereas in reality it is using an almost unconscious cue that humans use for each other's sake when talking in a group.

Speech Understanding without Recognition?

The final example is the most extreme, although it was in many senses a child of some of the techniques of Phone Slave. *Grunt*, aptly named, was an attempt to understand speech, in a very *limited context*, by analyzing the speech signal but employing no word recognition. It is the ultimate in illusion; it maintains a conversation, in many ways entirely rational and effective, yet understands not a single word. It takes advantage of a simple but somewhat robust dialog model to guess what the user may want.

Grunt [Schmandt, 1988] used speech synthesis to recite driving directions. Earlier work had studied the structure of directions and how to talk about them, but simply spewed out the entire route with no interaction or flow control from the user. But people help each other, using what are sometimes called *back channels* [Yngue, 1970; Kraut, Lewis, and Swezey, 1982], giving cues, perhaps visual, perhaps spoken though not necessarily lexical ("uh-huh") that indicate their degree of understanding (as well as interest in the topic and the talker, among others). Grunt listened, and tried to determine when the user understood, was confused, or simply needed more time to write down the directions.

Grunt broke directions into a series of short paragraphs, and paused after speaking each paragraph. It presumed a simplistic dialog structure, in which the human could make one of four types of response:

- *Implicit acknowledgment.* The listener says nothing; after a suitable period the talker assumes understanding and continues.

- *Acknowledgment.* The listener indicates that the conversation can proceed.
- *Failure.* The listener indicates lack of understanding. Confusion may be *local*, such as a misunderstood word, or *global*, as in inability to relate the route to some known landmark or expected intersection.
- *Synchronization.* The listener wishes the talker to slow down, usually because he is writing down the directions. "Hold on a second . . . "

Grunt then attempted to use some very simple but robust acoustical cues to classify the user's response into one of these groups. The primary classifier was utterance *length*. The affirmative responses ("uh-huh", "OK", "all right") are often very short (less than about 800 milliseconds). Clarification and synchronization requests are both longer, and Grunt could not distinguish between them.

Grunt's discourse strategy followed immediately from these response categories. After a relatively long time out, silence allowed Grunt to assume comprehension and continue, although repeated silences would generate some channel checking ("Are you there?") and encouragement ("It makes me nervous that you never say anything."). An affirmation would cut short the silence and allow Grunt to continue. After a longer utterance, Grunt would wait a few seconds; a synchronization request demands the floor, which will then be yielded by an affirmation, which is again usually short ("Just a moment . . . OK."). If this pattern happened, Grunt could continue, otherwise either silence or another longer response (perhaps repeating the original question) would trigger an attempt to explain the last set of directions more clearly.

One obvious flaw with the above is that several short questions (for example, "What?", "Where?", "Left?") are common indicators of confusion in this context, and would be falsely interpreted as acknowledgments. These questions, however, have a very different pitch contour (or intonation), which rises steeply midway through the vowel. Using real-time pitch-tracking hardware, we analyzed the intonation of such monosyllabic questions and obtained reasonably effective discrimination between them and the short affirmations.

How well did all this work? In some cases, it broke down completely, and often comically. In many cases (about 20 percent), however, the interaction was flawless; to the author, this is an amazing result for such a simple acoustic classifier. Most subjects in our experiments rapidly assumed they were talking to a very sophisticated recognizer. The illusion was successful, using acoustical cues that are much more speaker-independent than most recognizers.

Some of the breakdowns share common aspects and identify some classes of problems. Some subjects assumed speech recognition would work best

Discourse Function

Acknowledgement	Implicit Acknowledgement
Request Clarification	Synchronization

Figure 3: Grunt: Classification of user responses by discourse function.

Acoustic Evidence
(simple version)

Short Duration (<800 ms)	Silence
Long Duration (>800 ms)	Can't Distinguish

Figure 4: Grunt: Simple acoustical discriminators.

with discrete speech, and as a result spoke single words ("Repeat!"), which of course were incorrectly interpreted as acknowledgments. Others never gave any response to the system and remained mute through the directions, except when asked *"Are you still there?"* to which they dutifully responded "Yes, I am." Both of these behaviors seem to be artifacts of conversing with a computer, and are unlikely to occur in human-to-human dialog. Of course, this suggests a whole new area of interesting discourse studies.

Conclusions

Three examples of *illusory* interfaces have been described. All take advantage of constraints and expectations to act in a manner that may seem quite intelligent, or at least reasonable, for a particular kind of interaction. The first step toward the design of such systems must be observation of human behavior, in search of patterns and cues. The system will succeed to the extent that it can mimic and do the expected; when communication breaks down, the system may not be able to describe its limitations.

These examples were all motivated by difficulties in speech recognition, so they employed more robust devices, such as conversation protocols, acoustic consequences of body posture, and utterance length and pitch contours. Each had to be developed specific to a particular application, or, more precisely, to a specific conversational situation. All are very powerful when successful, suggesting that some aspects of illusion may be useful in masking artifacts of the user interface and allowing the application to proceed unimpaired.

New Directions
Introduction

THE PREVIOUS SECTION EXPLORED the ever-growing cornucopia of techniques and technologies that are available to interface designers. In this section, we will look at some of the ideas, theories, and paradigms that are on the frontiers of human-computer interface design.

The chapters in this section cluster around four primary themes. The first is the notion of interface agents—computational entities that perform work for users. As Alan Kay points out in his sermon, the notion of agents has been a leading paradigm for the future of the human-computer interface for at least a decade, and its existence as a science-fiction myth has been around for quite a while longer. In this section, Negroponte explores the fundamental idea and compares it to the direct-manipulation metaphor. Laurel delineates a set of functional and aesthetic criteria for interface agents. Oren et al. report work done at Apple on a prototypical agent-style interface to a database application. As a bridge between agents and natural-language issues, Don explores the applicability of narrative form and style as a means of representing point of view.

Natural-language interaction is a theme that is equally strong in terms of both popular futurism and real artificial-intelligence research. What does a computer have to know in order to carry on a "natural" conversation with a human user? What constitutes a "natural language" and how can it be incorporated in an interface? Brennan and Buxton describe two approaches to the natural-language interface paradigm.

Brenda Laurel

345

Most serious computer-game users have at one time or another been convinced that there is really an imaginary world on the other side of the screen—and a really good game lets us dive into it by suspending our disbelief. But all computer users are at one time or another aware of the interface as a barrier beween the user and unencumbered participation in an imaginary world (whether it is a spreadsheet or the land of Oz hardly matters). What would it take to create a computationally represented "reality" that is so persuasive that users can consistently feel themselves to be a part of it? Myron Krueger describes his pioneering work in integrating computers, humans, and video technology to create "alternate realities" for users. Scott Fisher gives us a look at the first full-blown virtual reality project at NASA Ames Research. John Walker, president and founder of Autodesk, explores the "generations" of user interface design and tells us why his company intends to make virtual reality systems a real product. Journalist and author Howard Rheingold offers some insight into the power and uses of the virtual reality paradigm.

The fourth theme is the multimedia paradigm that is currently evolving in a variety of contexts, including interactive videodiscs and CDs, interactive television, and multimedia educational and entertainment installations. Michael Naimark compares movies and computers to reveal core artistic and philosophical issues. Douglas Crockford discusses the limitations and potential of television as part of the multimedia mix. Tim Oren illuminates some of the artistic, political, and methodological issues involved in shaping a new medium.

Most robust paradigms begin with fantasies and grand "what-ifs." H. G. Wells imagines a manned moon mission; Čapek dramatizes the plight of robots; Vinge and Gibson chart the seas of Cyberspace. Real workers in the real world of technology must parse these visions—usually created by nontechnologists—into sets of tractable problems that quickly lose their glamor. Sooner or later, it devolves to us—the people who actually design human-computer interaction—to reconstitute the grand ideas in ways that incorporate notions about technique and technology, purpose and use, and strategies for research and development. These chapters provide focused visions of the future that can motivate and guide innovation.

Hospital Corners

WHEN I LEARNED TO MAKE MY BED, I was artfully taught and dutifully learned to make hospital corners. This simple fold had both functional and esthetic advantages, and with practice, added no time to the tedium of bedmaking. Today, notwithstanding this skill, I cherish the opportunity of delegating the task and have little interest in the *direct manipulation* of my bedsheets.

Likewise, I feel no imperative to manage my computer files, route my telecommunications, or filter the onslaught of mail, messages, news, and the like. I am fully prepared to delegate these tasks to agents I trust as I tend to other matters (which could be as banal as getting dressed) while those other tasks are brought to a satisfactory conclusion. For the most part today, these agents are humans. Tomorrow they will be machines. But what cannot change in the equation, in the transition, is *trust*.

Dynadots

Stalking the future is a curious game. More often than not we project our current images, sometimes unwittingly, with mere technological changes, which, in the case of computers, include speed, memory, and the exotica

Nicholas Negroponte

Professor of Media Technology
Director, Media Laboratory
Massachusetts Institute of Technology

A version of this chapter appears under the title, "An Iconoclastic View Beyond the Desktop Metaphor," in the *International Journal of Human-Computer Interaction,* Vol. 1, no. 1, pp. 109–113 (published by Ablex Publishing Corporation).

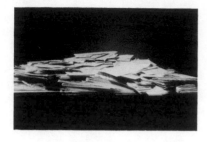

of I/O. In the text that follows, I have a view of the future not generally held, which affects the human interface enormously and is not a mere technological advance, but a fundamental departure from commonly held views.

The common assumption is that computers will move in the direction of paper and/or clipboard-like paraphernalia. Alan Kay's early vision of the *dynabook* is now beginning to find implementations in the back rooms of many corporate laboratories. The general portrait of that future machine is: about the size of *Time* magazine; maybe flexible; radio-transmitting; high resolution, color and bright display; stylus input; massive memory and lightning speed. When not in transport, such a machine might be hung on the wall in front of a keyboard for more traditional use. Anyway, that is the flavor of most people's view of the future personal computers and is clearly embodied in John Sculley's excellent videotape: "The Knowledge Navigator."

My view includes a slightly different mix of form factors and physical embodiments of computers. Many or most will be small objects (hence *dynadots,* to be in keeping with the jargon) that intercommunicate with each other, serving special needs. I expect to carry much more computing power on my wrist tomorrow than is in my office today. Agents, great and small, will be distributed all over the place.

The reason this dynadot view is important is twofold. For one, it leads to a wider computer presence, upon which truly personalized systems will be built. Computers will go underground. My refrigerator will know when it is out of milk, but will take appropriate action only after a conversation with my calendar or travel planning agent.[1] Yes, small, highly interconnected objects that compute form a *society of objects.*

The second consequence of this view of the future is that the form factor of such dynadots suggests that the dominant mode of computer interaction will be speech. We can speak to small things.

Speech Works in the Dark

Speech has other values too often overlooked. For example, it allows us to deal with computers out of arms' reach, it works around corners, it carries the richness and information content of tone and prosody, and it is frequently the free channel (for example, while driving, dressing, or reading).

Our tendency is to couple speech recognition with natural language understanding. Although this is surely a proper long-term view; it misleads

---

1 "Some terminals of the future will be all knowing rooms without walls. Others will be flat, thin, flexible touch-sensitive displays. And others will be wrist watches and cuff links with the right hand talking to the left by satellite." —"The Metaphysics of Television," N. Negroponte, *Methodology of Interaction,* Amsterdam, North-Holland Publishing Company, 1980.

us into believing that it is too far off to consider its current worth and usability.

The "space" of speech recognition is characterized by three axes:

- User-dependent versus user-independent
- Small vocabularies versus large vocabularies
- Discrete versus connected utterances

In this volume, the hardest corner is clearly:

- User-independent, large vocabularies, connected speech

Let's examine these issues one by one.

User-independent speech is a goal driven by two desires: not to require the machine to be trained for each word, and not to be limited to a single user. One desire is obvious and one is suspect. It is not necessarily true that user-dependent speech systems need to be trained word-for-word, rather than evolving over time. And, it certainly is not necessarily true that a system that can recognize anybody's speech is an asset. Sure, it should be able to cope with family, friends, and our dog's bark. But there is no real value in the ability to have such systems cope with random accents or strangers.[2]

Large vocabularies are also a myth. The secret is not size, but rapid downloading of speech subsets from a very large word space—call these *word windows*. At any one moment, the total number of utterances required in a machine at any single moment might be as small as 500. Context is the trigger of what needs to be folded into the system from instant to instant. And remember, we are not talking about discussing Thomas Mann, but delegating, which more or less means: issuing commands, asking questions, and passing judgments; more like drill sergeant talk.

To complete the "problem space" of speech recognition, consider the matter of *connected* speech. Surely we have little interest in talking to a machine in broken language. Much of this, in fact, can be achieved with multiword utterance recognition. This is not the right way to do connected speech, but it addresses the issue by widening the acoustic duration. And, alas, sometimes we just might have to use more discrete talk.[3]

The real problem in speech recognition is spatial independence, so that

---

[2] The telephone company might argue that such systems would allow for *anybody* to call American Airlines from *any* telephone and hold a discussion about flight plans. But I can call my personal computer or talk to my wrist watch, instead, and have either of them deal with the airline in ASCII. No. Speaker-independence has only niche applications, such as in vending machines and security systems.

[3] This is the weakest argument I have. It is a near-term solution. Added with the rest, I suggest that user-dependent, small vocabulary, discrete speech systems could be used today, if people really were interested in a plural human interface.

one can speak to computers from a distance, in the presence of noise and the like. Many people think that speech is primarily to liberate you from the keyboard in the sense of not having to type (which some people can't do or feel is beneath their station). I think it is indeed to liberate us from the keyboard, but in the different sense of not having to be near it or not having to try to use it while our hands are tending to something else. Also, right now for personal computers there is a real **captive audience** of people. One cannot deal with them *en passant*.

"About So Big"

Speech does not stand alone. "So big" might be the small distance between two of your fingers, the space between your cupped hands, the volume embraced by your arms, or the size of some huge mountain or building to which you are pointing in the distance. In short, the utterance is meaningless without the parallel channel of communication (in this case) of gesture.

Such plurality has another, and in my mind, greater significance: concurrence and redundancy. My classic (read: often used) story is that of dinner talk in a foreign country. If your hosts ask you, say in French, "Do you want some more wine?" or "Please pass the bread," you will understand them with and even without your high school French. Whereas, if they talk among themselves about politics, you will be totally at a loss unless your command of French is almost fluent.

Most people conclude that this is obvious because the first example is "baby talk," whereas a discussion about political matters engages all kinds of sophisticated metaphors, complex terms, grandiose concepts, and oblique referents. These differences are true, but they are not the important ones by far. The important difference is that in the baby talk, table talk scenario all the objects and subjects of discourse are in the same **space and time** as you (and your hosts). This suggests that when somebody says, "Please pass the water," his or her arm can be stretched out in the direction of the water pitcher, and his or her eyes can gaze upon the empty glass. What this means is that the message is enormously **redundant,** and you can pull the signal out of any of many **concurrent** channels. That's the real difference.

For this same reason, when you know a foreign language to a limited degree, a most painful task is to use that language over the telephone. In such situations you are at the mercy of a single channel. But that is the way we use computers today, with signal channels.[4]

---

[4] Note that when you talk on the telephone your face and body still emit expression, even though you know full well that the person at the other end can see none of it. This suggests that our human system of expression is quite tightly wired with the very same (somewhat uncontrollable) parallelism discussed above.

Why Winking Works

At a recent dinner party I winked at my wife,[5] and she knew all the *paragraphs* of information it would have taken me (otherwise) to explain the same to some stranger. The reason is quite obvious. A vast amount of shared experiences and robust models of each other make the epitome of communication **be the lack of it.**

In an agent model of computers, similar familiarity is required in order to preclude relentless explicitness that would destroy the value of agencies. In daily life it can often be the case that it is easier to do something oneself than to explain it to somebody "new." No, the computer must be an old friend with as many shared experiences (facts, at least) as the future *computer presence* will allow. This is absolutely critical to a new metaphor, beyond the desktop.

The Theatrical Metaphor

If you are prepared to accept the promise of **delegation** and the viability of speech, the desktop metaphor is subject to serious change, soon.[6]

---

[5] In some perverted measure of information theory, this could be construed as one bit.

[6] I have not addressed animation because I think it goes without saying that there will be a dramatic change in three-dimensional engines and low-cost, real-time, high-resolution animation will be as commonplace as *pull-down* menus.

My view of the future of desktop computing (versus dynadots in this case) is one where the bezel becomes a proscenium and agents are embodied to any degree of literalness you may desire. In the longer term, as holography prevails, little people will walk across your desk (if you have one) dispatched to do what they know how.

The picture is simple. The stage is set with characters of your own choice or creation whose scripts are drawn from the play of your life. Their expressiveness, character, and propensity to speak out are driven by an event (external) and a style (yours). If you want your agents to wear bow ties, they will. If you prefer talking to parallelpipeds, fine.

This highly literal model of agents can be dismissed as a foolish scheme to replace serious **icons** with *Snow White and the Seven Dwarfs*.[7] But this begs the question about delegation and speech. In some form we can expect surrogates who can execute complex functions, filter information, and intercommunicate in our interest(s).

Direct manipulation has its place, and in many regards is part of the joys of life: sports, food, sex, and for some, driving. But wouldn't you really prefer to run your home and office life with a gaggle of well-trained butlers (to answer the telephone), maids (to make the hospital corners), secretaries (to filter the world), accountants or brokers (to manage your money)[8], and on some occasions, cooks, gardeners, and chauffeurs when there were too many guests, weeds, or cars on the road?

---

[7] In 1977, I recall almost being laughed out of an auditorium when I suggested that a calculator icon would invoke that object on the screen and ease of use would naturally stem from familiarity.

[8] This one might make you nervous.

Interface Agents:
Metaphors with Character

The Case for Agents

ON THE BRIDGE OF THE USS ENTERPRISE, a decidedly clipped female voice announces that the computer is "working." On board the Nostromo, Ripley hunches over her console seeking advice from "Mother." On the moon, Adam Selene foments a revolution. HAL refuses to open the pod bay doors, and his sibling SAL wonders whether she'll dream when her creator powers her down.

Since the beginning of this century, people have dreamed about the new companions they might create with high technology. Some of those dreams are nightmares about malevolent computers enslaving mankind as techno-evolution catapults them far beyond our puny carbon-based brains. Most are wistful longings for new helpers, advisors, teachers, playmates, pets, or friends. But all of the computer-based personae that weave through popular culture have one thing in common: they mediate a relationship between the labyrinthine precision of computers and the fuzzy complexity of man.

Why is this tendency to personify interfaces so natural as to be virtually universal in our collective vision of the future?

Computers behave. Computational tools and applications can be said to have *predispositions* to behave in certain ways on both functional and stylistic levels. Interfaces are designed to communicate those predispositions to users, thereby enabling them to understand, predict the results of, and successfully deploy the associated behaviors.

When we think and communicate about behavioral predispositions, we

Brenda Laurel
Interactivist

naturally use metaphors based on living organisms. Even the most technologically savvy user will feel quite comfortable comparing the Macintosh and the IBM PC in terms of their "personalities" and may characterize software with adjectives based on a living-organism metaphor: WORD is fussy, my spelling checker is illiterate, EMACS is obtuse. Where agent-like activities already exist, they are often perceived as having character—one interface designer has described error messages as "wrist-slapping grannies."

An interface agent can be defined as a character, enacted by the computer, who acts on behalf of the user in a virtual (computer-based) environment. Interface agents draw their strength from the naturalness of the living-organism metaphor in terms of both cognitive accessibility and communication style. Their usefulness can range from managing mundane tasks like scheduling, to handling customized information searches that combine both filtering and the production (or retrieval) of alternative representations, to providing companionship, advice, and help throughout the spectrum of known and yet-to-be-invented interactive contexts.

Objections to Agents

Although the notion of interface agents seems natural and desirable to many, considerable resistance exists. One negative view can be described as the "agent as virus" problem. One of this book's authors characterized agents as "whining, chatting little irritants." She dreaded waking up one day to find "a whining little secretary stuck in my machine." Here the problem is not agents *per se*, but rather the traits that they are assumed to possess. One solution is to offer the user a number of agents from which to choose (rather like a job interview or theatrical audition); another is to provide an "identa-kit" whereby agents could be configured by their users.

Closely related to "agent as virus" is the notion that agents are just plain silly. "I would feel incredibly stupid pretending that there was a person in my computer," one programmer told me (however, this same person has often been observed shouting obscenities at his screen). In a lively conversation on the subject on the WELL (Whole Earth 'Lectronic Link), one user confided that he had been saving digitized images of his dog to immortalize him as an agent after his death. This idea was greeted with a mixture of derision and horror. Yet the idea of a canine agent (perhaps not one's own departed pet) readily suggests a class of activities (fetching the morning paper and announcing intruders, for instance), a level of competence (the agent will deliver the paper but will not provide commentary), and a kind of communication (a small repertoire of simple commands and an equally small repertoire of behavioral responses) that may be entirely appropriate.

For some users, the idea of agents smacks of indirection. "Why should

I have to negotiate with some little dip in a bow tie when I know exactly what I want to do?" The answer, of course, is equivocal. Few of us would hire an agent to push the buttons on our calculator; most of us would hire an agent to scan 5,000 pieces of junk mail. If I were looking for a specific book for a research project, I'd probably use a reference librarian; if I were browsing with an opportunistic eye, I'd want to go into the stacks. When I have to negotiate with UNIX, I call my husband. It doesn't feel like indirection when an agent does something for me that I can't or don't want to do myself. I have often railed against interfaces that force me to plead with a system (in exotic language) to do a very simple thing [Laurel, 1986a]. But that is quite different than having a competent agent at my beck and call. Agents, like anything else, can be well or poorly designed. A good one will do what I want, tell me all I want to know about what it's doing, and give me back the reins when I desire. Good interfaces usually allow for more than one way of doing things, too. Only users who want to use agents should have them; others should have other choices.

Perhaps a more thought-provoking objection to agents rests on an ethical argument that goes something like this: if an agent looks and acts a lot like a real person, and if I can get away with treating it badly and bossing it around without paying a price for my bad behavior, then I will be ecouraged to treat other, "real" agents (like secretaries and realtors, for instance) just as badly. This argument seems to hinge on the fear that humans will mistake a representation for the real thing, possibly first expressed by Plato when he banned the dramatic arts from his Republic on the same grounds. Yet few would trade the plays of Shakespeare and Molière for the apparent unambiguity of Plato's world. Today, many parents are concerned that their children will confuse the violence in the news with that in the latest commando movie (or video game). These are real issues that must be addressed by artists and citizens. The solution lies, I believe, not in repression of the form (which is a strategy that is bound to fail, if history is any indicator), but rather in the ethics of the artist, the entrepreneur, the parent, and the culture at large.

Another objection is that implementing agents would necessarily involve artificial intelligence, a discipline whose star is currently in eclipse. "AI doesn't work," the litany goes, "and even if it did, an agent would gobble up more cycles than it's worth." Two responses apply. First, although the grand platform of AI may not have been satisfactorily realized, there are numerous examples of the successful use of AI techniques. For example, Object Lens, an "intelligent groupware" system under development at the Sloane School of Management at MIT, enables users to create agents that can sort mail, issue reminders, and find things in object-oriented databases [Crowston and Malone, 1988]. Second, there are already examples of agents that employ no AI at all (see the chapter by Oren et al.). The problem here may be that an anthropomorphic agent is being confused with a full-blown "artificial personality," the implementation of which is, of course, a daunting prospect. But an agent can—indeed, must—be much simpler than that, as we shall see.

In Defense of Anthropomorphism

Anthropomorphizing interface agents is appropriate for both psychological and functional reasons. Psychologically, we are quite adept at relating to and communicating with other people. We utilize this ability in dealing with nonsentient beings and inanimate objects through the process of anthropomorphism. This mode of operating in the world is so natural that we often engage in anthropomorphizing objects in our daily lives—ships, countries, cars, and vacuum cleaners. Where an anthropomorphic persona is not readily apparent, one is often created for us by advertisers: Reddy Kilowatt, the Pillsbury Doughboy, and the California Raisins come to mind (indeed, the anthropomorphic Raisins are so attractive that they have generated more revenue than their fruity friends).

Anthropomorphism is not the same thing as relating to other people, but is rather the application of a metaphor with all its concomitant selectivity. Metaphors draw incomplete parallels between unlike things, emphasizing some qualities and suppressing others [Lakoff and Johnson, 1980]. When we anthropomorphize a machine or an animal, we do not impute human personality in all its subtle complexity; we paint with bold strokes, thinking only of those traits that are useful to us in the particular context.

The kinds of tasks that computers perform for (and with) us require that they express two distinctly anthropomorphic qualities: *responsiveness* and the *capacity to perform actions*. These qualities alone comprise the metaphor of agency. To flesh out a particular agent, the computer can be made to represent its unique skills, expertise, and predispositions in terms of character traits. As in drama, traits can be represented directly through appearance, sound, communication style (external traits), which in turn cause us to infer traits on the level of knowledge and thought (internal traits). Evaluating action taken by an agent provides a feedback loop through which we refine and embellish our understanding of the agent's character. The point here is that, as the ultimate device for making dynamic, mimetic representations, the computer is ideally suited to the task of manifesting agents as dramatic characters [Laurel, 1986b].

By capturing and representing the capabilities of agents in the form of character, we realize several benefits. First, this form of representation makes optimal use of our ability to make accurate inferences about how a character is likely to think, decide, and act on the basis of its external traits. This marvelous cognitive shorthand is what makes plays and movies work; its universality is what makes the same play or story work for a variety of cultures and individuals. With interface agents, users can employ the same shorthand—with the same likelihood of success—to predict, and therefore control, the actions of their agents. Second, the agent as character (whether humanoid, canine, cartoonish, or cybernetic) invites conversational interaction. This invokes another kind of shorthand—the ability to infer, co-create, and employ simple communication conventions. As Susan Brennan and Bill Buxton illustrate in their chapters, the essence of conversationality can be captured without elaborate natural language processing. Third, the metaphor of *character* successfully draws our attention to just those qualities that form the essential nature of an agent: responsiveness, competence, accessibility, and the capacity to perform actions on our behalf.

Key Characteristics of Interface Agents

AGENCY

In a purely Aristotelian sense, an agent is one who takes action. In social and legal terms, an agent is one who is empowered to act on behalf of another. Researcher Susan Brennan observes that most people whom we refer to as "our agents"—real estate agents, insurance agents, and the like—are not working for us at all, but rather for the companies who pay their salaries [Brennan, 1984]. An interface agent would exercise its agency entirely on behalf of the user. Alan Kay traces the development of the concept:

> The idea of an agent originated with John McCarthy in the mid-1950's, and the term was coined by Oliver G. Selfridge a few years later, when they were both at the Massachusetts Institute of Technology. They had in view a system that, when given a goal, could carry out the details of the appropriate computer operations and could ask for and receive advice, offered in human terms, when it was stuck. An agent would be a "soft robot" living and doing its business within the computer's world. [Kay, 1984]

Agents provide expertise, skill, and labor. They must of necessity be capable of understanding our needs and goals in relation to them (either explicitly or implicitly), translating those goals into an appropriate set of actions, performing those actions, and delivering the results in a form that we can use. They must also know when further information is needed from us and how to get it. In life, any person or institution who is empowered by us to take action on our behalf is an agent. Examples include secretaries, gardeners, craftspeople and laborers, teachers, librarians, and accountants.

What kinds of tasks do we perform with computers for which agents are appropriate? They are tasks with the same requirements as those for which we employ agents in real life: tasks that require expertise, skill, resources, or labor that we need to accomplish some goal and that we are

Figure 1: Kinds of tasks an agent might perform

Information
Navigation and Browsing
Information Retrieval
Sorting and Organizing
Filtering

Work
Reminding
Programming
Scheduling
Advising

Learning
Coaching
Tutoring
Providing Help

Entertainment
Playing against
Playing with
Performing

unwilling or unable to perform ourselves. Figure 1 provides examples of computer-related tasks where agents would be appropriate.

Some of these tasks are appropriate for an agent because they are too complex for either straightforward algorithmic solutions or for complete parametric specification by the human user. An obvious example is a search for information in a large database, which may involve linguistic, numeric, formal, and a variety of heuristic and stylistic concerns. The nature of the complexity of such problems makes them excellent candidates for an expert-systems approach [Hayes-Roth et al., 1983]. Like the human experts who give expert systems their not-so-metaphorical name, agents based on such systems probably require considerable detailing and subtlety in their character traits. Other kinds of tasks (such as sorting mail or preparing monthly invoices) require much less "intelligence"; the associated agents are valuable because they are diligent, quick, accurate, and impervious to boredom. Representing such agents would require relatively fewer, more simplistic traits. Both functional implementation and external representation (that is, character) will vary widely according to the nature of the agent's tasks.

RESPONSIVENESS

Because of its social contract with the user, an interface agent is a prime example of user-centered interface design. An agent succeeds or fails on the basis of its ability to be responsive to the user. What are the dimensions of responsiveness?

Most other forms of human-computer interface exhibit *explicit responsiveness*; that is, user and system communicate through a series of highly constrained, explicit transactions. Typically, a system accommodates users' expressions of goals and intentions only in ways that are formally compatible with its operating requirements. Even when commands are camouflaged in comfortable metaphors like "cut," "paste," or "paint," users must parse their actions and intentions in terms dictated by the system (and therefore the interface) and must express them explicitly.

Because it is the function of an agent to take action on behalf of a user, it follows that the value of the agent derives, at least in part, from its ability to formulate and execute a set of actions solely on the basis of a user's goals. Whether those goals are explicitly stated by the user or inferred by the system, the way an agent interprets and attempts to meet them constitutes *implicit responsiveness*. This is the principal means whereby an agent amplifies the user's personal power.

One aspect of implicit responsiveness is the ability of an agent to tune its actions to the user's traits and preferences. If my French tutor notices that I'm a theatre buff, she'll enhance my learning process by assigning readings in Molière. Noting my intransigence regarding the three-comma rule, my writing coach should probably beat on me mercilessly until I either succumb to the new grammar or exchange him for Edgar Allan Poe. Knowledge about the user can be both obtained explicitly (by questioning) and inferred (by noticing).

Users also change over time. Even when the user's goals are explicitly the same from day to day, the way they should be interpreted changes. If I ask my news agent to tell me what's going on in the Middle East, for instance, he should not present me with the same article I read yesterday. And if he's smart, he'll notice that I seem to have become especially interested in the Persian Gulf and will gather materials accordingly. Responsiveness therefore requires that the agent have access to a dynamic model of the user, or at the very least, a log of his experience in a particular application or environment with rules for interpreting that experience when formulating actions.

Depending upon how it is implemented, an interface agent may be associated primarily with a single user or with an application or environment that has multiple users. In the latter case, the agent must be able to distinguish among users, at least on the basis of experience and preferences, in order to be genuinely responsive.

Interface designers often have a strong aversion to implicit responsiveness because it requires inference, and inference is fuzzy. The belief is that an incorrect inference is more disturbing to the user than no inference at all (that is, insistence on explicit transactions). But a failed inference need not be painful if it results only in a request for more information. If a system knows enough to generate an error message, it also knows enough to ask a question. The risk of incorrect inference can be mitigated by a variety of strategies for disambiguation, including dialogue, user modeling, and the creation of redundancy through the use of multiple input channels (see the chapter by Chen and Leahy and that by Mountford and Gaver).

COMPETENCE

Suggestions about building and employing the first area of competence, knowledge about the user, are included in the discussion of responsiveness above. Clearly, an interface agent must also be competent in the domain of the application or environment in which it operates. An agent can be said to have access to all of the information and possible operations in its domain by virtue of its being part of the same system. But in order to serve the user well, an agent must possess (or be able to generate) both meta-knowledge and multiple representations.

By *metaknowledge* we mean knowledge about problem-solving in a domain. If the domain is a database, knowledge is required about both the information content and the process of retrieving and representing that information to the user. If the domain is a table of airline schedules and fares, the metaknowledge consists in knowing how to formulate a travel plan based on both domain information and the preferences of the traveler, and then knowing how to present it in a clear and actionable way.

The ability to provide multiple representations of information is a key aspect of responsiveness. Brennan observes:

> Multiple representations increase the odds that the user and the system will be able to communicate effectively and that ambiguities in one representation will be disambiguated by another; multiple representations also provide a basis for a learning environment. Good teachers and good students are skilled at providing feedback by trading multiple representations back and forth. . . . [Brennan, 1984]

At the very least, competence consists of knowing how to select from among multiple representations already extant in a single database. Ultimately, however, such limited competence will prove to be inadequate. Users will eventually want agents to assemble information from multiple sources containing huge volumes of information in a wide variety of forms. It seems impractical to create a new information-linking industry where humans attempt to stitch all the information in the world together so that we can build interfaces that simply follow the threads. It also seems impractical to include multiple representations for every item in even a small database. Competence ultimately will include the ability to both retrieve and generate alternate representations of information according to the needs and personal styles of users. Agents will be selected or configured by users partially on the basis of their distinctive searching heuristics and representation-making abilities.

ACCESSIBILITY

An agent's traits and predispositions must be made accessible to the user. Perceptually, users must be given cues by the external representation of an agent that allow them to infer its internal traits. Selection of the modes of representation (for example, visual, verbal, auditory, etc.) should be driven by a consideration of the whole character, the environment, and the traits in question. For some agents and environments, text is just enough (ELIZA's disembodied phrases may be its greatest strength), whereas for others completely different modalities are required (imagine capturing Marilyn Monroe without a picture or Donald Duck without a voice). For example, in the Guides project (see the chapter by Oren et al. in this volume), graphical icons that minimize facial detail and emphasize emblematic props are adequate for distinguishing among points of view in the task of navigating through the textual database, but for providing alternate representations of information in storytelling style, motion video and character voice are required.

On the conceptual level, an agent is accessible if a user can predict what it is likely to do in a given situation on the basis of its character. Equally important is the criterion that an agent must be conceived by users as a coherent entity. It is in the area of accessibility that the idea of structuring agents as dramatic characters has the greatest value.

Design and Dramatic Character

The case for modeling interface agents after dramatic characters is based on both the familiarity of dramatic characters as a way of structuring thought and behavior and the body of theory and methodology already in place for creating them. Most cultures have a notion of dramatic form, and people are quite familiar with both the differences and the similarities between characters and real people. Character traits function as stereotypic "shorthand" for understanding and predicting character behavior [Schank and Lebowitz, 1979].

Somewhat ironically, dramatic characters are better suited to the roles of agents than full-blown simulated personalities. The art of creating dramatic characters is the art of selecting and representing only those traits which are appropriate to a particular set of actions and situations [Schwamberger, 1980]. For most uses, an interface agent, like a dramatic character, must pass a kind of anti-Turing test in order to be effectively understood and employed by the user. We want to know that the choices and actions of our agents, whether computational or human, will not be clouded by complex and contradictory psychological variables. In most cases, we want to be able to predict their actions with greater certainty than those of "real" people.

Although designers and scholars like Alan Kay worry that oversimplification of character will destroy the illusion of lifelikeness [Kay, 1984], the fact is that, thanks to well-internalized dramatic convention, we can enjoy (and believe in) even one-dimensional dramatic characters. In fact, when a minor dramatic character possesses only one or two functional traits, audience members will impute elaborate histories and motivations as needed to make it believable [Schwamberger, 1980]. Whether the character is as simple as Wiley Coyote or as complex as Hamlet, we take pleasure when—and *only* when—even the surprises in a character's behavior are causally related to its traits.

Happily, the selectivity and causality inherent in the structure of dramatic characters simplifies the task of representing them computationally [Laurel, 1986b]. In the area of story generation, James Meehan, Michael Lebowitz, and others have created functional and entertaining characters from a small cluster of well-conceived traits that are realized as goal-formulating and problem-solving styles [Meehan, 1976; Lebowitz, 1984]. Increasingly in the world of adventure and role-playing computer games, designers are implementing characters with traits that are *dynamic* (modified by learning and experience) and *relational* (modified in relation to objects and situations).

The artistic side of the design problem is to represent the character (in this case, an interface agent) to the user in such a way that the appropriate traits are apparent and the associated styles and behaviors can be successfully predicted. External traits like diction and appearance must be shaped to suggest those internal traits (values, heuristics, etc.) which determine how a character will make choices and perform actions. A character is coherent—whole—when its traits are well-integrated through careful selection and planned interaction. The designer can look to the considerable body of work on playwriting, as well as to the area of modeling and representing character traits computationally for guidance [see, for instance, Carbonell, 1980].

An R & D Agenda

As we are discovering with all types of interfaces, good design is no longer the exclusive province of the applications programmer, the graphic designer, the AI researcher, or even the multimedia hacker. In the effort to make interface agents a reality, several areas of technology and design must be explored simultaneously.

In the theoretical arena, work must proceed on the analysis of user needs and preferences vis-à-vis applications and environments. What are the qualities of a task that make it a good candidate for an agent-like interface? What kinds of users will want them, and what are the differences among potential user populations? How might interface agents affect the working styles, expectations, productivity, knowledge, and personal power of those who use them?

In terms of design, the meatiest problem is developing criteria that will allow us to select the appropriate set of traits for a given agent—traits that

Figure 2: Two versions of "Phil," a semi-intelligent agent who appeared in various Apple promotional videotapes. Different representations of an agent character may set up different user expectations. The bow tie becomes an iconic costume element, making the character recognizable in both representations. Although "Phil" is not a working program, similar agents have been implemented in the "Guides" project (see the chapter by Oren, et al.). "Phil" was created by Doris Mitsch of Apple Creative Services. The video "Phil" was enacted by Scott Freeman of the American Conservatory Theater.

can form coherent characters, provide useful cues to users, and give rise to all of the necessary and appropriate actions in a given context. Contributions will be needed from the disciplines of dramatic theory and practice, literary criticism and storytelling, and aspects of psychology and communication arts and sciences.

In the area of implementation, much ongoing work can be appropriated. We must explore and refine existing AI techniques for understanding, inference, and computational representation of character. Techniques for constructing and enacting characters can also be imported from the field of computer game design. Expert-systems techniques can be applied to such "soft" problems as learning and assimilating the user's style and preferences, developing navigational strategies, and creating alternate representations. Work on such technologies as language and speech processing, paralinguistics, story generation, image recognition, and intelligent animation can be refocused and revitalized by the agents' platform.

Finally, rapid prototyping techniques must be developed to facilitate user testing and evaluation. If we can continue to gather feedback from individual users and inspiration from popular culture as a whole, the notion of agents will evolve—as it should—in collaboration with the people from whose fantasies it arose.

Guides:
Characterizing the Interface

The Design Problem

THE GUIDES METAPHOR EMERGED in the process of designing an interface for an educational hypermedia database. The content, acquired from a number of sources, was American history from 1800 to 1850. Grolier Electronic Publishing was the primary content provider and contributed the text and related indexes. This material, based on the Americana series of encyclopedias, influenced the selection of images, maps, and sound. Bettmann Archive provided the images, which were digitized and retouched at Apple. R.R. Donnelley Cartographic created several series of animated maps. Folkways Records supplied the music. Apple's HyperCard software served as the delivery medium. [Technical details of the project are further described in Salomon, 1989.]

The author of a hypertext that is to be used in an educational setting is faced with severe challenges. It has been widely noted that hypertext systems are characterized by user disorientation, or "getting lost" while attempting to find a way among the myriad connected documents and links [Conklin, 1987; Halasz, 1988]. The hypertext author's purpose may be to provide an educational experience, but the cognitive load posed by navigating among the various items may be so great that the user has little energy left for absorbing the content.

Therefore, one of our design goals was to reduce the cognitive load on users that is created by "navigating" while trying to learn. For this reason, we wanted to provide a way of structuring and presenting the content that

Tim Oren
Gitta Salomon
Kristee Kreitman
Advanced Technology Group
Apple Computer, Inc.

and

Abbe Don
New York University
Summer Intern, Apple Computer, Inc.

avoided the navigation metaphor. The essential question for the interface to answer is "What should I read next, what's my best choice?" rather than requiring the user to work through a large list of alternatives.

We discussed providing a reasonable "next choice" as an alternative to free browsing, which would form paths through the database. By simply following them, the user could examine the full content in large topical chunks. These paths would be fixed by the database creator, not created in response to a user's actions. However, if the paths were strictly specified, would we be making good use of the dynamics of the new medium? In order to avoid this rigidity, we started looking for ways to make the paths adapt to the user's needs and actions.

In pursuing a linear, experiential user metaphor in preference to a formal database taxonomy, we were venturing close to narrative [Oren, 1987]. The database content, history, also suggested that a storylike approach would be appropriate. Because of this, we began looking at the use of characters and the human figure to suggest a storylike structure and get the user involved in a search for relationships among the various pieces of information.

The Guides Metaphor

Guides first appeared in the form of travel agents. We considered centralizing the interface around one agent, a survey-type expert with an intriguing personality, perhaps like Alistair Cooke in "Masterpiece Theater" or Vincent Price in "Mystery." We thought of the character of Rudyard Kipling in the film "The Man Who Would Be King," and his richly textured surroundings, full of skulls, beads, and maps. The user would "enter" a sitting room and get a feel for the period through the objects in the environment. The central figure would introduce users to interesting stories and to other people—guides—who would accompany the user on his "travels" in the database.

The travel guides were to be of the modern period, each biased towards a particular type of information. A user could select a historian and get his point of view through his selection of documents, and then choose the geographer and be shown maps. The artist would bring out the paintings; the musician would select pieces of music. A user could consult multiple agents who would always be available to help users generate the next move or to help them find relevant materials.

This design raised several questions: Was it important for the interface, in this case the travel agents, to be clearly represented as separate from the database, existing in a distinct context, or should they share the same context—in this case, a historical one? The fact that the database and interface were both created and represented using the same tool (Hyper-Card) makes such a choice possible and necessary.

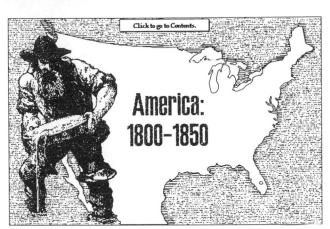

Figure 1: A title card followed by a picture sequence introduces the database.

Figure 2: The Contents Card appears at the end of the sequence and provides several entry points into the database.

Figure 3: Tours composed of images, music, and narration introduce new users to prominent themes. Users can branch from a tour into an article in the database by clicking on the "related article" icon.

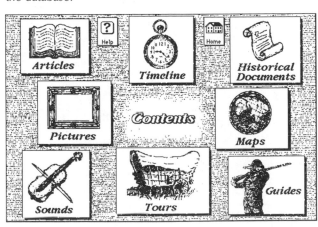

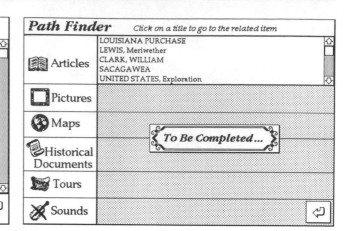

LEWIS AND CLARK EXPEDITION

LEWIS AND CLARK EXPEDITION, the widely celebrated geographical and scientific exploration in 1804-1806 of a vast, uncharted territory of the United States, much of it newly acquired by the Louisiana Purchase. Commissioned by the U.S. government, Meriwether Lewis and William Clark led a band of some 40 soldiers and civilians up the Missouri River, across the Rocky Mountains, and down the Columbia River to the Pacific Ocean, returning by a similar route.

President Thomas Jefferson had long planned such an expedition, even when the entire region to be crossed belonged to European powers, and Congress had authorized the venture before France sold the Louisiana Territory to the United States in 1803. Jefferson had made Meriwether Lewis his private secretary, or aide, in 1801, perhaps for the express purpose of training him to lead the expedition.

Figure 4: The article card presents several options to users along the bottom of the screen.

Figure 5: By clicking on the "Pathfinder" icon, users are shown a list of links from the current location.

Figure 6: Clicking on the "Guides" icon presents users with the available guides. Once a guide is selected, the guide's "first choice" article is displayed and a user can choose to go to it.

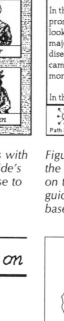

PROSPECTING

PROSPECTING is the search for deposits of valuable minerals. The term is usually associated with the great gold and silver rushes of the early American West, but it also includes the search for copper, lead, uranium, and other metals as well as for coal and petroleum.

In the decades following the discovery of gold in California in 1848, droves of prospectors combed the mountains, canyons, and rivers of the Western states looking for the bonanza that might bring them fabulous riches. The great majority of them were disappointed in their quest, and thousands died of disease or from the violence that filled the lawless frontier towns and mining camps. A few did make fortunes, and the stories of their success attracted still more thousands to each new gold or silver strike.

In the years that followed, major finds of gold, silver, or copper were made in

Figure 7: Alternatively, the user can go to any article and the chosen guide will suggest a "next choice" article based on the current location. The user can change to a different guide at any time and receive a different set of suggestions, based on the particular guide's interests.

Figure 8: When a guide is active, its name is shown in the Pathfinder screen.

Figure 9 (right): Map card as shown on screen.

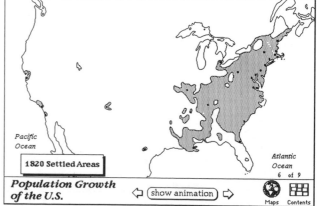

We decided to change the interface so that it, including the travel agents, all looked like part of the historical period. We wanted to add visual richness, provide a context, and seduce users into the mood of the database from the start. Also, we had in mind that if we later designed a database for a different period, we could change the look in order to distinguish visually between time periods. In the finished design (see figure 2), the interface carries many graphic elements that refer to the period.

After deciding that the interface should have a historical look and feel, we moved towards embedding the "travel guides" in the database. Each guide would be a stock character of the period itself. They would have a set of specific interests in the historical period and could suggest different things for the user to view.

We wanted the resulting database to have a narrative feel, to be like a story told to the user, unfolding one move at a time. The database could be relinearized by combining a guide's point of view with the user's current position. We decided guides should try to use or hint at narrative, avoiding a third-person presentation. When people perceive even the simplest relatedness among items, they will often assume—or unconsciously superimpose—narrative structure on the materials. We wanted to encourage people to work out how the articles interrelate and to figure out connections, which is often a part of the learning process.

Implementing Guides

Grolier had supplied a hierarchical topical index of over 200 items. It contained major topic such as "Transportation," with more specific terms such as "Ships and Shipping" underneath it, and even more specific terms such as "Clipper Ships" underneath that. Every article was classified by one or more terms from this index.

The guide's point of view was created by assembling collections of these topics. A list of "interests" for each guide was built using the master topic list. A program then compared each guide's interest list with the specific index terms for each article. The more terms that appeared in both, the more interest the guide would have in a particular article. Ranked interest lists of articles were created for each guide.

These lists allowed the current guide to dynamically offer a "next choice" or favorite article (figure 7). If the user was not interested in the "next choice," other choices could be reached by clicking on the guide's icon. A modified link display showing all connected articles of interest to the guide, in order of relevance, would appear (figure 8). The user could obtain a different set of suggestions for the next move by changing guides. Guides were successful in hiding a complicated algorithm behind an interface that simply stated, "Here's the next move." In comparison to the complex interfaces of earlier electronic encyclopedias intended for educational use [Marchionini, 1987, 1988], we felt this was a breakthrough.

The first guides, such as the slave, were nothing more than a collection of the topics nested under slavery in the index. For later guides, we made up "life stories" to help choose topics. For instance, the preacher was supposed to have been born in upstate New York during the Reformist Period, was a left-winger for his time, was active in the Abolition movement, and later became a missionary to the Oklahoma Indian territory. It was easier to pick topics based on this description of the preacher's life and times, and the resulting guide seemed more interesting, because it would lead to connections that were real but not obvious. However, once a guide had been created, there was no way for a user to find out the guide's "story."

User Reactions

The database was first shown at an Apple Multimedia Open House. People seemed intrigued, and they found guides engaging. Because much of our design had been based on intuition about how to draw people in, this provided the first evidence of validity. However, we still needed to find out if guides worked for the reasons we thought they should, and why and where they did not work. Abbe joined the team around this time and informally observed educators at an Apple University Consortium meeting and students at Palo Alto High School.

CHARACTERIZING THE INTERFACE

One question commonly asked was, "Why did the guide bring me to this article?" Users wanted to know each guide's "life story" and how it related to the choices that were being made. Often, they also tried to identify the guide with a particular character. For instance, because many articles are biographies, the first item a guide selects is often about a real person. The scout guide chooses the James Bridger article first and the inventor's "first choice" is the article on Samuel Morse. In these situations, users often assumed Bridger or Morse was now their guide.

Users also anticipated that each guide's point of view would be embodied in the content. They expected the guide to do more than just point out interesting items. For instance, the slave guide brought a user to the Andrew Jackson article, and he specifically wanted to know: "Am I now seeing this from the slave's point of view, and would I, in fact, see a different part of the article if the Indian had brought me here?" Though the role we had assigned the guides was navigation only, users wanted them to deliver content as well.

Users appeared to be ascribing emotions to the guide and their relationships to the guide. For example, the preacher guide brought one student to the Illinois history article, and she could not figure out why. The student actually got angry and did not want to continue with the guide. She felt the guide had betrayed her. In another example, a software bug caused the guide to disappear when there was no link from an article. One student interpreted this as " . . . the guide got mad, he disappeared." He wanted to know " . . . if I go back and take his next choice, will he come back and stay with me?"

Users assumed or wanted characterization behind the iconic guide figures, although we never explicitly tried to develop them as characters. This reflects the power of the human figure to suggest personality. The guides could have been represented by object icons. If we had used a gold pan and a nugget to represent a miner or a covered wagon to represent a settler, it's doubtful that users would express the same desire for characterization.

Computer scientists have tended to shy away from personifying machines, but we felt we were seeing a call for it from users. We were reminded of the reactions to Weizenbaum's psychologist program ELIZA in the 1960s. Some users actually sent observers out of the room because they were having a private conversation, though they knew their partner was a computer [Weizenbaum, 1976]. Also, we believe there is difference between portraying characters within the database versus anthropomorphizing the machine itself. The projection that occurred with ELIZA was not "a computer is a person," but rather "there is a doctor in the machine." Similarly, none of our users said *the computer* is betraying me or *the computer* is mad at me. Rather, the relationship occurred between the user and the image of the guide.

APPROPRIATENESS OF MEDIA

We had assumed that users would find the tours (figure 3) the most attractive way to get into the database for the first time. They provide a dramatic introduction by depicting a "slice of life" theme expressed in pictures, music, and narration while allowing users to exert some control over the presentation. For instance, a user could stop a tour, rewind it, or jump into a related part of the database.

Creating the tours was labor-intensive and similar to filmmaking in that it required storyboarding, choosing and editing pictures, creating a layered soundtrack, and working out timing. To our dismay, users indicated that tours were of little interest. The visuals and third-person narration reminded them of filmstrips or slide shows. They seemed to interact with the tours in the same way they interact with these conventional media—that is, not at all. Few seemed to notice the ability to branch into the database.

In retrospect, tours were a technical success but an interface and media failure. We attempted to draw people into the database using the capabilities of a new technology, but we found ourselves imitating a familiar presentation medium. Ironically, the more we succeeded in that imitation, the more we failed to get users to see the new possibilities.

In contrast, the maps in the database also used simple animation, to give the illusion of change over time, but they were surprisingly well received (figure 9). The maps allowed users to see time "collapsed" and moving fast—something they cannot see in the real world with a traditional static map. By using the computer to move beyond the limits of normal cartography and to depict dynamic processes, the maps broke new ground in media use.

Video Guides

DESIGNING THE VIDEO VERSION

In the video version, we explored the storytelling role of guides by expanding the settler guide into a character. Abbe wrote first-person scripts based on women's journals on the Overland Trail [Schlissel, 1982; Ross, 1985]. We wanted to confront the two main questions users had: "Why did the guide bring me here?" and "Am I seeing this article from the guide's point of view?"

To answer the first question, "navigation tip" stories were created to provide sneak previews and offer reasons why the guide would take the user to a particular article. These stories were built around the topics in both the guide's interest list and the article's index term list. These were the same lists used in the first version.

To answer the "point of view" question, content stories were written that supplied the settler woman's view on a specific article. For example, the Forty-Niners article is about men in the mining towns. In order to provide an alternative point of view, the settler guide narrated a "content story" that was drawn from first-person accounts of women who also settled there and became self-sufficient.

Video guides as we constructed them differed from the earlier guides in their form, content, and function:

	Original Guides	Video Guides
Form	generic historical characters	specific character on video
Content	where should I go next	first-person stories
Function	next-move generator	next-move generator and content-provider

Conclusions and Issues

At this writing, the video version of guides has not been widely tested with users. Our conclusions are based on user reactions to the first version of the project, our own and colleagues' perceptions of the video guides, and the experiences of designing and building both versions. Many of the issues that emerged during the project remain unresolved and thus provide grounds for further exploration. They are discussed below.

Figure 10 (right): The Settler Guide card is reached from the main Guide card via a new button called "Meet the Guide." Where the previous Guide page allowed the user to choose a guide and go to just the "first choice article," the Settler Guide card offers the user multiple starting points.

Based on my experiences as a settler, I recommend the list of articles below.

Click on a ▶ to see a navigation tip.
Click on an article title to go to that article.

Settler Introduction

▶ PRAIRIE SCHOONER
▶ FORTY-NINERS
▶ PUBLIC LAND
  SOD HOUSE
▶ FOLK ART, American
▶ THE COURSE OF WESTWARD SETTLEMENT
▶ FRONTIER LIFE
▶ WAGON TRAINS

Guides   Contents

Figure 11 (below): Clicking on the "Settler Introduction" activates an animated transition between the Mac screen and the video monitor. The animation is followed by a video introduction in which the actress, out of costume, explains how a guide works and what her interests are.

Figure 12: By clicking on the triangle associated with the Forty-Niners article, for example, the user activates a video "navigation tip" that suggests why the Settler would go to the Forty-Niners article. A user can view several previews and then choose an article, or move ahead immediately by clicking on an article title, in this case by clicking on the Forty-Niners article title.

Figure 13: A video icon has been added to the original article screen design. Clicking on the video icon activates the settler guide's "content story" which in this example is her first person perspective on Forty-Niners. The guide's list of next moves is displayed in a new "pop-up" pathfinder. Some are marked to indicate that a navigation story may be accessed.

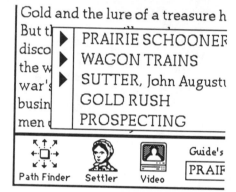

THE VALUE OF GUIDES

Our design was driven by the need to construct a simple interface that did not confront a user in a learning situation with the cognitive load of a complex hypertext map, or the arcane structure of a traditional query interface. We believe that guides have succeeded in this respect. They point the way to a merger of browsing and search in a single metaphor. Also, because the guide metaphor does not expose the underlying algorithms, these methods can be modified and improved without the need for the user to relearn the interface.

We have also found value in the deliberate personification of the interface, in introducing the conventions of storytelling, point of view, and character into the computing milieu. This seems to result in engagement, projection, and suspension of disbelief on the part of users. We find that users desire to carry this process further, to see point of view expressed in content, perhaps in the form of explicit storytelling by the guides. Teachers have suggested that the dramatic video character could provide a new learning model. Kids could create their own stories, too—get dressed in costumes or use storytelling as a new way of doing a classroom report.

Guides also indicate the degree to which simple implementations of interface ideas may succeed if they engage the expectations and desires of users. Like Schmandt's "Grunt" interface (see Schmandt's chapter in this volume), guides create a successful illusion within a limited domain, in this case exploiting the natural fit between the information at hand and a narrative, characterized presentation.

MULTIPLE POINTS OF VIEW

Initially, we wanted to encourage users to make connections between articles in their heads. Now, based on their desire for point of view, we might reorganize each article into a central factual nugget of names, dates, places, with a constellation of points of view around it (see Don's chapter in this volume). The choice of facts would represent the encyclopedia's point of view and the various guides would offer different interpretations of the subject addressed in the encyclopedia article. For example, the "fact nugget" for The Age of Jackson article might include the years Jackson was in office, the name of his vice-president, major wars and skirmishes that occurred, significant acts or laws passed during his term, etc. Then the settler guide could provide point-of-view material on land claim issues, the Indian guide could provide material on Indian affairs, and so on for each guide that had relevant information for that article.

Children often assume educational material is objective and comprehensive, but in fact any encyclopedia has a particular perspective. For instance, the articles chosen for inclusion in this database and the way they are presented reflect Grolier's editorial bias on American history. Guides suggest a natural way to present multiple voices and points of view. Rather than a singular, omniscient voice, users would be presented with multiple voices and would be placed in a position to draw their own conclusions. Closure resides with the users as they interact with the database.

The video version was also designed under the assumption that we would eventually provide multiple video guides. Their different perspectives would be expressed through different navigation and content stories. When multiple guides are implemented, we will need to experiment with interface designs that show the user that other points of view are available. Several techniques have already been suggested.

We could use a "Hollywood Squares" metaphor in which several guides are always sitting on the periphery of the screen. Some yawn because they have nothing to do with the current article, while others try to get the user's attention. Or perhaps the guides could grab the user's attention in an animated Monty Python-like way, for example, by sticking their heads in from the side of the screen. Or maybe a user could peel away the text and see various characters running around underneath. They would be carrying information, carting it to different places, and some would be trying to garner attention as if they knew more than the others.

Another approach might be the dramatic recreation of historical figures in both "historical" and "comparative" scenarios. A historical scenario might include Harriet Tubman taking the user along the underground railroad. A "comparative" scenario would allow the user to suggest ways characters might interact. For example, suppose there were eight characters and a user could request "I'd like to see what these two would say to each other about this topic"—like Karl Marx speaking with Queen Victoria about class politics.

RELATION OF GUIDES AND THE DATABASE

The database is primarily text taken from an encyclopedia and is written in an omniscient, third-person voice. The content is frozen, so the first guides were able only to change the user's path. However, users desired to see point of view within the text, which would require a rewrite of the content. The addition of other first-person sources such as memoirs would also help. The interesting point is that in designing an interface to a textual database, we have found that the writing style adapted to the print medium is not optimal for the computing medium. This is a warning that there may be sharp limits to the notion of "repurposing"; that is, moving existing content to a new medium by simple format conversion.

Because the text base was fixed, expanding the guide's role in the video version required adding content in the video sequences. The result is that the richness of the video image currently dominates the user's experience. The text appears flat and boring in comparison. This may indicate that the mode of presentation of a guide needs to match the modes of the underlying data. In a purely textual database, a static graphic image such as the first version of guides is appropriate. If the underlying database is multimodal, containing sound and video, then a video representation of the guide should not be as jarring.

APPROPRIATENESS OF VIDEO FOR GUIDES

The impact of video has raised a number of issues. With video, what you see is what you get, and that's it. It's the nature of the medium. The original notion behind guides—to evoke people's interest in figuring out the connections by themselves—might be lost because of the enforced literality of the video navigation stories.

There is a risk in trying to make a film out of a fantasy. Tolkien wrote, "Drama is naturally hostile to Fantasy" [Tolkien, 1966]. There was an urge to fantasize and project onto the iconic guides. Does that urge still exist in the video version? Consider voice-only story telling situations, such as Garrison Keillor in *A Prairie Home Companion*. The images and associations in the listener's head can be even richer and more powerful than those explicitly offered by video. We also need to avoid the trap we fell into with tours. If it looks like television, people may react as if it *is* television.

What is important and necessary when representing the character of the guide? The original guides, presented in 32-by-32-pixel icons, required the use of a user's imagination. In the video version the user watches a "talking head," the image of the actress portraying the guide. Is it necessary to be so literal with character? Would it be better to use a voice-over and a sequence of relevant images?

FRAMING

The actress portraying the settler guide appears out of costume during the video segment that explains her role to the user. This introduction was built on a Brechtian model from theatre and explicitly acknowledges the computer system as a representational medium. This was done for two reasons: 1) to address the issue of provenance and bias of information and 2) as a frame around the user interaction with the database.

The content of the database is past history, but the user is in the 20th century operating a computer. The introduction was intended as a vehicle through which both the user and the system designers agree to play "make-believe," while acknowledging the user's ability to move freely between the present and the past. The present contains the computer, the research or learning experience that the user has undertaken, and the actress out of costume. The past contains the events represented by the database, and the actress in costume enters this world as a guide.

Does the implementation accomplish its goals? We're uncertain for several reasons. Audiences have learned the representational conventions that enable them to suspend their disbelief when reading a piece of fiction or viewing a movie. Standard theatrical conventions do not prepare an audience to be suddenly confronted with actors out of costume. Thus, the use of explicit framing could introduce nuances that are lost on the average user and that could create confusion.

Although accuracy and consistency in representation are important, they should not be taken to the point that they sabotage engagement. In this medium, frames may want to collapse in, to dissolve into the content. For example, the first interface worked better when we broke down the distinction between the modernistic controls and the historic content. The same thing may occur with video guides.

Our guides are now generic characters with historical interests, and none of them is expert on the whole database or system functions. Hence the only way to give information about the operation of the computer system itself is to put the words into the mouth of a "historical" character. Perhaps framing should occur at a higher level, using a guide with an omniscient view who "understands" the themes and structure of the database and how the system works. This omniscient-view guide is analagous to a T.V. anchorperson who has an overview of the nightly broadcast and who introduces reporters who have more in-depth knowledge on a particular topic. A generalist guide could embody metalevel expertise and point of view. James Burke of the television series *Connections*, for instance, could be a good model for such a guide if his unique way of examining relations [Burke, 1978] could be simulated.

NAVIGATION VERSUS CONTENT

In the first version, users did not understand that guides were only providing navigation as a "next move" generator. The video version offers both navigation and content in the form of stories, but now it appears that people have trouble recognizing the difference between the two. The settler video guide is perceived as an additional content provider, regardless of whether she is providing a navigation tip or content story.

The intent was to script the video in two distinct storytelling modes. The user accesses navigation tip stories *between* articles, "on the links." They offer information about why the guide is bringing the user to an article. The second type of story, which occurs *at* the article, provides first-person points of view with an anecdotal flavor. The navigation stories can be viewed as a commentary on the primary content and therefore as another layer. Because there are additional facts and content in both types of stories, we have a figure and ground problem. What is a link, what is an article? When you put stories on the links, they may become articles themselves from the user's viewpoint, however implemented.

Users might find it confusing because both types of stories are written in the first person. We may need to emphasize the distinction by explicitly indicating when the guide is navigating in the text and speech. We might only need to have the guide say, "You know, you might try to go look at pioneers or wagon trains right now."

Alternatively, for the navigation tips, we could provide an environment full of props in which the guide is sitting out of costume talking about her interests or experiences. The user would get a sense of what constitutes form and what constitutes content, where the guide is navigating, where she is telling about something she knows "in character." We might use the out-of-costume framing notion as an interface device, but we need to first find how users react to this device.

We are finding out as much about the way people want to receive content as we are about navigation. We have uncovered a lot about what engages in the interface, but we have also discovered that the interface is deeply intermeshed with the content.

GUIDES AND AGENTS

The relation between guides and agents should be noted. Agents are, or should appear to be, autonomous software entities that make choices and execute actions on behalf of the user. They embody the expertise to find and present information to the user, responding dynamically to the user's changing goals, preferences, learning style, and knowledge. In many contexts, this implies the ability to find or create alternate representations of information (see Laurel's chapter in this volume). The aspect of autonomy requires some degree of intelligence in the agent, and, given the current state of artificial intelligence, of preexisting structure in the underlying information.

Guides are related to agents in that they can alter the user's course through the data, and, in the video version, offer alternate views of the content through the stories they tell. It should be noted that these alternate views are "canned" additions to the database, rather than intelligent reformulations of the content. Guides are a simple form of agents who assume the roles of storytellers, and their success is to be measured not by the stringent requirements of full-blown intelligent agents, but against the softer criteria of plausibility and suspension of disbelief.

We have been asked by teachers whether they might add their own guides to the system, or have a personal guide to represent them, pointing out things emphasized in a class and drawing in data from other sources. Giving teachers the means to create such guides would necessitate developing capabilities that would bring the guides concept closer to the stature of agents.

This project is a demonstration of the concept of agents rather than a true implementation. The interesting result here is that guides were readily accepted in an educational setting. This is heartening in that it confirms that users react positively to agentlike interfaces, and that education may be an appropriate setting for both interface agents and narrative-style presentations of information.

Narrative and the Interface

Anecdote

Abbe Don

Interactive Telecommunications Program
New York University
Summer Intern, Apple Computer, Inc.

Abbe: Why did you have cows in the city?

Annie: My mother didn't like to ask my father for all the money that she wanted to send to Europe for the families. Everybody was poor. There were no rich people. So a friend of hers had cows. So she says to my father, we have a stall and you are renting it out to six horses. So why don't we get some cows there? So, they got the cows. They used to milk at six o'clock in the morning. Then my brothers, your great-great-uncles, Julius and Wolf, and my sister, Aunt Fannie, and I, we had to deliver the milk in the morning, during the winter and summer. I must have been about eight years old so it was, let me see, I was born in 1891, so it was before the turn of the century. They used to put a pail here, a pail there, a pail here, and a pail there, on a pole, across my shoulders, like you see in the movies, and we had to go from house to house to house to deliver the milk. Toward evening, they milked the cows again, and we had to do the same thing all over. And once it was so slippery, and so cold, I fell and I spilled the milk. I was afraid to go home, I'd get killed for spilling the milk, I remember I was going by Tantela Rosie, in the backyard. Oh, did I hate those cows . . . . And we had cows wherever we moved, the cows used to come with us—every year or so they went to the stockyards to get new cows. I hated it like hell. And the neighbors used to complain. My father used to pay off the alderman.

And my mother used to make her own cheese, her own butter, her own sour cream. And she had them 'til she died—she was 76 years old. My children remember those cows.

Learning from Personal Experience

As my great-grandmother told stories, she weaved in and out of the past and present, the old country and America, English and Yiddish, business and family, changing voice from first person to direct address to third person. As I design interactive, multimedia knowledgebases, I am reminded of how she structured and conveyed information, each detail part of the narrative continuum and potentially linked to several other stories or digressions, some of them new, some of which I had heard before. However, both content and meaning were affected by the context: the presence of other visitors, whether we were baking together, looking at photos in her scrapbook, or if I interrupted the flow of the story to ask for more details. It was as if she had a chronological, topical, and associative matrix that enabled her to generate stories in which structure, content, and context were interdependent. Using my great-grandmother as a model, I began to investigate the characteristics of oral storytelling and multimedia interface design.

Narrative includes both the story being told (content) and the conditions of its telling (structure and context). Similarly, creating a multimedia knowledgebase involves selecting or generating information as well as representing the structure and the content to the user through the interface. All too often, these activities occur separately. A narrative approach to multimedia interface design provides a framework that allows the structure and content of the knowledgebase to evolve together while accommodating a variety of contexts defined by the user's needs and interests. Within that framework, interface designers can adopt strategies from narrative theory, such as including multiple representations of events and information, or using characters as a means of representing material with an explicitly acknowledged point of view. New tools need to be developed in order to implement these strategies in a computer environment. Such tools would enable both designers and users to take advantage of the power of the computer by dynamically generating material as well as reconfiguring it based on a multitude of cross-references.

Speaking of Media

Electronic media, and especially computers, are used as both a thought-generating tool and a thought-storing medium. But this relationship between creating and storing new human experiences has engendered a new task: the need to organize and access the knowledge that we have generated and stored. Currently, researchers, consumers, or travelers learn a different set of interface conventions in order to find information whether they are in a library, at a record store, or pressing buttons on their touchtone phone to make plane reservations. In most systems, there is little continuity between the structure and the content, let alone the context of the experience.

However, the activities involved in generating, storing, manipulating, and distributing multimedia knowledgebases, which may include text, graphics, still photographs, animation, full-motion video, dialogue, music, and sound effects, are beginning to converge (see Oren's chapter). But, because contemporary cultural codes perpetuate the myth that information represented by or generated by computers is true, objective, and comprehensive, we tend to forget that computer hardware and software are mediated and constructed, produced and consumed, within a particular culture at a particular point in history. Instead, various media come across our computer or television screens (and increasingly they will become one screen) as "neutral" information. In order to address the consequences of this convergence, interface designers need to consider 1) the relationship between content, structure, and context, 2) the multiple representations of knowledge outlined above, and 3) the politics of information.

Narrative, and in particular oral storytelling, can provide both system designers and users with idiosyncratic, personal tools for performing the range of activities involved in producing and using multimedia knowledgebases. Storytelling is a cross-cultural activity that most individuals are exposed to or engaged in from childhood through adulthood. Some stories are experienced in a social or ritualistic context, often as a means of cultural reproduction [Masayevsa, 1984; Turner, 1987], and others are told in the privacy of one's bedroom. In either case, most people have learned something about the conventions of storytelling simply by exposure to them.

As individuals, we represent ourselves to ourselves and others by constructing a sense of self through a variety of media such as diaries, photo albums, phone conversations, and home movies. Even corporate annual reports can be thought of as the "story of what a company did this year." Although bar charts and graphs may be the best way to represent financial data, the interpretations of the data can be presented in narrative form. Did the fourth quarter sales drop as a result of unsustainably high sales in the third quarter, bad weather, a nationwide economic slump, or because the Redskins did not make it to the playoffs? In a narrative, the reader assumes that everything "noted is notable" [Barthes, 1977]. And notable elements, whether they are part of the character's traits, the setting, the action, or the cultural codes of production, can serve as an associative index that points to other levels of meaning. Unlike random browsing, a digression occurs within the context of the story.

The Limits of the Alphabetic Index

The alphabetic index developed as "a crossroads between auditory and visualist cultures." Because traditional oral storytelling is represented exclusively in a temporal mode, once it is spoken, there is no way to "point" back to it. Writing, on the other hand, enables a spatial representation on the page. With the development of a tangible page, information could be physically "located" in space. The index was transformed from an oral storytelling convention in which it "had originally been thought of as vaguely, 'places' in the mind where ideas were stored" to a written list in which "these vague psychic 'places' became quite physically and visibly localized" [Ong, 1982].

Ironically, in the computer environment, we continue to represent items in an index in order to locate them alphabetically or topically, but we have lost the physical, concrete entity of the page and re-replaced it with a vague "virtual" space. A "false" spatial representation is then created in order to orient the viewer. In a database with limited records that is organized strictly by topic or that can be accessed meaningfully by keywords, such as an address file, this false spatial representation is not a major drawback. But in multimedia knowledgebases, one of the goals is to take advantage of the fact that items are not fixed in space so that they can be dynamically organized by a multitude of cross references or searched for by associations. A narrative approach can enable designers to consider the components of multimedia knowledgebases as "events" experienced in a dynamic, temporal sequence rather than as objects in space.

In addition to the more abstract concerns already described, a narrative approach to interface design may also facilitate answering some recurring design questions (see the chapter by Oren et al.):

- What is the relationship between navigation and content? How should the screens and the transitions between them look and feel? Scientific? Lyrical? Comicbook-like?

- What conventions, if any, exist for moving between data represented as text, still pictures, video, and sound? Can these different media be integrated so that the user is not thrust abruptly from one medium to another?

- What are the tasks and goals of users in this particular context? How can the information be structured so that users can find what they are looking for based on what they already know or are familiar with rather than a positivist approach that requires them to know how the system is organized in order to use it?

Characteristics of Oral Narrative

The most obvious distinction of an oral narrative is that it requires the presence of a storyteller addressing an audience. A traditional oral storyteller used a pattern of recurring themes and formulas as mnemonic devices to create an episodic structure. However, the telling of each story changed with each performance, because for the storyteller "narrative originality lodges not in making up new stories but in managing a particular interaction with this audience at this time—at every telling the story has to be introduced uniquely into a unique situation, for in oral cultures an audience must be brought to respond, often vigorously" [Ong, 1982]. A storyteller relied on feedback from the audience, who responded not only to the spoken words but also to "gestures, vocal inflections, facial expression, and the entire human, existential setting which the real, spoken word always occurs" [Ong, 1982].

Similarly, a system designer manages the interaction with the user. Where the storyteller has direct interaction with the audience, the system designer and user must interact via a "representation" [Laurel, 1986] in order to generate and manipulate information as well as to provide feedback. In multimedia databases, the storyteller can take the form of different characters who either store the information or assemble it from existing source material in the knowledgebase. In a more sophisticated (future) system, the character would generate the information. In addition, both the user and the characters represented by future systems should be able to speak, as well as to convey emotion through voice inflection, facial expression, and other gestures.

For example, in the anecdote that begins this chapter, selected from "We Make Memories" [Don, 1989] an interactive multimedia project about family history, Annie is the character of my great-grandmother, whose "knowledge" is stored as audio segments on a videodisc. Considered in isolation, her story is an amusing, personal anecdote about a child's dislike for performing chores. Considered as part of an urban history database, or in conjunction with an alderman character, the story serves as an entry point to a discussion of Chicago politics, in particular the relationship between Jewish immigrants and the Democratic machine. When considered in the context of my grandmother's and my mother's stories, it becomes more about dietary laws and the role of women in Jewish family life. Although the content of the story stays the same, the meaning of the story shifts depending on the structure and context of the user's interaction with the system.

A further distinction of oral storytelling is the way in which oral narrators traditionally embedded names, lists, how-to instructions, or other "facts" in the context of a storyline so that knowledge was experienced as events unfolding in time, rather than as objects outside of the audience's experience. By embedding the information in action, they were able to represent different types of information within the storytelling framework.

Multiple representations of knowledge inevitably require addressing the politics of information by explicitly acknowledging where information originates. Who is telling the story, to whom are they telling it, and why?

In "We Make Memories," the "knowledge" is stored as family photo-

Figure 1: *Screen from "We Make Memories." Clicking on the faces in the corners activates video segments in which each character provides her point of view on the current topic, defined by the center picture on the screen. Clicking on the center picture activates a sequence of images on the Macintosh screen.*

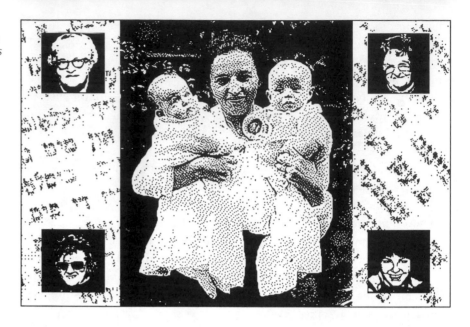

graphs and home movies, point-of-view video segments, and my first-person "written text" that describes the events that took place after my great-grandmother's death. However, common themes occur throughout the various media, so by presenting the viewer with more than one form, a richer experience ensues. In addition, the viewer can choose which elements to view. For example, some users find the family photographs digitized on the Macintosh screen to be the most interesting element, though most express a preference for the oral storytelling segments. Many of the photos also appear in conjunction with the video so that they have a multiplicity of meaning depending on the context in which the user encounters them. For example, the image of my great-grandmother holding her twins (figure 1) is part of a sequence of mother and child images when viewed "sequentially" on the Mac. However, the image recurs during a story about childbirth in which my great-grandmother, my grandmother, and my mother discuss bearing children. Within the context of the discussion, controversial topics arise, such as attitudes about birth control and abortion. My great-grandmother describes going to a doctor in 1915 to have an abortion and then deciding not to do it. Rather than being a moralistic tale that supports the "right to life" or a pro-choice position that supports a woman's right to control her own body, in the context of the other stories, this tale evokes multiple readings so that the user must draw her own conclusions.

In oral narrative, heroes with predictable character traits "served a specific function in organizing knowledge" in story form [Ong, 1982]. As a consequence, audiences learned conventions about what to expect from certain characters, such as clever Odysseus or furious Achilles. Similarly,

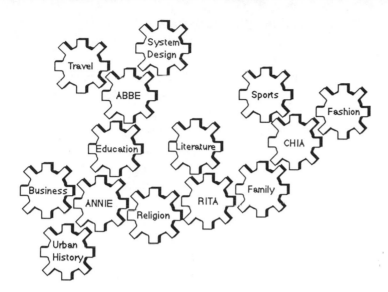

Figure 2: The context gears.

characters can serve the purpose of representing different points of view in the interface (see Laurel's chapter in this volume). An ideal representation is through first-person storytelling in which the character informs the user about the source of the information: was this tale experienced directly, passed down in narrative form from some other source, or sought out based on a request from the user that intersected with the character's "knowledge"? And, within the computer context, users should have the ability to define the type of characters they prefer. For example, when visiting an art museum, I would much rather hear about the paintings from a passionate curator than from a whiney docent.

The Context Gears

While working on the video version of the Grolier's Guides, Tim Oren and I had several "what if?" conversations in which we tried to develop a model for designers to represent multiple points of view in a database (see the chapter by Oren et al.). Based on those conversations, I developed the context gear model (figure 2), which organizes information around clusters of characters whose different interests or knowledge are represented by the cogs emanating from their individual gears. Each character gear intersects with a subject gear, whose cogs represent subtopics. The gears are interlocked but shifting as the user's interests shift, enabling the dynamic assembly of the information in the knowledgebase. Users can specify which topics they are interested in, intersecting with the context gears, as the characters provide content through their point of view.

The movement of the gears provides a way of representing a change over time as the material is dynamically assembled based on the context of the user's experience, the form of the information presented, and the point of view of the character presenting the information.

The context gears also provide designers with a model for developing gateways to additional multimedia databases. For example, "We Make Memories" is a fairly small, personal knowledgebase. However, both its content and formal representational strategies could segue with the YIVO Institute for Jewish Research videodisc project, "People of 1000 Towns, A Photographic Encyclopedia of Jewish Life in Eastern Europe, 1880–1940." The YIVO videodisc contains 17,000 still photographs from their pre-World War II photo collection. The current incarnation was built with dBASE III (a questionable interface for general public use) but the images have been indexed by photographer, place, date, people in the photograph, as well as a description of the image. While the images are being indexed, researchers have been conducting "The Talking Pictures" project, which interviews "informants" who grew up in the towns depicted on the video-disc. As they look at photographs on the disc, the "informants" are video-taped while they provide additional historical or anecdotal information about daily life in the towns or while they identify specific people in the photographs. Currently, these videotapes exist as auxiliaries to the database and are viewed separately from the videodisc. Although there are some technical limitations to seamlessly hooking up multiple videodisc players or videotape machines, a narrative interface could be developed using the context gears to connect the "encyclopedia" of still images with the "Talking Pictures" videotapes, which in turn would provide a series of attachable gears to the model used to structure "We Make Memories."

Tales for the Future

As the ranks of anonymous "information providers" grow, it is increasingly important for both system designers and users to be conscious of the politics of information. Who is providing the information, to whom are they providing it (or not providing it as the case may be), and why?

Storytelling is not only an effective and familiar means of communication, but it also enables multimedia interface designers to use characters to convey information from an explicitly acknowledged point of view. However, using characters to represent multiple points of view collapses the distinctions between what we usually think of as "the interface" and what we usually consider to be "the content" of a multimedia knowledgebase. Instead, characters play the dual role of navigation aids and content sources. The result is a heuristic interface that emerges out of the material represented in the knowledgebase, rather than a control-structure interface that is slapped onto the content after it is assembled.

In the short term, this may require each new multimedia knowledgebase to have its own specialized interface. Further research, however, should investigate which characteristics of narrative can be applied as an interface to a variety of multimedia knowledgebases. This research can lead to the development of a narrative *genre* of multimedia interfaces (see Oren's chapter).

Meanwhile, the context gears model does suggest a first step toward integrating knowledgebases generated from different sources or by different institutions. Theoretically, one series of gears (such as those in figure 2) can be attached to another series from a different multimedia knowledgebase as a way of enlarging the domain of each. This task will initially be easier to accomplish with knowledgebases that overlap in content or that share similar representational strategies.

The power of the context gears model rests in its ability to account for changes over time as material is dynamically assembled from the multimedia elements in the knowledgebase. The character gears, the topic gears, and the user's interests interact to retrieve information already represented. Eventually, information could be generated based on these intersecting criteria, or new "gear" characteristics might be added, such as a chronology gear in order to generate stories from a chronological, topical, and associative matrix.

Although my great-grandmother never attended high school, she left behind a deftly constructed sense of herself in the form of her scrapbooks, complete with her eighth-grade graduation certificate, numerous family photographs, and an extensive collection of homemade greeting cards created by her great-grandchildren. She also left us all the stories she told as she prepared for the holidays or visited with family and friends, who in turn told them to one another. Her most moving stories were personal tales that were neither didactic nor overbearing but that taught us about going out into the world with confidence in ourselves and concern for others. I hope that my tales for the future will be as powerful and long-lasting as hers.

Acknowledgments

I would like to thank Andres Edwards, Brenda Laurel, Pat Quarles, and the Asilomar Group for their feedback on earlier versions of this essay.

Conversation as Direct Manipulation:

An Iconoclastic View

SOME PEOPLE INSIST that *direct manipulation* interfaces are superior to *conversational* interfaces. In direct manipulation, the elements on the screen behave as if they *are* the objects that they represent. The distinguishing features of direct manipulation are claimed to be 1) continuous representation of the objects of interest, 2) physical actions instead of complicated syntax, and 3) rapid, incremental, reversible operations with immediate visual feedback [Shneiderman, 1982; Hutchins, Hollan, and Norman, 1985]. Direct manipulation is also easy for new users to learn, easy for intermittent users to use, and easy for experts to extend. Another of its virtues is that users can operate upon the output representations and use them as input back to the system [Draper, 1986].

But the dichotomy between direct manipulation and conversation is a false one, as I'll argue here. First, direct manipulation interfaces succeed *because* they share important features with real conversations. Second, when so-called "conversational" interfaces fail, it is because they lack these pragmatic features—that is, words alone do not a conversation make. Third, real conversations actually fulfill many of the criteria for direct manipulation. For example, two people talking to each other continuously represent the things of mutual interest within their separate mental models. They can refer to anything that's within their common ground, and they can do this with less effort than it takes to point to a screen with a mouse. As they talk, they introduce new material to each other, relate it to old,

Susan E. Brennan

Department of Psychology, Stanford University
and
The Natural Language Project, Hewlett-Packard Labs

coordinate their attention, and negotiate their understanding, step by step. When they understand each other, they end up behaving as if they shared a single mental model—a virtual workspace containing entities available for inspection and manipulation by both.

My second claim is that people's expectations about human/computer interaction are often inherited from what they expect from human/*human* interaction. Thus, psychological models of human communication are good sources of principles for designing and evaluating interfaces that take account of a user's perspective. If we take the liberty of thinking of the user's input as *utterances within a conversation*, we can explain why some characteristics of an interface work and others do not.

The View from the Tower of Babel

There is some confusion about what conversational interfaces are. It seems that any interface involving primarily textual input and enforcing alternating turns between the user and the system is fair game. Sometimes formal query languages and natural language interfaces are grouped together under "high-level languages," which, along with command languages, get categorized as "conversational." So we see comparisons of the Macintosh desktop to UNIX, which conclude, not surprisingly, that direct manipulation interfaces are better than conversational ones, at least for the average person.

However, few would argue that using UNIX is much like having a conversation (those who would, probably have different kinds of conversations than the rest of us). One of UNIX's major failings as conversation is its lack of informative feedback after a user takes a turn. Imagine trying to talk with someone who, half the time, stared unblinkingly at you in silence after you said something, and the rest of the time, responded with a lengthy monologue. UNIX is powerful and flexible, but it is counterintuitive, inconsistent, and notoriously difficult for people to learn [Norman, 1981]. In fact, it was never meant to be a human/computer interface. Thus, it's no surprise that the average person should prefer shuffling icons around on a Mac desktop—that is, talking to the furniture—to "conversing" with an autistic UNIX system.

Direct Manipulation as Conversation

Appropriately enough, the first great conversational human/computer interface was also the first great direct manipulation one. Ivan Sutherland's *Sketchpad* enabled a user and a computer "to converse rapidly through the medium of line drawings" [Sutherland, 1963]. This style of interaction was primarily graphical, yet it exhibited some of the important features of human conversation. A user conversed with Sketchpad by pointing. The system responded by updating the drawing immediately, so that the relationship between the user's action and the graphical display was clear. In fact, because the feedback was so timely and relevant, it could be considered analogous to *backchannels*, or secondary speech in human/human communication [Yngve, 1970; Schegloff, 1982]. Backchannels are not considered separate turns or attempts to take over the floor, but can be simultaneous with primary speech. A hearer reacts to a speaker with eye contact, nods, and *um hmm*'s. So whether or not words are the principle currency between user and computer, the conversation metaphor applies.

In the model of action proposed by Norman to cover the human use of computers (and tools and controls in general), a user must overcome two kinds of gulfs. First, the user must figure out how to translate her intentions into the input language allowed by the interface, thus overcoming the *gulf of execution*. Then, she must interpret the system's response and figure out if she's getting any closer to her goals—this is the *gulf of evaluation* [Norman, 1986]. This model addresses the problem of why interfaces don't work by helping the designer pinpoint exactly where the mappings between goals and tools break down [see Hutchins, Hollan, and Norman, 1985]. But it does *not* reflect the user's perspective about what she thinks she is doing as she interacts with her system. This model leaves the goals-to-tools mapping entirely up to the designer. It does not lead to specific predictions about which system behaviors will violate her expectations, en route to her goal. Could a metaphor that is different from "direct manipulation"—one based on human/human conversation—be used to develop a more informative model of human/computer interaction?

THE CONVERSATION METAPHOR

Let us consider some models of human communication. The information-processing model or message model of communication assumes that an agent with some goal generates a message, which is input to another agent, who sends back some output to be processed. Traditional psycholinguistics divides the territory similarly, into comprehension and production, two activities that roughly correspond to overcoming Norman's gulfs of evaluation and execution. But people are not just information processors sending out messages into the void to be picked up by other information processors. The models that assume that they are fail to explain how and why human language use *works* so well. People do many things with language, and sometimes in ways that would make a prescriptive grammarian quite ill:

Herb: Right! now, next week. [Looks at Susan.]

Susan: Ok, I will.

Herb: Good. [The twelve people in the room stand up and start to leave.]

Here, Herb adjourns his research group meeting by getting Susan to agree to present her data at their next meeting. Examples like this, when taken out of context, are utterly incomprehensible (which leads some people to insist that natural language is inherently ambiguous). But to the participants, such a conversation is as concrete as a desktop. Herb and Susan and the other members of the group share *common ground* [Stalnaker, 1978; Clark and Carlson, 1981; Clark and Marshall, 1981], and they expect one another to understand what they mean. Shared context is not enough by itself to ensure understanding, though. People use a system of *turn-taking* [Sacks, Schegloff, and Jefferson, 1974]. Turns are typically in the form of adjacency pairs [Schegloff and Sacks, 1973]; for instance, a question/answer sequence is an adjacency pair, with the question turn as the first part and the answer turn as the second part. But in our example above, what if Susan had looked at Herb blankly (as she often does)? Herb would have tried again. People in conversation keep at it until they get it right (or right enough for current purposes). The *collaborative model* says that in a conversation, every contribution must be understood and accepted (whether explicitly or implicitly) before the participants go on [Clark and Schaefer, 1988; 1989].

The Cooperative Principle

> Our talk exchanges do not normally consist of a succession of disconnected remarks, and would not be rational if they did. They are cooperative efforts to some degree. Each participant recognizes in them, to some extent, a common purpose or set of purposes, or at least a mutually accepted direction. [Grice, 1975]

Human conversation is inherently *cooperative*. The philosopher Grice's cooperative principle and its maxims are summarized in figure 1.

Computer interfaces often violate the maxim "be relevant." Many systems do not assume any connectivity whatsoever between user actions. The notions of incoherence and nonsequitur do not exist for these systems; rather, these interfaces treat *all* user utterances as if they were nonsequiturs.

Another problem facing the user is understanding where system messages come from. Grice distinguished between two types of meaning: 1) symptoms, clues, or other effects that do not originate intentionally from an agent but that are essentially side effects *caused* by the thing they mean, and 2) the meaning that occurs when a hearer recognizes the intention of a speaker to cause an effect simply by saying something. This second type of meaning corresponds to the notion of *speaker's meaning* [Levinson, 1983]. In the design of an interface, the failure to give due consideration to how the system represents itself to the user conflates these two types of meanings.

> **Maxims of quantity:**
> Make your contribution as informative as is required.
> Do not make your contribution more informative than is required.
>
> **Maxims of quality:**
> Do not say what you believe to be false.
> Do not say that for which you lack adequate evidence.
>
> **Maxims of manner:**
> Be perspicuous.
> Avoid obscurity of expression.
> Avoid ambiguity.
> Be brief.
> Be orderly.
>
> **Maxim of relation:**
> Be relevant.

Figure 1: Grice's cooperative maxims. [*Grice, 1975*]

Consider error messages. "SEGMENTATION VIOLATION!" or "ERROR #13" seem like either dire digital disasters inside the system or messages designed for somebody else. Error messages often violate the maxim of manner, "avoid obscurity of expression." Other error messages violate the maxim "be relevant"—for instance, "ERROR #42." Error messages should be relevant and informative. They should express a cooperative intention by giving the user some inkling of how to repair the error. But gratuitous user friendliness in the form of canned messages can be misleading. Here Eleanor, a typical polite Stanford undergraduate, interacts with SOCRATES, a reference-finding program in the campus library.

```
SOCRATES:    PLEASE SELECT COMMAND MODE
Eleanor:     > Please find an author named Octavia Butler.
SOCRATES:    INVALID FOLIO COMMAND: PLEASE
```

This is a successful error message, in that Eleanor knew exactly how to repair the problem. But it came up in the first place because she expected the system to use only words it could understand (we expect this of people, too, unless they are reading from a Berlitz phrasebook!). Lewis and Norman [1986] point out that error should be considered a normal part of operation, not an exception. They stress that people cooperate in making repairs, and suggest taking this into account when designing error messages for systems. They are right, but the conversation metaphor needs to be applied not only to repairs, but to other aspects of human/computer interaction as well.

Reference Resolution

In conversation, referring is a mutual activity [Clark and Marshall, 1981; Clark and Wilkes-Gibbs, 1986; Isaacs and Clark, 1987; Schober and Clark,

1989]; people negotiate the referring expressions they use. In a fluent conversation, what is said can be divided into given and new information [Clark and Haviland, 1977; Prince, 1981]. The given information links the current utterance with what has been said or done before and enables the partner to integrate the new information appropriately into the discourse (so that it too becomes given). Direct manipulation interfaces enable people to refer to given information—that is, to icons that exist on the screen—by pointing, and this is one area where direct manipulation interfaces really shine. But as we have seen, natural language allows this as well. In fact, one of the great things about natural language conversation is that a speaker can refer to something that isn't even there as far as the hearer is concerned—by using an indefinite noun phrase (as in "there's a big, rabid raccoon behind you"). Her hearer will create a mental entity for that reference, which can then be referred to by either of them using a definite noun phrase or pronoun (or else fled from).

To summarize the argument so far, thinking of user interfaces in terms of real conversation leads both to more specific predictions about how people will behave and to more informative explanations of why interface features succeed or fail. The hope is that employing the conversation metaphor will lead to insights in the kinds of architectures and features that are necessary to support cooperation between people and computers.

Natural Language: When a Word Is Worth a Thousand Icons

If people's expectations about conversation enable us to explain some of their expectations about interacting with computers, then what about natural language interfaces? Are they better conversationalists? How are conversations via words different from conversations via icons or formal languages? What is the best way to get information out of a database?

According to a position expressed by Shneiderman, an advocate of direct manipulation, the only advantage of a natural language interface is that it relieves the user of the burden of learning the syntax of a query language. He also says:

> People are different from computers, and human-human interaction is not necessarily an appropriate model for human operation of computers. Since computers can display information 1,000 times faster than people can enter commands, it seems advantageous to use the computer to display large amounts of information and allow novice and intermittent users simply to choose among the items. [Shneiderman, 1986]

But this is no solution. Just because a system can display all that information doesn't mean that the user wants to see it (recall Grice's maxim of quantity). Another problem is that a menu interface enforces its own hierarchy on the user's goals. Menus are well-trodden paths. You can do only what some designer thought of allowing you to do. You cannot combine and filter the elements of your virtual world in novel ways.

What about direct manipulation? Again, this solution is fine for very small worlds, if what you want to do can be represented by dragging around icons. What about hypertext? Hypertext interfaces provide the ability to link and browse huge amounts of information in meaningful ways. But there is always the possibility of getting lost in hyperspace.

Some things simply can be accomplished more easily using a natural language such as English. These things include negation, quantification, searching very large databases, issuing commands over entire sets of things, distinguishing individuals from kinds, filtering and requesting information in ways the interface designer hasn't already thought of, building up a complex query that takes more than a single turn, and doing anything that's not in the here and now.

How about command languages? Some are designed to resemble natural language, although what they're really doing is mapping exact strings and arguments to interpretations. Perhaps if the command set contained enough variations of particularly likely queries, the user's attempt would be sure to succeed. Or would it? Here's an exercise for the imaginative reader: try to estimate how many ways there are to ask a simple question about, say, *programmers who work for department managers*, using plain old everyday English. (Those who are too impatient to guess, see the caption to figure 2.)

There are many different approaches to building natural language interfaces, and each has its own limits. Outside of science fiction movies, most of them begin with the assumption that the input will be a string of characters and that it will be interpreted in light of one particular application. The idea is to get from an English sentence to some kind of logic or other formal language representation that can then be executed to carry out the user's command or request. So the only sense in which a natural language program can be said to *understand* a query is in the mapping of its formal interpretation onto a program capable of taking some action in the virtual world of the application.

Some natural language interfaces make the additional assumption that the sentences a user types will be well-formed. These will fail at anything that an eighth-grade English student couldn't diagram. However, interactive human language use is wildly unruly by traditional standards; speakers constantly make errors and repairs and rely upon their listeners to fill in the gaps. Those interfaces that don't assume input is well-formed have the advantage that they sometimes seem more tolerant; some even ignore syntax altogether and respond only to keywords. In these cases, much of their success is due to *false positives* (luck).

A linguistically sound approach to processing is necessary in a natural

List programmers department managers supervise.
What programmers work for department managers?
List programmers working for department managers.
List programmers who work for department managers.
List any programmers department managers supervise.
Which programmers work for managers of departments?
Which programmers do department managers supervise?
List all programmers working for department managers.
List each programmer a department manager supervises.
List all programmers who work for department managers.
List programmers whose supervisors manage departments.
List all programmers that department managers supervise.
Which of the programmers work for department managers?
Who are the programmers department managers supervise?
List every programmer any department manager supervises.
List every programmer supervised by a department manager.
Which programmers are supervised by department managers?
Who are the programmers working for department managers?
List programmers with supervisors who manage departments.
Who are the programmers who work for department managers?
List every programmer whom a department manager supervises.
List programmers whose supervisors are department managers.
List each programmer that any department manager supervises.
List all of the programmers who work for department managers.
Which programmers are there working for department managers?
List each programmer who is working for a department manager.
Which of the programmers are department managers supervising?
Which of the programmers are working for department managers?
Which of the programmers do managers of departments supervise?
Who are all of the programmers working for department managers?
List the programmers who are supervised by department managers.
List each of the programmers supervised by a department manager.
Which of the programmers are supervised by department managers?
List any programmer whose supervisor is a manager of a department.
Who are the programmers being supervised by department managers?
Who are all of the programmers that department managers supervise?
List any programmers there might be working for department managers.
List everyone who is a programmer supervised by a department manager.
List each of the programmers who is supervised by a department manager.
Which of the programmers are being supervised by department managers?
Who are the programmers whose supervisors are managers of departments?
List any programmer with a supervisor who is the manager of a department.
Which of the programmers are being supervised by managers of departments?
Which of the programmers have supervisors who are managers of departments?
List all programmers working for supervisors who are managers of departments.
List any programmer who has a supervisor who is the manager of a department.
List all programmers who work for anyone who is the manager of a department.
Which of the programmers have supervisors who are the managers of departments?
List each of the programmers who is supervised by anyone managing a department.
Who are all of the programmers who have supervisors who are department managers?
(etc.)

Figure 2: How shall I ask thee? Let me count the ways. (From 7000 Variations on a Single Sentence, by the Hewlett-Packard Natural Language Project, 1986.)

language interface to a database query system. It can't be faked.[1] That is why natural language interfaces have taken so long to be developed, and the technology will continue to improve as more of the problems are solved. But in order to live up to their potential, natural language interfaces must treat language as a conversation and not as disembodied grammatical sentences composed of strings of characters. For this we need to apply the psychology of language use further. The following four examples represent steps in this direction.

Questions and Answers

Questions and answers, common adjacency pairs in human language use, tend to parallel one another in their syntax and words [Levelt and Kelter, 1982]. An answer that uses different words than its projecting question may indicate that a distinction is being made or that there is a misunderstanding. Natural language interfaces that do not preserve this parallelism between questions and answers do not seem particularly conversational (see figure 3a). Those that preserve parallelism (figure 3b) are more cooperative [Brennan, 1988].

Talking to Strangers

When people talk to one another, they design their utterances with their partners in mind [Clark and Murphy, 1983; Bell, 1984; Milroy, 1987]. They can accommodate a wide range of partners: friends, strangers, the hard of hearing, disembodied voices on the telephone, readers who will come along after they are gone, groups, foreigners, children, dogs. This flexibility in *audience design* (that is, designing what you say explicitly *for* your audience) has been documented even among the very young. For

```
User:        Who has a terminal?
System:      Shall I do the following? Create a
             report showing the full name and
             the manager and the equipment from
             the forms on which the equipment
             includes 'TERMINAL'?
```

Figure 3a: Dialogue from commercially available software product.

```
User:        Who has a terminal?
System:      DAN FLICKINGER HAS A TERMINAL.
```

Figure 3b: Dialogue from HPNL, Hewlett-Packard Labs.

---

[1] For examples of how far you can go with illusory intelligence for scripted interaction, see Schmandt's chapter in this volume.

instance, five-year-olds speak differently to younger siblings than to adults [Shatz and Gelman, 1973]. But how do people target what they say when their partner is a natural language interface to a computer?

Recently, I ran a *wizard of Oz* experiment to find out [Brennan, 1989]. In a wizard of Oz experiment, the user's keyboard input is intercepted by an experimenter, who either modifies it so that the computer will be able to handle it, or else simulates the system's responses entirely. In this particular experiment, people were led to believe that their partner was either another person or a natural language interface to a database. I played the role of the wizard, and I was blind to whether subjects thought I was a person or a computer so that I could behave consistently in both conditions. This allowed me to systematically compare transcripts of the language used by subjects who thought they had a human partner with the language used by subjects who thought they had a computer partner. I also examined how the kinds of responses people received shaped their language use to both kinds of partners.

The results: Although most people expected only their human partners to be sensitive to the social context surrounding the conversation, they expected some degree of *context dependence* in the conversation (that is, connectedness between turns) regardless of whether a partner was human or computer. In addition, people whose partners responded with complete sentence answers were much more likely to type complete sentence questions. Similarly, short answers shaped users to type short questions (that is, phrasal, elliptical, or keyword). This finding is relevant because many natural language interfaces can interpret only complete sentences. It is consistent with the finding that polite or informal responses from a system can shape commands from users to be more polite or informal [Richards and Underwood, 1984]. So a natural language interface should present itself and design its responses in a way that is informative about the kind of a conversational partner it is. This will help in painlessly constraining users from typing certain kinds of input that the system can't handle.

Talking to the Furniture

A group of software engineers and computational linguists at Hewlett Packard has connected a natural language interface (HPNL) to a desktop interface to a workstation.

"What a bizarre idea," you may think. "Why would I want to plead with my desktop to copy a file when I can just grab it with my mouse and drag it?" Skeptical, you sit down to a desktop filled with folders and spreadsheets and mail messages and function icons and pull-this-way-and-that-way menus. Although they look familiar, you've never seen these particular icons before, and there sure are a lot of them, and lots of windows too. Perhaps it's someone else's desktop you're visiting; perhaps it's a desktop shared by a group of you working together. At any rate, it's going to take you a whole bunch of clicks even to find the thing you want to copy. Resigned, you start opening folders up one at a time, searching for your file.

What if you could filter all that clutter in some idiosyncratic way that would help you find what you're looking for? What if you could ask the desktop itself for help? As soon as the screen contains more things than can be visible all at once, it becomes more like a database than a desktop.[2] A natural language interface to the desktop treats it like one. So you can say, "How many folders are there on the desktop?" and then, "Give me all the ones named annual report," and even, "Mail them to Lew tomorrow." Here, natural language is good at filtering large amounts of information, at providing random access to a particular item, at referring to something in a previous utterance, and at doing things that are not in the here and now.

Animated Language

One way to make a natural language interface more conversational is to integrate it with a graphic interface that, when appropriate, provides the user with additional clues as to how her utterance has been interpreted with respect to the application. The goal is to make these clues analogous to (though not slavishly imitative of) backchannels in human/human conversation (see Schmandt's chapter).

A first requirement for the integration of language and graphics is that the interface must provide consistent access across multiple modes; it must support referring via both typing at the keyboard and pointing with a mouse or touch screen. Certain actions are more easily done gesturally/spatially (as direct manipulation enthusiasts have noticed), others are more easily done with language (as I have argued), and some can be done with either, or with a combination of both. Pointing and language go together naturally; for instance, when two people work together in front of the same screen, there is typically a certain amount of touching the screen as well as talking and typing.

A second requirement is that the system must support the negotiation of meaning and the interactive repair of errors. Ambiguity and failure can arise at any stage of processing in a natural language interface (for example, in spelling, morphology, syntax, semantics, disambiguation, or pragmatics). People are particularly good at letting other people know whether or not they've understood an utterance. If users of a natural language interface have the *option* of attending to a graphical display that's percolating away on the corner of the screen as an adjunct to the textual part of the conver-

---

[2] The Macintosh interface seems to acknowledge this by including the Find File program.

sation, they can get additional evidence regarding whether the system has understood them. In addition, they can make repairs by editing the text of the last turn, taking a new textual turn, or by pointing at and manipulating the graphic display.

Conclusion

The fundamental ability of human beings to adapt to their conversational partners makes the whole human/computer enterprise possible. As we have seen, the way a conversational partner represents itself and the style in which it responds influence how a user designs utterances for that partner. Thus, the natural constraints imposed by the act of conversing should be exploited so that a user will be painlessly constrained from falling off the edge of the interface.

The following strategies are derived from what we know about human/human conversation: 1) don't continue until an understanding that is sufficient for current purposes is reached; 2) assume that errors will happen and provide ways to negotiate them; 3) articulate the answer or response in a way that preserves the adjacency with (and apparent relevance to) the question or command; 4) represent the interface in a way that invisibly constrains the user to act in ways the system understands and to stick to the application domain; and 5) integrate typed input with pointing and other input/output channels. Applying these strategies should make interaction with a computer more *conversational*, whether it's via a desktop or a natural language interface.

The "Natural" Language of Interaction:

A Perspective on Nonverbal Dialogues[*]

THERE IS LITTLE DISPUTE that the user interface is a bottleneck restricting the potential of today's computational and communications technologies. When we begin to look for solutions to this problem, however, consensus evaporates. Researchers and users all have their own views of how we should interact with computers, and each of these views is different. If there is a thread of consistency, however, it is generally in the view that user interfaces should be more "natural." Within the AI community, especially, this translates into "natural language understanding systems," which are put forward as the great panacea that will free us from all of our current problems.

The question is, is this hope realistic? The answer, we believe, lies very much in what is meant by *natural language*.

What is normally meant by the term is the ability to converse using a language like English or German. When conversing with a machine, such conversations may be coupled with speech understanding and synthesis, or may involve typing using a more conventional keyboard and CRT. Regardless, our personal view is that the benefits and applicability of such

Bill Buxton

Rank Xerox EuroPARC
and
University of Toronto

---

[*] This is a revision of a paper that previously appeared under the same title in *Proceedings of CIPS '87*, Intelligent Integration, Edmonton, Canadian Information Processing Society, pp. 311–16, and *INFOR Canadian Journal of Operations Research and Information Processing*, 26(4), pp. 428–38.

systems will be limited, largely because of the imprecise and verbose nature of such language.

But we do not want to argue that point, because it has too much in common with arguments against motherhood or about politics and religion. More importantly, it is secondary to our principal thesis: that this class of conversation represents only a small part of the full range of natural language.

We argue that there is a rich and potent gestural language that is at least as "natural" as verbal language, and that—in the short and long term—may have a more important impact on facilitating human-computer interaction. And, despite its neglect, we argue that this type of language can be supported by existing technology, so we can reap the potential benefits immediately.

Another View of Natural Language

There is probably little argument that verbal language coexists with a rich variety of manual gestures (a variety that seems to increase in range as one approaches the Mediterranean Sea). The real question is, what does this have to do with computers, much less with natural language? What we are going to argue is that such gestures are part of a nonverbal vocabulary that is natural and that is a language capable of efficiently communicating powerful concepts to a computer.

The burden of proof, therefore, is to establish the communicative potential of such a language, and to show that it is, in fact, natural. Our approach is to argue by demonstration and by example. We will provide some concrete demonstrations of how such language can be used and will argue that it is natural in the sense that users come to the system with the basic requisite communication skills already in place. Our main hope is that we may be able to cause some researchers to rethink their priorities and direct more attention to this aspect of interaction than has previously been the case.

The Macintosh as Victim

Before going too much further, it is probably worth making a few comments about my approach and my examples. As will become pretty evident, the Apple Macintosh takes a bit of a beating in what follows. Some readers may view this as evidence of contempt for its design. From my perspective, it is evidence of respect. Let me explain.

User interface design today is plagued by an unhealthy degree of complacency. We live in a world of copy-cat unimaginative interface products, where major manufacturers put out double-paged color spreads in *Business Week* announcing " . . . our system's user interface is as easy to use as the most easy to use microcomputer [that is, the Mac]" (or words to that

At this stage I want to change the order of the sentences. The third sentence, that which follows, I want to preceed this one. The third sentence, this one, I want to preceed number two. I can specify this using proofreader's notation.

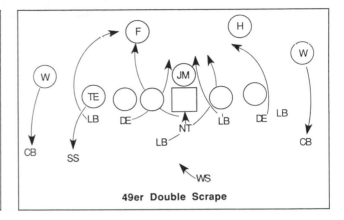

49er Double Scrape

Figures 1a and 1b: Similar notations for two types of information. Figure 1a (left) illustrates the use of proofreader's notation to specify a spatial relationship within a document. Figure 1b (right) uses a similar notation to specify a spatial relationship over time in the context of a football play.

effect). In what other industry can you get away with stating that you're as good as the competition, rather than better? Especially when the competition's product is more than four years old!

The best ideas are the most dangerous, because they take hold and are the hardest to change. Hence, the Macintosh is dangerous to the progress of user interfaces precisely because it was so well done! Designers seem to be viewing it as a measure of success rather than as a point of departure. Consequently, it runs the risk of becoming the COBOL of the 90s.

I criticize the Macintosh precisely because it is held in such high regard. It is one of the few worthy targets. If I can make the point that there are other design options, and that these options appear to have a lot of potential, I may help wake people up to the fact that it is an unworthy design objective to aim for anything less than trying to do to the Macintosh what the Macintosh did to the previous state of the art.

Enough of the sermon. Let's leave the pulpit for some concrete examples.

Of Proofreaders and Football Coaches

Let us start off with a "real" computer-relevant example. Of all applications, text editing has perhaps been the most studied in terms of human factors. Within text editors (and command-line interfaces in general), perhaps no linguistic construct has received more attention and been more problematic than that of a verb that has both a direct and an indirect object.

The classic examples of this construct, largely because they are so ubiquitous, are the move and copy operations. In fact, the problems posed by verbs having two different types of operand are such that in programs like MacWrite, move and copy have each been replaced by two operations (cut-and-paste and copy-and-paste, respectively). Each step of these compound operations has only one operand (the second being implicit, the "magic" operand, the clipboard).

What is clear, however, to anyone who has ever annotated a document or seen a football playbook, is that there exists an alternative notation (read "language") for expressing these concepts. This is characterized by the gestural proofreader's move symbol. Whether intended in the spatial or temporal sense, the notation is clear, succinct, and is known independently of (but is understandable by) computers.

Figure 1a shows how the proofreader's move symbol can be used to specify a verb with two objects (direct and indirect) without any ambiguity. Figure 1b illustrates the use of essentially the same notational language in a very different context. This time it is being used to illustrate plays in a football game. Despite the context, the notation is clear and unambiguous, will virtually never result in an error of syntax, and is known to the user before a computer is ever used. Also, it can be used to articulate concepts that users traditionally have a great deal of trouble expressing.

Could this type of notation be the "natural" language for this type of concept? More to the point, do any of today's "state-of-the-art" user interfaces even begin to let us find out?

Natural Languages Are Learned

The capacity for language is one of the things that distinguishes humans from the other animal species. Having said that, nobody would argue that humans are born with language. Even "natural" languages are learned. Anyone who has tried to learn a foreign language (a language that is "natural" to others) knows this. We are considered a native speaker if and when we have developed fluency in the language by the time we are required to draw upon those language skills.

If we orient our discussion around computers, the same rules apply. A language could be considered "natural" if, upon approaching the computer, the typical user already has language skills adequate for expressing desired concepts in a rich, succinct, fluent, and articulate manner.

By this definition, most methods of interacting with computers are anything but natural. But is there an untapped resource there, a language resource that users bring to the system on first encounter that could provide the basis for such "natural" dialogues?

Yes!

What's Natural to You Is Foreign to Me

One of the problems with arguments in favor of natural language interfaces is the unspoken implication that such systems will be universally accessible. But even if we restrict ourselves to the consideration of verbal language, we must accept the reality of foreign languages. German, for example, is different than English in both vocabulary and syntax. There is no universally agreed placement of verbs in sentences, for example.

The point to this train of thought, which is a continuation of the previous comments about languages being learned, is that so-called natural languages are only natural to those who have learned them. All others are foreign.

If we start to consider nonverbal forms of communication, the same thing holds true. The graphic artist's language of using an airbrush, for example, is foreign to the house painter. Similarly, the architectural drafts-person has a language that includes the use of a drafting machine in combination with a pencil. Each of these "languages" is natural (albeit learned) for the profession.

But the argument will now be raised that I am playing with words, and that what I am talking about are specialized skills developed for the practice of particular professions, or domains of endeavor. But how is that different from verbal language? What is conventional verbal language if not a highly learned skill developed to enable one to communicate about various domains of knowledge?

Where all of this is heading is the observation that the notion of a universally understood natural language is naive and not very useful. Each language has special strengths and weaknesses in its ability to communicate particular concepts. Languages can be natural or foreign to concepts as well as speakers. A true "natural language" system is achieved only when the language employed is natural to the task, and the person engaged in that task is a native speaker. But perhaps the most important concept underlying this is acknowledging that naturalness is domain specific, and we must, therefore, support a variety of natural languages.

Where There's Language There Must Be Phrases

Let us accept, therefore, that there is a world of natural nonverbal languages out there waiting to be tapped for the purpose of improved human-computer interaction. Then where are the constructs and conventions that we find in verbal language? Are there, for example, concepts such as sentences and phrases?

Let us look at one of our favorite examples [Buxton, 1986b]. Consider making a selection using a pop-up menu. Conceptually, you are doing one thing: making a choice. But if we look more closely, there is a lot more going on (as the underlying parser would tell you if it knew how). You are "uttering" a complex sentence that includes:

1. Mouse button down: to invoke the menu
2. A one-dimensional locate: moving the mouse to the item to be selected
3. Mouse button up: to cause the currently highlighted item to be selected

While you generate each of these tokens, you are not aware of the mechanics of doing so. The reason is that from the moment that you depress the mouse button, you are in a non-neutral state of tension (your finger). Although you may make a semantic error (make the wrong selection), everything in the system is biased towards the fact that the only reasonable action to conclude the transaction is to release your finger. There is virtually no cognitive overhead in determining the mechanics of the interaction. Tension is used to bind together the tokens of the transaction just as musical tension binds together the notes in a phrase. This is a well-designed interaction, and if anything deserves to be called natural, this does.

But let us go one step further. If appropriate phrasing of gestural languages can be used to reduce or eliminate errors of syntax (as in the pop-up menu example), can we find instances where lack of phrasing permits us to predict errors that will be made? The question is rhetorical, and we can find an instance even within our pop-up menu example.

Consider the case where the item being selected from the menu is a verb, like cut, which requires a direct object. Within a text editor, for example, specifying the region of text to be cut has no gestural continuity (that is, is not articulated in the same "phrase") with the selection of the cut operator itself. Consequently, we can predict (and easily verify by observation) a common error in systems that use this technique: that users will invoke the verb before they have selected the direct object. As a result, they must restart, select the text, then reselect cut.

To find the inverse situation, where the use of phrasing enables us to predict where this type of error will not occur, we need look no further than the proofreader's symbol example discussed earlier. The argument is, if the language is fluid and natural, it will permit complete concepts to be articulated in fluid connected phrases. That is natural, and if such a criterion is followed in language design, learning time and error rates will drop while efficiency will improve.

On Head-Tapping and Stomach-Rubbing

If there is anything that makes a language natural, as the previous discussion emphasized, it is the notion of fluidity, continuity, and phrasing. Let us push this a little farther, using an example that moves us even further from verbal language.

One of the problems of verbal language, especially written language, is that it is single-threaded. We can parse only one stream of words at a time. Many people would argue that anything other than that is unnatural, and would be akin to the awkward party trick of rubbing your stomach while tapping your head. The logic (so-called) seems to be based on the belief that because we can speak and read only one stream of words at a time, languages based on multiple streams are unnatural (after all, if God had wanted us to communicate in multiple streams, she would have given us two mouths).

But this argument is so easy to refute that it is almost embarrassing to have to do so. Imagine, if you will, a voice-activated automobile. (If this is too hard, imagine yourself as an instructor with a student driver.) Your task is to talk the car down London's Edgware Road, around Marble Arch, and along Park Lane. If anything will convince you that verbal language is unnatural in some contexts—even spoken and coupled with the ultimate speech understanding system (a human being, in the case of the student driver)—this will. The single stream of verbal instructions does not have the bandwidth to simultaneously give the requisite instructions for steering, gear shifting, braking, and accelerating.

(The AI pundits will, of course say, that the solution here is to couple the natural language system with an expert system that knows how to drive. Fine. Then replace the student driver with an expert, but one who has never driven in London before and go out at rush hour. The odds are still less than 50:50 of making it around Marble Arch. If you aren't in an accident, you will be bound to cause one. QED)

There are some things for which verbal language is singularly unsuited. For our purposes, we will characterize these as tasks in which the single-threaded nature of such language causes us to violate the principles of continuity and fluidity in phrasing, as outlined above. That is what was happening in the car driving example, what would happen if one tried to talk a pianist through a concerto, and what does happen in many common computer applications, which are—likewise—inappropriately based on single-threaded dialogues.

From Marble Arch to MacWrite

We can use the Apple Macintosh, in particular the well-known word processor MacWrite, to illustrate our statements about continuity and multithreaded dialogues. The example is based on an experiment that Brad Myers and I undertook [Buxton and Myers, 1986].

The study was motivated by the observation that a lot of time using window-based WYSIWYG text editors was spent switching between editing text and navigating through the document being edited. In the direct manipulation type systems that we were interested in, this switching took the form of the mouse being used to alternatively select text in the document and to navigate by manipulating the scroll bar and scroll arrows at the side of the screen.

This type of task switching occurs when the text that one wants to select is off screen. Hence, what is conceptually a "select text" task becomes a compound "navigate / select text" task. Because each of the component tasks (navigate and select) were independent, we decided to design an alternative interface in which each task was assigned to a separate hand.

Assuming right-handed users, the right hand manipulated the mouse and performed the text-selection task. The left hand performed the navigation task (using two touch-sensitive strips: one that permitted smooth scrolling, the other that jumped to the same relative position in the document as the point touched on the strip).

We implemented the new interface in an environment that copied MacWrite. What we saw was a dramatic improvement in the performance of experts and novices. In particular, we saw that by simply changing the interface, not only did performance improve, but the performance gap between experts and novices was narrowed. Perhaps most important, it was clear that using both hands in this manner caused no problem for experts or for novices. Clearly they had the requisite motor skills before ever approaching the computer, and the mapping of the skills employed to the task was an appropriate one.

Why did this multihanded, multithreaded approach work? One reason is that each hand was always in "home position" for its respective task (assuming that they were not on the keyboard, in which case, each hand could be positioned on its own device about as fast as one hand could be placed on the mouse—which is the normal case). Hence, the flow of each task was uninterrupted, preserving the continuity of each.

The improvements in efficiency can be predicted by simple time-motion analysis, such as is obtainable using the Keystroke level model of Card, Moran, and Newell [1980]. Because each hand is in home position, no time is spent acquiring the scroll gadgets or moving back to the text portion of the screen. Having both hands simultaneously available, the user can (and did) "mouse ahead" to where the text will appear while still scrolling it into view. That users spontaneously used such optimal strategies is a good argument for the naturalness of the mode of interaction.

Another Handwaving Example

Is this just one of those interesting idiosyncratic examples, or are there some generally applicable principles here? We clearly believe the latter. Most "modern" direct manipulation systems appear to have been designed for Napoleon, or people of his ilk, who want to keep one hand tucked away for no apparent purpose.

But everyday observation gives us numerous examples in which people assign a secondary task to their non-dominant hand (or feet) in order to avoid interrupting the flow of some other task being undertaken by the dominant hand. Although this is common in day-to-day tasks, the single-threaded nature of systems biases greatly against using these same techniques when conversing with a computer. Consequently, in situations in which this approach is appropriate, single-threaded dialogues (and this includes verbal natural language understanding systems) are anything but natural.

Figure 2: *Grabbing the page in MacPaint. In order to expose different parts of the "page" in Macpaint, one selects the hand icon from the menu on the left, then uses the hand to drag the page under the window (using the mouse).*

But it is not just a case of time-motion efficiency at play here. It is the very nature of system complexity. If a single device must be time-multiplexed across multiple functions, there is a penalty in complexity as well as time. This can be illustrated by another example taken from the Macintosh program, MacPaint.

Like the previous example, this one involves navigation and switching between functions using the mouse. In this case, the tasks are inking (drawing with the paint brush), and navigating (moving the document under the window).

In this example, imagine that you are painting the cat shown in figure 2. Having finished the head, you now want to paint the body. However, not enough of the page is exposed in the window. The solution is to move the appropriate part of the page under the window. We then go on painting.

Let us work through this in more detail, contrasting two different styles of interaction.

1. Assume that our initial state is that we have been painting (having selected the "brush" icon in the menu).

2. Assume that our goal (target end state) is to paint on a part of the page not visible in the window.

3. Our strategy is to move the page under the window until the desired part is visible, and then resume painting.

4a. The official method, as dictated by MacPaint:

   a. Move the tracking symbol (using the mouse) from the paint window to the menu in the left margin.

   b. Select the "hand" icon.

   c. Move to the paint window.

   d. Drag the page under the window (as shown in figure 2). This may involve multiple "strokes," that is, releasing the mouse button, re-positioning the mouse, then dragging some more.

   e. Move the tracking symbol from the paint window back to the menu in the left margin.

   f. Select the "brush" icon.

   g. Move back to the paint window.

   h. Resume painting.

4b. Our multihanded, multithreaded method: Assume that the position of the page under the window is connected to a trackball that is manipulated by the left hand, while painting is carried out (as always) with the mouse in the right hand. The revised method is:

   a. Drag the page under the window (which may involve multiple "strokes" of the trackball).

It is clear that the second method involves far fewer steps and is far more respectful of the continuity of the primary task, painting. It is likely that it is easier to learn, less prone to error, and much faster to perform (we don't make this claim outright because there can be other influences when the larger context is considered, and we have not performed the study). It also means that the nonintuitive hand icon can be eliminated from the menu, reducing complexity in yet another way. It is, within the context of the example, clearly a more natural way to perform the transaction.

An important part of this example is the fact that the initial and final (goal) states are identical except for the position of the page in the window. In general, when this situation comes up during task analysis, bells should go off in the analyst's head prompting the question: if the start and goal state involve the performance of the same task, is the intermediate task a secondary task that can be assigned to the other hand? Can we preserve the fluidity and continuity of the primary task by so doing?

In many cases, the answer will be yes, and we are doing the user a disservice if we don't act on the observation.

Is It That Simple? Learning from History

To be fair, at this point it is worth addressing two specific questions:

- At first glance, many of these ideas seem pretty good. Is it really that easy?

- Are these ideas really new?

The answer to both questions is a qualified "no." Furthermore, the questions are very much related. Many of the ideas showed potential and were demonstrated as long as twenty years ago. However, developing a good idea takes careful design and the right combination of ingredients.

Although many of these ideas have been explored previously, the work was often ahead of the technology's ability to deliver to any broad population in a cost-effective form. A human nature issue also arises from the fact that once a technique has been tried without follow-through, people frequently seem to adopt a "that's been tried, didn't catch on, so must not have worked" type of attitude.

In addition, there are some really deep issues that remain to be solved to support a lot of this work, and certainly, the leap from a lab demo to a robust production system is nontrivial, regardless of the power or "correctness" of the concept. For example, gesture-based systems generally require a stylus and tablet whose responsiveness to subtle changes of nuance is beyond what can be delivered by most commercial tablets (and certainly any mouse). IBM, among others, has spent a lot of time trying to get a tablet/stylus combination with the right feel, amount of tip-switch travel, and linearity suitable for this type of interaction.

The last point (not in importance) concerning the degree of acceptance of gestural and two-handed input—despite isolated compelling examples having been around for a long time—has to do with user testing. Demos, there have been. Carefully run and documented user testing and evaluation, however, can be noted only by their scarcity. The only published studies that I'm aware of that tried to carry out formal user testing of gestural interfaces are Rhyne and Wolf [1986], Wolf [1986], and Wolf and Morrel-Samuels [1987]. The only published formal study that I am aware of involving user tests of two-handed navigation-selection and scaling-positioning tasks was by Buxton and Myers [1986].

One of the most illuminating, glaring (and depressing) points stemming from the above is the huge discrepancy (in computer terms) between the dates of the first prototypes and demonstrations (mid 60s – early 70s), and the dates of any of the published user testing (mid-late 80s). I think that this says a lot about why these techniques have not received their due attention. Change is always hard to bring about. Without testing, we never get anywhere near an optimal understanding or implementation of the concept, and we never get the data that would otherwise permit us to quantify the benefits. In short, we simply are handicapped in our ability to fight the inertia that is inevitable in arguing for any type of significant change.

Summary

We have argued strongly for designers to adopt a mentality that considers nonverbal gestural modes of interaction as falling within the domain of natural languages. Although verbal language likely has an important role to play in human-computer interaction, it is not going to be any type of general panacea.

What is clear is that different forms of interaction support the expression of different types of concepts. "Natural" language includes gestures. Gestures can be used to form clear fluid phrases, and multithreaded gestures can capitalize on the capabilities of human performance to enable important concepts to be expressed in a clear, appropriate, and "natural" manner. These include concepts in which the threads are expressed simultaneously (as in driving a car, playing an instrument, or mousing ahead), or sequentially, where using a second thread enables us to avoid disrupting the continuity of some primary task by having the secondary task articulated using a different channel (as in the MacPaint example).

We believe that this notion of a natural language understanding system can bring about a significant improvement in the quality of human-computer interaction. To achieve this, however, requires a change in attitude on the part of researchers and designers. Hopefully the arguments made above will help bring about such a change.

Acknowledgments

The research reported in this paper has been undertaken at the University of Toronto, with the support of the Natural Sciences and Engineering Research Council of Canada, and at Rank Xerox's Cambridge EuroPARC facility in England. This support is gratefully acknowledged. We would like to acknowledge the helpful contributions made by Thomas Green and the comments of Rick Beach, Elizabeth Churchill, Michael Brook, and Larry Tesler.

Videoplace and the Interface of the Future

I SAT AT A TABLET and drew on the image of a student's hand. She was a little embarrassed at this attention and moved her hand. I followed her hand with the stylus. It looked as if she had drawn the line. Picking up the idea, she moved her finger where she wanted me to draw.

This scene occurred in 1970 at the University of Wisconsin. It was an experimental artistic environment, called METAPLAY, set up to explore ways in which humans might like to interact with machines.

METAPLAY was quite elaborate for its time. A camera pointed at a graphic computer that displayed the drawing created with the tablet. The computer image was transmitted across campus, where it was superimposed over the live image of people standing in the gallery of the student union. The composite image was rear-screen-projected so that this audience could see themselves. It was then transmitted back to the computer center, where it was displayed on the monitor to provide feedback for the drawing process.

Despite its antiquity, this environment had many attributes that would be desirable for the human interface of the future.

- The participants were standing in the middle of a room unencumbered by any instrumentation.
- They saw themselves as part of the image they were creating.

Myron W. Krueger

Artificial Realities

417

- They saw their fingers in that image as tools that could be used for drawing.
- They were physically involved in the experience they were having.
- They were involved in a discovery process that converted computer illiterates into active users almost instantaneously.
- The interface had a playful personality.
- The system perceived the participants rather than just receiving input.
- A true dialogue took place, with both the participants and the computer system injecting novelty into the experience.

Epiphany

During this exhibit we were working on an additional form of perception. We had built an array of hundreds of pressure sensors that would track each person's footsteps as he or she moved around the room. We were transmitting the position information from the floor to the graphic computer in the computer center. We were discussing a transmission problem, on the phone, when I realized that we had a better alternative.

There was an early PDP 12 in the gallery that had a low resolution graphic display. I asked the operator in the gallery to display the signal transmitted on the gallery computer while I displayed the signal received on the graphic computer in the computer center. We were then both looking at the same video image consisting of two superimposed computer images.

To facilitate our conversation, we each pointed to the signals displayed on our respective computer screens. Both of our hands appeared in the composite image. We were able to converse, pointing to features of the signals as we talked exactly as we would if we were sitting together on the same side of a table with a piece of paper between us. The sense of being together was very strong. When I moved my hand, in order to point at something, and my image inadvertently overlapped the image of his hand, he moved it out of the way. The idea of personal distance had arisen spontaneously in a situation that had never occurred before. In later experiments, some people reported a sensation in their finger when they touched the image of another person on the point. It is enough that individuals have a very proprietary sense about their image. What happens to it happens to them. What touches it, they feel.

Related to this observation was the idea that our teleconference created a place that consisted of the information we both shared. As long as we focused our attention on that place, we were there. This place was named VIDEOPLACE. VIDEOPLACE is an instance of a broader concept, a world in which full physical participation would be possible. This world is an "artificial reality." This concept is the basis of my 1974 doctoral thesis,

"Computer Controlled Responsive Environments," later published as *Artificial Reality* (Addison-Wesley, 1983).

The kind of interface suggested in the METAPLAY exhibit has been under continuous investigation and development since the early 1970s. A version of VIDEOPLACE has been in operation since 1976.

In VIDEOPLACE, you enter a darkened room and see a real-time image of your silhouette on a large video projection screen. A camera aimed at you sends information about what you are doing to the computer system. This system perceives your image in motion, analyzes it, understands what it sees, and responds instantaneously with graphics, video effects, and synthesized sound. Your individual movements determine what you will experience.

There are 30 interactions in the VIDEOPLACE repertoire, with new ones being added on a continuous basis. You can really draw on the video screen, without the intervention of a hidden collaborator, by holding up your finger while standing in the middle of a room (figure N in the color insert). If you close your hand, you can move it without drawing. Holding up five fingers erases the drawing.

You can play with a graphic creature, called CRITTER, who will chase your image. If you hold out your hand, CRITTER will land on it and attempt to climb up your silhouette, performing a celebratory jig if it reaches the top of your head. An open hand attracts CRITTER, and with a little coaxing it will dangle from a fingertip. If you move that finger abruptly, CRITTER will plunge to the bottom of the screen and splat, only to be instantly resurrected. CRITTER is also aware when it has been captured by two encircling hands. It tries desperately to escape. Failing that, it explodes—and appears elsewhere a moment later (figure O in the color insert).

In many of the interactions, the participant's image is shown life-sized. However, in some interactions the participant's image is reduced in scale in order to explore new relationships. With more space to move around in, the participant can fly around the screen, jump from a graphic object, and fall under moon gravity. The participant can also swing from one object to another or form a chorus line with a series of his previous images.

In a telecommunications interaction the image of a second person, in a different location, appears on the screen. The second person can exist on a different scale. Thus, we have juxtaposed the giant hands of one person with the shrunken image of another (figure P in the color insert). These hands can lift a tiny person and suspend him from a graphic string, dangled from a giant finger. Inevitably, the tiny people wonder if it is possible to swing on the string. Sure enough, when they move from side to side, imparting energy to their images, they begin to swing back and forth. An opportunity has been offered and accepted without a word being spoken or a manual consulted.

VIDEOPLACE is a deliberately informal and playful arena for exploration of the human interface. However, because we do a great deal of development, we have a number of tools we can operate standing within the VIDEOPLACE environment. Being able to stand while working is a valuable addition to the inventory of user interface options. Overcoming the sedentary tyranny of existing systems is one of VIDEOPLACE's ongoing goals.

In the VIDEODESK environment, a camera is mounted over the desk and aimed at the clear surface of the desk. The camera sends information about the position and actions of the user's hands and fingers to the computer system. We have implemented a number of traditional demos with this interface, showing the value of multipoint control. Two fingers can be used to define the endpoints of a line or the opposite as corners of a box as well positioning an object on the screen in one motion. Similarly, the user can mix colors by using one hand to control the amount of red in the image and the other hand to control the amount of green. The distance between the two hands can be used to control the amount of blue.

The most dramatic VIDEODESK demonstration of multipoint control is the use of the thumb and forefingers of the operator's two hands as control points for a spline curve (figure Q in the color insert). If this curve is used to define the aperture of an extruding device and graphic stuff is squeezed through as the user changes the shape of the spline, a complex three-dimensional solid can be created very rapidly (figure R in the color insert). We have done some work with true three-dimensional perception of the user's hands using multiple cameras and a stereographic display.

What to Wear

Although I originally coined the term *artificial reality* to describe VIDEO-PLACE, I considered VIDEOPLACE an instance of a larger concept including data gloves, suits, and stereo glasses, and described these options in *Artificial Reality*. However, I have a profound personal prejudice against wearing devices on any regular basis. I suspect that I am not alone. Therefore, I believe that human interface research will branch in two directions. One fork will have the objective of completing an artificial reality technology that includes force and tactile feedback, using whatever intrusive and encumbering means that are necessary. The other fork will pursue an interface that merges seamlessly with the rest of our environment.

For example, goggles are used in the NASA VIEW environment to display events in the artificial reality (see Fisher's chapter). A major problem with goggles is that they isolate people and therefore do not mix well with the other activities that take place in a work environment. In *Artificial Reality*, I suggested the possibility of glasses that can go from solipsistic to transparent simply by focusing through. However, even with such glasses the transition would certainly be jarring.

The Short-term Future

The more likely short-term trend for human interaction is toward the disintegration of the traditional user interface, which exists as an isolated function. We will no longer "go to the computer" and sit down. Instead, voice and gesture will free us from physical contact with the computer. Familiar devices, like pencils, will be acceptable as input devices as long as there are no wires. A computer presence will permeate the workplace and the home, available whenever a need is felt.

Fully comprehended natural language will not be necessary. Precise English is attempted only in legal contracts and is wholly inadequate for the programming task. However, it will be sufficient to operate applications. Consider the use of language among people who already understand each other. Incomplete sentences, jargon, and other shorthand abound. Communication is not limited to one-way commands. Clarifications are often requested. Much is anticipated and explanation is truncated. Language and gesture will be used in a very similar way, for when the domain is restricted and much is already understood, language can become verbal gesture (see the chapters by Brennan, Buxton, and Kurtenbach and Hulteen).

Artificial Reality

The important thing about artificial reality concepts is not so much whether they will be used immediately, but the fact that they bring more of the ultimate vocabulary of potential human-machine interface to the table. Use of the whole body, tactile and force feedback, and speech input and output are all part of that vocabulary. These concepts also introduce a host of new issues that must be considered.

The premise of an artificial reality is that our ability to interact physically with objects and spaces is an important aspect of our intellectual heritage. However, this physical metaphor is complex, existing on three levels.

On the first level, actions can be used as gesture commands that have no direct relationship to the physical context. For instance, both VIDEO-PLACE and the NASA VIEW system use an open hand to erase a drawing. These gestures are a departure from the intent of the physical metaphor and may be confused with it. Although they are useful when used sparingly, they require the user to learn a kind of sign language rather than just acting naturally.

On a second level, a gesture is recognized by the system as intending a physical action. For example, back and forth motions on the part of a person dangling from the end of a string are probably attempts to swing. The system responds in terms of simulated physics.

The third level, which has not yet been implemented, integrates the first two and accomplishes complete realization of the metaphor. It depends on a simulation so complete that there is no confusion, on the part of the user or the system, regarding what will happen if the user moves in a certain way in a given context.

Realism will be an interesting issue. We can be sure that there will be an initial desire to depict a realistic world. However, as we become more comfortable in our artificial realities, we may find that we want to introduce elements, for comfort or convenience, that have no antecedents in the real world (see Rheingold's chapter).

Artificial realities will have the same relationship to the real one that our homes have to the natural environment. Our homes are abstract spaces, partly defined by economics but primarily by our aesthetic sense. Similarly, artificial realities will be limited by our ability to adapt conceptually, but need not conform to physical reality any more than our homes mirror the outside environment. Physics will be employed if desired but may be turned off if it is not convenient.

Artificial reality will also be a composable medium and, as such, a new form of human expression and human experience. Even more than previous media, it will challenge our sense of reality philosophically and give us a new view of ourselves and existence. Just as is often the case with novels, plays, and television, we will not recognize that this new kind of experience is as real in its way as our other experience.

When judging user interfaces, our usual standard of goodness is the efficiency with which one can progress from point A to point B using the application. At some point we must recognize that our lives are spent in between. As more of our commercial and personal transactions are accomplished through computers, the quality of the experience provided by the computer interface has bearing on the quality of life itself. Therefore, the aesthetics of interaction will be as important as the efficiency.

Virtual Interface Environments

On the morning of July 29, 2001, Helen and Graham Lesh commuted to work in their accustomed manner. They got up from the breakfast table, kissed each other goodbye for the morning, and walked down the hall to their respective workspaces, where they slipped into their datasuits and donned their virtual environment headsets.

An outside observer would see Helen standing almost immobile in the center of her dimly lit space, making a series of fine movements with her hands. An outside observer would not be seeing the same environment that Helen saw, however. Helen, a plastic microsurgeon, found herself, as expected, in full sensory contact with her virtual operating theater: The bright white lights, the blue-garbed OR crew, and the phalanxes of equipment that surrounded them, looked and sounded exactly as they would in a real operation. Reaching for a scalpel, murmuring commands to her interface, Helen prepared for an hour of intensive rehearsal for the operation that would take place in the real, life-and-death operating theater at University Hospital the following day.

While Helen was zooming her view in on facial capillaries modeled on those of tomorrow's patient and etching virtual tissue a few hundred molecules at a time with a micromanipulated laser scalpel, Graham was in his workspace, trying to create a new pharmaceutical. An outside observer would think that Graham was miming a wrestling match with himself, or recapitulating his infancy, for Graham was on all fours, his

Scott S. Fisher

Aerospace Human Factors Division
NASA Ames Research Center

Figure 1: The user's end of the NASA Ames Virtual Environment Workstation with head-coupled, stereoscopic display and DataGloves for virtual object manipulation. Photo courtesy of NASA.

head aimed at a point in space near one corner of the workspace. In Graham's reality, he was crawling around a complex molecule, reaching for other molecules and trying to fit them together, like a kind of dynamic tinkertoy.

For the time being, Graham and Helen are fictitious, but they are using perfectly plausible technological descendants of the virtual environment display systems that have been developed over the past four years at NASA's Ames Research Center in the Aerospace Human Factors Research Division [Fisher et al., 1986,1987,1988].[1]

Here, in fact, there is a graphic simulation of a hemoglobin molecule that a person can fly through and move around in physically, as if reduced to molecular size. A head-mounted, wide-angle, stereoscopic display system controlled by operator position, voice, and gesture has been developed for use as a multipurpose, multimodal interface environment (figure 1). The

[1] The principal project team at NASA is C. Coler, S. Fisher, M. McGreevy, W. Robinett, and E. Wenzel. At Sterling Software: S. Bryson, J. Humphries, R. Jacoby, D. Kaiser, D. Kerr, and P. Stone.

system provides a multisensory, interactive display environment in which a user can virtually explore a 360-degree synthesized or remotely sensed environment and can viscerally interact with its components. Our objective has been to develop a new kind of interface that would be very closely matched to human sensory and cognitive capabilities. The effect of immersing one's sensoria in even the crudest prototypes of these interfaces has led many who have experienced it to refer to the experience as a kind of *virtual reality*. We prefer to use the term *virtual environment* to emphasize the ability to completely immerse a subject in a simulated space with its attendant realities.

A Bit of History: The Evolution of Personal Simulation and Telepresence Environments

Matching visual display technology as closely as possible to human cognitive and sensory capabilities in order to better represent "real" experience has been a major ambition for research and industry for decades. One example is the development of stereoscopic movies in the early 1950s, in which a perception of depth was created by presenting a slightly different image to each eye of the viewer. In competition with that during the same era was Cinerama, which involved three different projectors presenting a wide field of view display to the audience. Because the size of the projected image was extended, the viewer's peripheral field of view was also engaged. More recently, along the same lines, the Omnimax projection system situates the audience under a huge hemispherical dome, and the film image is predistorted and projected on the dome; the audience is now almost immersed in an image surround.

The idea of sitting inside an image has been used in the field of aerospace simulation for many decades to train pilots and astronauts to safely control complex, expensive vehicles through simulated mission environments. More recently, this technology has been adapted for entertainment and educational use. "Tour of the Universe" in Toronto and "Star Tours" at Disneyland are among the first entertainment applications of simulation technology and virtual display environments; about 40 people sit in a room on top of a motion platform that moves in synch with a computer-generated and model-based image display of a ride through a simulated universe.

The technology has been moving gradually toward lower-cost personal simulation environments in which viewers are also able to control their own viewpoint or motion through a virtual environment. An early example of this is the Aspen Movie Map, done by the M.I.T. Architecture Machine Group in the late 1970s [Lippman, 1980]. Imagery of the town of Aspen, Colorado was shot with a special camera system mounted on top of a car, filming down every street and around every corner in town, combined with shots above town from cranes, helicopters, and airplanes and also with

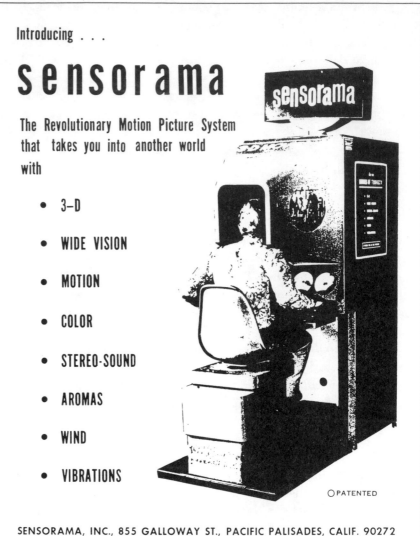
Figure 2: "Sensorama" — A multi sensory simulation environment developed by Morton Heilig. Invented and produced by Morton L. Heilig.

shots inside buildings. The Movie Map gave the operators the capability of sitting in front of a touch-sensitive display screen and driving through the town of Aspen at their own rate, taking any route they chose, by touching the screen, indicating what turns they wanted to make and what buildings they wanted to enter. In one configuration, this was set up so that the operator was surrounded by front, back, and side-looking camera imagery so that, again, they were completely immersed in a virtual environment.

Another notable virtual environment developed for entertainment applications was "Sensorama" (figure 2). This was an elegant prototype of an arcade game designed by Morton Heilig in the mid-1960s and one of the first examples of a multisensory simulation environment that provided more than just visual input. When you put your head up to a binocular viewing optics system, you saw a first-person-viewpoint, stereo-film-loop of a motorcycle ride through New York City and you heard three-dimensional binaural sound that gave you sounds of the city of New York and of the motorcycle moving through it. As you leaned your arms on the handlebar platform built into the prototype and sat in the seat, simulated vibration cues were presented. The prototype also had a fan for wind simulation that combined with a chemical smell bank to blow simulated smells in your face.

Conceptual versions of virtual environments have been described by science fiction writers for many decades. One concept has been called *telepresence*, a technology that would allow remotely situated operators to receive enough sensory feedback to feel like they are really at a remote location and are able to do different kinds of tasks. Arthur Clarke has described "personalized television safaris" in which the operator could virtually explore remote environments without danger or discomfort. Heinlein's "waldoes" were similar, but were able to exaggerate certain sensory capabilities so that the operator could, for example, control a huge robot. Since 1950, technology has gradually been developed to make telepresence a reality. Research continues at other laboratories, such as the Naval Ocean Systems Center in Hawaii and MITI's Tele-existence Project in Tsukuba, Japan, to develop improved systems to help humans operate safely and effectively in hazardous environments such as undersea or outerspace.

One of the first attempts at developing a telepresence visual system was done by the Philco Corporation in 1958. With this system, an operator could see an image from a remote camera on a CRT mounted on his head in front of his eyes and could control the camera's viewpoint by moving his head [Comeau, 1961]. A variation of the head-mounted display concept was done by Ivan Sutherland in the late 1960s, first at M.I.T.'s Draper Lab in Cambridge, Massachusetts and then later at the University of Utah [Sutherland, 1968]. This helmet-mounted display had a see-through capability so that computer-generated graphics could be viewed superimposed onto the real environment. As the viewer moved around, the computer-generated objects would appear to be stable within that real environment and could be manipulated with various input devices (figure 3).

The Virtual Environment Workstation project at NASA Ames (VIEW) is based upon yet another kind of helmet-mounted display technology and, in addition, provides auditory, speech, and gesture interaction within a virtual environment.

Figure 3: Don Vickers wearing the University of Utah Head-Mounted Display. Photo courtesy of Technology Information Systems Program, Lawrence Livermore National Laboratory.

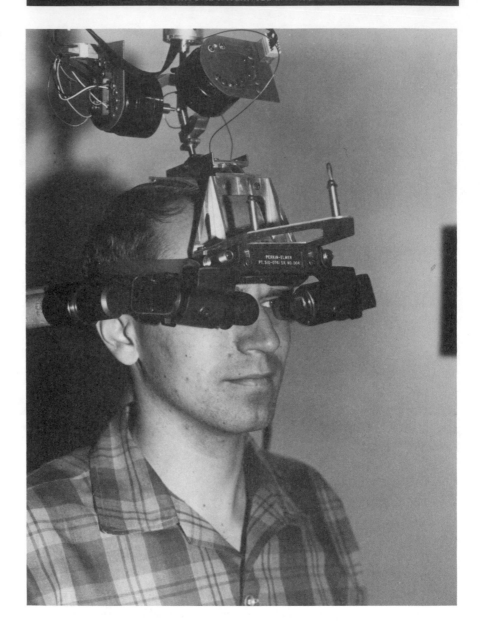

The Ames Virtual Environment Workstation

The first virtual environment display system developed at Ames was literally a motorcycle helmet with a visor attachment containing two small liquid crystal display screens of 100-by-100-pixel resolution. Several iterations of this first prototype have resulted in a much lighter, less claustrophobic headset, with a long-term goal of designing a visor-like display package worn on the head. We are currently assembling five versions of this third prototype for use in various research environments (figure 4). Included on the headset is a microphone for connected speech recognition, earphones for 3-D sound cueing, and a head-tracking device, as well as the package to hold the LCD display screens and viewing optics for each eye.

The liquid crystal display screens are inexpensive, flat panel displays that draw very little power and that have been used specifically for safety reasons and for their lightness. The current resolution is 640 pixels by 220 pixels. These transmissive displays accept a standard NTSC video signal and require some form of backlighting. In the first version, an LED backlight array was used, and, currently, very bright, miniature fluorescent tubes are being used. Another key part of the display is the very wide-angle optics through which the liquid crystal displays are viewed. The objective is to present a wide-angle field of view that closely matches human binocular visual capabilities rather than just a small window into this 3-D world. These optics allow the displays to completely fill your visual field of view, thus helping to achieve a sense of presence in the 3-D virtual environment.

On the helmet is a tracking device that tells the host computer where you're looking within the three-dimensional virtual environment. We're now using an electromagnetic device that measures where the head is within a magnetic field emitted by a source. Azimuth elevation and roll information of the head is combined with XYZ position at a resolution of .03 inch and .10 degree accuracy. When this information is received by the host computer, it's sent to the graphics system or remote camera system so that, as you turn your head, the new position is recorded and a new image that matches that position of regard is displayed. As you turn your head, new

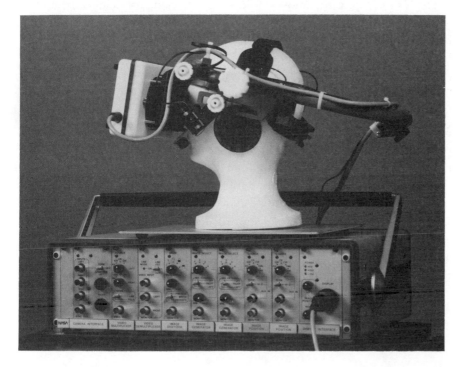

Figure 4: Head-mounted wide-angle, stereoscopic display and electronics support with microphone for speech recognition and headphones for three-dimensional sound cues developed at NASA Ames Research Center. Photo courtesy of NASA.

images are being drawn so quickly that you feel like you're completely immersed in the virtual environment. Another sensing technology that we're investigating may provide the ability to track eye position in order to display a three-dimensional cursor within this environment. Eye-tracking will tell us where your eyes are converged in three-dimensional space so that, for example, you'll be able to trigger menus with your eyes; we'll also be able to present different kinds of depth-of-field information, which is yet another depth cue that has been lacking in typical simulation display systems to date.

Virtual environments in the Ames system are synthesized with 3-D computer-generated imagery, or are remotely sensed by user-controlled, stereoscopic video camera configurations. The computer image system enables high-performance, real-time 3-D graphics presentation at resolutions of 640 by 480 and 1,000 by 1,000 pixels. This imagery is generated at rates up to 30 frames per second as required to update image viewpoints in coordination with head and limb motion. Dual independent, synchronized display channels are used to present disparate imagery to each eye of the viewer for true stereoscopic depth cues. For real-time video input of remote environments, two miniature CCD video cameras are used to provide stereoscopic imagery. Development and evaluation of several head-coupled, remote camera platform and gimbal prototypes is in progress to determine optimal hardware and control configurations for remotely controlled, free-flying, or telerobot-mounted camera systems.

As this display technology evolved to give a feeling of being surrounded by virtual objects or being inside a virtual environment, we also began to develop means of interacting with that virtual world—of literally reaching in and touching the virtual objects, picking them up, interacting with virtual control panels, etc. Earlier research in this area had been done for various applications that required manipulation of remote objects with reasonable dexterity and feedback to the operator. For example, in 1954, Ralph Mosher at General Electric developed the "Handyman" system—a complicated exoskeleton around the operator's arm that was used to control a remote robotic arm device. Although operationally useful, this control system was rather large and unportable.

We were interested in getting away from such an invasive device and in 1985 contracted VPL Research, Inc. to develop a "dataglove"—a lightweight, flexible glove instrumented with flex-sensing devices to measure the amount of bend of each joint of the fingers and the amount of abduction, the splay between fingers [Fisher, 1986] (figure S in the color insert).[2]

Information from the glove is transmitted to the host computer to represent what the hand is doing at any moment. In the current, commercially

---

[2] The principal project team at VPL was T. Zimmerman, C. Blanchard, S. Bryson, and J. Grimaud.

available DataGlove, the amount of bend is measured by light attenuation within fiber optic bundles covering the fingers, and magnetic tracking devices give absolute position and orientation of the hand within the 3-D space. Position and orientation combined with the finger bend is used to control a graphic model of the hand in the virtual environment or to control a remote robot hand. With this capability the user can pick up and manipulate virtual objects that appear in the surrounding virtual environment [Foley, 1987]. We've also programmed the dataglove so that gestures can be recognized, similar to American sign language. The operator can make a particular gesture and the host will recognize it as user input to trigger a particular command or subroutine. For example, pointing with one finger moves your viewpoint through the computer-generated environment as if you were flying through that space, with the distance between your finger and your body determining your velocity; making a fist lets you grab different objects; and using a three-finger point invokes a menu floating in visual space that you can then use to choose other subroutines or information displays. In actual use, operators can design their own set of gestures as preferred (figure 5).

Additional work in progress for the glove will provide the capability for tactile feedback. An array of very small solenoid actuators has been assembled that will present a sense of texture as you touch a virtual object and, for example, if you're touching an edge of a virtual cube, as you intersect the edge of the cube, one line of the array of solenoids is triggered to present some sense of edgeness. In future scenarios, detailed virtual environment databases or tactile sensors on remote robot end-effectors will transmit tactile information to arrays such as this integrated in the DataGlove. A further requirement for tactile feedback to the operator is force reflection, through which some sense of solidity and surface boundaries of virtual objects is communicated back to the operator. Now, if the hand is closed on a virtual object, the fingers will pass right through the object. Interim solutions include the use of auditory feedback to the operator to indicate contact with and forces applied to virtual objects. In the longer term, technology is required that will constrain the user's fingers so that they will close only to the outside boundary of that virtual object; eventually, full arm and body interaction will need to be enabled.

The auditory channel is another major part of our sensory input and display research. The auditory display in the VIEW project is capable of presenting a wide variety of binaural sounds to the user via headphones using sound-synthesis technology developed for music synthesizers. The primary function of this display is to provide both discrete and dynamic auditory cues to augment or supply information missing from the visual or gestural displays. For example, discrete sound cues can signal contact between telerobot end-effectors and target objects; alert the operator to attend

Figure 5. Various gestures can be used for system commands or interaction with virtual objects in the Ames Virtual Environment Workstation. Photos courtesy of NASA.

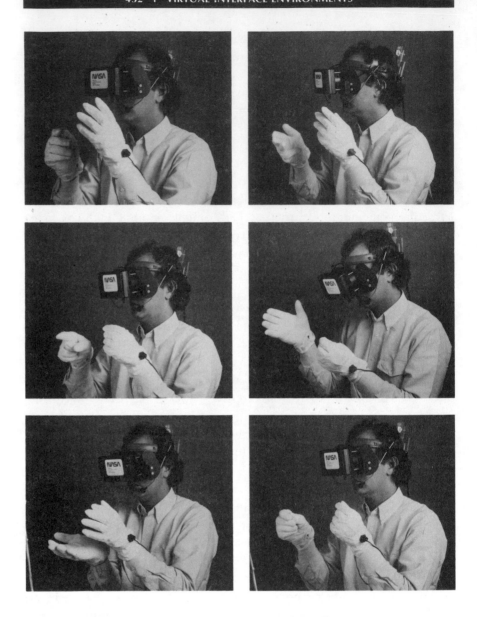

to information in a data window that is currently out of the field of view; or indicate successful recognition of a hand gesture. Similarly, auditory parameters can be dynamically modulated and coordinated with the other subsystem displays to represent, for example, the relative positions of other objects moving within the virtual environment. In the real world, we also have a very good sense of where sounds are coming from around us. Additional research at Ames has developed an auditory display prototype called the Convolvotron that is capable of synthetically generating three-dimensional sound cues in realtime. These cues are presented via headphones and are perceived outside of the user's head at a discrete distance and direction in the 3-D space surrounding the user. When it is integrated into the VIEW system, the position of the operator can be monitored in real-time and the information used to maintain up to four localized sound cues in fixed positions or in motion trajectories relative to the user. This capability will further aid the operator's situational awareness by augmenting spatial information from the visual display and providing navigational and cueing aids from outside the field of view [Wenzel et al., 1988].

The VIEW system also includes commercially available, speaker-dependent, connected speech-recognition technology that allows the user to give voice input in a natural, conversational format that cannot be achieved with highly constrained discrete word recognition systems or through keyboard input. Typical speech-mediated interactions are requests for display/report of system status, instructions for supervisory control tasks, and verbal commands to change interface mode or configuration. Taken together, the capabilities of the Virtual Environment Display system described enable a wide range of applications.

Applications

SPACE AND TELEPRESENCE

This system has been developed primarily for space applications, and will be used as a tool for the design, development and evaluation of user interface requirements for different NASA missions, such as the Space Station scheduled for launch in the mid-1990s. One of the unique interface requirements in this environment will be to allow an operator on board to remotely control semi-autonomous robots outside the station. If the robot encounters a task beyond its programmed ability, an astronaut would be alerted to take over control in telepresence mode. Using the Virtual Environment Workstation, the robot's camera system would provide stereo images to the operator's head-mounted display while precisely miming his head movements, and the robot's dexterous end-effectors would be controlled by dataglove gestures (figure 6). The astronaut would receive a sufficient quantity and quality of sensory feedback to feel present at the remote task site and would be able to carry out repairs or detailed inspections as if he were actually there [Fisher et al., 1987].

NAVIGATING INFORMATION-SPACE

It's more likely that most of an astronaut's time in a highly automated Space Station environment will be spent in a "supervisory" control mode: monitoring the structure's subsystems, communications, and science activities, as well as monitoring external activities like spacecraft docking or working robots. User interface requirements for these tasks are more closely related to information management than remote manipulation and pose a

Figure 6: Virtual interface environment for telepresence and telerobot control. Picture courtesy of NASA.

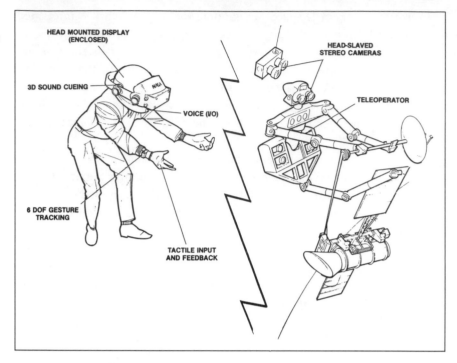

formidable challenge to interface design. To meet these needs, control environments have been proposed that require over 200 different control panels with more than 3,000 display and control elements for all of them. One problem is that none of the workstations will necessarily have the same control language or the same input requirements. This would obligate users to learn different input sequences for all the different workstations.

With the Virtual Environment Workstation, we are developing a capability for users to interact with a virtual representation of these control panels as a more efficient alternative to a hardware-based control station requiring maintenance and spare part inventory. The main objective is to develop a kind of generic workspace in which the interface can be tuned specifically to an operator's skill and training and can be easily reconfigurable for different tasks as required [Fisher et al., 1986, 1988].

Ken Knowlton, while working for Bell Labs, developed one of the first virtual information environments [Knowlton, 1977]. He built a virtual workspace for the phone operators who had complex tasks to do that required a changing keypad configuration as they went through their work. The display that he developed was a half-silvered mirror placed above a blank keyboard. Above that, a monitor displayed computer graphic key overlays so that as the operators looked into the half-silvered mirror, they'd see virtual keypad labels spatially correspondent with the keyboard and could also see their hands, working the keyboard. This device was also a virtual space that could be reconfigured depending on what the operator

Figure 7: Telepresence in Dataspace with the Ames Virtual Environment Workstation. Picture courtesy of NASA.

needed to see and do for a particular task. Later, at M.I.T., a modified version of Knowlton's display was built using the same configuration, without a keyboard in it. By using a six-degree-of-freedom tracking device and stereo viewing glasses, the user could actually draw in three-space, manipulate the objects he had drawn, and literally configure a limited virtual world [Schmandt, 1983] (see figure T in the color insert).

The current virtual environment research at Ames is an attempt to extend this cubic meter of virtual workspace to a complete virtual information surround. One of the first implementations of this virtual information environment enables users to literally (verbally) call up windows of information, use the glove to grasp the windows, move them around, and anchor them in virtual space and then interact with virtual control panels as they would with a real control panel (figure 7). Another piece of technology in development for this particular configuration of dataspace gives us the ability to insert live video windows in combination with the computer-generated world in order to present a mix of computer-generated background and live video from a remote camera, from videodisc, or from video tape. These windows can be formatted as any size that the operator requests or chooses and then can be placed within that environment.

In part, this concept is a three-dimensional extension of a unique interface developed in the mid-1970s at M.I.T.'s Architecture Machine Group in Cambridge, Massachusetts, called the "Spatial Data Management System" [Herot, 1980; Negroponte, 1981]. The prototype SDMS presented a whole wall of video information to the user, who sees an 8 1/2'-by-12' rear-projected video image of what was called *dataland*. To the operator's left is a touch-sensitive monitor that shows an overview of dataland. On the right is a touch-sensitive monitor that shows a table of contents of various ports of information that you can dive into in dataland. The operator sits in a chair instrumented with very small joysticks and touch pads on each arm of the chair so that he can literally helicopter above dataland and then drop into each port of information, depending on what task he needs to do. The Virtual Environment Workstation takes this from a two-dimensional, or two-and-a-half-dimensional, representation of dataspace, into a full, three-dimensional surround of information, where the operator literally flies through dataspace. This system provides a unique interface as well as a research tool to evaluate this and many other possible graphic representations of multidimensional data and information.

Another potential application of virtual dataspace involves the development of a portable information environment for an astronaut working outside of a spacecraft. With the ability to display imagery on the transparent visor of a spacesuit helmet, complex tasks such as maintenance or repair of a satellite could be aided by presentation of virtual information windows. On request, the operator could have access to detailed part schematics or dynamic repair scenarios that could be placed in virtual space near the work site for reference when needed or even superimposed on the site itself.

PERSONAL SIMULATION: ARCHITECTURE, MEDICINE, ENTERTAINMENT

In addition to remote manipulation and information management tasks, the VIEW system also may be a viable interface for several commercial applications. So far, the system has been used to develop simple architectural simulations that enable the operator to design a very small 3-D model of a space, and then, using a glove gesture, scale the model to life size, allowing the architect/operator to literally walk around in the designed space. A similar design application has been developed specifically to help engineers better visualize complex three-dimensional phenomena such as air flow over a wing surface or fuel flow through a rocket engine. In these scenarios, the operator can walk around in the three-dimensional data representations and literally get inside the vortex of turbulence or fly through the particle flow. A next step will be to use the datagloves as realtime interactive design tools to provide an aeronautical designer with the ability to change the shape of an airplane wing and then look at the change in flow turbulence in real time. Seismic data, molecular models, and meteorological data are other examples of multidimensional data that may be better understood through representation and interaction in a virtual environment.

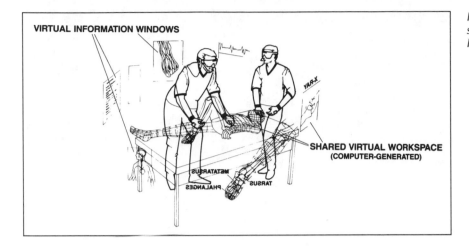

Figure 8: A virtual interface for surgical simulation and training. Picture courtesy of NASA.

Another virtual environment scenario in progress involves the development of a surgical simulator for medical students and plastic surgeons that could be used much as a flight simulator is used to train jet pilots. As the pilot can literally explore situations that would be dangerous to encounter in the real world, surgeons can use a simulated "electronic cadaver" to do pre-op planning and patient analysis. The system is also set up in such a way that surgical students can look through the eyes of a senior surgeon and see a first-person view of the way he or she is doing a particular procedure. As illustrated in figure 8, the surgeon can be surrounded with the kinds of information windows that are typically seen in an operating room in the form of monitors displaying life support status information and x-rays. Eventually, this technology will evolve to a capability for doing remote surgery or microsurgery, where the operator could use this kind of interface to control a micromanipulator doing, for example, brain surgery. Using the gloves to control the micromanipulator, the motion of the hand can be adjusted so that a very gross motion of the operator's hand can be scaled down to a very small motion of the micromanipulator while viewing a stereo image from a binocular microscope or miniature telerobot camera.

Entertainment and educational applications of this technology could be developed through this ability to simulate a wide range of real or fantasy environments with almost infinite possibilities of scale and extent. The user can be immersed in a 360-degree fantasy adventure game (figure 9) as easily as he or she can viscerally explore a virtual 3-D model of the solar system or use a three-dimensional paint system to create virtual environments for others to explore.

TELECOLLABORATION

A major near-term goal for the Virtual Environment Workstation Project is to connect at least two of the current prototype interface systems to a common virtual environment database. The two users will participate and

Figure 9: *Visceral interaction in a multimodal virtual environment. Photo courtesy of NASA.*

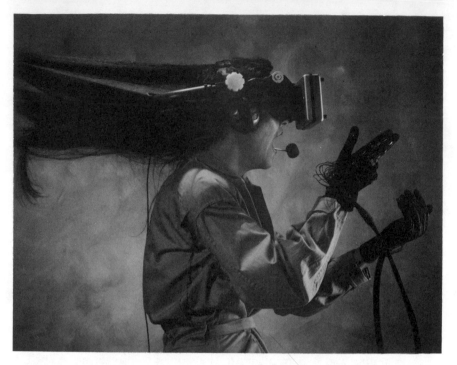

interact in a shared virtual environment, but each will view it from their relative, spatially disparate viewpoints. The objective is to provide a collaborative workspace in which remotely located participants can virtually interact with some of the nuances of face-to-face meetings while also having access to their personal dataspace facility. This could enable valuable interaction between scientists collaborating from different locations across the country or even between astronauts on a space station and research labs on Earth. With full body tracking capability, it would also be possible for users to be represented in this space by life-size virtual representations of themselves in whatever form they choose—a kind of electronic persona. For interactive theater or interactive fantasy applications, these styles might range from fantasy figures to inanimate objects, or different figures to different people. Eventually, telecommunication networks may develop that will be configured with virtual environment servers for users to dial into remotely in order to interact with other virtual proxies.

Although the current prototype of the Virtual Environment Workstation has been developed primarily to be used as a laboratory facility, the components have been designed to be easily replicable for relatively low cost. As the processing power and graphics frame rate on microcomputers quickly increases, portable, personal virtual environment systems will also become available. The possibilities of virtual realities, it appears, are as limitless as the possibilities of reality. They can provide a human interface that disappears—a doorway to other worlds.

Through the Looking Glass

TODAY'S FASCINATION with "user interfaces" is an artifact of how we currently operate computers—with screens, keyboards, and pointing devices—just as job control languages grew from punched card batch systems. Near-term technological developments promise to replace contemporary user interfaces with something very different.

John Walker

Autodesk, Inc.

User Interaction Generations

From the users' standpoint, how they interact with the computer is an issue surpassingly more important than what the computer is built from. Let's try to redefine computer generations in terms of modalities of operation.

Generation	Means of Operation
First	Plugboards, dedicated set-up
Second	Punched card batch, RJE
Third	Teletype timesharing
Fourth	Menu systems
Fifth	Graphical controls, windows

FIRST GENERATION: KNOBS AND DIALS

By this reckoning, ENIAC and the tabulating equipment that preceded it were first-generation systems—set up to solve specific problems by specialists with detailed and precise knowledge of the operation of the hardware.

Many of the popular images of computers in the 1950s—the computer stretching from floor to ceiling, covered with knobs, dials, and oscilloscope screens, attended by mad scientists—derive from the reality of first-generation operation. In the first generation, the user went one-on-one with the computer, in the computer room, operating the computer at the switch and knob level. Because the user was the operator of the machine and controlled it with little or no abstraction, there was essentially no mediation between the computer and its expert user.

SECOND GENERATION: BATCH

After ENIAC, virtually all general-purpose digital computers were programmable without hardware reconfiguration. Even though until late in the 1950s most programming was done in machine language, requiring detailed knowledge of the hardware, the machine could be turned from task to task as rapidly as new programs could be loaded into memory. Computers built from vacuum tubes or discrete transistors were so expensive that extensive efforts were devoted to maximizing the productivity of a computer. As the 1950s waned, the original model of computer usage—an individual user signing up for dedicated time on the machine—was supplanted by the batch shop, with a specialist computer operator running a stack of jobs.

The user's image of the computer during the second generation often revolved around a countertop. It was across the counter that the users handed the card deck containing their programs and data, and across the same counter that, some time later, their cards would return, accompanied by a print-out they hoped would contain the desired result (but more often consisted of a cryptic error message or the Dreaded Core Dump).

Second-generation operation introduced many important levels of mediation and abstractions between the user and the computer hardware. First and probably most important was the time shifting performed by a batch system and the autonomy this gave to the computer (or its operator) at the expense of the user's direct control. Because the computer did the user's bidding without an opportunity for user intervention, time limits, resource scheduling, recovery from unanticipated errors, and the like became a shared responsibility of the user and the autonomous computer operating system.

This led to the development of job control languages, which provided a powerful (though often arcane) means of controlling the destiny of a task being performed by the computer without the user's involvement. The card deck, print-out, countertop, and job control language form the heart of the user's view of a second-generation system.

THIRD GENERATION: TIMESHARING

Throughout the second-generation period, operating system technology progressed toward the goal of squeezing more and more performance from computers. Because many programs did not use the full capacity of the computer, but rather spent much of their time reading and writing much slower peripheral devices, operating systems were eventually generalized to allow concurrent execution of multiple jobs, initially in the hope of maximizing the usage of scarce CPU and memory resources, and later with subsidiary goals, such as providing more responsive service for small tasks while larger jobs were underway.

If a computer's time could be sliced or shared among a small number of batch jobs, why couldn't it be chopped into much smaller slices and spread among a much larger community of interactive users? This observation, and a long-standing belief that the productivity of computer users (as opposed to the productivity of the computer itself) would be optimized by conversational interaction with the computer, led to the development of timesharing systems in the 1960s.

Timesharing promised all things to all people. To the computer owner it promised efficient use of computing power by making available a statistical universe of demands on the computing resource which would mop up every last CPU cycle and core-second. It promised batch users the same service they had before, plus the ability to compose their jobs interactively and monitor their progress on-line. And it offered interactive, conversational interaction with the computer to a new class of users.

The interactive character device, whether a slow printing terminal such as a teletype, or an ASCII "glass teletype" running at speeds of up to 960 characters per second, led to the development of conversational computing. The user types a line of input to the computer, which immediately processes it and responds with a reply (perhaps as simple as a prompt indicating it's ready for the next line). The conversational mode of interaction was the Turing test made real—the users "conversed" with the computer, just as they might with another human on a teletype-to-teletype connection.

FOURTH GENERATION: MENUS

Although conversational systems broadened the accessibility of computers, they still fell far short of the goal of making computers accessible to a large segment of the populace. The development of fast alphanumeric terminals (1,000 characters per second and up) made it possible to present large amounts of information to the user almost instantaneously. This allowed the computer to present the user with a "menu" of choices, from which selections could be made simply by pressing one or two keys.

Menu command selection, coupled with data entry modeled on filling in a form, rapidly became the standard for application systems intended to be operated by non-computer-specialists. Hundreds of thousands of people spend their entire working day operating systems of this design, although people who have studied how users actually learn and use these systems, in applications ranging from credit card transaction entry to targeting tactical nuclear weapons, often find that users see them in a very different way than the designers intended—frequently moving from menu to menu by rote learning of keystroke sequences, leaving the carefully crafted menus unread.

FIFTH GENERATION: GRAPHICS

When monolithic integrated circuits drove down the cost of computer memory, full-screen raster graphics moved from a laboratory curiosity or specialized component of high-end systems to something that could be imagined as an integral part of every computer. Alan Kay and others at the Learning Research Group at the Xerox Palo Alto Research Center saw that this development, along with development of fast, inexpensive processors, data networks, and object-oriented programming techniques, could lead to the development of totally new ways of interaction with computers. In the mid-1970s they explored the potential of these technologies on the Alto computer with the Smalltalk language.

Being able to express interaction with a computer on a two-dimensional graphics screen allows many metaphors that can be only vaguely approximated with earlier technologies. The screen can be turned into a desktop, complete with pieces of paper that can be shuffled (windows), accessories (tools), and resources (applications). The provision of a pointing device such as a mouse allows direct designation of objects on a screen without the need to type in names or choose from menus as in earlier systems. This property has caused such systems to be referred to as direct manipulation systems. For example, file directories can be displayed as file folders on a screen, each folder containing a number of documents. If users wish to move a document from one directory to another, they need only grasp it with the pointing device and drag it from one folder to another.

In addition, the availability of a graphics screen allows much more expressive means of controlling programs and better visual fidelity to the ultimate application of the computer. When documents are edited, font changes can actually be shown on the screen. Controls that would otherwise have to be expressed as command names or numbers can be shown as slider bars, meter faces, bar or line charts, or in any other form suited to the information being presented.

It is ironic that five generations of user interaction with computers have brought us back to the starting point. Users of the first computers had dedicated access to the computer and direct control over its operation. The development of personal computers has placed the computer back in the user's hands as a dedicated machine, and event-driven interaction that places the user in immediate command of the computer's operation restores the direct control over the computer that disappeared when the user was banished from the computer room in the second generation. Use of graphics to express operating parameters is even restoring to computer applications the appearance of the computer control panels of the first generation, replete with meters, squiggly lines moving across charts, and illuminated buttons. This isn't to say we haven't come a long way—the meters on a Univac I console read out things like the temperature of the mercury delay line memories, and the switches allowed the user to preset bits in the accumulator. Today's displays and controls generally affect high-level parameters inside applications and allow the user, for example, to vary the degree of smoothing of a surface patch by moving a slider bar while watching a three-dimensional shaded image change on the screen.

What Next?

In the last forty years we've taken the computer user, who was initially in direct control of a dedicated computer, operating it by switches and gazing at huge arrays of blinking lights, to greater and greater distances from the computer and direct interaction with it, then back again to contemplating a virtual control panel on a glowing screen filled with slide pots, radio buttons, meters, all providing direct and expressive control over what's going on inside the computer. It appears that we've finally reached the end of the road—individuals have at their fingertips, for no more than the price of an automobile, dedicated computing power in excess of what existed in the world in 1960, with applications carefully tailored to provide intuitive control of the powerful tasks they perform, and a growing ability to move between applications at will, combining them as needed to address whatever work the user needs done.

It's interesting to observe the extent to which the term *user interface* has emerged as a marketing and, more recently, legal battleground following the introduction and growing acceptance of fifth-generation user interaction. Many people would probably fail to identify anything before a fourth-generation menu system as a "user interface" at all.

I believe that conversation is the wrong model for dealing with a computer—a model that misleads inexperienced users and invites even experienced software designers to build hard-to-use systems. When you're interacting with a computer, you are not conversing with another person. You are exploring another world.

The problem is that once a programmer has created a world intended for use by others, some poor user has to wander into it, armed only with the sword of his wits, the shield of The Manual, and whatever experience in other similar worlds he or she may have painfully gleaned, then try to figure out the rules. The timeless popularity of adventure games seems to indicate that at least some people enjoy such challenges, but it's much easier to exult in the discovery that the shiny stones cause the trolls to disappear when exploring the Cave of Befuddlement than finally to learn that only if you do a preview will the page breaks be recalculated correctly for the printer when the boss is waiting for the new forecast spreadsheet.

If what's inside the computer is a world instead of another person, then we should be looking at lowering the barriers that separate the user from the world he's trying to explore rather than at how to carry on a better conversation. Let's look at the barriers that characterize each generation of user interaction:

Generation	Barrier
First	Front panel
Second	Countertop
Third	Terminal
Fourth	Menu hierarchy
Fifth	Screen

Now we're at the threshold of the next revolution in user-computer interaction: a technology that will take the user through the screen into the world "inside" the computer—a world in which the user can interact with three-dimensional objects whose fidelity will grow as computing power increases and display technology progresses. This virtual world can be whatever the designer makes it. As designers and users explore entirely new experiences and modes of interaction, they will be jointly defining the next generation of user interaction with computers.

Through the Screen to Cyberspace

To move beyond the current generation of graphics screen and mouse, to transport the user through the screen into the computer, we need hardware and software that provide the user a three-dimensional simulacrum of a world and that allow interaction in ways that mimic interaction with real-world objects. *Cyberspace* means a three-dimensional domain in which cybernetic feedback and control occur.

I define a cyberspace system as one that provides users a three-dimensional interaction experience that includes the illusion they are inside a world rather than observing an image. At the minimum, a cyberspace system provides stereoscopic imagery of three-dimensional objects, sensing the user's head position and rapidly updating the perceived scene. In addition, a cyberspace system provides a means of interacting with simulated objects. The richness and fidelity of a cyberspace system can be extended by providing better three-dimensional imagery, sensing the user's pupil direction, providing motion cues and force feedback, generating sound from simulated sources, and further approximating reality almost without bounds.

The idea of transporting users in some fashion into a computer and allowing them to interact directly with a virtual world has been extensively explored in science fiction. Fredrick Pohl's later Heechee books, writers of the "cyberpunk" genre such as William Gibson and Rudy Rucker, and movies including *Tron* have explored what we will find and what we will become when we enter these worlds of our own creation. It's no wonder the idea of entering a computer world is so fascinating—it is the ultimate realization of what fiction has been striving for since sagas of the hunt were told around Paleolithic campfires. The images that prose and poetry create in the mind, that the theatre enacts on stage, that motion pictures and television (aided by special effects) bring to millions, through the cyberspace interface paradigm not only can be given three-dimensional substance but also can be made interactive, replacing passive viewing with active participation.

Ivan Sutherland, who invented so much of what we now consider commonplace in the computer graphics industry, realized in the 1960s that using two small CRTs to provide stereoscopic images to the eyes and sensing head position to compute the viewpoint was the way to three-dimensional realism. In 1968, Sutherland built a helmet with two CRTs, attached to the ceiling with a set of linkages and shaft encoders to determine head position [Sutherland]. This contraption, called the "Sword of Damocles" because of all the hardware dangling above the user's cranial vault, really had only one serious flaw—it was twenty years ahead of its time in the computer power required to make it practical.

Now that fast CPUs and special-purpose graphics hardware have made real-time generation of realistic 3-D images widely available at reasonable cost, and every expectation is that the ongoing trend of increasing performance at decreasing cost will soon bring that power to personal computers, the technological groundwork is in place to bring Sutherland's prototype into the mainstream of computer graphics. As Scott Fisher describes it in another chapter of this volume, the "Virtual Environment Display System" created by the group at NASA Ames is the first modern cyberspace system [Fisher et al.].

Building Cyberspace

Exploring cyberspace requires specialized hardware and software. To provide the illusion of being within cyberspace, the system should provide a stereoscopic image that tracks head position. A system that does this can be built by using two small video monitors mounted on a helmet the user wears. Affixed to the helmet is a head-tracking device, such as the Polhemus Navigator (made by a subsidiary of McDonnell Douglas), which provides eighth-inch position and quarter-degree angular accuracy without attached wires.

The video displays can be fabricated from components salvaged from LCD pocket televisions, or camcorder viewfinders can be used as-is. (The current NASA design uses custom displays to achieve a wide field of view, but their first prototype used commercial LCD displays). Each monitor is attached to a separate graphics controller that renders the view of the three-dimensional model of the world from that eye's viewpoint, updating the display as the head translates and rotates.

One could configure an initial experimental cyberspace system using, for example, two personal computers as rendering engines, fed a three-dimensional model created with AutoCAD or AutoSolid by a control computer that monitors head position and sends viewpoint updates to the rendering engines.

For user interaction with the cyberspace environment, one could use the VPL DataGlove, which, with available software, allows recognition of commands from hand gestures and, with a Polhemus navigator attached to the glove, pointing and grasping of objects in cyberspace. Other input devices such as joysticks and foot pedals could also be explored. The entire hardware complement needed for this initial cyberspace exploration and demonstration system would cost less than $15,000 (not counting the control computer, which would not be dedicated to the system in any case) and could easily be transported and set up wherever required. This system is so simple and transportable that I call it "cyberspace in a briefcase." Improving the realism of cyberspace systems can use all of the capacity of the next several generations of graphics hardware (while being useful even with currently affordable products).

For initial explorations of cyberspace, software should consist of a toolkit that allows rapid prototyping of cyberspace environments. Because cyberspace is so new and the fundamentals of how one should interact with it remain to be discovered, we should attempt to prescribe as little of the interaction as possible in the toolkit itself, but make it easy for those who use the kit to define their own environments.

Initial cyberspace environments will literally represent three-dimensional models. Because cyberspace is the most natural way to work in three dimensions, we expect that three-dimensional design will be the first major application area for cyberspace systems. But as William Gibson says, "The street finds its own uses for things." Just as AutoCAD has been applied to many tasks well outside the traditional bounds of the "CAD market," cyberspace can be expected to grow rapidly in unanticipated directions. If video games are movies that involve the player, cyberspace is an amusement park where anything that can be imagined and programmed can be experienced. The richness of the experiences that will be available in cyberspace can barely be imagined today.

As conventions develop for defining cyberspace environments, cyberspace will be applied in increasingly abstract ways. A cyberspace system may turn out to be the best way to implement a hypertext browsing system, or for visualizing scientific data in multidimensional space (one could imagine a "transdimensional cyberspace Harley" that lets you ride along any vector in the state space).

In designing interactive systems we must distinguish between abstractions introduced because of the limitations of the medium (for example, abbreviations to compensate for a slow teletype) and abstractions that add power or intuitiveness to the interface (such as the ability to create macros to perform repetitive tasks). By creating a very rich environment, cyberspace allows us to dispense with the abstractions of compromise and explore the abstractions that empower the user in new ways.

Cyberspace is a general-purpose technology of interaction with computers—nothing about it is specific to 3-D graphical design any more than fifth-generation interfaces based on raster graphics screens are useful only for two-dimensional drawing. New technologies, however, tend to be initially applied in the most obvious and literal ways. When graphics displays were first developed, they were used for obvious graphics applications such as drawing and image processing. Only later, as graphics display technology became less expensive and graphics displays were widely available, did people come to see that appropriate use of two-dimensional graphics could help clarify even exclusively text- or number-oriented tasks.

So it will be with cyberspace. Cyberspace represents the first three-dimensional computer interface worthy of the name. Users struggling to comprehend three-dimensional designs from multiple views, shaded pictures, or animation will have no difficulty comprehending or hesitation to adopt a technology that lets them pick up a part and rotate it to understand its shape, fly through a complex design like Superman, or form parts by using tools and seeing the results immediately. Those who had to see shaded pictures to appreciate the value of rendering software and to experience their first fly-through to consider animation something more than a gimmick are sure to appreciate cyberspace only after they have stepped into it the first time.

The ability to place users in computer-generated three-dimensional environments and allow them to interact with simulated objects will begin to break down the barrier between the user and the world inside the computer. It will usher in totally new ways to interact with computers, new applications for computers, and, ultimately, new ways of thinking about computers themselves.

What's the Big Deal about Cyberspace?

The primary research instrument of the sciences of complexity is the computer. It is altering the architectonic of the sciences and the picture we have of material reality. Ever since the rise of modern science three centuries ago, the instruments of investigation such as telescopes and microscopes were analytic and promoted the reductionalist view of science. Physics, because it dealt with the smallest and most reduced entities, was the most fundamental science. From the laws of physics one could deduce the laws of chemistry, then of life, and so on up the ladder. This view of nature is not wrong; but it has been powerfully shaped by available instruments and technology.

The computer, with its ability to manage enormous amounts of data and to simulate reality, provides a new window on that view of nature. We may begin to see reality differently simply because the computer produces knowledge differently from the traditional analytic instruments. It provides a different angle on reality.
—*Heinz Pagels [1988]*

A "DIFFERENT ANGLE ON REALITY" can make a world of difference. The realm outside our skins, where coffee cups and computers exist, is a designed world. And the realm inside our heads, where concepts and symbolic models exist, is a simulated world. Cyberspace systems will change both these worlds in ways we can only begin to imagine.

Today, it is possible to use a glove-based input device and head-mounted display to pull users' perceptions through the screen and into the world depicted by the computer. The resulting experience isn't just a total wrap-around audio-visual display. As John Walker points out, cyberspace is an immersion in another world, a simulated world you can view and touch directly (see Walker's chapter in this volume). Cyberspace is a human-computer interface, but it is also a mind-space, the way mathematics and music and myth are mind-spaces—mind-space you can walk around in and grab by the handles.

Cyberspace is more than a sexy new way to operate a computer. You have to consider the NASA Ames prototype as a Kitty Hawk version of a new technology that is bound to evolve rapidly. The "cyberspace in a briefcase" version as it exists at Autodesk, assembled from off-the-shelf components, is the Spirit of Saint Louis. The 747 version, however, will transport users directly to the interior of simulated worlds virtually indistinguishable from external reality. And it will enable them to externalize the symbolic worlds inside their minds in spectacular new ways. This

Howard Rheingold
Author

capability for total sensory transport gives cyberspace the potential to become a major historical lever like printing presses and computers. Ask anyone who has tested a prototype: the graphics are still crude, and the toolkit is nonexistent, but cyberspace feels like one of those developments that come along unexpectedly and radically alter everyone's outlook forever after.

The scientific and technological applications of professional and mass-market cyberspace systems will be fairly big business as they phase in over the next two to ten years. Cyberspace as a scientific visualization tool is bound to generate a revolution of its own. In fundamental research in the sciences of complexity—from meteorology and high-energy physics to epidemiology—the use of conventional graphics-intensive computer modeling systems already has been instrumental in the cross-disciplinary revolution known as chaos theory. The advent of a general tool for three-dimensional, hand-manipulable scientific visualization will lead to unforeseeable breakthroughs in otherwise unrelated fields, just as surely as the microscope led to modern medicine.

Combined with robotics, cyberspace interfaces won't lack for commercial applications. The evolution of telepresence systems will extend the reach and judgment of surgeons and space shuttle technicians and save the lives of miners, undersea operators, and others in hazardous environments. The first visible changes in the world around us will come over the next five years, as cyberspace-aided-design kicks into gear: cyberspace systems allow you to use your hand and eye where conventional CAD systems constrain you to your mouse and the screen. The most profound implication of cyberspace, however, is not that it is a useful human interface for practical tasks people want to accomplish with the aid of a computer, but that the experience of immersion in a virtual world will change the way people perceive the world outside the computer.

The cyberspace experience is destined to transform us because it is an undeniable reminder of a fact we are hypnotized since birth to ignore and deny—that our normal state of consciousness is itself a hyper-realistic simulation. We build models of the world in our minds, using the data from our sense organs and the information-processing capabilities of our brains. We habitually think of the world we see as "out there," but what we are seeing is really a mental model, a perceptual simulation that exists only in our brains. That simulation capability is where human minds and digital computers share a potential for synergy. Give the hyper-realistic simulator in our heads a handle on computerized hyper-realistic simulators, and something very big is bound to happen.

Cognitive simulation—mental model-making—is what humans do best. We do it so well that we tend to become locked into our own models of the world by a seamless web of unconscious beliefs and subtly molded perceptions. And computers are model-making tools par excellence, although they are only beginning to approach the point where people might confuse simulations with reality. Computation and display technology are converging rapidly on hyper-real simulation capability. That point of convergence is important enough to contemplate in advance of its arrival. The day computer simulations become so realistic that people cannot distinguish them from nonsimulated reality, we are in for major changes.

We still have a few years, but this technology is arriving at a rapid rate. Today, it is possible to put a lightweight helmet on your head and an input glove on your hand and fly around inside a wire-frame model of a space shuttle or a protein molecule. It pays to remember that today's prototypes will seem as crude as ENIAC when enough computation power is integrated into cyberspace systems. The wire-frame graphics will be replaced by solid modeling, full color, animation, high resolution, eye-tracking. That helmet will look like a Walkman with a pair of sunglasses to go along with the earphones. Or it might simply be built into the room. The dataglove might become a datasuit. Ideally, advances in input and display technologies will approach a smooth, mind-in-glove fit between human and computer model-building capacities.

We are approaching a breakpoint where the quantitative improvement in that model-building interface will trigger a qualitative quantum leap. In coming years, we will be able to put on a headset or walk into a media room, and surround ourselves in a responsive simulation of startling verisimilitude. Our most basic definitions of reality will be redefined in that act of perception, as Jean Baudrillard claims in this passage:

> Abstraction today is no longer that of the map, the double, the mirror or the concept. Simulation is no longer that of a territory, a referential being or a substance. It is the generation by models of a real without origin or reality: a hyperreal. The territory no longer precedes the map, nor survives it. Henceforth, it is the map that precedes the territory. [Baudrillard, 1983]

The advent of technology-generated hyper-reality could be the nightmarish "consensual hallucination" described by William Gibson in the novel *Neuromancer*, in which the word *cyberspace* originated [Gibson]. Or the result might be an increase in human freedom and power, akin to the aftereffects of printing and communication technologies. Which way it will go—dystopia or empowerment—depends in part upon how people react to the unmasking of reality as a cognitive-perceptual construct. People tend to react in different ways to the news that reality might be an illusion, depending on their personal emotional attachment to their brand of reality. Denial, cognitive dissonance, resistance, and satori are all possible psychological reactions to the truth we are forced to face in the illusory realm of cyberspace, in roughly descending order of popularity.

"Film is truth at 24 frames per second," Jean-Luc Godard used to say. That projection rate is the threshold at which the separate photographic images projected on a movie screen fuse in the human perceptual system into the consensual hallucination we know as cinema. Cyberspace is where the Turing machine hits 24 frames per second.

The advancement of many of the key qualities we think of as human is linked to the evolution of world views—to the emergence and invention of new ways to see the world. As Jacob Bronowski put it:

> We cannot separate the special importance of the visual apparatus of man from his unique ability to imagine, to make plans, and to do all the other things which are generally included in the catchall phrase "free will." What we really mean by free will, of course, is the visualizing of alternatives and making a choice between them. In my view . . . the central problem of human consciousness depends on the ability to imagine. [Bronowski, 1978]

Given a tool for visualizing and modeling, how might we use it to help us make plans, imagine, and otherwise exert conscious influence on an increasingly complex environment? Can we imagine ways to apply it to the very real problems of the world? Or will we watch the unleashing of the ultimate escape drug? Part of the answer depends on what cyberspace does to our way of seeing the world.

Visually-oriented computer interfaces, film, photography, and before them, painting and drawing, all changed the way people see the world. People ran screaming out of movie houses at the sight of the first extreme close-ups of giant faces on the screen. The Renaissance was influenced as much by the introduction of perspective as by the rediscovery of Greek philosophy. It is part of a cultural evolutionary process: every time a widely seen visual paradigm breaks into a new dimension, reality shifts a little. In the case of the cyberspace transformation (because of the nature of the digital computer), it looks like reality is going to change a lot.

It was a long uphill battle to get people to see the first graphics-capable computers as models for future human-computer interfaces, simply because they were perceived as flashy narrow-purpose machines for doing computer graphics. Computer graphics is indeed a rich niche, but the use of graphical displays is a general amplification of human-computer communication capabilities. Don't forget that the first computers were a general amplification of human information-manipulating capabilities, even though they started out as fancy calculators and were stubbornly perceived that way by computer designers for decades [Rheingold, 1988].

The route from today's prototypes to tomorrow's cyberspace will start with the world of design and diffuse from there—the way spreadsheets and personal computers started from the financial side of business and diffused from there. Cyberspace is direct manipulation par excellence. The interface maps directly onto the task, because the interface consists largely of a simulation of the task. With today's typical aerodynamic analysis tool, for instance, the user interface is at worst a series of mathematical expressions and at best a manipulation of pointers and cursors controlling various processes and points of view. The interface is overlaid on the task. In the aerodynamic simulation of the future, a designer will be able to "walk" around (and through and inside) the structure of the aircraft, pulling and pushing things into new positions (within constraints beyond which they will not budge), and view the aerodynamic results in real time from multiple vantage points by moving naturally.

Designers of automobiles and molecules, appliances and architecture, will be the first to find immediate use for cyberspace, just as graphics applications spawned CAD in the first place (see the chapters by Walker and Fisher in this volume). And any breakthrough in CAD is certain to have wide ripple effects. As Don Norman points out in this volume, we live in a designed world. Economists such as Paul Hawken believe this increasing emphasis on designed products is one manifestation of the "informative economy" that is emerging around the world, in which the amount of information that goes into a product has become more valuable than the mass or energy required to manufacture it [Hawken, 1983]. The raw materials in a Parisian gown, a Japanese automobile, or an American television program are not what give it value; the information embedded in the product's design is what gives it value. In this regard, a design revolution is bound to be at once an economic revolution and a change in world view.

Pervasive as design might be, it is still a niche. Cyberspace has the potential for more. As Brenda Laurel put it:

> Reality has always been too small for human imagination. The impulse to create an "interactive fantasy machine" is only the most recent manifestation of the age-old desire to make our fantasies palpable—our insatiable need to exercise our imagination, judgment, and spirit in worlds, situations, and personae that are different from those of our everyday lives. Perhaps the most important feature of human intelligence is the ability to internalize the process of trial and error. When a man considers how to climb a tree, imagination serves as a laboratory for "virtual" experiments in physics, biomechanics, and physiology. In matters of justice, art, or philosophy, imagination is the laboratory of the spirit. [Laurel, 1986]

As with other technologies, cyberspace is not an either-or case. It will be both-and. People will use it as a hybrid of entertainment, escape, and addiction. And other people will use it to navigate through the dangerous complexities of the 21st century. It might be the gateway to the Matrix. Let us hope it will be a new laboratory of the spirit—and let's see what we can do to steer it that way.

Realness and Interactivity

Michael Naimark
Media Artist

Legend has it that a gentleman once approached Picasso on the street and criticized his paintings as distorting reality. Seeming to change the subject, the artist asked the gentleman if he had a girlfriend. He did, and produced a small picture of her from his wallet. "She's beautiful," replied Picasso, "but she's so tiny."

This paper is about how reality is a funny thing, now that we are beginning to simulate it, and where the clues may lie in understanding styles of function and aesthetics about virtual realities.

Virtual Realities Require Realness and Interactivity

Realness and interactivity have various meanings. We usually use the term *realness* to mean our sense-ability: what our senses sense. This "sense of presence" is independent of whether the material is derived from the real world or from a fantasy-based one (perhaps *thereness* is a more appropriate word than *realness*). The term *interactivity* usually means our effectability: what our effectors affect. Though interactivity always requires information flowing in both directions, it is our input and its effect that distinguishes it from noninteractivity, where the flow is always one-way.

The ultimate virtual reality is, by definition, indistinguishable from reality, where all our effectors are sensed and all our sensors are affected. This is a rather formidable task. Such models exist in the fantasy literature:

the family media room in Ray Bradbury's story "The Veldt" and "cyber-space" in William Gibson's *Neuromancer* are popular examples of total immersion in virtual realities (and most certainly include created worlds as well as real ones). Other models, theoretical ones, have been proposed from the points of view of media technology [Negroponte, 1981], cybernetic theory [Bricken, 1983], and drama [Laurel, 1986]. The combination of realness with interactivity is a new frontier where experienced pioneers today are few, and come from such diverse worlds as flight simulation, dream research, and experimental theater.

Clearly there is an attraction to experiencing the jaw-dropping impact of a seven-story-high IMAX movie controlled by a video game-style steering wheel (which is very much what present-day flight simulators really do). Or having a conversation with a Disney-style talking head interacting in a way that dwarfs the ELIZA psychoanalyst program (which very much doesn't exist today in any form of media). We can expect such progress on the technological front, but there is a bit of a communication problem.

The sense-ability experts and the effect-ability experts come from different worlds. And their uses of each others' terms are grossly miscalibrated.

The Movie World Understands Realness But Not Interactivity

If you want a mediated experience to look and sound (and feel and smell) real, go to the motion picture industry. From the beginning, the trend has been toward better sound, color, scale, depth, spatial resolution, and temporal resolution. Today we have various "enhanced-format" theaters at theme parks and worlds' fairs offering "more reality." These include big movies like IMAX and OMNIMAX (horizontally formatted 70mm film), panoramic movies like CircleVision (nine 35mm screens arranged in a cylinder), deep movies like Twin-70mm stereo (two 70mm projectors and polarized glasses), and smooth movies like Showscan (70mm film shot and projected at 60 frames per second).

Other tricks are known by the motion picture industry to achieve even more reality. The use of a concave mirror to achieve infinity focus is used in today's flight simulators to allow the users' eyes to focus at infinity, as they normally do when viewing landscapes. Disney pioneered relief projection, projecting movies on a screen the same shape as the image, such as the "talking heads" in the Haunted Mansion. He also pioneered the use of a single room-size half-silvered mirror to produce 3-D ghost-like images seen in the Haunted Mansion's ballroom. Lucasfilm recently introduced the use of a motion platform synchronized with image and sound in their "Star Tours" ride, giving the audience a parallel kinesthetic sensory input channel.

What has been restricted to the film world has begun to enter the video world. High-definition television, with its various and opposing formats, has forced some of these parameters to be surveyed and formalized (Schrieber, 1984).

So when people from the motion picture industry say they can give you a sense of reality, they can, as they say, knock your socks off. But if they say they can give you an interactive experience, don't come running.

The world's first interactive movie (as it was billed) was produced by the Czechs for EXPO '67 in Montreal. The audience had "yes/no" buttons and every few minutes they were given a choice. This database of movie scenes was so sparse that after the end, the audience was asked if they would like to see the *other* end ("vote yes or no"), which acknowledged what the experience really was: a clever and perhaps prophetic gimmick. (Incidentally, it was more clever and less technological than the audience may have imagined. Each choice was carefully structured so that either option would end at the same next choice, where the audience vote told the projectionist on which of the two synchronized projectors to put the lens cap.)

Today, most of the interactivity known to the motion picture industry is in the form of interactive videodiscs, because they share common production hardware and techniques with conventional cinema. Most interactive videodisc applications are poke-and-see movie snippets with just slightly more options than the Czech's film. In a Sony advertisement a few years ago, a Cuisinart kiosk was shown with a monitor and ten push buttons numbered one through ten, presumably allowing the user one of ten short linear programs. (Sardonically, the words on the screen flashed "PUSH BUTTON SIX." One can't help but wonder who's controlling whom here.)

You can't conduct a symphony orchestra, or carry on a rich conversation, or drive a car this way.

The Computer World Understands Interactivity But Not Realness

If you want an interactive mediated experience, go to the computer world. But because it is younger and less evolved than the world of cinema, it has addressed interactivity more in the context of here-and-now practicalities than in the context of future sensory-rich virtual realities, where theoretical factors such as simultaneity, memory, and interruptibility become essential [Lippman, 1985].

All interactive media experiences require user input. With a little imagination, one can envision human-machine interaction beyond a keyboard and mouse to the natural and kinesthetic way we encounter the real world. Input devices for our hands, arms, head, eyes, body, and feet can sense position, gesture, touch, movement, and balance.

Video games are primitive examples of this sort of interactivity. Driving games such as "Pole Position" offer user control as tight linked as real world power steering. Even the first arcade video game, "Pong," had an input channel many times the bandwidth of practically any "interactive" videodisc system today.

But don't ask computer people about a sense of media reality: their perceptions are warped by current hardware constraints.

Go to any computer graphics film show and listen when the audience applauds. A few years ago I was at the annual SIGGRAPH film show, the largest of these events, standing next to a young security guard in a mobbed colosseum. After a couple minutes a shot of a (fractal) mountain scene appeared on the screen and the audience applauded. I noticed the security guard getting tense. Shortly after that, (ray traced) shiny steel balls were shown hovering over a chessboard. More applause. Then a (atmospheric) foggy outdoor forest scene appeared and the audience exploded. At this point, the security guard snapped. He grabbed my arm ("something weird is going on here, man") and demanded an explanation.

More recently, I attended a demo of a new chip capable of unlimited real-time movement through a 3-D database of limited cartoon-like quality. A very excited representative of a well-known computer maker kept exclaiming how real this was, and continued to refer to the little green cones as "trees."

Who're we kidding?

Bandwidth Is Not Enough

But if virtual reality-making follows moviemaking (or any other media form), then throwing more bandwidth at the medium doesn't automatically make it better. Being artful with what you have does.

In early motion pictures, shots were long in duration, camera movement, if any, was slow, and scenes were edited for perceptual continuity. Audiences were cautiously led through the virtual space of cinema, careful not to get "lost." As the language of cinema evolved and audiences grew more sophisticated, more inferences could be made. Conceptual continuity replaced perceptual continuity. One might speculate that the Lucas/Spielberg-style fast-paced thriller would have been impossible for early movie watchers to have followed. The evolution of aesthetic style results in massive bandwidth compression.

We have little basis for aesthetic style in virtual realities yet, and we have much to learn. For starters, we still have only a meager understanding of the use of scale in media. Nor do we have more than a hint of a cinematic language of interactivity. We have little understanding of the roles of acculturation and habituation in media. And we have no experience at all in creating behavior as well as image.

We do know that these media issues have something to do with context and its relationship to medium (remember McLuhan), as we are creating media forms with vast new capabilities. This has created a particularly critical role for artists today, if we are to believe that artists of the future will create landscapes that you walk through and portraits that you converse with.

Integrating Computers and Television

TELEVISION is perhaps the most important form of communication ever invented. It is certainly the most popular and influential in our society. It is an effortless window on the world, requiring of the viewer only the right time and the right channel, or for the nondiscriminating viewer, any time and any channel (except channel one).

Computer presentation of information could certainly benefit from the color, motion, and sound that television offers. Television viewers could similarly benefit from the control and personalization that is promised by computer technology.

Combining the two seems irresistible. They already seem to have much in common, such as CRT screens and programs and power cords. But they are different in significant ways, and those differences are barriers to reasonable integration.

The problems on the computer side will get fixed in the course of technological evolution, which should continue into the next century. We've been fortunate so far that not one of the early computer systems has been so popular that it couldn't be obsoleted (although we are dangerously close to having that happen with UNIX, and there is now some doubt as to whether even IBM can displace the PC). The worst features of computers, that they are underpowered and designed to be used by nerds, will improve over the long haul.

Television, unfortunately, has been spectacularly successful, and so is

Douglas Crockford
Lucasfilm Ltd.

461

still crippled by the limitations of the electronics technology of 40 years ago. There are many new television systems on the horizon, a few of which promise to solve the integration problem, but for the time being we are stuck with what we've got.

These limitations are not noticed by audiences, and could be completely ignored if they were merely the esoterica of television engineers. Unfortunately, the television medium is far more specialized than you might suppose. Interface designers who ignore its limitations do so at their own peril.

Venue

Computer displays are generally designed for close viewing, usually in an office environment—most often as a solitary activity. The display is sharp and precise. Displays strongly emphasize text, sometimes exclusively so. Graphics and color are sometimes available. Displays are generally static. Only recently have computers been given interesting sound capabilities. There is still little understanding of how to use sound effectively beyond BEEPs, which usually indicate when the machine wants a human to perform an immediate action.

Television, on the other hand, was designed for distant viewing, usually in a living room environment, often as a group activity. The screen is alive with people, places, and products. The screen can present text, but viewers are not expected to receive much information by reading. The sound track is an essential part of the viewing experience. Indeed, most of the information is carried audibly. (You can prove this yourself. Try this demonstration: Watch a program with the sound turned all the way down. Then watch another program with the sound on, but with the picture brightness turned all the way down. Then stop and think.)

Television was designed for distant viewing because the electronics of the 1940s couldn't handle the additional information required to provide sufficient detail for close viewing. Television has lower resolution than most computer displays, so you have to get some distance from it for it to look good.

The correct viewing distance for a television viewer is as much as ten times what it is for a computer user. Where is the best place to sit in order to enjoy fully integrated interactive television, the arm chair or the desk chair? Many of the current generation of multimedia products, such as Compact Disc-Interactive, suffer from this ambiguity. The color images are best viewed from a distance, but the cursor-oriented interface wants to be close.

Overscan

Every pixel on a computer display is precious. Because the visible window is a rectangle, and the corners of CRTs are curved, the visible rectangle is

Field Dominance

Right   Wrong

inset, with sufficient black border to assure that even the corner pixels will be visible. Television, unfortunately, does not use such a border.

The first picture tubes used in television were more oval than rectangular. It was decided that the picture should fill every bit of the face of the screen, even if that meant that viewers would be unable to see the portions of the images that were near the edges, particularly in the corners.

This was well suited to the distant viewing assumption, but the uncertainty of what is visible on a viewer's screen (it can vary from set to set) causes problems even for producers of television programs. They had to accept conventions of Safe Action Area and Safe Title Area, which are smaller rounded rectangles within the television frame. Most actions that happen within the Safe Action Area will be visible on most sets. All text should be confined to the Safe Title Area, which is visible on virtually all sets.

30 FPS

Many computer systems have displays that run at 30 or 60 frames per second, because it is commonly believed that television runs at a rate of 30 frames per second. This is incorrect for two reasons:

• Television doesn't really have frames, it has fields. A field is a half of a picture, every other line of a picture (sort of like looking through blinds). There is no guarantee that two fields make a coherent picture, or even which fields (this one and that one, or that one and the next one) make up a frame. This is the field dominance problem, and it makes television hostile to treating individual frames as discrete units of information.

- If television did have a frame rate, it would be 29.97 frames per second. The original black and white system was 30, but it was changed when color was introduced. This can make synchronization difficult. Movies transferred to television play a little longer, and the pitch in the sound track is lowered slightly. It also causes problems with timecode.

  Timecode is a scheme for identifying every frame with a unique number, in the form hour:minute:second:frame, similar in function to the sector and track numbers on computer disk drives. For television, there are assumed to be 30 frames per second, but because the true rate is 29.97, over the course of a half hour you would go over by a couple of seconds. There is a special form of timecode called Drop Frame Timecode, which skips every thousandth frame number, so that the final time comes out right. However, it can be madness dealing with a noncontinuous number system in a linear medium, particularly if frame accuracy is required.

Interlace

Computers want to be able to deal with images as units. Television doesn't, because it interlaces. *Interlace* is a scheme for doubling the apparent frame rate at the price of a loss of vertical resolution and a lot of other problems. Pictures are transmitted as alternating fields of even lines and fields of odd lines.

Images coming from a television camera produce 59.94 fields per second. Each field is taken from a different instant in time. If there is any motion in the scene, it is not possible to do a freeze frame, because the image will be made up of two fields, forcing the image to flutter forward and backward in time. A still can be made by taking a single field and doubling it to make a frame, with a loss of some image quality.

Twitter is a disturbing flicker caused by the content of one line being significantly different than its interfield neighbors. In extreme cases, it can cause the fields to separate visibly. Twitter can be a big problem for computer generated images, because twittery patterns are extremely common, particularly in text, boxes, and line drawings. The horizontal stripes in the Macintosh title bar cause terrible twitter. Twitter can be removed by filtering, but with a loss of detail and clarity.

Field dominance, as mentioned above, is the convention of deciding what a frame is: an odd field followed by an even, or an even field followed by an odd. There are two possible ways to do it; neither is better than the other, and neither is generally agreed upon. Some equipment is even, some is odd, some is random. This can be critical when dealing with frames as discrete objects, as in collections of stills. If the field dominance is wrong, instead of getting the two fields of a single image, you will get a field each of two different images, which looks sort of like a superimposition, except that it flickers like crazy.

Color

RCA Laboratories came up with an ingenious method for inserting color into a television channel that could still be viewed by unmodified black-and-white sets. But it didn't come for free. The placing of all of the luminance and color information into a single composite signal causes some special problems.

The color space of television is not the same as that in a computer RGB system. A computer can display colors that television can't, and trying to encode those colors into a composite television signal can cause aliasing. (*Aliasing* means "something you don't want.")

Television cannot change colors as quickly as a computer display can. This can also cause aliasing and detail loss in computer-generated pictures on television. There are other problems, such as chroma crawl and cross-color, which are beyond the scope of this chapter. But they're there.

Videotape

In the Golden Age, there was no good way to save programs, so all programs were produced live. Videotape was developed years later.

Our problems with videotape are due to two causes. First, the design of television gave no thought to videotape or videodisc, which results in the generation loss problem. Second, the control aspects of interactive television require greater precision than broadcasters require, which creates the frame accuracy problem.

Generation loss is the degradation in the quality of a program that happens every time it is copied. Because videotape is not spliced, the only way to assemble material is by copying it, and with each copy it gets worse. This problem is being corrected by the application of digital computer technology, and can be considered solved, at least in some locations. It remains to make digital video recording cheap and widely available.

The frame accuracy problem is another story. A computer storage device that, when requested to deliver a particular sector, instead delivered a different sector would be considered defective. In the world of videotape editing, it is often considered normal. In a commercial or situation comedy, no one can notice that an edit is off by 1/29.97 seconds, so precise, accurate-to-the-frame behavior is not always demanded of professional video gear. This can make the production of computer-interactive video material extremely difficult, because if your interest is in a particular frame, the off-by-one frame is totally wrong.

Other Television

This chapter has mostly concentrated on the NTSC system used in the United States. Other countries use the PAL and SECAM systems, which have their own worlds of problems. These are compounded for the designer who wants to make programs that work in all nations.

A number of new television systems are being proposed to replace or enhance the existing systems. To the extent that these have progressive scan (noninterlaced), component color (not composite), a frame rate that can be expressed as a whole number (60 fps, not 59.94 fps), and digital encoding (not analog), then computers and television can be integrated successfully, and the limitations listed above will be techno-historical trivia.

The convergence of television and computer media is extremely desirable. Computer technology would benefit from animated displays and high-bandwidth digital video storage. Camcorders could be wonderful computer input devices. Television technology would benefit from being less mysterious and more straightforward to use, eliminating the video priesthood in much the same way that good interface design will eliminate the computer priesthood.

Although desirable, this convergence is not inevitable. Some of the worst use of computers is in television engineering. Some of the worst television is "desktop video." The full power of a new medium based on the well-considered unification of computer and television technology is distant and elusive. The design challenge is not technologically difficult. It requires only a commitment to excellence and a willingness to accept change.

This New Television could make the tools of production available to every individual. The New Media Literacy could grant to people a significant power over the technology of the Information Age. The New Television could perhaps be the most important form of communication ever invented.

Designing a New Medium

THOUGH CURRENT COMPUTER-ASSISTED "multimedia" systems are clumsy and expensive, progress at the hardware level is accclerating. What has not kept pace is our understanding of software and content design for the multimedia environment. Particularly, there has been little examination of the implications for computer-human interaction to be found in the emerging use of the computer as a medium.

Computers are usually viewed as tools, instruments for storing and manipulating data that ultimately will be printed out. But now the computer is beginning to be used as a medium in itself, a means of communication in which the content is never reduced to print. Examples include multimedia education systems, collaborative computing environments, and desktop presentations. The computing medium has both real-time and stored forms and is multimodal, incorporating text, voice, music, graphics, video, and animation.

We should now begin thinking of the computer-human interface as a media process. This means enlarging our study to include issues such as the psychology of media, evolution of genre and form, and societal implications of media biases—issues heretofore peripheral to computing. The shift of focus to the media level may give us a new language in which to describe such choices and to analyze the prior evolution of computer systems. It suggests that attention to artists employing the computing medium,

Tim Oren
Advanced Technology Group
Apple Computer, Inc.

and the incipient genres they will originate, is a source of inspiration and understanding for user interface and computer systems designers.

Taking Control of Media

The forms of existing media, such as television, have been largely determined by opportunism. The first technically feasible configuration is rushed to market and exploited and then sets an *ad hoc* standard for form and content in that medium. Television shows are certainly designed, but they are set in a framework of hardware and marketplace over which the writer has no control. Altering a medium based on obsolete hardware is extremely difficult, as the current high-definition television (HDTV) controversy shows.

In contrast, the computer medium is malleable and tunable—"soft." As hardware improves, the face that the computing medium presents to the user and author is increasingly determined by the design and limits of software. Because software is more easily manipulated than hardware, the computing medium is craftable, a metamedium. Its existence implies, for the first time, a design space that may be *deliberately* explored.

The wrong way to deal with this situation is to muddle about until we hit gold, and then let the marketers take over. The current status of interactive media is a prime counterexample, with its proliferation of specifications: CD-ROM, CD-I, DVI, CD-V, LV-ROM and so on and on. All of these were motivated by market positions that might be obtained by leveraging current hardware products. None of them involved prior attention to what content and forms might make interactivity an attractive option, or to the biasing characteristics of the medium that would result.

The choices designers make, or the decision to leave the matter to the vagaries of the marketplace, will have far-reaching consequences. Our society increasingly communicates its knowledge and values and conducts its affairs through media, rather than face to face. Each medium has its own set of biases and proclivities that alter and govern the form of information it transmits. The growth of institutions around a medium is likewise influenced by its biases. For instance, the effects of network television on public debate and education are widely perceived [Mander, 1978].

The computing media described in this book and elsewhere [Ambron, 1988] are proposed as vehicles for collaborative work, learning, and play and particularly for the education of the young. Media biases in such systems will have a powerful effect on our culture, as they govern what may be discussed, created, and transmitted now and from generation to generation.

If we as designers want to take control of the process, there must be a vocabulary in which to articulate choices. At present, much of the computer-human interface field is committed to the detailed study and modeling of low-level cognitive phenomena [Newell, 1985], an inappropriate level at which to address media issues. We should instead consider whether the language of media and criticism is a useful next stage to our understanding of systems of humans and machines.

The Evolution of Media

in-cu-nab-u-lum [fr. L *incunabula*, pl., swaddling clothes, cradle, fr. *in-* + *cunae* cradle] **1**: a book printed before 1501 **2**: a work of art or of industry of an early period

What can we learn about the new computing medium by looking at the past? Every medium goes through an early incunabular stage in which old forms persist into the new medium before being modified and finally replaced with new, better adapted, forms. For example, the text shown in figure 1 replicates in early movable type the interlineation and marginalia typical of a hand-written manuscript. With its detailed cross-references among six parallel streams of text, it resembles the notion of hypertext more than it does a modern book.

What happened to this form? It was driven out in part by the difficulty of typesetting such pages. With early printing technology, each character had to be placed individually on the page and replaced in the type fount after use. New forms of content, such as outlines, tables of contents, alphabetical indexes, and footnotes, arose to fill similar functions while simplifying the layout problem and reducing the number of typefaces needed. These forms are now so stamped in our consciousness as to be thought essential for scholarly literature.

In this early day of computer media we are also using incunabular forms. We are busily replicating hierarchically organized books on CD-ROM and distributing libraries of still photos on videodisc. To get beyond this stage and exploit the computing medium, we will have to invent forms and genres that are more than borrowings. Thomas Edison created the movie camera, but D. W. Griffith and Sergei Eisenstein invented filmmaking. Likewise, the advances of the new medium will be defined by seminal visions of those who are expressing themselves in ways heretofore impossible. This is the key to success of the computer medium, not digital video, broadband fiber networks, or some other hardware advance.

The problem is harder now, however. The limits of the film and cameras of the time set essential parameters for Griffith and Eisenstein. In the computer, above the essential hardware substrate, both form (user interface) and content (data) may be implemented in software. For instance, a HyperCard stack stores both interface and content in the same way. Not only is the form defined in software and therefore malleable, but the boundary between form and content is itself plastic. Without some guiding

Figure 1 : Image of incunabular Biblical commentary. Text and two parallel commentaries, interlinked with numeric references.

notion of conventional form, the viewer may have trouble distinguishing the two. Indeed, the traditional separation of form and content is called into question by the computing medium.

DEFINING THE DESIGN SPACE

What are the conceptual dimensions of the new design space? Our experience is too limited for any conclusive answer, but the following will be considered below: What is the human role in the range from active to passive—is it user, viewer, or participant? To what extent do the author or editor and final viewer of content share the same environment? Are the means of creation widely distributed or centralized, costly or inexpensive? Is the medium suited for a mass or an elite audience?

This design space is so large that a perception that all computer-based media (CD-I and DVI, for instance) must compete with one another is superficial. Rather, the *forms* built of these technologies will compete amongst themselves and with older forms for the time and attention of potential authors and audiences. The expressive range of the forms, the types of messages that can be sent, and their potential to engage the human participant, will be the grounds of comparison. The psychology of the media experience must be investigated if we are to have a notion of *a priori* design for engagement [Laurel, 1986a].

It should also be obvious that in such a space there is unlikely to be "one true user interface." A stubborn adherence to known methods would cripple the potential of new media by restricting expressive range. The knowledge won in the Desktop setting on the Macintosh now has to be tested against a wider set of choices, and we must look for overarching principles that can explain both the Desktop and the multimedia experience.

GENRE

Genres are conventional, familiar ways of setting expectations of the experience to come. All works in a given genre have certain underlying ideas and themes in common. One does not expect to pick up a romance novel and have it suddenly turn into a police procedural, nor to have a soap opera change into a variety show. Genre recognition invokes our memories of conventional stories, characters, and handling of form and leaves us free to enjoy the nuances of the story of the moment, rather than relearning basics. In order to gain the advantages of a particular genre, an artist must work within its boundaries. Artists may choose to break the boundaries of a recognized genre for several reasons. They may wish to comment on the conventions of a form by satirizing or burlesquing it, for instance, or they may deliberately violate the established conventions of a genre for the sake of innovation. Whenever artists depart from a known genre, they risk losing the benefits of genre recognition. But successful innovation in a particular work can feed the genre and cause it to evolve.

As older, fixed media have found a necessity for genre, so we may suspect that the new flexible computing medium will have a greater need. With the range of design available, there must be a means of setting expectations and transferring knowledge from past exposures, if the content itself is to be appreciated.

Because of the role of genre in setting expectation, borrowings into the computing medium from existing media must be approached with caution.

For instance, a value of computers is interaction. Use of an established noninteractive genre for the sake of familiarity may sabotage this value by lulling the user into old, established habits, which do not include an active user role (see the chapter by Oren et al. in this volume). One also risks comparison with the highly evolved and intense production values employed by established media, such as print and video.

The notion of genre has already arrived on the computer, under a different name: *metaphor*. *Metaphor* as applied to the interface is a different sense of the word than its literary use. In the literary definition of metaphor, our interfaces are hopelessly mixed: We place *windows* on our *desktop*, then put *folders* within the *windows*, thus forming a *tree*. What an odd collection of natural, architectural, and office imagery! And yet it doesn't seem to matter. If we instead think of the so-called Desktop metaphor as a *genre*, a developed set of expectations for content and form, then it seems reasonable, because a genre can embrace many metaphors. And indeed, the Desktop's appeal to skill transfer from program to program is solving the same problem as the evolution of genre. It at once sets user expectations and self-enforced limits of expression.

Because of the familiarity and strength of its underlying ideas, the Desktop has burgeoned into a genre with many individual expressions. Other genres of the computing medium are discussed in the trade periodicals daily: spreadsheets, WYSIWYG text editors, draw and paint programs. Each has one breakthrough ancestor that established it in the public's eye, and a succession of new, innovating programs that influence and refine the underlying genre. Try thinking of Bill Atkinson as Edgar Allen Poe, and MacPaint as "The Murders in the Rue Morgue."

CONVENTION AND PHRASING

Existing media have established conventions that punctuate the viewer's experience. For instance, an establishing shot is conventionally used in film before a close-up is done. A cut from one head shot to another facing the opposite way indicates conversation. If creepy music starts playing just before the hero opens a door, you can be sure he's in for a nasty surprise. Like genre, media conventions set expectations and allow a focus on content, but they do it on a different scale. Media conventions cut across genre lines; for instance, the filmic conventions mentioned above are employed in all genres of movies, from horror to comedy to adventure.

The punctuation of experience is even more important in computer media systems. For instance, the perceptual jump between a color video and black-and-white computer text can be abrupt. To ease such jumps, we will need segue conventions that set up expectations for the transition. We will also need standard ways for setting context in nonlinear media. The common occurrence of interface features such as maps, backtrails, paths, and tours in current multimedia prototypes may indicate that they are becoming recognized conventional uses that address this problem.

For conventions in new media to have value, much of the potential audience must be "media literate," conscious of the media conventions. This process has already begun. A videotape control panel would not have been recognized by most people ten years ago but is now the prime means that most consumers have of dealing with "interactive" sound and video.

Most computer interface ideas can be recognized as directed at this simple, media-wide level of convention. Heretofore, simplicity and even "monotony" have been recognized as important characteristics of interface [Raskin, 1986]. Experience from more mature media suggests that a progressive unfolding of depths of sophistication is a more likely final outcome. The surface story of film or novel is accessible to all, but a lifetime may be spent studying their forms and gaining a richer understanding and appreciation of the works. Future computer systems may have simple surface conventions and many layers of sophistication for those willing to learn.

Conversational Systems

The ruling paradigm of the Macintosh interface is the combination of a passive, tool-like computer with an active human. The machine is to be nonmodal and reactive, and should intrude as little as possible on the task at hand. A traditional medium like television is in sharp contrast. The human is the passive observer of the content, and the machine is the active element.

Between these poles may be options for new media that are *participatory*; that is, where all actors, both machine(s) and human(s) may take active or passive roles at various times. We will need conventions for the exchange of initiative between the actors in the system. Such conventions need to be modeless; in other words, it should be possible for any actor to ask to "take the floor" at any time. Let us call a participatory system with conventions for such exchange of initiative a *conversational system*, taking human conversation as a metaphor (though not implying the necessary use of human language).

Conversational systems are needed because the knowledge of the human is incomplete. For instance, the novice cannot begin to use a system unless there is some volunteering of information on operation. A student cannot use an educational multimedia work effectively if there are no starting points, no examples or concepts that are offered spontaneously. Also, the sheer quantity of information available in present and predicted systems overwhelms attempts to keep it mentally organized, and the computer, acting as agent, must volunteer the information and organization as needed, in response to the human's explicit or inferred needs (see Laurel's chapter in this volume). In computer games, the entire experience is the interaction between the player and the behavior of the program.

A comparison of written and spoken language shows the enormous impact that conversational systems will have on form. In published media, the author produces a finished work, which relies on culture and knowledge that the eventual reader is assumed to share in order to ground the discussion. Face-to-face communication is an iterative process in which meaning is negotiated, with the ability to digress to explain a cryptic referent if understanding breaks down (see Brennan's chapter in this volume). Anyone who has tried to turn a recording of a conversation into a published article has experienced the difference in forms firsthand.

This use of spoken and written language as an example does not imply that a conversational medium must use human language. In a system that includes computers as well as humans, the methods evolved for human-human communication may or may not be appropriate for any particular situation. The "utterances" of computer-human conversations may take many nonverbal forms (see Buxton's and Schmandt's chapters in this volume). But whatever the type of utterance, a conversational medium should be capable of flexible exchange of initiative, two-way transfer of information, and maintenance of context through the analysis of discourse.

What are the current prospects for building conversational abilities into computer media? The ability to mock a conversational entity is the so-called Turing Test, and this task falls within the bounds of artificial intelligence (AI). As yet, AI has failed to produce a system for discourse understanding that is at once general and robust. Formal symbolic methods suffer from brittleness when they venture outside constrained domains. Attempts to improve them with "common sense" suffer from the so-called knowledge acquisition bottleneck: the need for human intelligence to encode knowledge into a prescribed format and to ensure consistency with the remainder of the system.

There are other, nonsymbolic, approaches to giving the computer the ability to act independently. Connectionist methods show some promise for spontaneous generalization, but their use in large, unconstrained domains is unproven and their workings are often unexplainable to the user.

The methods of information retrieval in unstructured text deserve notice. Information retrieval attempts to break the knowledge acquisition bottleneck by automatic indexing and searching of text. But there are no "reliable" retrieval methods; all retrieval is inherently probabilistic as a result of the imprecise use of words by authors and readers and the computer's inability to fully understand context.

The prospect, then, is that the intelligence of the human participants in a conversational medium will dominate that of the computer for the foreseeable future. The advantages of the machine are an eidetic memory, infinite patience, and its role as the mediator of all interactions. It is able to watch as you work and communicate. But a robust portrayal of a conversational entity that can operate across contexts is beyond us at this time.

Storytelling

> A story is a little knot or complex of that species of connectedness called relevance.—Gregory Bateson [Bateson, 1980]

One way around the current lack of generalized conversational systems is to consider subclasses of conversation. For instance, some collaborative work systems use the formalized conversation of business [Winograd, 1985]. Here I will consider the possibility that storytelling, viewed as a constrained conversation, may be a tractable approach, with the potential to engage the human participant at deep symbolic levels as well as explicit cognitive levels.

Like conversation, a storytelling metaphor departs from a responsive tool-like model for the computer. But rather than free interchange of initiative, a storyteller holds the content and structures its presentation to achieve a dramatic effect, partially in response to the spoken and unspoken reactions of the audience at hand. Thus, it has some conversational aspects. This can be contrasted with pure drama, where the form is supplied by the artist, or again with real or simulated worlds, where we follow a self-determined path through space and time and form and meaning are self-supplied.

The so-called "navigation" of databases is similar to this wandering of a real world [Oren, 1987], because the items are viewed in a linear sequence. Interpretation is up to the user: if we are successful in casting the items in terms of our own experience, we may assimilate the information contained [Mandler, 1984]. The role of a storyteller in such a system could be to arrange the narratization of content into useful patterns, by constraining and guiding the choice of what to read or view. This is one origin of the "what's next?" question that led to the formulation of guides (see the chapter by Oren et al. in this volume).

Results from the guides experiments suggest that people find the addition of storytelling and personification to the interface to be intriguing and engaging, particularly in comparison to third-person, omniscient voice text and narration. There seems to be a desire for more carefully defined characters and associated points of view within the database. We are led to suspect that the further extension of storytelling method into new media is worth examining.

Storytelling has the convention of describing only what deviates from the expected and is significant to the advancement of the plot. This dovetails with the finding that humans do not encode, recognize, or recall something that is *expected* in a context [Mandler, 1984]. Mentioning any low-level detail raises its perceived importance to the story (see Don's chapter in this volume). The convention is so strong that the mention of a seemingly unrelated item in the course of a story may instigate a search for its relevance. This may be the psychological basis of foreshadowing (and the entire mystery genre), and is precisely the user behavior desired with guides: to produce a suspension of belief such that plausible connections will be investigated before the narrative explanation is discarded.

The goal of the story is to evoke the user's engagement at both conscious and unconscious levels. Given the limits of intelligence in the computer, we must create a storyteller that can "tell more than it says." The medium becomes as much a mirror to the user as a window on the data. Myron Krueger suggests that: "Ambiguity is an instrument of efficient communication, for while you may not have succeeded in saying one thing clearly, you have suggested several ideas at the same time" [Krueger, 1983].

The imprecision enforced by our poor tools may work in our favor in the storytelling mode, if it is not so dissonant as to break suspension of disbelief.

Our present understanding of creating and portraying story elements in computing media is crude. But there are intriguing questions here: can we heighten engagement by moving from generic characters to figures who are very individualized, even flawed, or which develop with time? How can we represent elements such as plot, tension, and catharsis in the computer, and is their usage in the new media appropriate and helpful [Laurel, 1986b]? How can these elements be maintained while using the human participant as a source of unpredictability? How can interaction best be introduced to the storytelling process: branching, point-of-view shift, some form of interest feedback, or some extension of next-move generation? The best guidance available may be from studies of previous changes in media [Ong, 1982] and criticism of innovative literary forms [Lem, 1984; LeGuin, 1989].

In introducing story to the computer under the guise of new media, we move from the symbolic logic of AI to the class of subconscious symbol described by Jung and Campbell [Jung, 1968; Campbell, 1988]. We begin to explore whether the computer can transmit the "affective image" that speaks in archetypal terms. Examination of the computer human interface in these terms is unprecedented. The best parallels are in the psychological and critical analysis of myth and film. This is not unfitting, for the computer is one of the greatest artifacts of power of our time, an embodiment of the creation archetype for those who can wield it. The public fascination with the computer as Frankenstein and its power to attract young hackers have a mythic quality. We have spent a great deal of effort on the Appolonian side of the computer; perhaps the advent of new media will usefully engage the Dionysian aspects as well.

Media and Markets

> Convivial tools are those which give each person who uses them the greatest opportunity to enrich the environment with the fruits of his or her vision.—Ivan Illich [Illich, 1973]

Existing commercial media, such as television, radio, and most print and computer software forms, are mainly mass media. They are characterized by a marketplace with centralized production and distributed consumption. The ability to have a voice in a mass medium is regulated by one's access to the costly, centralized means of production.

Let us borrow *convivial* from Illich to describe other media in which all participants have the possibility to be authors or readers. Examples include the telephone and many electronic messaging and bulletin board systems. If we believed conviviality to be a desirable property of new media, how would we go about designing for it?

An essential principle is symmetry—that the same authoring tools be available to all. In the mass video medium, the networks have megadollar studios, whereas the consumer may have a single camera. In electronic messaging systems, a symmetric medium, everyone writes using the same tool. In a computing medium, the question is whether a potential artist needs a quarter-million-dollar budget to even begin. Symmetric media produce a talent-limited creative process; in mass media, the process is economically limited. We see that tools make the medium as much as its delivery vehicle.

We should also prefer "low thresholds" of accessibility to "high ceilings" of bandwidth and modality. Low thresholds let in authors with minimal resources. It is possible to "sketch" without a great commitment of time and expense. High ceilings yield a medium that is capable of absorbing a great deal of production value, which correlates to production costs. High production costs lead to the need for a mass market to amortize the expense, or for an audience able to subsidize production costs. We end up with "Three's Company"—the subjection of content to titillation, or with Broadway shows—content for the affluent few.

A medium may trade off production value against *salience* in gaining the attention of a user. *Salience* is the pertinence of a piece of information to a particular person's needs at the time it is presented. For instance, targeted direct mail advertising is an attempt to increase the salience of the message, as opposed to the intense production values that characterize television commercials. If, through devices such as agents, we are able to create personalized adaptive media that optimize salience, we may be able to compete with the production values of mass or elite media.

It may be useful for a convivial medium to have the property of collage-ability, that is, the ability to create new works by combining old ones from the same or other media. This admits the possibility that a legitimate expression may consist of the meaningful juxtaposition of existing works. It opens up the medium to those who are not primary creators in some of its forms. Collage-ability requires gateways, the technical means to bring information into the medium. Video digitizers, scanners, and optical character recognizers are examples of gateways. Once in, the medium should not erect artificial boundaries to the joint use of information from various sources. Collage-ability is desirable for convivial media, but raises many legal and ethical issues, such as the status of copyright and royalty in collage works, and the ability of artists to control the context of use of their work.

To promote understanding, propagation, and improvement of new forms, a convivial medium should be inspectable. It should be possible to "look under the hood" and see how an effect was achieved. This alone is not enough—though film and video are mostly in the open and literal, the tools are not yet accessible. But inspectable software is increasingly a thing of the past, with the replacement of hacker sensibilities by commercial interests. This trend should be reexamined if we are to move to new media where the value of content outweighs any transient advantage of programming.

One final aspect at which computing has been notoriously poor is the survivability of content. By *survivability* I mean the possibility to move the bulk of content and structure from one system to another. Music moves easily from vinyl to tape to CD, video from tape to disc to digital format. But software seldom goes anywhere at all, and the problems of moving a file system from an obsolete computer to a new one are notorious. If artists and commercial organizations are to make investments in new media, this must stop.

It is interesting to note that Apple's HyperCard has some characteristics of a convivial medium. It is not convivial in a true sense, because access requires purchase of a rather expensive computer system. However, for the community of Macintosh owners, it is symmetric, because everyone gets the same version. It emphasizes easy access over high production items such as color and digital video. It displays collage-ability of sound, digitized images, and scanned or typed text. Scripts are inspectable, and the sale and swapping of "buttons" is a recognizable phenomenon. The various updates have all been able to accept content from previous versions. Insofar as HyperCard has succeeded as a "Volksmedium," it is because it shares these aspects of convivial media.

Technologists Should Be Listening to Artists

Building a new medium is a talent-limited process because we are early in the evolution of genre, searching for seminal visions and rallying points. As with Edison and film, it is unlikely that the inventors of the technology will be the creators of such visions. This is more likely to fall to the authors, educators, and artists who have something to say and who find that the new medium offers them a way to say it for the first time. Early forms of the computer medium, such as HyperCard, are significant in providing this expressive opportunity to many.

Because these original uses and forms were not envisioned during the design of existing computing systems and interfaces, they are likely to produce points of strain as these tools are applied. Designers of such systems should get feedback by paying close attention to the problems experienced by artists who are pushing the edge. These observations can guide the construction of the next generation of computing media so that they are better fitted to evolving forms rather than replicating old ones.

Postscript:
On Visions, Monsters, and Artificial Life

THE DISCIPLINE OF INTERFACE DESIGN seems timid in a peculiar way. We thread our way through an enormous number of constraints. As Roy Pea puts it, it's like putting on a straitjacket and then wondering why you're so uncomfortable.

Brenda Laurel

At the deepest level, our visions are bound—like a genie in a bottle—by incantations, taboos, hexes. The power in the bottle is unknown, and so fears are endlessly embroidered by imagination. It is an old taboo, cross-cultural, that says: do not presume to imitate God—and even: do not presume to imitate life. The interdiction spans a spectrum from Platonist to Hebrew to Balinese, from grandmother to toddler, from conceptual artist to computer engineer.

Why is our vision so constrained? Besides this first archetypal taboo, there are four kinds of fears. The first is that, if we attempt to create computational "entities" that are modeled after sentient beings, we will succeed only in constructing crude and lifeless representations—scarecrows, talismans, dolls. It is the fear of failure.

The second fearsome vision is that we will succeed, like Dr. Frankenstein, in creating "life" that grossly amplifies our own shortcomings and flaws—and that suffers and makes us suffer in return. This is the fear of our human fallibility. It is beaten into us by war, poverty, the rape of the environment, the spectre of extinction. In this view, nothing that we can create can be good—but we have a special gift, it would seem, for creating monsters.

The third fear is that if we succeed in transforming computers into augmentation devices as empowering and indispensable as the opposable thumb, we will transform ourselves into something "less" than humans—slaves to a cybernetic symbiosis. It is the fear of losing our identity.

The final fearsome vision is that there really *is* a genie in the bottle. When some threshold of knowledge and capability is reached, a new kind of sentience will emerge. Whether we are parents or midwives hardly matters, for this is the fear, not of God, nor even of usurping God's creational prerogative, but rather the fear of alien life.

Yet just as surely as these fears will slow and subvert our progress, we will continue to pursue our age-old desire to give form to imaginary worlds. It is our nature—and our gift. Plato banned the art of drama from his Republic because he thought that humans were in danger of confusing art and life. Yet few regret the ability to weep with Antigone or laugh with Falstaff. The theatre answers a universal hunger for animate and malleable representations of our experiences, our condition, and ourselves.

It is the same with interactive media. The same objections will be raised; the same doubts and arguments will nip at our heels. But the idea of empowerment through representation will continue to drive us to create. We can't help it. This new medium, like all the others before it, will absorb and transform our hopes and fears, our archetypes and myths. There they will grow and change and take on new shapes and powers. They will be the stuff new visions are made of.

How fast can we invent the future? Will this book be obsolete in five years, two, or one?

Let's hope so.

Interface Evolution:

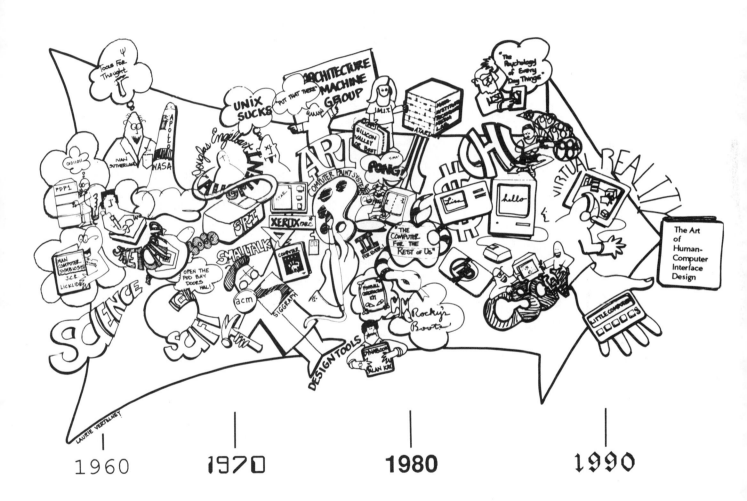

A Collective Timeline

References

An Interview with Don Norman

Gould, J. D., S. J. Boies, S. Levy, J. T. Richards, and J. Schoonard. "The 1984 Olympic message system: A test of behavioral principles of system design." *Communications of the ACM* 10:758–769.

Rubenstein, R., and H. Hersh. *The Human Factor*. Burlington, MA: The Digital Press, 1984.

Interface and the Evolution of Pidgins: Creative Design for the Analytically Inclined

Holm, John. *Pidgins and Creoles, Volume 1: Theory and Structure*. Cambridge, England: Cambridge University Press, 1988.

Polya, G. *How to Solve It*. Second edition. Princeton, NJ: Princeton University Press, 1957.

Tools and Techniques for Creative Design

Adams, J. L. *Conceptual Blockbusting*. Third edition. Reading, MA: Addison-Wesley Publishing Company, 1986.

Alexander, C. *Notes on the Synthesis of Form*. Cambridge, MA: Harvard University Press, 1964.

Arnheim, R. *Visual Thinking*. Berkeley, CA: University of California Press, 1969.

Baecker, R., and A. Marcus. *Human Factors and Typography for More Readable Programs*. Reading, MA: Addison-Wesley Publishing Company, 1990.

Buxton, W. "The Role of the Artist in the Laboratory." (German and English translation). In *Meisterwerke der Computer Kunst*. C. Schopf, ed. Bremen, Germany: TMS Verlag, 1988.

Deken, J. "Machines and Metaphors." *Proceedings of the Fifteenth Symposium on Computer Science and Statistics*. (March, 1983):80–83.

Edwards, Betty. *Drawing on the Artist Within*. New York: Simon and Schuster, 1986.

Fitter, M., and T.R.G. Green. "When Do Diagrams Make Good Computer Languages?" *International Journal of Man-Machine Studies*. Vol. 11 (1979):235–61.

Galileo. *Galileo's Discori e Dimonstrozioni Mathematiche Intorno a Due Nuove Scienze*. Leyden, 1638.

Hanks, Kurt, and Larry Belliston. *Rapid Viz*. San Mateo, CA: William Kauffman, 1980.

Harman, W., and H. L. Rheingold. *Higher Creativity*. Los Angeles: Tarcher, 1984.

Heckel, Paul. *The Elements of Friendly Software Design*. Second edition. New York: Warner Software, Warner Books, 1984.

Koestler, Arthur. *The Act of Creation*. New York: Macmillan, 1964.

Lakoff, G., and J. Johnson. *Metaphors We Live By*. Chicago: University of Chicago Press, 1980.

Laurel, Brenda. "Interface as Mimesis." In *User-Centered System Design: New Perspectives on Human-Computer Interaction*. D. A. Norman and S. Draper, eds. Hillsdale, NJ: Lawrence Erlbaum Associates, 1986.

MacCormac, Earl R. *A Cognitive Theory of Metaphor*. Cambridge, MA: M.I.T. Press, Bradford Books, 1985.

McKim, R. H. *Experiences in Visual Thinking*. Boston: P. W. S.-Kent Publishers, 1972.

Papanek, Victor. *Design for the Real World, Human Ecology and Social Change*. Second edition. Chicago: Academy Chicago Publishers, 1985.

Pile, John F. *Design: Purpose, Form and Meaning*. Amherst, MA: University of Massachusetts Press, 1979.

Thomas, F., and R. Johnston. *Disney Animation: The Illusion of Life*. New York: Abbeville Press, 1984.

Tufte, E. *Visual Display of Quantitative Information*. Cheshire, CT: Graphics Press, 1983.

Verity, J. "Graphically Speaking with Dr. Edward R. Tufte." *Datamation*. Vol. 20, no. 7 (July, 1985):88–90.

von Oech, R. *A Kick in the Seat of the Pants*. New York: Harper Row, 1986.

Wurman, R. S. *Information Anxiety*. New York: Doubleday, 1989.

y Gasset, José Ortega. *The Dehumanization of Art; and Other Essays on Art, Culture, and Literature*. Translated from Spanish by Albert Lee McVitty, Jr. Princeton, NJ: Princeton University Press, 1968. Original version of "The Dehumanization of Art" (1925) was distributed privately.

Interdisciplinary Collaboration

Kim, Scott. "Viewpoint: Toward a Computer for Visual Thinkers." Ph.D. Dissertation, Computer Science Department, Stanford University, 1988.

Koberg, Don, and Jim Bagnall. *The Universal Traveler*. Los Altos, CA: William Kauffman, 1973. (Reference on breaking down barriers between disciplines.)

Designing the Whole-Product User Interface

Berryman, Gregg. *Notes on Graphic Design and Visual Communication*. Los Altos, CA: William Kaufmann, 1984.

Lucie-Smith, Edward. *A History of Industrial Design*. New York: Van Nostrand Reinhold, 1983.

Working with Interface Metaphors

Apple Computer, Inc. *Human Interface Guidelines: The Apple Desktop Interface*. Reading, MA: Addison-Wesley Publishing Company, 1987.

Lakoff, George, and Mark Johnson. *Metaphors We Live By*. Chicago and London: The University of Chicago Press, 1980.

Consistency

Smith, D. C., C. Irby, R. Kimball, W. Verplank, and E. Harslem. "Designing the Star User Interface." In *Integrated Interactive Computing Systems*. P. Degano and E. Sandewall, eds. Amsterdam: North-Holland Publishing Company, 297–313.

Koko's MAC II: A Preliminary Report

Patterson, F. *Koko's Kitten*. New York: Scholastic Books, 1985.

Patterson, F. *Koko's Story*. New York: Scholastic Books, 1987.

Patterson, Francine, and Ronald Cohn. "Gorilla Use of Computer-Generated Speech I: Koko Chooses a Voice." The Gorilla Foundation, *Gorilla Journal*. Vol. 13, no. 1 (December 1989).

Interfaces for Learning: What Do Good Teachers Know That We Don't?

Bruner, Jerome. *On Knowing: Essays for the Left Hand*. Cambridge, MA: Harvard University Press, 1962.

Hawkins, Jan. "Practices of Novices and Experts in Critical Inquiry." In *Mirrors of the Mind: Patterns of Experience in Educational Computing*. Roy D. Pea and Karen Sheingold, eds. Norwood, NJ: Ablex Publishing, 1986.

Lawler, Robert, and Masond Yazdani. *Artificial Intelligence and Education*. Volume 1. Norwood, NJ: Ablex Publishing, 1987.

Nicol, Anne. "Children Using HyperCard." In *HyperCard in Education*. Sueann Ambron, ed. Apple Computer, Inc., in press (1989).

Salomon, Gavriel. "AI in Reverse: Computer Tools That Become Cognitive." Presented at the Annual Meeting of the American Educational Research Association, New Orleans, April 5–9, 1988.

Wenger, Etienne. *Artificial Intelligence and Tutoring Systems*. Los Altos, CA: Morgan Kaufmann Publishers, 1987.

Lessons Learned from Kids: One Developer's Point of View

Cignarella, Patty. "Girls Just Want to Have Fun." *Adweek's Marketing Computers*. Vol. 9, no. 6 (June, 1989):18–22.

Malone, Thomas W. "What Makes Things Fun to Learn? A Study of Intrinsically Motivating Computer Games." XEROX Palo Alto Research Center, August, 1980.

Markoff, John. "Computing in America: A Masculine Mystique." *The New York Times*. February 13, 1989.

Office of Technology Assessment, Congress of the United States. "Power On! New Tools for Teaching and Learning." Washington, DC, 1988.

A Writer's Desktop

Preminger, Alex, ed. *The Princeton Encyclopedia of Poetry and Poetics*. Princeton, NJ: Princeton University Press, 1974.

Saffo, Paul. "Desktop Publishing." *Personal Computing*. Vol. 12, no. 1 (December, 1988):69.

Saffo, Paul. "The Paper Revolution." *Personal Computing*. Vol. 11, no. 7 (July, 1987):43.

Building User-centered On-line Help

Borenstein, N. S. *The Design and Evaluation of On-line Help Systems*. Ph.D. thesis, Carnegie Mellon University, 1985.

Erlandsen, J., and J. Holm. "Intelligent Help Systems." *Information and Software Technology*. Vol. 29, no. 3 (1987):115–21.

Hysell, D. A. "Planning Considerations for Online Documentation." *Proceedings of the IEEE Professional Communication Society*. 1986 International Professional Communications Conference, Charlotte, North Carolina, pp. 61–66.

Miyata, Y., and D. A. Norman. "Psychological Issues in Support of Multiple Activities." In *User Centered System Design* (pp. 265–84). D. A. Norman and S. W. Draper, eds. Hillsdale, NJ: Erlbaum, 1986.

Norman, D. A. "Cognitive Engineering." In *User Centered System Design* (pp. 31–61). D. A. Norman and S. W. Draper, eds. Hillsdale, NJ: Erlbaum, 1986.

O'Malley, C. E. "Helping Users Help Themselves." In *User Centered System Design* (pp. 377–98). D. A. Norman and S. W. Draper, eds. Hillsdale, NJ: Erlbaum, 1986.

O'Malley, C. E., P. Smolensky, L. Bannon, E. Conway, J. Graham, J. Sokolov, and M. L. Monty. "A Proposal for User Centered System Documentation." *Proceedings of the CHI '83 Conference*, Boston, MA, pp. 282–85.

Owen, D. "Answers First, Then Questions." In *User Centered System Design* (pp. 361–75). D. A. Norman and S. W. Draper, eds. Hillsdale, NJ: Erlbaum, 1986.

Managing the Mundane

Smith, David Canfield. *Pygmalion: A Computer Program to Model and Simulate Creative Thought*. Basel, Switzerland: Birkhaüser-Verlag, 1976.

Smith, David Canfield. "Pygmalion: A Creative Programming Environment." Ph.D. dissertation, Department of Computer Science, Stanford University, 1975.

An Environment for Collaboration

Greif, Irene, ed. *Computer-Supported Cooperative Work: A Book of Readings*. San Mateo, CA: Morgan Kaufmann Publishers, 1988.

Malone, T. W., K. R. Grant, F. A. Turbak, S. A. Brobst, and M. D. Cohen. "Intelligent Information-Sharing Systems." *Communications of the ACM*. Vol. 30, no. 5 (May, 1987):390–402.

National Research Council. "A Report from the 1985 Workshop on Advanced Technology for Building Design and Engineering." Washington, DC: National Academy Press, 1986.

Panko, R. R. "Office Work." *Office: Technology and People (Netherlands)*. Vol. 2, no. 3 (October, 1984):205–38.

Stefik, M., and G. Foster. "Beyond the Chalkboard: Computer Support For Collaboration and Problem Solving in Meetings." *Communications of the ACM*. Vol. 30, no.1 (January, 1987):32–47.

Tisch School of the Arts. *Interactions, The Interaction Telecommunications Program Newsmagazine*. New York: New York University (December, 1988):8.

Groupware and Cooperative Work: Problems and Prospects

Aucella, A. F. "Voice: Technology Searching for Communication Needs." In *Proc. CHI+GI '87 Human Factors in Computing Systems*, Toronto, April 5–9, 1987, pp. 41–44.

Bjerknes, G., P. Ehn, and M. Kyng, eds. *Computers and Democracy—A Scandinavian Challenge*. Aldershot, UK: Gower, 1987.

Bodker, S., P. Ehn, J. Knudsen, M. Kyng, and K. Madsen. "Computer Support for Cooperative Design." In *Proc. CSCW '88 Conference on Computer-Supported Cooperative Work*, Portland, OR, September 26–28, 1988.

Ehrlich, S. F. "Social and Psychological Factors Influencing the Design of Office Communication Systems." In *Proc. CHI+GI '87 Human Factors in Computing Systems*, Toronto, April 5–9, 1987, pp. 323–29.

Ehrlich, S. F. "Strategies for Encouraging Successful Adoption of Office Communication Systems." *ACM Transactions on Office Information Systems*. Vol. 5 (1987):340–57.

Fanning, T., and B. Raphael. "Computer Teleconferencing: Experience at Hewlett Packard." In *Proc. CSCW '86 Conference on Computer-Supported Cooperative Work*, Austin, TX, December 3–5, 1986.

Greif, I., ed. *Computer-supported Cooperative Work: A Book of Readings*. San Mateo, CA: Morgan Kaufmann, 1988.

Grudin, J. CSCW '88: Report on the conference and review of the proceedings. *SIGCHI Bulletin*. Vol. 20 (1989):80–84.

Grudin, J. "Why Groupware Applications Fail: Problems in Design and Evaluation." *Office: Technology and People*. Vol. 4, no. 3 (1989):245–264.

Kling, R. "The Social Dimensions of Computerization." Plenary address given at CHI+GI '87 Human Factors in Computing Systems, Toronto, April 5–9, 1987.

Kraemer, K., and J. King. "Computer-based Systems for Cooperative Work and Group Decision-making." *ACM Computing Surveys*. Vol. 20 (1988):115–46.

Kraut, R. E., C. Egido, and J. Galegher. "Patterns of Contact and Communication in Scientific Research Collaboration." In *Proc. CSCW '88 Conference on Computer-Supported Cooperative Work*, Portland, OR, September 26–28, 1988.

Lai, K. Y., and T. W. Malone. "Object Lens: A 'Spreadsheet' for Cooperative Work." In *Proc. CSCW '88 Conference on Computer-Supported Cooperative Work*, Portland, OR, September 26–28, 1988.

Levy, S. *Hackers*. Garden City, NY: Anchor Press/Doubleday, 1985.

Malone, T. W., J. Yates, and R. I. Benjamin. "Electronic Markets and Electronic Hierarchies." *Communications of the ACM*. Vol. 30, no. 6 (1987):484–97.

McCracken, D. L., and R. M. Akscyn. "Experience with the ZOG Human-Computer Interface System." *Int. J. Man-Machine Studies*. Vol. 21 (1984):293–310.

Mintzberg, H. "A Typology of Organizational Structure." In *Organizations: A Quantum View*. D. Miller and P. H. Friesen, eds. Englewood Cliffs, NJ: Prentice-Hall, 1984.

Perin, C. "Electronic Social Fields in Bureaucracies." American Anthropological Association, Organized Session, "Egalitarian Ideologies and Class Contradictions in American Society." Washington, DC, November 15, 1989.

Perlman, G. "USENET: Doing Research on the Network." *UNIX/World*. (December, 1985):75–81.

Rowe, C. J. "Identifying Causes of Failure: A Case Study in Computerized Stock Control." *Behaviour and Information Technology*. Vol. 4 (1985):63–72.

Rowe, C. J. "Introducing a Sales Order Processing System: The Importance of Human, Organizational and Ergonomic Factors." *Behaviour and Information Technology*. Vol. 6 (1987):455–65.

Sathi, A., T. E. Morton, and S. F. Roth. "Callisto: An Intelligent Project Management System." *AI Magazine*. (Winter, 1986):34–52. Reprinted in Greif, I., ed. *Computer-supported Cooperative Work: A Book of Readings*. San Mateo, CA: Morgan Kaufmann, 1988, pp. 269–309.

Suchman, L. "Office Procedures as Practical Action: Models of Work and System Design." *ACM Transactions on Office Information Systems*. Vol. 1 (1983):320–28.

Whiteside, J., J. Bennett, and K. Holtzblatt. "Usability Engineering: Our Experience and Evolution." In *Handbook of Human-Computer Interaction*. M. Helander, ed. Amsterdam: North-Holland, 1988.

User Interface: A Personal View

Bruner, Jerome. *Towards a Theory of Instruction*. New York: W. W. Norton and Company, 1966.

Dawkins, Richard. *The Blind Watchmaker*. New York: Penquin Books, 1986.

Gallwey, Tim. *The Inner Game of Tennis.* New York: Random House, 1974.

Haber, R. "How We Remember What We See." *Scientific American.* Vol. 222 (1970):104–112.

Hadamard, Jacques. *An Essay on the Psychology of Invention in the Mathematical Field.* New York: Dover, 1945.

McLuhan, Marshall. *Understanding Media: The Extensions of Man.* New York: McGraw-Hill, 1964.

Minsky, Marvin, and Seymour Papert. *Perceptrons: An Introduction to Computational Geometry.* Cambridge, MA: M.I.T. Press, 1969.

Mumford, Lewis. *The Myth of the Machine.* 2 vols. New York: Harcourt, Brace and World, 1967–70.

————. *Technics and Civilization.* New York: Harcourt, Brace and Company, 1934.

Piaget, Jean. *Judgment and Reasoning in the Child.* New York: Harcourt, Brace and Company, 1928.

————. *The Language and Thought of the Child.* New York: Harcourt, Brace and Company, 1926.

————. *The Origins of Intelligence in Children.* New York: International Universities Press, 1952.

Suzuki, Shinichi. *Nurtured by Love: A New Approach to Education.* New York: Exposition Press, 1969.

Why Interfaces Don't Work

Norman, D. A. *The Psychology of Everyday Things.* New York: Basic Books, 1988.

The Evolution of Thinking Tools

Bergson, Henri. *Creative Evolution.* Trans. by Arthur Mitchell. New York: Henry Holt and Company, 1911.

Kay, Alan. "Computer Software." *Scientific American.* (September, 1984):52+.

Levine, Howard, and Howard Rheingold. *The Cognitive Connection.* New York: Prentice-Hall Press, 1987.

Russell, Bertrand. *Human Knowledge: Its Scope and Limits.* Part II. New York: Simon and Schuster, 1948.

Winograd, Terry. "Computer Software for Working with Language." *Scientific American.* (September, 1984).

The Interpersonal, Interactive, Interdimensional Interface

Gibson, William. *Neuromancer.* New York: Ace, 1984.

Nelson, Ted. *Computer Lib/Dream Machines.* Revised edition. Redmond, WA: Microsoft Press, 1987 (originally published, 1974).

The Right Way to Think about Software Design

Nelson, T. *Computer Lib/Dream Machines.* Revised edition. Redmond, WA: Microsoft Press, 1987.

Nelson, T. "The Crime of Wizzywig." *Mondo 2000.* (August, 1989).

Technique and Technology: Introduction

Heckel, Paul. *The Elements of Friendly Software Design*. Second edition. New York: Warner Software, Warner Books, 1984.

Animation at the Interface

Baecker, R. M. "Digital Video Display Systems and Computer Graphics." *Computer Graphics*. Vol. 13, no. 2 (1979):48–56.

Baecker, R. M. "Introduction to the Panel Session on Program Visualization." *Computer Graphics*. Vol. 20, no. 2 (1986):325.

Baecker, R. M. "Picture-Driven Animation." *Proceedings of the 1969 Spring Joint Computer Conference*. (1969):273–88.

Baecker, R. M. *Sorting Out Sorting*. 30-minute color sound videotape. Distributed by Morgan Kaufmann, Publishers, 1981.

Baecker, R. M., and J. Buchanan. "A Visually Enhanced and Animated Programming Environment." (Submitted for Publication.)

Baecker, R. M., and W.A.S. Buxton. *Readings in Human-Computer Interaction: A Multidisciplinary Approach*. Palo Alto, CA: Morgan Kaufmann, 1987.

Bentley, J. L., and B. W. Kernighan. "A System for Algorithm Animation." Computing Science Technical Report No. 132, AT&T Bell Laboratories, Murray Hill, NJ, 1987.

Brown, M. *Algorithm Animation*. Cambridge, MA: M.I.T. Press, 1988.

Burtnyk, N., and M. Wein. "Computer-generated Key-frame Animation." *Journal of the Society of Motion Picture and Television Engineering*. Vol. 80, no. 3 (1971):149ff.

Danahy, J. "Exploring Design through 3-Dimensional Simulations." *Landscape Architecture*. (July-August, 1988):64–71.

Eames, C. *Powers of Ten*. Animated film. IBM Corporation, 1971.

Kurlander, D., and S. Feiner. "Editable Graphical Histories." *Proceedings of the 1988 IEEE Workshop on Visual Languages*. (1988):127–34.

Lasseter, J., W. Reeves, et al. *Luxo Jr*. Animated film, Pixar Corporation, 1986.

Lasseter, J., W. Reeves, et al. *Red's Dream*. Animated film, Pixar Corporation, 1987.

Laybourne, K. *The Animation Book*. New York: Crown Publishers, 1979.

The Learning Company. *Robot Odyssey 1*. Computer game, 1984.

Martin. Private communication. Appears in Baecker, "Picture-Driven Animation." *Proceedings of the 1969 Spring Joint Computer Conference*. (1969):273–88.

McLaren, N. *Pas de Deux*. Animated film. National Film Board of Canada, 1967.

McLaren, N. Quotation displayed at Expo-68 in Montreal. Appears in Baecker, "Picture-Driven Animation." *Proceedings of the 1969 Spring Joint Computer Conference*. (1969):273–88.

Myers, B. "The Importance of Percent-Done Progress Indicators for Computer-Human Interfaces." *Proceedings of the Conference on Human Factors in Computing Systems*. (CHI '85):11–17.

Myers, B. "The User Interface for Sapphire." *Computer Graphics and Applications.* Vol. 4, no. 12 (1984):13–23.

Reynolds, C. "Computer Animation with Scripts and Actors." *Computer Graphics.* Vol. 16, no. 3 (1982):289–96.

Shoup, R. "Color Table Animation." *Computer Graphics.* Vol. 13, no. 2 (1979):8–13.

Sproull, R. F. "Frame-Buffer Display Architectures." *Annual Review of Computer Science.* Vol. 1 (1986):19–46.

Sukaviriya, P. "Dynamic Construction of Animated Help from Application Control." *Proceedings of the ACM SIGGRAPH Symposium on User Interface Software.* (1988):190–202.

Verrall, R. *Cosmic Zoom.* Animated film. National Film Board of Canada, 1968.

New Uses for Color

Albers, Joseph. *The Interaction of Color.* New Haven, CT: Yale University Press, 1963.

Barrett, Cyril. *An Introduction to Optical Art.* New York: E. P. Dutton and Company, 1971.

Claus, R. James, and Karen S. Claus. *Visual Environment: Sight, Sign and By-Law.* Don Mills, Ontario: Collier-Macmillan Canada, Ltd., 1971.

Cox, Donna J. "Using the Supercomputer to Visualize Higher Dimensions: An Artist's Contribution to Scientific Visualization." *Leonardo.* Vol. 21, no. 3 (1988):233–42.

De Grandis, Luigina. *Theory and Use of Color.* New York: Harry N. Abrams, 1986.

Greenberg, Donald, Aaron Marcus, Allan H. Schmidt, and Vernon Gorter. *The Computer Image: Application of Computer Graphics.* Reading, MA: Addison-Wesley Publishing Company, 1982.

Jam Session. Version 1.1. San Rafael, CA: Broderbund Software, 1987.

Keates, John S. "The Perception of Colour in Cartography." *Proceedings of the Cartographic Symposium,* University of Glasgow, 1962, pp. 19–28.

Lassen, Niels A., David H. Ingvar, and Erik Shinkøj. "Brain Function and Blood Flow." *Scientific American.* Vol. 239, no. 4 (October, 1978):62–71.

Mantei, Marilyn. "Capturing the Capture Lab Concepts: A Case Study in the Design of Computer Supported Meeting Environments." *Proceedings of the Conference on Computer-Supported Cooperative Work.* (September, 1988):257–70.

Marcus, Aaron. "The Ten Commandments of Color." *Computer Graphics Today.* Vol. 3, no. 10 (November, 1986):7–9.

Murch, Gerald M. "Color Graphics—Blessing or Ballyhoo?" In *Readings in Human-Computer Interaction: A Multidisciplinary Approach.* R. M. Baecker and W.A.S. Buxton, eds. Los Altos, CA: Morgan Kaufmann Publishers, Inc., 1987.

Olson, Judy M. "Color and the Computer in Cartography." In *Color and the Computer.* H. John Durrett, ed. Orlando, FL: Academic Press, 1987, pp. 205–220.

Olson, Judy M. "Spectrally Encoded Two-Variable Maps." *Annals of the Association of American Geographers*. (1981):259–76.

PowerPoint. Version 2.0. Redmond, WA: Microsoft Corporation, 1988.

Reising, John M., and Anthony J. Aretz. "Color Computer Graphics in Military Cockpits." In *Color and the Computer*. H. John Durrett, ed.. Orlando, FL: Academic Press, 1987, pp. 151–70.

Salomon, Gitta, and James Chen. "Using Neural Nets to Aid Color Selection." *Society for Information Display International Symposium Digest of Technical Papers*. Vol. 20 (May, 1989):326–29.

Wagner, Annette, and Gitta Salomon. "Color Finder Survey Results." *Confidential Apple Technical Report*. January, 1988.

Wyszecki, Gunter, and W. S. Stiles. *Colour Science*. New York: John Wiley and Sons, 1982.

Recognizing the Symptoms of Hypertext and What to Do about It

Bush, Vannevar. "As We May Think." *Atlantic Monthly*. (July, 1945):101–108.

Byte Magazine. Special Issue on Hypertext. Vol. 13, no. 10 (October, 1988).

Communications of the ACM. Special Issue on Hypertext. Vol. 31, no. 7 (July, 1988).

Conklin, Jeff. "Hypertext: An Introduction and Survey." *IEEE Computer*. (September, 1987):17–41.

Gittins, David. "Icon-based Human-Computer Interaction." *Int. J. Man-Machine Studies*. Vol. 24 (1986):519–43.

Halasz, Frank. "Reflections on Notecards: Seven Issues for the Next Generation of Hypermedia Systems." *Communications of the ACM*. (July, 1988):836–52.

Pea, Roy D. "Human-Machine Symbiosis: Exploring Hypermedia as New Cognitive and Cultural Technologies." Draft, in *Computers, Cognition and Epistemology*. S. Larsen and K. Plunketts, eds. Hillsdale, NJ: Lawrence Erlbaum Associates, 1988.

Smith, John B., and Stephen F. Weiss. "An Overview of Hypertext." *Communications of the ACM*. (July, 1988):816–19.

Van Dam, Andries. "Hypertext '87 Keynote Address." *Communications of the ACM*. (July, 1988):887–95.

Weiland, William J., and Ben Shneiderman. "Interactive Graphics in Hypertext Systems." Human-Computer Interaction Laboratory, University of Maryland, Jan. 4, 1988.

A Design for Supporting New Input Devices

Apple Computer, Inc. "The Toolbox Event Manager." In *Inside Macintosh*. Vol. 1, ch. 8. Reading, MA: Addison-Wesley Publishing Company, 1985.

Brooks, F. "Grasping Reality Through Illusion—Interactive Graphics Serving Science." *Proceedings of SIGCHI'88*. (May 1988):1–11.

Buxton, W., and B. A. Myers. "A Study in Two-Handed Input." *Proceedings of SIGCHI'86*. (April, 1986):321–26.

International Standards Organization. "Information Processing-Graphical Kernel System (GKS) Functional Description." International Standards Organization, ISO/DP 7942.

Mantei, M. "Capturing the Capture Lab Concepts: A Case Study in the Design of Computer Supported Meeting Environments." *Proceedings of the CSCW '88 Conference*, Portland, OR, September 26–28, 1988. New York: ACM, 1988.

Nexus, *SideBand™*. A Macintosh program. Brisbane, Australia: Nexus Development, 1989.

Stefik, M., G. Foster, D. Bobrow, K. Kahn, S. Lanning, and L. Suchman. "Beyond the Chalkboard: Computer Support for Collaboration and Problem Solving in Meetings." *Communications of the ACM*. Vol. 30, no. 1 (January, 1987):32–47.

Sun Microsystems. *NeWS™ 1.1 Manual*. Chapter 3, "Input." Part No: 800–2146–10. Mountain View, CA: Sun Microsystems. Revision A of 15 January 1988.

Watterson, B. *Something Under the Bed Is Drooling, A Calvin and Hobbes Collection*. Kansas City, MI: Andrews and McMeel, 1988, pp. 101–104.

Gestures in Human-Computer Communication

Bolt, R. "*Put That There*': Voice and Gesture at the Graphics Interface." SIGGRAPH '80 Proceedings. Published as *Computer Graphics*. Vol. 14, no. 3 (July, 1980):262–70.

Buxton, W., and B. Myers. "A Study in Two-Handed Input." *CHI '86 Conference Proceedings*. (April, 1986):321–26.

Ehrlich, S. (moderator), T. Bikson, W. MacKay, and J. Tang. "Tools for Supporting Cooperative Work Near and Far: Highlights from the CSSW Conference (Panel)." *CHI '89 Conference Proceedings*. (1989):353–56.

Fisher, S. "Telepresence Master Glove Controller for Dexterous Robotic End-Effectors." SPIE Cambridge Symposium on Optical and Optoelectronic Engineering, October 26, 1986, Cambridge, MA.

Krueger, M. *Artificial Reality*. Reading, MA: Addison-Wesley Publishing Company, 1983.

Kurtenbach, G. "Hierarchical Encapsulation and Connection in a Graphical User Interface: A Music Case Study." Master's Thesis, University of Toronto, Dept. of Computer Science, 1988.

Mountford, S. J., R. Penner, and P. Bursch. "Pilot Command Interfaces for Discrete Control of Automated Nap-of-Earth Flight." *Proceedings of the AIAA/IEEE 6th Digital Avionics Systems Conference*. (1984):386–92.

Petajan, E., B. Bradford, and D. Bodoff. "An Improved Automatic Lipreading System to Enhance Speech Recognition." *CHI '88 Conference Proceedings*. (May, 1988):19–25.

Schmandt, C. M., and E. A. Hulteen. "The Intelligent Voice-Interactive Interface." *Proceedings of Human Factors in Computing Systems*. (March 15–17, 1982):363–66.

Suen, C., M. Berthold, and S. Mori. "Automatic Recognition of Handprinted Characters—The State of the Art." *Proceedings of IEEE*. Vol. 68, no. 4 (April, 1980):469–87.

Sutherland, I. "A Head Mounted Three-Dimensional Display." *Fall Joint Computer Conference*. (1968):757–64.

Zimmerman, T., J. Lanier, C. Blanchard, and S. Bryson. "A Hand Gesture Interface Device." *CHI + GI '87 Conference Proceedings*. (April, 1987):189–92.

Talking and Listening to Computers

Apple Computer, Inc. *Inside Mac*. Vol. 5. Reading, MA: Addison-Wesley Publishing Company, 1988.

Baumgarten, H. S., and V. J. Schiavone. "A Voice-Input Computerized Dental Examination System." *Speech Technology*. Vol. 4, no. 3:42–45.

Bernabe, B. "Technology and Programming Perspectives on Interactive Voice for Military Aircraft." *Proceedings of the Voice I/O Systems Applications Conference, AVIOS*. San Francisco, CA, October, 1988.

Blattner, M., D. Sumikawa, and R. Greenberg. "Earcons and Icons: Their Structure and Common Design Principles." *Human-Computer Interaction*. Vol. 4, no. 1 (1989):11–44.

Bly, S. "Sound and Computer Information Presentation." (UCRL – 53282). Doctoral Dissertation, Lawrence Livermore National Laboratory and University of California, Davis, 1982.

Brooks, R., P. Millar, I. Cameron, and A. Bain. "Voice Controlled Banking." *Proceedings of the Voice I/O Systems Applications Conference, AVIOS*. San Francisco, CA, October, 1988.

Buxton, W. "Introduction to This Special Issue on Non-speech Audio." *Human-Computer Interaction*. Vol. 4, no. 1 (1989).

Buxton, W. "There's More to Interaction Than Meets the Eye: Some Issues in Manual Input." In *User Centered System Design: New Perspectives on Human-Computer Interface*. D. A. Norman and S. W. Draper, eds. Hillsdale, NJ: Lawrence Erlbaum Associates, 1986.

Corrick, D. and D. Warren. "'ELTON' Takes Orders for New Zealand Wines and Spirits." *Speech Technology*. Vol. 4, no. 3:82–86.

Diethrlich, E. "Voice Recognition and Voice Synthesis in the Cardiac Intensive Care Unit." *Speech Technology*. Vol. 4, no. 3 (1988):46–50.

Digital Equipment Corporation. "Online Sales Reporting with DECtalk." *Straight Talk*. Vol. 2, no. 1 (1985):2–4.

Edwards, A. "Soundtrack: An Auditory Interface for Blind Users." *Human-Computer Interaction*. Vol. 4, no. 1 (1989):45–66.

Eddy, D. A. "Registration via Telephone—The Friendly Alternative." *Proceedings of the Voice I/O Systems Applications Conference, AVIOS*. San Francisco, CA, October, 1988.

Firman, T. R. "Empowering the Macintosh Interface with Speech Recognition." *Proceedings of the Voice I/O Systems Applications Conference, AVIOS*. San Francisco, CA, October, 1988.

Franz, G., J. Reimer, and W. Wotiz. "Julie: The Application of DSP to a Consumer Product." *Speech Technology*. Vol. 4, no. 3 (1988):82–86.

Gaver, W. W. "Auditory Icons: Using Sound in Computer Interfaces." *Human-Computer Interaction*. Vol. 2 (1986):167–77.

Gaver, W. W. "Everyday Listening and Auditory Icons." Doctoral Dissertation, University of California, San Diego, 1988.

Gaver, W. W. "The SonicFinder, an Interface That Uses Auditory Icons." *Human Machine Interaction*. Vol. 4, no. 1 (1989).

Hutchins, S. E. "Computer-Animated Speech Processing for Speech Therapy." *Proceedings of the Voice I/O Systems Applications Conference, AVIOS*. San Francisco, CA, October, 1988.

Hutchins, E. L. "Metaphors for Interface Design." Paper presented at NATO Workshop on Multimodal Dialogues including Voice. Venaco, Corsica, France, 1986.

Hutchins, E. L., J. D. Hollan, and D. A. Norman. "Direct Manipulation Interfaces." In *User Centered System Design: New Perspectives on Human-Computer Interaction*. D. A. Norman and S. W. Draper, eds. Hillsdale, NJ: Lawrence Erlbaum Associates, 1988, pp. 87–124.

Laurel, B. "Interface as Mimesis." In *User Centered Design: New Perspectives on Human-Computer Interface*. D. A. Norman and S. W. Draper, eds. Hillsdale, NJ: Lawrence Erlbaum Associates, 1986.

Liang, M. D., and K. A. Narayanan. "Voice Controlled Microscope Facilitates Intricate Microsurgical Procedures." *Speech Technology*. Vol. 4, no. 3 (1988):52–54.

Love, J. M. "Automated Voice Wireless Dispatching." *Proceedings of the Voice I/O Systems Applications Conference, AVIOS*. San Francisco, CA, October, 1988.

Mansur, D. L., M. M. Blattner, and K. I. Joy. "Sound-graphs: A Numerical Data Analysis Method for the Blind." *Proceedings of the 18th Hawaii International Conference on System Sciences*. (January, 1985):63–174.

Mezrich, J. J., S. Frysinger, and R. Slivjanovski. "Dynamic Representation of Multivariate Time Series Data." *Journal of the American Statistical Association*. Vol. 79: 34–40.

Mountford, S. J., R. Penner, and P. Bursch. "Pilot Command Interfaces for Discrete Control of Automated Nap-of-Earth Flight." *Proceedings of Sixth Digital Avionics Systems Conference*, Baltimore, MD, December, 1984.

Mountford, S. J., and J. Schwartz. "Speech Technology Enhancements of Automatic Target Recognition." *Proceedings of Fifth Digital Avionics Systems Conference*. Seattle, WA, November, 1983.

North, R. A., and S. J. Mountford. "Applications of Speech Technology in Manned Penetration Bombers." *Proceedings of the Human Factors Society, 24th Meeting*. Los Angeles, CA, October, 1980.

North, R. A., S. J. Mountford, and L. A. Krueger. "A Voice-Interactive Kit Verification Station." *Proceedings of Voice-Data Entry Systems Applications Conference*. CA, September, 1982.

North, R. A., and W. A. Lee. "The Application of Advanced Speech Technology in Manned Penetration Bombers." Final Report, AFWAL/TR/82/3004, Wright-Patterson Air Force Base, 1982.

Petajan, E., B. Bischoff, D. Bodorff, and N. M. Brooke. "An Improved Automatic LipReading System to Enhance Speech Recognition." *Proceedings of CHI.* (1988):19.

Peterson, I. "Picture This." *Science News.* (June 20, 1987).

Pickover, Clifford. "From Noise Comes Beauty (Generating Textures in Computer Graphics)." *Computer Graphics World.* Vol. 11, no. 3 (March, 1988):115–17.

Rao, D., and M. Llief. "Talking to Maclow." *Proceedings of the Voice I/O Systems Applications Conference, AVIOS.* San Francisco, CA, October, 1988.

Reed, J. T. "Welcome to the Metropolitan State College Touchtone Information System Please Enter a Service Code." *Proceedings of the Voice I/O Systems Applications Conference, AVIOS.* San Francisco, CA, October, 1988.

Schmandt, C. "The Intelligent Ear: A Graphical Interface to Digital Audio." *Proceedings of the International Conference on Cybernetics and Society.* (1981):393–97.

Schmandt, C., and B. Arons. "Phone Slave: A Graphical Telecommunications Interface." *Proceedings of the Society of Information Display.* Vol. 26, no. 1 (1985).

Schmandt, C. M., and E. A. Hulteen. "The Intelligent Voice-Interactive Interface." *Proceedings of Human Factors in Computing Systems.* (March 15–17, 1982):363–66.

Schuster, R. E. "B.R.U.T.U.S: Better Registration Using Touch-Tone Phones for University Students." *Proceedings of the Voice I/O Systems Applications Conference, AVIOS.* San Francisco, CA, October, 1988.

Searcy, G. "Butler-in-a-Box." *Proceedings of the Voice I/O Systems Applications Conference, AVIOS.* San Francisco, CA, October, 1988.

Sprouls, C. "Voice in the Everyday Activities of a Management Class." *Proceedings of the Voice I/O Systems Applications Conference, AVIOS.* San Francisco, CA, October, 1988.

Wickens, C. D., S. J. Mountford, and W. Schreiner. "Multiple Resources, Task-Hemispheric Integrity and Individual Differences in Time-Sharing." *Human Factors.* Vol. 23, no. 2 (1981):211–29.

Witten, I. H., and D. H. C. Madams. "The Telephone Enquiry Service: A Man-Machine System Using Synthetic Speech." *International Journal of Man-Machine Studies.* Vol. 9:449–64.

Illusion in the Interface

Davis, James R., and Julia Hirschberg. "Automatic Generation of Prosodic Support for Discourse Structure." *Proceedings of the Association for Computational Linguistics.* (1988):187–93.

Flanagan, James L. "Analog Measurements of Sound Radiation from the Mouth." *Journal of the Acoustic Society of America.* Vol. 32, no. 12 (1960).

Kojima, H., J. Nishi, and L. Gomi. "A Voice Man-Machine Communication System Based on Statistical Information Received from Telephone Conversations." *Proceedings of 1987 Conference*, American Voice I/O Society, October, 1987, pp. 101–110.

Kraut, Robert E., Steven H. Lewis, and Lawrence W. Swezey. "Listener Responsiveness and the Coordination of Conversation." *Journal of Personality and Social Psychology.*Vol. 41, no, 4 (1982):718–31.

Sakoe, H., and S. Chiba. "Dynamic Programming Algorithm Optimization for Spoken Word Recognition." *IEEE Transactions on Acoustics, Speech, and Signal Processing.* Vol. 26 (February, 1978):43–49.

Schmandt, Chris. "Employing Voice Back Channels to Facilitate Audio Document Retrieval." *Proceedings.* ACM Conference on Office Information Systems. (1988):213–18.

Schmandt, C., and B. Arons. "A Conversational Telephone Messaging System." *IEEE Trans. on Consumer Electr.* Vol. 30, no. 3 (1984):xxi–xxiv.

Schmandt, C., and B. Arons. "Phone Slave: A Graphical Telecommunications Interface." *Proc. of the Soc. for Information Display.* Vol. 26, no. 1 (1985):79–82.

Schmandt, Chris, and Barry Arons. "A Robust Parser and Dialog Generator for a Conversational Office System." *Proceedings of 1986 Conference.* American Voice I/O Society. (1986):355–65.

Schmandt, Christopher, Barry Arons, and Charles Simmons. "Voice Interaction in an Integrated Office and Telecommunications Environment." *Proceedings.* American Voice Input Output Society. (1985).

Yngve, Victor H. "On Getting a Word in Edgewise." *Papers from the Sixth Regional Meeting.* Chicago Linguistics Society. (1970):567–78.

Interface Agents: Metaphors with Character

Brennan, Susan. "Interface Agents." Unpublished paper, 1984.

Crowston, Kevin, and Thomas W. Malone. "Intelligent Software Agents." *Byte.* Vol. 13, no. 13 (December, 1988):267–74.

Carbonell, Jaime G. "Towards a Process Model of Human Personality Traits." *Artificial Intelligence.* Vol. 15 (1980):49–50.

Hayes-Roth, Frederick, Donald A. Waterman, and Douglas B. Lenat, eds. *Building Expert Systems.* Teknowledge Series in Knowledge Engineering, no. 1. Reading, MA: Addison-Wesley Publishing Company, 1983.

Kay, Alan. "Computer Software." *Scientific American.* Vol. 251, no. 3 (September, 1984):52–59.

Lakoff, George, and Mark Johnson. *Metaphors We Live By.* Chicago: The University of Chicago Press, 1980.

Laurel, Brenda. "Interface as Mimesis." In *User-Centered System Design: New Perspectives on Human-Computer Interaction.* D. A. Norman and S. Draper, eds. Hillsdale, NJ: Lawrence Erlbaum Associates, 1986.

Laurel, Brenda. "Toward the Design of a Computer-Based Interactive Fantasy System." Ph.D. Dissertation, The Ohio State University, 1986.

Lebowitz, Michael. "Creating Characters in a Story-Telling Universe." *Poetics.* Vol. 13 (1984):171–94.

Meehan, James Richard. "The Metanovel: Writing Stories by Computer." Ph.D. Dissertation, Yale University, 1976.

Schank, Roger C., and Michael Lebowitz. "The Use of Stereotype Information in the Comprehension of Noun Phrases." Alexandria, VA: Defense Technical Information Center, 1979.

Schwamberger, Jeffrey. "The Nature of Dramatic Character." Ph.D. Dissertation, The Ohio State University, 1980.

Guides: Characterizing the Interface

Burke, James. *Connections*. Boston: Little, Brown and Company, 1978.

Conklin, Jeff. "Hypertext: An Introduction and Survey." *IEEE Computer*. Vol. 20, no. 9 (September, 1987):17–41.

Halasz, Frank G. "Reflections on NoteCards: Seven Issues for the Next Generation of Hypermedia Systems." *Communication of the ACM*. Vol. 31, no. 7 (July, 1988):836–52.

Marchionini, Gary, and Ben Shneiderman. "Finding Facts versus Browsing Knowledge in Hypertext Systems." *IEEE Computer*. (January, 1988):70–80.

Marchionini, Gary, Diane Patrick, and Jerry Teague. "Children's Use of a CD-ROM Encyclopedia: A Look at Electronic Information-Seeking Strategy." *NECC Conference Proceedings*. June, 1987.

Oren, Tim. "The Architecture of Static Hypertexts." *Hypertext '87 Papers*. University of North Carolina, Chapel Hill, NC, November 13–15, 1987, pp. 291–306.

Ross, Nancy Wilson. *Westward the Women*. San Francisco: North Point Press, 1985.

Salomon, Gitta, Tim Oren, and Kristee Kreitman. "Using Guides to Explore Multimedia Databases," *Proc. 22nd Hawaii International Conference on System Sciences*, Kailua-Kona, Hawaii, January 3–6, 1989, pp. 3–12.

Schlissel, Lillian. *Women's Diaries of the Westward Journey*. New York: Schocken Books, 1982.

Tolkien, J. R. R. "On Fairy Stories." In *The Tolkien Reader*. New York: Ballantine, 1966.

Weizenbaum, Joseph. *Computer Power and Human Reason*. San Francisco: W. H. Freeman, 1976, pp. 2–7.

Narrative and the Interface

Barthes, Roland. "Introduction to the Structural Analysis of Narrative." In *Image Music Text*. New York: Hill and Wang, 1977.

Barthes, Roland. *S/Z*. New York: Hill and Wang, 1974.

Chatman, Seymour. *Story and Discourse: Narrative Structure in Fiction and Film*. Ithaca, NY: Cornell University Press, 1978.

Don, Abbe. "We Make Memories." Master's Thesis. Interactive Telecommunications Program, New York University, 1989.

Eagleton, Terry. *Literary Theory*. Minneapolis, MN: University of Minnesota Press, 1983.

Fischer, Michael. "Ethnicity and the Post-Modern Arts of Memory." In *Writing Culture*. James Clifford and George Marcus, eds. Berkeley, CA: University of California Press, 1986.

Laurel, Brenda K. "Interface as Mimesis." In *User Centered System Design, New Perspectives on Human-Computer Interaction*. D.A. Norman and S. Draper, eds. Hillsdale, NJ: Lawrence Erlbaum Associates, 1986.

de Lauretis, Teresa. "Desire in Narrative." In *Alice Doesn't: Feminism, Semiotics, Cinema*. Bloomington, IN: Indiana University Press, 1984.

Masayevsa, Victor. *Itam Hakim, Hopiit*. (We, The People, The Hopi.) Videotape produced by IS Productions, Hotevilla, Arizona, 1984.

Ong, Walter. *Orality and Literacy: The Technologizing of the Word*. London: Methuen, 1982.

Turner, Terry. "From Cosmology to Ideology: Resistance, Adaptation and Social Consciousness Among the Kayapo." (English text of communication presented to the Symposium, "Pesquisas Recentes em Etnologia e Historia Indigena da Amazonia," sponsored by the Associacao Brasileira de Antopologia, Museum Goeldi, Belem do Para, Brazil, December 7–10, 1987.)

YIVO Institute for Jewish Research. "People of 1000 Towns, a Photographic Encyclopedia of Jewish Life in Eastern Europe, 1880–1940." New York: YIVO Institute for Jewish Research, 1988.

Conversation as Direct Manipulation: An Iconoclastic View

Bell, A. "Language Style as Audience Design." *Language in Society*. Vol. 13 (1984):145–204.

Brennan, S. E. "Conversation with and through Computers." Submitted for publication, 1989.

Brennan, S. E. "The Multimedia Articulation of Answers in a Natural Language Database Query System." *Proceedings, Second Conference on Applied Natural Language Processing*. Association of Computational Linguistics, Austin, TX, 1988, pp. 1–8.

Clark, H. H., and T. B. Carlson. "Context for Comprehension." In *Attention and performance IX*. J. Long and A. Baddeley, eds. Hillsdale, NJ: Lawrence Erlbaum Associates, 1981.

Clark, H. H., and S. E. Haviland. "Comprehension and the Given/New Contract." In *Discourse Production and Comprehension*. R. O. Freedle, ed. Hillsdale, NJ: Lawrence Erlbaum Associates, 1977.

Clark, H. H., and C. R. Marshall. "Definite Reference and Mutual Knowledge." In *Elements of Discourse Understanding*. A. K. Joshi, B. Webber, and I. A. Sag, eds. Cambridge, England: Cambridge University Press, 1981.

Clark, H. H., and G. L. Murphy. "Audience Design in Meaning and Reference." In *Language and Comprehension*. J. F. LeNy and W. Kintsch, eds. Amsterdam: North-Holland Publishing Company, 1982.

Clark, H. H., and E. F. Schaefer. "Collaborating on Contributions to Conversations." *Language and Cognitive Processes*. Vol. 2 (1987):1–23.

Clark, H. H., and E. F. Schaefer. "Contributing to Discourse." *Cognitive Science*. Vol. 13 (1989):259–94.

Clark, H. H., and D. Wilkes-Gibbs. "Referring as a Collaborative Process." *Cognition*. Vol. 22 (1986):1–39.

Draper, S. W. "Display Managers as the Basis for User-Machine Communication." In *User Centered System Design*. S. W. Draper and D. A. Norman, eds. Hillsdale, NJ: Lawrence Erlbaum Associates, 1986.

Grice, H. P. "Logic and Conversation." (From the William James lectures, Harvard University, 1967.) In *Syntax and Semantics 3: Speech Acts*. P. Cole and J. Morgan, eds. New York: Academic Press, 1975.

Hewlett-Packard Natural Language Project. "7000 Variations on a Single Sentence." Unpublished draft, 1986.

Hutchins, E. L., J. D. Hollan, and D. A. Norman. "Direct Manipulation Interfaces." In *User Centered System Design*. S. W. Draper and D. A. Norman, eds. Hillsdale, NJ: Lawrence Erlbaum Associates, 1986.

Isaacs, E. A., and H. H. Clark. "References in Conversation Between Experts and Novices." *Journal of Experimental Psychology: General*. Vol. 116 (1987):26–37.

Levelt, W. J. M., and S. Kelter. "Surface Form and Memory in Question Answering." *Cognitive Psychology*. Vol. 14 (1982):78–106.

Levinson, S. C. *Pragmatics*. Cambridge, England: Cambridge University Press, 1983.

Lewis, C., and D. A. Norman, "Designing for Error." In *User Centered System Design*. S. W. Draper and D. A. Norman, eds. Hillsdale, NJ: Lawrence Erlbaum Associates, 1986.

Milroy, L. "Style-Shifting and Code-Switching." In *Observing and Analyzing Natural Language*. Lesley Milroy, ed. New York: Blackwell, 1987.

Norman, D. A. "Cognitive Engineering." In *User Centered System Design*. S. W. Draper and D. A. Norman, eds. Hillsdale, NJ: Lawrence Erlbaum Associates, 1986.

Norman, D. A. "The Trouble with UNIX." *Datamation*. Vol. 27 (1981):139–50.

Prince, E. F. "Toward a Taxonomy of Given-New Information." In *Radical Pragmatics*. P. Cole, ed. New York: Academic Press, 1981.

Richards, M. A., and K. M. Underwood, "How Should People and Computers Speak to One Another?" *Proceedings, Interact '84: First IFIP Conference on "Human-Computer Interaction."* London: International Federation for Information Processing, 1984, pp. 33–36.

Sacks, H., E. A. Schegloff, and G. A. Jefferson. "A Simplest Systematics for the Organization of Turn-taking in Conversation." *Language*. Vol. 50 (1974):696–735.

Schegloff, E. A. "Discourse as an Interactional Achievement: Some Uses of 'Uh Huh' and Other Things That Come Between Sentences." In *Analyzing Discourse: Text and Talk*. D. Tannen, ed. 32nd Georgetown University Roundtable on Languages and Linguistics 1981. Washington, DC: Georgetown University Press, 1982, pp. 71–93.

Schegloff, E. A., and H. Sacks. "Opening Up Closings." *Semiotica*. Vol. 8 (1973):289–327.

Schneiderman, B. *Designing the User Interface: Strategies for Effective Human-Computer Interaction*. Reading, MA: Addison-Wesley Publishing Company, 1986.

Schneiderman, B. "The Future of Interactive Systems and the Emergence of Direct Manipulation." *Behavior and Information Technology*. Vol. 1 (1982):237–56.

Schober, M. F., and H. H. Clark. "Understanding by Addressees and Overhearers." *Cognitive Psychology*. Vol. 21 (1989):211–32.

Shatz, M., and R. Gelman. "The Development of Communication Skills: Modifications in the Speech of Young Children as a Function of Listener." *Monographs of the Society for Research in Child Development*. Vol. 38, no. 5 (1973):1–37.

Stalnaker, R. C. "Assertion." In *Syntax and Semantics: Pragmatics 9*. P. Cole, ed. New York: Academic Press, 1978.

Sutherland, I. E. "Sketchpad: A Man-Machine Graphical Communication System." M.I.T. Lincoln Laboratory Technical Report no. 296, Lexington, MA, 1963.

Yngve, V. H. "Getting a Word in Edgewise." *Papers from the Sixth Regional Meeting of the Chicago Linguistic Society*. Chicago, IL, 1970, pp. 348+.

The "Natural" Language of Interaction: A Perspective on Nonverbal Dialogues

Baecker, R., and W. Buxton. *Readings in Human-Computer Interaction: A Multidisciplinary Approach*. Los Altos, CA: Morgan Kaufmann, 1987.

Buxton, W. "Chunking and Phrasing and the Design of Human-Computer Dialogues." *Proceedings of the IFIP World Computer Congress*. Dublin, Ireland, September 1–5, 1986, pp. 475–80.

Buxton, W. "An Informal Study of Selection-Positioning Tasks." *Proceedings of Graphics Interface '82*. (1982):323–28.

Buxton, W. "Lexical and Pragmatic Considerations of Input Structures." *Computer Graphics*. Vol. 17, no. 1 (1983):31–37.

Buxton, W. "There's More to Interaction than Meets the Eye: Some Issues in Manual Input." In *User Centered Systems Design: New Perspectives on Human-Computer Interaction*. D. Norman and S. Draper, eds. Hillsdale, NJ: Lawrence Erlbaum Associates, 1986, pp. 319–37.

Buxton, W., and B. Myers. "A Study in Two-Handed Input." *Proceedings of CHI'86*. (1986):321–26.

Rhyne, J. R., and C. G. Wolf. "Gestural Interfaces for Information Processing Applications." Computer Science Technical Report RC 12179, IBM T.J. Watson Research Center, Distribution Services 73–F11, P.O. Box 218, Yorktown Heights, NY, 1986.

Wolf, C. G. "Can People Use Gesture Commands?" *ACM SIGCHI Bulletin*. Vol. 18, no. 2 (1986):73–74.

Wolf, C. G., and P. Morrel-Samuels. "The Use of Hand-Drawn Gestures for Text-Editing." IBM Technical Report RC 12523 (#56294), 2/19/87. To appear in the *International Journal of Man-Machine Studies*, (in press).

VIDEOPLACE and the Interface of the Future

Foley, James D. "Interfaces for Advanced Computing, " Scientific American. Vol. 257, no. 4, pp. 126–135.

Krueger, M. W. Artificial Reality. Reading, MA: Addison-Wesley Publishing Company, 1983.

Krueger, M. W. "Computer Controlled Responsive Environments." Ph.D. Dissertation, University of Wisconsin, 1974.

Krueger, M. W. "Responsive Environments." Proceedings of National Computer Conference. 1977.

Krueger, M. W. "VIDEOPLACE—An Artificial Reality," Proceedings of the ACM Conference on Human Factors in Computing Systems, April, 1985.

Krueger, M. W. "VIDEOPLACE: A Report from the ARTIFICIAL REALITY Laboratory." Leonardo. Vol. 18, issue 3 (October, 1985).

Krueger, M. W. "VIDEOPLACE Sampler." SIGGRAPH Video Review. (1986).

Virtual Interface Environments

Comeau, C., and J. Bryan. "Headsight Television System Provides Remote Surveillance." Electronics. (Nov. 10, 1961):86–90.

Fisher, Scott S. "Telepresence Master Glove Controller for Dexterous Robotic End-Effectors." Advances in Intelligent Robotics Systems, D. P. Casasent, ed. Proc. SPIE 726, 1986.

Fisher, S. S., M. McGreevy, J. Humphries, and W. Robinett. "Virtual Environment Display System." ACM 1986 Workshop on 3D Interactive Graphics, Chapel Hill, North Carolina. October 23–24, 1986.

Fisher, S. S., M. McGreevy, J. Humphries, and W. Robinett. "Virtual Interface Environment for Telepresence Applications." In Proceedings of ANS International Topical Meeting on Remote Systems and Robotics in Hostile Environments. J. D. Berger, ed. 1987.

Fisher, S. S., E. M. Wenzel, C. Coler, and M. W. McGreevy. "Virtual Interface Environment Workstations." Proceedings of the Human Factors Society 32nd Annual Meeting, Anaheim, CA, October 24–28, 1988.

Foley, James D. "Interfaces for Advanced Computing." Scientific American. Vol. 257, no. 4 (1987):126–35.

Herot, C. "Spatial Management of Data." ACM Transactions on Database Systems. Vol. 5, no. 4 (1980).

Knowlton, K. C. "Computer Displays Optically Superimposed on Input Devices." The Bell System Technical Journal. Vol. 56, no. 3 (March, 1977):367–83.

Lippman, Andrew. "Movie-Maps: An Application of the Optical Videodisc to Computer Graphics." Computer Graphics. Vol. 14, no. 3 (1980):32+.

Negroponte, N. "Media Room." Proceedings of the Society for Information Display. Vol. 22, no. 2 (1981):109–13.

Schmandt, C. "Spatial Input/Display Correspondence in a Stereoscopic Computer Graphic Work Station." Computer Graphics, Proceedings of ACM SIGGRAPH '83. Vol. 17, no. 3 (1983):253+.

Sutherland, I. E. "Head-Mounted Three-Dimensional Display." *Proceedings of the Fall Joint Computer Conference*. Vol. 33 (1968):757–64.

Wenzel, E. M., F. L. Wightman, and S. H. Foster. "A Virtual Display System for Conveying Three-Dimensional Information." *Proc. Hum. Fac. Soc.* (1988).

Through the Looking Glass

Fisher, S. S., M. McGreevy, J. Humphries, and W. Robinett. "Virtual Environment Display System." ACM 1986 Workshop on 3D Interactive Graphics, Chapel Hill, NC, October 23–24, 1986.

Sutherland, I. E. "A Head-Mounted Three Dimensional Display." *Proceedings of the Fall Joint Computer Conference*. (1968). Washington DC: Thompson Books, 1968, pp.757–64.

What's the Big Deal about Cyberspace?

Baudrillard, Jean. *Simulations*. New York: Semiotext(e), Inc., Columbia University Press, 1983.

Bronowski, Jacob. *The Origins of Knowledge and Imagination*. New Haven, CT: Yale University Press, 1978.

Fisher, S. S., M. McGreevy, J. Humphries, and W. Robinett. "Virtual Environment Display System." ACM 1986 Workshop on 3D Interactive Graphics, Chapel Hill, NC, October 23–24, 1986.

Gibson, William. *Neuromancer*. New York: Berkley, 1984.

Hawken, Paul. *The Next Economy*. New York: Holt, Rheinhart, and Winston, 1983.

Laurel, Brenda. "Toward the Design of a Computer-Based Interactive Fantasy System." Ph.D. Dissertation, The Ohio State University, 1986.

Pagels, Heinz. *The Dreams of Reason*. New York: Simon and Schuster, 1988.

Rheingold, Howard. *Tools for Thought*. New York: Prentice-Hall, 1985.

Realness and Interactivity

Bricken, W. "A Model Interface Model." Atari Research Memo. Sunnyvale: Atari Sunnyvale Research Laboratory, 1983.

Laurel, B. K. "Toward the Design of a Computer-Based Interactive Fantasy System." Ph.D. Dissertation. Department of Theater, The Ohio State University, 1986.

Lippman, A. "Imaging and Interactivity." Media Lab report. Cambridge, MA: Massachusetts Institute of Technology, 1985.

Negroponte, N. *Media Room*. SID 22, no. 2 (1981):109–13.

Schrieber, W. "Psychophysics and the Improvement of Television Image Quality." *SMPTE*. Vol. 93, no. 8 (1984):717–25.

Designing a New Medium

Ambron, Sueann, and Kristina Hooper, eds. *Multimedia in Education*. Redmond, WA: Microsoft Press, 1988.

Bateson, Gregory. *Mind and Nature*. New York: Bantam, 1980.

Campbell, Joseph, and Bill Moyers. *The Power of Myth*. New York: Doubleday, 1988.

Illich, Ivan. *Tools for Conviviality*. New York: Harper and Row, 1973.

Jung, Carl G. *Man and His Symbols*. New York: Dell, 1968.

Krueger, Myron W. *Artificial Reality*. Reading, MA: Addison-Wesley Publishing Company, 1983.

Laurel, Brenda. "Interface as Mimesis." In *User-Centered System Design: New Perspectives on Human-Computer Interaction*. D. A. Norman and S. Draper, eds. Hillsdale, NJ: Lawrence Erlbaum Associates, 1986.

Laurel, Brenda K. "Toward the Design of a Computer-Based Interactive Fantasy System." Ph.D. Dissertation, The Ohio State University, 1986.

LeGuin, Ursula. *Dancing at the Edge of the World*. New York: Grove Press, 1989.

Lem, Stanislaw. *Microworlds*. New York: Harcourt Brace Jovanovich, 1984.

Mander, Jerry. *Four Arguments for the Elimination of Television*. New York: Morrow, 1978.

Mandler, J. M. *Stories, Scripts, and Scenes: Aspects of Schema Theory*. Hillsdale, NJ: Lawrence Erlbaum Associates, 1984.

Newell, Allen, and Stuart K. Card. "The Prospects for Psychological Science in Human-Computer Interaction." *Human Computer Interaction*. Vol. 1 (1985):209–42.

Ong, Walter J. *Orality and Literacy*. New York: Methuen, 1982.

Oren, Tim, "The Architecture of Static Hypertexts." *Hypertext '87 Papers*. Chapel Hill, NC: University of North Carolina, November 13–15, 1987, pp. 291–306.

Raskin, Jef. "Human Interface Design (Interview)," *Doctor Dobb's Journal*. (May, 1986):32–38.

Winograd, Terry, and Fernando Flores. *Understanding Computers and Cognition: A New Foundation for Design*. Norwood, NJ: Ablex, 1985.

Michael Arent
Advanced Technology Group
Apple Computer, Inc.

Ronald Baecker
Dynamic Graphics Project
Computer Systems Research Institute
and Department of Computer Science
University of Toronto

Sue Booker
Special Products, Apple Products
Apple Computer, Inc.

Susan E. Brennan
Department of Psychology, Stanford University
and
The Natural Language Project,
Hewlett-Packard Labs

Michael Chen
Advanced Technology Group
Apple Computer, Inc.

Chris Crawford
Computer Game Designer

Douglas Crockford
Lucasfilm Ltd.

Allen Cypher
Advanced Technology Group
Apple Computer, Inc.

Abbe Don
Interactive Telecommunications Program
New York University
Summer Intern, Apple Computer, Inc.

Thomas D. Erickson
Advanced Technology Group
Apple Computer, Inc.

Scott S. Fisher
Aerospace Human Factors Division
NASA Ames Research Center

Kathleen Gomoll
Advanced Technology Group
Apple Computer, Inc.

Jonathan Grudin
Human Interface Laboratory
MCC

Kathleen Gygi
Interactive Telecommunications Program
New York University
Summer Intern, Apple Computer, Inc.

Joyce Hakansson
President, Joyce Hakansson Associates

Eric A. Hulteen
Advanced Technology Group
Apple Computer, Inc.

Scott Kim
Look Twice, Inc.

Gordon Kurtenbach
University of Toronto
Summer Intern, Apple Computer, Inc.

Henry Lieberman
Visible Language Workshop, Media Laboratory
Massachusetts Institute of Technology

Michael Naimark
Media Artist

Anne Nicol
Human Interface Group
Apple Computer, Inc.

Tim Oren
Advanced Technology Group
Apple Computer, Inc.

Howard Rheingold
Author

Gitta Salomon
Advanced Technology Group
Apple Computer, Inc.

Chris Schmandt
Media Laboratory
Massachusetts Institute of Technology

Abigail Sellen
University of California at San Diego
Summer Intern, Apple Computer, Inc.

Ian Small
Dynamic Graphics Project
Computer Systems Research Institute
and Department of Computer Science
University of Toronto

Bruce Tognazzini
Product Engineering
Apple Computer, Inc.

Harry Vertelney
Advanced Technology Group
Apple Computer, Inc.

Laurie Vertelney
Advanced Technology Group
Apple Computer, Inc.

Annette Wagner
Product Engineering
Apple Computer, Inc.

Subject Index

511

Name Index

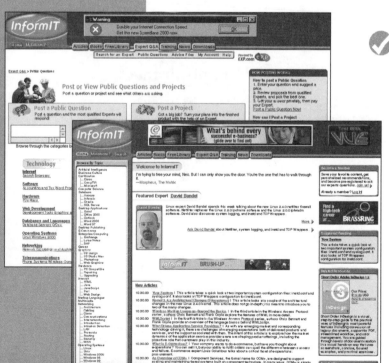

AutoCAD® 2012 & AutoCAD LT® 2012 Bible

Published by
Wiley Publishing, Inc.
10475 Crosspoint Boulevard
Indianapolis, IN 46256
www.wiley.com

This book is printed on acid-free paper. ∞

For general information about our other products and services, please contact our Customer Care Department within the United States at (877) 762-2974, outside the United States at (317) 572-3993 or fax (317) 572-4002.

Library of Congress Control Number: 2011930299

Trademarks: Wiley, the Wiley logo, and related trade dress are trademarks or registered trademarks of John Wiley & Sons, Inc. and/or its affiliates, in the United States and other countries, and may not be used without written permission. AutoCAD and AutoCAD LT are registered trademarks of Autodesk, Inc. All other trademarks are the property of their respective owners. Wiley Publishing, Inc. is not associated with any product or vendor mentioned in this book.

Wiley also publishes its books in a variety of electronic formats and by print-on-demand. Not all content that is available in standard print versions of this book may appear or be packaged in all book formats. If you have purchased a version of this book that did not include media that is referenced by or accompanies a standard print version, you may request this media by visiting http://booksupport.wiley.com. For more information about Wiley products, visit us www.wiley.com.

AutoCAD® 2012
& AutoCAD LT® 2012
Bible

Ellen Finkelstein

WILEY

Wiley Publishing, Inc.